Identity, Conflict, & Counter-Narratives

Identity, Conflict, & Counter-Narratives

Dalit Experiences in Culture, Politics, and Stigmatisation

Edited by

Yagati Chinna Rao and **Raj Sekhar Basu**

Orient BlackSwan

IDENTITY, CONFLICT, AND COUNTER-NARRATIVES: DALIT EXPERIENCES IN CULTURE, POLITICS, AND STIGMATISATION

ORIENT BLACKSWAN PRIVATE LIMITED

Registered Office
3-6-752 Himayatnagar, Hyderabad 500 029, Telangana, India
e-mail: centraloffice@orientblackswan.com

Other Offices
Bengaluru, Chennai, Guwahati, Hyderabad
Kolkata, Mumbai, New Delhi, Noida, Patna

First published by Orient Blackswan Private Limited 2025

ISBN 978-93-5442-920-0

040929

Typeset in
Arno Pro 11.5/12.75
by Le Studio Graphique, Gurgaon 122 007

Printed in India at
Avantika Printers Private Limited, New Delhi 110 020

Published by
Orient Blackswan Private Limited
3-6-752, Himayatnagar, Hyderabad 500 029, Telangana, India
e-mail: info@orientblackswan.com

In memory of

Professor Sabyasachi Bhattacharya (1938–2019)

Contents

Tables

Abbreviations

AGI	Attorney General of India
AIADMK	All India Anna Dravida Munnetra Kazhagam
AP	Andhra Pradesh
BJP	Bharatiya Janata Party
BSP	Bahujan Samaj Party
CCPA	Cabinet Committee on Political Affairs
CMS	Church Missionary Society
CPI(M)	Communist Party of India (Marxist)
GO	government order
ICS	Indian Civil Services
IPR	intellectual property rights
LMS	London Missionary Society
MPA	Madras Presidency Association
MRPS	Madiga Reservation Porata Samiti
NCSC	National Commission for Scheduled Castes
NCSCSC	National Commission to examine the issue of Sub-Categorization of Scheduled Castes
NSS	Nair Service Society
NTR	N. T. Rama Rao
OBC	Other Backward Classes
RSS	Rashtriya Swayamsevak Sangh
RTC	Round Table Conference
SC	Scheduled Caste
SCF	Scheduled Castes Federation
SIUC	South India United Church

SNDP	Sree Narayana Dharma Paripalana Yogam
SNM	Sri Narayana Movement
SP	Samajwadi Party
ST	Scheduled Tribe
TDP	Telugu Desam Party
UNESCO	United Nations Educational, Scientific and Cultural Organization
UT	Union Territory
WIPO	World Intellectual Property Organization
WTO	World Trade Organization

Preface

The essays in this volume were originally presented at a special panel on 'Dalit History and Politics' held at the seventy-seventh session of the Indian History Congress in 2016 in Thiruvananthapuram. It is the story of that panel which also serves as the story of this volume, a story originating in the peculiar paradox that reigns over the province of Indian history concerned with those formerly known as 'untouchables'. Despite the many seemingly radical perspectives that pervade history writing in India, a credible, critical, and reflexive historiography of untouchable pasts has remained conspicuous by its absence. Verily, there has been a concerted effort by a small community of historians to evolve and craft a particular perspective in this regard, but this has met with dismissal from mainstream historians on grounds of epistemic incorrectness and ahistorical methods (notwithstanding the honorary status imparted to collective perspectivism by broader ideological frameworks and institutions). A typical argument about Dalit historiography functions on a principle whereby its practitioners are not only accused of failure but also saddled with the burden of proving their innocence—their rigour—both within academia and outside it. Indeed, Dalit history is seen to exist at a point of seemingly impossible convergence—historical sources, methods, ideas, and speculation all come to naught when discussing the history of untouchables.

It is difficult to ignore the suspicion that this is the ultimate gesture of self-exoneration by those who stand indicted by histories of the oppressed. It is true that, despite the progress made over the decades in bringing historicism to explorations of caste, these explorations have been marked by a certain inadequacy in terms of critical reflections on methods, conceptual frameworks, and the question of sources; but, while those questions ought to eventually be critically examined, what they signify more than anything else is the failure of the discipline to evolve a broader intellectual vision of engaging with the 'other', to shed the appalling bias that has indeed been legitimised as normative practice. It is, in other words, a lack of collective consciousness and will rather than any other epistemic or intellectual lack that accounts for this inadequacy or failures.

In September 2016, the editors of this volume were visiting fellows at the Dipartimento Istituto Italiano di Studi Orientali (ISO) of Sapienza Università di Roma, and professors Sabyasachi Bhattacharya and Yagati Chinna Rao were finalising the introduction to the then forthcoming volume, *The Past of the Outcaste: Readings in Dalit History* (Orient BlackSwan, 2017). Working on this introduction and reckoning with Indian historians' apathy towards Dalit history prompted Prof. Bhattacharya to write, somewhat exasperatedly, in an email to Prof. Rao, 'How long will these accusations persist? Isn't it time to form a panel? Not at your university, not in my town, but right under the nose of the Indian History Congress!' Then, after a long interval, Prof. Bhattacharya wrote in another mail, 'Who could be better qualified than you to undertake the initiative?'

Prof. Rao shared the idea of the panel with Prof. Raj Sekhar Basu and enquired if he would be willing to join the panel as a co-coordinator. Prof. Basu's positive and enthusiastic response began the process of giving the idea the shape in which it was presented to the then general secretary of the Indian History Congress, Prof. Ishrat Alam, who readily granted them permission to organise a parallel special panel on 'Dalit History and Politics'. Since then, the editors have been organising this panel regularly.

Importantly, theirs was not the first panel on Dalit history at the Indian History Congress. In 2010, the Congress in its seventieth session held in Delhi a special panel on the 'History and Historiography of Dalits', made possible with generous financial assistance from the University Grants Commission under its then chairman, Prof. S. K. Thorat, and organised by the Institute of

Development Studies, Kolkata, under its then director, Prof. Amiya K. Bagchi. However, there were no attempts to continue or revive the panel after that session—until this one.

The idea of a panel of scholars engaging with untouchable histories was in synchrony with what Prof. Bhattacharya in the early 90s had persuasively made a case for: 'a new perspective on our past', through a 'history from below' or the people's history or a history of the oppressed, in the true spirit of the historians' creed. He envisioned a merging of the ideational and the empirical from the perspective of the oppressed, without losing sight of its other, i.e., the elite, predicated on the collective Asian, African, and Latin American experience within a post-colonial framework. Hence, for being the inspiration for this special panel, we dedicate this volume to Prof. Sabyasachi Bhattacharya.

We thank all the contributors, and Dr Priyadarshini Vijaisri, Dr Sudarshana Bhaumik, Arvind Suraj, Asif Equbal, and Mrs Poonam Chauhan for their help and assistance at various stages.

We also thank profusely our publishers for their stewardship of the process of converting these essays into the present volume.

The Editors

Introduction

Y. Chinna Rao & Raj Sekhar Basu

I

'Dalit' and 'Dalit identity' are widely discussed terms in the social sciences and in literature, with a voluminous literature on Dalits having emerged in the last two decades.[1] The term 'Dalit' denotes a vast social category and the identity associated with it is anchored in not only social but also economic, political, and historical ground realities, among which that of caste or *jati* is primary. Understanding the caste system is a prerequisite to understanding the social location of Dalits, as all Dalit castes occupy the lowest rungs of the caste hierarchy.[2] And yet, while there is no dearth of social science texts on caste, the study of caste by social scientists has, until fairly recently, remained largely ignorant of Dalits. Although 'the study of Dalits necessitates the understanding [of] caste', sociologists did not consider an 'examination of Dalits' to be 'essential or indispensable' to achieving this understanding.[3] The life world of Dalits is always presented from a Brahminical point of view or within the framework of Hindu theology rather than that of a 'value-neutral' ethnography or 'field view',[4] an approach that has only recently been adopted by the social sciences in India. The same is largely true of Indian history, which has neglected and systematically marginalised the history of the lower castes.[5] Even the Subaltern School of history that emerged in the 1980s and adopted a post-colonial and Marxist approach failed to recognise the Dalit life world.[6]

The indiscriminate use of the term 'Dalit' in contemporary Indian social sciences and humanities has been significantly influenced by international scholarship.[7] 'Dalit', which broadly means oppressed or 'depressed classes',[8] is a constructed identity rooted in the oppression and exploitation embedded in the Indian caste system and in opposition to the higher castes. The term is of Sanskrit and Marathi origin—derived from the word '*dal*' which literally means to crack, split, break, or turn[9]—and traces its history to the nineteenth century, when Mahatma Phule, a social reformer from the Mali or gardener community of Maharashtra, used it to refer to those oppressed by the caste system.[10] Contemporary usage of the term, linking it to the centuries-old practice of caste-based oppression, is inseparably associated with Dr B. R. Ambedkar as well as the Dalit Panther movement of the 1970s.[11] Today, the term is used by Dalits as a symbol of self-assertion, pride, change, revolution, and as a positive identity rooted in their generational struggle against caste oppression and the rejection of Brahminical Hindu theology, traditions, texts, and notions of god, rebirth, fate, and heaven.[12]

There are two sets of scholarly arguments for redefining 'Dalit' as a category. The first rests on the notion of an 'out of date history', as proposed by Romila Thapar, who argues that certain categories like '*arya*' and '*anarya*' have lost their significance. She contends that 'there is a political necessity for holding on to the Dalit category',[13] which replaced colonial terminologies liked 'Depressed Classes' and 'untouchables' that were favoured in the first half of the twentieth century. However, she also cautions against generalising the Dalit category on a pan-India basis, as that would mean neglecting important regional as well as cultural distinctions.[14] On the other hand, Ramnarayan Rawat, in his works on the Chamars of north India, establishes that colonial and nationalist identities have always been questioned by Dalit writers, historians, and activists—this notion becomes central to the second set of arguments.[15] Gopal Guru and V. Geetha cite the work of K. N. Panikkar, who draws a relationship between caste and class to argue that Dalit self-perception is shaped by social exploitation based on caste, culture, and class. Panikkar cites Premchand's short story 'Sadgati', which presents caste as an ideological weapon of class oppression, in support of his argument.[16]

Dalit assertion has been shaped by social and religious movements for a long time. In contemporary literature, 'non-Brahmin' is used as an umbrella term for these social and religious movements and is associated with a vision of a society liberated from 'the slavery of class, caste and women.'[17] Scholars suggest that the analysis of these movements can be done by the Ambedkarian or the Phuleian approaches, both of which share the commonality of emphasising education as an important mechanism for social uplift but differ in that Phule, although he propagated the idea of '*bahujan samaj*' to include all oppressed and marginalised groups, did not explicate a clear position on politics or conversion.[18] The critique of the Brahminical order in Dalit writings of the nineteenth and twentieth centuries relies intellectually and spiritually on certain early traditions of Indian philosophy, namely the Lokayata, Charvaka, Jain, and Buddhist traditions, as well as the Bhakti movement.[19] Among these, Buddhism, which began to be revived in the form of neo-Buddhism in the early years of the twentieth century by organisations like the Mahabodhi Society and Theosophical Society that were interested in the religious beliefs of communities regarded as untouchable, remains instrumental in shaping the assertion and political identity of Dalits.[20]

In fact, voices pleading the Dalit cause have been raised since the very beginning of Tamil literature in the first century AD. Nearly two millennia later, writers like Subramania Bharati, Sivaram Karanth, Thakazhi Sivasankara Pillai, and Mulk Raj Anand wrote about the life and struggles of Dalits without once staking claim to any kind of position within the Dalit literature tradition, for they believed that Dalit literature had to consist of the writings of Dalits.[21] Starting around 1958, contemporary Dalit writing began to gain prominence, particularly in Maharashtra but also in south and north India. Capitalist expansion in Maharashtra—both before and after Independence—along with the flight of Mahars to cities in search of jobs and education laid the ground there for a literary movement[22] that was an extension of the protest movement against caste-based inequality.[23] It was at the first Maharashtra Dalit Sangh conference in Mumbai in 1958 that the term 'Dalit literature' was first recognised and used, and a demand for its inclusion in university curriculums was also raised. The emergence of the Dalit Panthers later paved the way for writers like Namdeo Dhasal and Arjun Dangle.

The Dalit autobiography also emerged as a separate genre, serving as a powerful means of expressing the real pain and anger of the community.[24] The first Dalit autobiography was Hazari's *Untouchable: The Autobiography of an Indian Outcaste,* published in 1951,[25] and it was followed in the next few decades by pioneering works like Daya Pawar's *Baluta,* which highlights atrocities committed against Mahars,[26] and Aravind Malagatti's *Government Brahmana,* which deals with upper-caste mockery of the reservations granted by the government to Dalits.[27] The first English translation of a Dalit piece of writing was *Poisoned Bread,* published in 1992,[28] and the same year also saw the publication of Mulk Raj Anand and Eleanor Zelliot's *Anthology of Dalit Literature.* These English translations helped make Dalit literature accessible to a global readership.[29]

Dalit literary movements soon proliferated in other Indian states. *Joothan,* the autobiography of Om Prakash Valmiki, was published in 1997 and came to be considered the first Dalit autobiography in Hindi. The *mangalkavya*[30] narratives of pre-colonial Bengal could also be linked to these movements and viewed in the context of the marginalised history of the lower orders of Bengal.[31] Challenging the mainstream understanding of caste, Romila Thapar argued that caste mobility existed in the subcontinent during the pre-colonial era.[32] Both Hitesranjan Sanyal and Sekhar Bandyopadhyay observed that, in the sixteenth century, groups of individuals had broken away from certain castes to form new castes with occupations different from those of the parent castes, which led to social mobility. Sanyal has discussed three factors—the clearing of wastelands, technological innovation, and commercial success—as being pivotal to the upward social mobility of the lower castes of Bengal. All these factors were clearly reflected in the *Chandimangal* of Kavikankan Mukundaram Chakravarti, which describes, for instance, the goddess Chandi instructing the hunter Kalketu to clear the forests to build her temple. The 'upward economic movement and consequent social differentiation' had started long before the arrival of the British—the Mughal advance into Bengal in the sixteenth century led to land reclamation and peasantisation in the south-western part of the region.[33] Thus, starting in the deep south in the sixth century, gradually spreading northward through Karnataka and Maharashtra and engulfing north India and Bengal from the fifteenth century onwards, these movements from below were watersheds in Indian history, not only in religious and literary terms but also within their broader socio-cultural contexts.[34]

Understanding the complexity and dynamism of Indian society requires an understanding of the non-Brahmin perspective, for that is where the entry of 'the perspective from below' can be situated[35]—the perspective of those who form a homogenised bottom but, now partially emancipated and empowered, are demanding their legitimate share of representation in the production of knowledge. However, the study of these perspectives is also influenced by the difference approach adopted;[36] while the emic approach views Dalit self-conceptualisation or self-identification as an idea that is always emancipatory,[37] Dalit autobiographies are perfect examples of a combination of emic and etic approaches. On the other hand, it also worth noting that the 'perspective from below' is very different from the subaltern perspective due to subaltern historiography's Marxist focus on 'the circles of elite politics' with an emphasis on 'insurrectionary activities.'[38] Although the Dalit movement does run contrary to 'the dominant social trends in its analysis of national identity, religion, socio-economic development',[39] Gail Omvedt believes that this analysis goes beyond Marxism, because Marxism has failed to provide an analysis of caste.[40]

Against this backdrop of complex historiographical and ideological debates, it becomes important to explore the historicity of the term 'Dalit' and the process of Dalit identity formation from the perspective of Dalits themselves. The present volume attempts such an exploration with a view not only to conducting a socio-historical analysis of Dalit identity formation but also to addressing the marginalisation and exclusion of Dalits in the mainstream development discourse.

II

Caste is an important feature of the Indian social system. It is a purely South Asian phenomenon that is not only found in Hinduism but also in South Asian strains of Islam, Sikhism, and Christianity. It is a system that ascribes status to individuals within a social hierarchy based on purity and pollution and has evolved over a long span of time; at least 3,000 years, according to S. V. Ketkar.[41] Romila Thapar argues that caste structure took on a distinct shape in lineage-based society and that the *varna* model tied together all the available stratifications in that society.[42] Braj Ranjan Mani has argued that the Shudras, who were, according to this model, people engaged in production work and were superior in number and physical strength to the higher orders, resented their humiliation and subordination. For all we know, they may have joined hands with the *vratyas*—groups of those who were defeated by dominant political powers in the first millennium BC—and other non-Aryans to destroy the Brahminical order; sources of the ancient period do not reveal this.[43]

Several anthropologists, sociologists, and historians have tried to define caste. Colonial administrators-cum-anthropologists also tried to define it in different census reports. Herbert H. Risley defines a caste as

> a collection of families or groups of families bearing a common name; claiming common descent from a mythical ancestor, human or divine; professing to follow the same hereditary calling; and regarded by those who are competent to give an opinion as forming a single homogenous community.[44]

Risley further observes that the name of a caste usually also denotes the specific occupation of that caste. Endogamy is another feature of caste that S. V. Ketkar has emphasised, along with hereditary membership, in his definition of caste.[45] G. S. Ghurye, in his anthropological analysis of caste, argues that the social philosophy of caste comprises six features: i) segmental division of society; ii) hierarchy; iii) restrictions on feeding and social intercourse; iv) different civil and religious disabilities and privileges for different sections; v) restrictions on choice of occupation; and vi) restrictions on marriage.[46] After the publication of *Who Were the Shudras?* in 1946, B. R. Ambedkar wrote a sequel titled *The Untouchables,* in which he recognised 50 million 'untouchables' as a class.[47] He severely critiqued 'Hindu civilisation' on the basis of the presence of this divide, questioning the notion of a civilisation in which a mass of people were treated as 'an entity beyond human intercourse and whose mere touch is enough to cause pollution'.[48] Examining the origin of untouchability, Ambedkar uses the phrase 'broken man': '... the distinction between the Hindus and the Untouchables in its original form, before the advent of untouchability, was the distinction between tribesmen and broken men from alien tribes.'[49] Ambedkar distinguishes 'the impure' from untouchables, contending based on historical research that, while the impure as a class had existed since the time of the Dharma Shastras, it was difficult to trace untouchables as a class before 400 AD.

One of the earliest Western works on caste was that of German scholar Max Weber. In it, Weber describes castes as 'status groups' and declares them to be features of all pre-capitalist societies.[50] French scholar Célestin Bouglé suggests, on the other hand, that caste as a system of inequality developed within the Hindu religion as a synthesised form of all the basic components that are omnipresent in all societies, viz. specialisation, hierarchy, and repulsion.[51] Louis Dumont, another French scholar, subscribing to Bougle's view, examines caste as a peculiarly Hindu phenomenon. In *Homo Hierarchicus,* Dumont describes the caste system as an extreme form of social stratification that goes against the tenets of egalitarianism[52] and identifies three fundamental characteristics of the system: separation, division of labour, and hierarchy.[53] While discussing the historical emergence of caste, Dumont clearly explains that Hindu scriptural texts have masked or hidden the emergence of the fifth *varna,* that of the untouchables.[54] In this connection, it is worth noting Dumont's observation that *varna* exists only in the classical texts while caste exists in the real sense. Common to both is the remarkable feature of Brahminical supremacy, with the Brahmin representing the highest form of purity and holding the key to religious interpretation; the king, who controls the political domain, acts on the aid and advice of the Brahmin. *Varna* can be described as an all-India model or system of hierarchy in which castes that vary from region to region can be fitted. Regional specificities impacted the possibilities of mobility between different hierarchical rungs of this model, and these possibilities were used politically by certain castes—in the early census reports, for instance, people who claimed new lands and thus gained power registered themselves as members of castes higher in the ritual hierarchy than the ones they were originally documented as belonging to.[55]

Another view of caste in social history is that it is a colonial construction. Nicholas B. Dirks argues that 'caste (again, as we know it today) is a modern phenomenon, that it is, specifically, the product of an historical encounter between India and Western colonial rule.'[56] Dirks opines that caste is 'a single term capable of expressing, organizing, and above all "systematizing" India's diverse forms of social identity, community, and organization.'[57] He also suggests that the census was a purely imperial exercise to classify the entire Indian population on the basis of caste and the process of Sanskritisation was legitimised under colonial rule.[58] However, suggesting that caste is but the outcome of a colonial project is futile. It is believed by most historians that, before the arrival of the British, all regional societies in the subcontinent were based on norms and conventions and ranked into a social hierarchy based on order and function, i.e. they were already classified according to the caste system.[59]

Dirks has also produced a critique of Dumont's work. The Dumont analysis is based on a notion of separation of religion and political power, while Dirks highlighted the fact that 'in many medieval Hindu contexts, kings derived much of their power from worship, and bestowed their emblems and privileges in a cultural atmosphere permeated by the language and attitudes of worship.'[60] The expansion of Islam and merged boundaries between religious texts and political ideologies served as evidence of this fact.[61] Citing examples of Kallars and other Poligar communities of south India, Dirks emphasises that the relationships between the royal and religious classes were pivotal to the social organisation of caste and kinship, for, in one sense, the intervention of the Brahmin priests defined and lent credence to the idea of sovereignty—indeed, it is clear that, in places like Pudukottai, groups that established regional supremacy through war were able, despite low positions on the social scale, to claim royal status by securing the support of Brahmins. Politics is underlined by Dirks as foundational to the process of hierarchisation and the formation of units of identity,[62] and this insight remains crucial to the analysis of contemporary Dalit identity and assertion. The anthropological notion of caste as it exists today is based on earlier studies of the practices of regional societies. The emergence of caste in its present form is, therefore, not a sudden occurrence; the institution has undergone a gradual process of modification and translation since ancient times.[63] But the elements of tradition (as it exists today) have been shaped by deliberate colonial practices that began in the early eighteenth century, guided by the logic of expanding Western power through regional state-building. In the early nineteenth century, the norms of caste and ideology were sharpened by an authoritative colonial government. The introduction of representative government has further bolstered the presence of caste in the political realm. The assertion of caste through various intersectionalities can be seen in this framework.[64]

III

The publication of McKim Marriott's edited series *Village India* in the 1950s is considered a point of departure for an understanding of caste not only in terms of internal factors in a village or the village as a site of study but also in terms of factors external to the village.[65] *Village India* is a collection of research articles[66] that attempted to understand continuity and change among Indian villages in terms of 'little traditions' and 'great traditions'.[67] In his essay on the social system of a Mysore village,[68] M. N. Srinivas notes that the lower castes have historically been known to adopt the rituals and other practices of Brahmins and other double-born or higher castes to improve their caste status, a practice he terms 'Sanskritisation', and identifies the institutionalisation of patron–client relationships between different castes.

Srinivas also proposes that the social hierarchy on the basis of purity can be overturned by the presence of a 'dominant caste',[69, 70] which, over the course of a century at the time, had found new areas to operate in and had taken on new meanings as a result of constitutional safeguards. British rule, according to Srinivas, had erased the territorial boundaries of caste regimes that had existed in the pre-British era:

> [I]ncreased economic mobility led to increased social mobility, and the traditional process of Sanskritization ensured that such mobility did not lead to revolution. But, untouchables, by and large, seem to be unable to take advantage of it. This is one indication that the problem of the untouchables is different from that of the other low castes; the latter have a means of pushing themselves up in the system, while the former do not.[71]

It is evident that only those castes benefitted from British rule which were already prosperous. The higher castes took advantage of Western education and became the first nationalists. The British policy towards the lower castes was based on the notion of humanitarian work, but the protectionist impulse also boosted nationalism among Brahmins and other higher castes.[72] Srinivas predicted that relations between dominant castes and Scheduled Castes would become more bitter and violent, with the slow pace of change within the parameters of political democracy contributing to resentment. The rise of Dalit Panthers and the production of a body of protest literature can be seen as an expression of this resentment, with Dalit literature rejecting caste inequalities and exploitation and also contributing to the militancy of other sections of society.[73]

Village India contains revealing and insightful analyses by several other scholars. Kathleen Gough observes a transition taking place in a Tanjore village[74] inhabited by Brahmins and Adi Dravidas (the so-called 'exterior castes' of Tanjore): the village was moving from what was a closed, stationary system, governed by religious law and having the characteristics of a feudal economy, to a more open system governed by secular law and having the characteristics of an expanding capitalist economy. Detailing an account of the attempts by Chamars—traditional leatherworkers and agricultural labourers who are regarded as untouchable—to raise their social status and take control of their identity in villages of Uttar Pradesh,[75] Bernard Cohn underlines the vernacular usage of the term '*achut*' and also the abusive connotation of 'Chamar', as in the phrase 'dirty as a Chamar'—in response to which the Chamars of Madhopur village had started calling themselves 'Raidasi' while the Chamars of Azamgarh had renamed themselves 'Harijan Thakurs'. Cohn also shows how recent changes in the political environment had helped Chamars win village council elections; among other factors, he lists the development of railroads, the Arya Samaj movement, and the rise of the Noniya caste.[76] Alan Beals examines the interplay among factors of change in a Mysore village, describing the rise of the Madiga caste in Namhalli and the prosperity of the village during times of war[77] and explaining how cultural contact with other communities changed Madiga and other 'middle-class' castes. Andre Beteille, in his study of Sripuram, argues that 'today it is possible to achieve a variety of economic and political positions in spite of one's birth in a particular caste, although the latter is still very important in setting limits within which choice in the former is possible.'[78]

Based on the above, it can be concluded that caste 'attributes drawn from the notion of a pure ritual hierarchy would certainly not resonate with facts on the ground.'[79] Ritual dominance, in other words, is not a determinant of the nature of caste interactions in contemporary Indian society.[80] A profusion of assertive caste identities now jostle for space in the body politic; untouchable castes that were once considered supine and docile are now militant, aggressive and conscious of their power and rights in a democratic polity. New ideals fuel the political activism of castes that were once dominant, leading to caste antagonism that manifests in contradictory hierarchies.[81] Amidst all of this, the alternative identities of lower-caste people represent the ongoing Dalit struggle for identity.

IV

History is an everlasting process of constructing and reconstructing narratives to which episodes are added and deleted and in which blame is accepted and denied,[82] and this process is consciously used as a political weapon by 'the marginalised and oppressed communities ... [to seek] an honourable alternative place within the caste centred hierarchical Indian society.'[83] 'Mainstream' history has always involved the 'dehistoricisation of Dalits',[84] which Dalits have identified and responded to by denying the characterisation of them as passive objects. This denial takes the form of a search for their own history,[85] one that is not dependent on borrowings from any earlier historiographies.[86]

Dipesh Chakraborty mentions that history as a formal discipline was introduced to Indians by the British, who accorded centrality to historical evidence and ideas of truth and reality. History as a discipline has remained anchored in this idea of evidence in the post-colonial period as well. Common to discursive trends in national historical narratives, both within the liberal as well as Marxist frameworks, is the tendency to not acknowledge non-elite and non-Brahmin contributions to the national movement. Often, the acts of these outcastes are dubbed 'parochial', 'pro-colonial', or even 'anti-national' in nature.[87] Suvira Jaiswal argues that the history of 'the impure caste' or untouchables did not receive much attention in the nationalist phase of Indian historiography, which was characterised by an interest in the glorification of India's past.[88] This is in keeping with the civilisational approach to the analysis of history, which focuses on 'material achievements' and fails to recognise the 'victims' of these material achievements.[89] Similarly, Cambridge historiography, though it contests the ideological basis of the nationalist narrative, does not initiate a dialogue with the social periphery, instead projecting the 'lower' castes as mere passive followers of elite leaders. Marxist historians too, tended to work within rigid class parameters and showed a marked reluctance to address issues related to caste.[90] The study of Dalits, therefore, has generally been left to anthropologists and sociologists.

As a result, the history of the marginalised people or castes has been linked to the concept of 'history from below', which later came to be known as subaltern history. The Subaltern School critiqued traditional Indian historiographies, both colonial and nationalist, and sought to remove all elitist biases in the writing of history.[91] Two major themes that emerged in the writings of the subaltern scholars were peasant resistance and peasant consciousness in colonial India and the relationship between the peasantry and the national movement.[92] These studies highlight religion as the major weapon used by the so-called lower classes to defend themselves. As has been noted by Christian Lee Novetzke, Partha Chatterjee understands religion to be a common fabric shared by both elite and subaltern but reconstructed by the subaltern to mark their insurgency, and the importance of religion in understanding subaltern militancy and the subaltern worldview have been explored by Sumit Sarkar, Shahid Amin, and Ishita Banerjee Dube as well.[93]

Ranajit Guha takes the position that 'colonial elitism' and 'bourgeois nationalist elitism' have dominated national historiography as ideological products of British India[94]—both have vested interests in the portrayal of the making of the Indian nation and nationalism as elite achievements, and the involvement of the elite classes in these processes was calculated to further their 'share in wealth, power and prestige' under colonial structures instead of the 'nation's good.' This school of historiography has consistently failed to recognise the independent contributions of the non-elites.[95] In his autobiography *Jhompri se Rajbhavan* (From Hut to Palace), Mata Prasad too questions the scope of Indian nationalism, citing its neglect of the humiliation of Dalits by caste Hindus. He argues that Indian nationalism was an outcome of the everyday humiliation—economic inequalities along with cultural and social exclusion—experienced by members of the Indian elite classes like Gandhi and Bose under colonial rule.[96] Only in recent times has the study of caste and its interpretation received the attention of social scientists and historians.[97]

The Europeans were the first to take the initiative to understand the significance of the world of 'untouchables'. Historically, census reports have provided administrators, and scholars, in-depth and exhaustive information about untouchables across the subcontinent; however, they also reflected the biases of the officials responsible for collecting census data and compiling the reports.[98] Laura Dudley Jenkins highlights the debates on contemporary demands for reservation and the classification of groups by the state in India. She argues that official classifications used by the state fail to identify the 'complexities of caste, race, class, religion, gender and other forms of social identities' and that '[procedures of] official identification have unintended side effects on identity politics.'[99] She strengthens her argument by highlighting the importance of the distinction between a self-defined entity and an externally defined entity and drawing attention to how they can impact each other, with official categories influencing groups and groups asserting themselves to reshape the official categories.

Reservation is no doubt a redistributive mechanism based on the concept of caste. The criteria for classifying communities for the purposes of reservation range from anthropological parameters to administrative and legal definitions, and the validation of identity claims by communities falls under the purview of the Supreme Court of India. Discussing the complications that riddle this process, Jenkins highlights cases of inter-caste marriages, reconversions, and 'desanskritization' and argues that 'legal hardenings of caste have colonial objectives behind them.'[100] She also questions 'official' anthropological accounts by citing the Anthropological Survey of India's People of India project. Contending that the ultimate aim of the project is to profile each community of India on the basis of caste, she argues, quoting Dirks, that it is similar to Risley's work in that both treat caste as the fundamental and overpowering unit of analysis:

> Caste was just one category out of many others, one way of organizing and representing identity. Moreover, caste was not a single category or even logic of categorization... To read and organize social difference and deference—pervasive features of Indian society—solely in terms of caste thus required a striking disregard for ethnographic specificity, as well as systematic denial of the political mechanisms that selected different kinds of social units as most significant at different times.[101]

According to Jenkins, the People of India project has been reduced to a tool for making decisions related to quota policies.[102] She thus highlights the relationship between anthropology, politics, and administration, a relationship that can be traced back to colonial ethnographers and their engagement with the political contexts in which they operated.

Examining the role of the post-colonial census in the creation of official identities on the basis of caste, tribe, and religion, Jenkins notes that, as the census results form a basis for affirmative action policies, after each census, new castes demand Scheduled Caste status. Census reports, however, never reveal the kinds of social changes—including internal divisions—that have impacted social groups or how.[103] Moreover, as the caste of an individual is verified against official state-level schedules and a caste listed as a Scheduled Caste in one state might not be listed as a Scheduled Caste in another state,[104] Jenkins argues that the official identity arrived at through this process may not match the personal identity in every case.[105] She goes on to observe that the extension of reservations to Other Backward Classes (OBCs) and their demands for a comprehensive caste census are evidence of the failure of the postcolonial hope that caste would fade away with the embrace of modernity.

Owing to their extremely dehumanised and degraded position in Indian society, Dalits in colonial India attracted the interest of missionaries and colonial ethnographers, and though their studies were valuable, the historical point of view expressed in them is often incomplete and incoherent. Perhaps the earliest and most exhaustive and systematic work on any Dalit caste was conducted by G. W. Briggs in the 1920s, who was not a historian by discipline.[106]

Briggs was working for a Christian mission and his work was focused on the historically significant urban centres of Agra and Oudh. Briggs traced the history of the Chamar caste back to the Rig Veda.[107] He also traced the origins of the caste to the categories of 'Dasyu' and 'Chandala', with Chandalas having been defined as those with polluted Aryan blood and Dasyus as those who had been conquered. They were treated as unclean but served the village community during times of death and disease. Their knowledge of exorcism and magical rites helped them find a place in society. Chamars, who in Bengal were menial workers similar to Chandalas, trace their origins to the '*charmakara*' ('skin workers') of the past. Briggs argues that, according to the Manu Code, even though the Chamars were defined as Karavara, a community of low origin, they led respectable lives, as did the Chandals.[108]

Recent claims made by members of the Chamar community through references to stories such as those of the *mangalkavya* tradition also trace their ancestry to 'high-born' persons who were downgraded into the leatherworkers' group. Briggs argues that 'the caste itself had its origin in that occupational class on the borders of the ancient village.'[109] The features described by him show variations and attest to the notion of Chamars being a mixed-race caste that was expanded through large-scale recruitments from above; some of them are described as fair, while others are described as dark-skinned and short and can be grouped with the pre-Aryan type. The 'higher' features of many Chamar women are assumed to be the result of illicit relations with higher castes. Some clans are reported to share similarities with Jats; Briggs believes that demands of livelihood drove some Jats into the leatherworking profession. Briggs also uses census data to draw inferences about the pan-India presence of Chamars: Madigas in Telugu country, Chakliyans in Tamil Nadu, Mochis in Bengal, Satnamis in Central Provinces, Jaiswars in the east (Bengal and North-East India), and Jatiyas as a dominant group in Meerut and Ballia, some of whose clans are even reported to share surnames with Rajput clans.[110] They are associated with low moral standards, a conclusion deriving from the normalcy of illicit relationships as well as divorces. Theirs is a 'saturated world with animistic ideas',[111] for they are described as treating every tree, plant, and animal as an abode of spirits: 'the range of the Chamar's superstitions and beliefs begins with the primitive notions of animism, and reaches up through the worship of nature deities.'[112] At the same time, many Chamars are reported to have been influenced by Ramananda and other reformers—Briggs refers to them as followers of Kabirpanth, Nanakpanth, and Rae Das[113]—and have named themselves after these reformers. They were also reported as employers of degraded Sarwariya Brahmins and Gurra Brahmins.[114] In the end, Briggs claims that, just before the 1911 census, a large number of Chamars received conversion offers from Arya Samaj and Mohammedan communities. Since Briggs was there on Christian missionary work, he argues in favour of Christianity, opining that 'Jesus offers to the Chamars a satisfactory place in the social order and a satisfactory religious life.'[115]

Post-colonial India witnessed its first anthropological work on Nimar Balahis in Madhya Pradesh by Stephen Fuchs, who was also involved in missionary work.[116] By studying the social structure and culture of 'untouchables', Fuchs made an attempt to fill the gaps in the anthropological literature on the marginalised sections of Indian society. In the foreword to Fuch's seminal work *The Children of Hari*, Christoph von Fürer-Haimendorf describes this work as 'concrete proof of the anthropological approach, i.e. the combination of verbal enquiry with direct observation',[117] but critiques Fuchs for not investigating the origins of the caste and opines that 'sooner or later the historical position of the depressed classes will have to be clarified.'[118] Furthermore, he argues against Fuchs' theory that tribes were reduced to the status of untouchables by invaders, stating that, while it was possible that this had occasionally been the case, it was no longer believed to be the explanation for the emergence of the untouchable castes. The relative socioeconomic positions of the tribes and the untouchables was evidence of the weakness of this theory, as was the fact that the racial features of the untouchable castes were much closer to those of the local Hindu castes than to those of the invaders.[119]

Fuchs regards Balahis as being from Dravidian or Austro-Asiatic stock. He argues that the term 'Balahi' is a Dravidian term and traces it to the southern terms 'Parayan' or 'Pulayan'.[120] The racial features of the caste cannot be generalised, as they are reported to have 61 clans, of which only some were founded by their ancestors. Studying census reports, Fuchs concludes that Chamars, Mahars, Koris, and Kolis are but different branches of the same race.[121] The different sub-groups of Balahis are reported to each have a headman known as *mukhya-jat-patel*. Inter-dining and marriage were considered the ways to join the Balahi community, with only a few castes treated as non-admissible, namely Chamars, Dhobis, Basors, and Mangs. Castes having customs objectionable to the Balahis were debarred.[122]

Fuchs notes that a considerable number of Balahis had started resenting caste discrimination. He favours the use of Christian education to bring about social change among Balahis but notes that 'most of the Balahis assumed the Christian religion as superficially as a cloak under which to hide their former self.'[123] As they continued to practise customs and rituals objectionable to caste Hindus after converting to Christianity, Balahis were considered as low as they were before conversion and thus seen as an insult to Christianity.[124] Balahis were reported to have the *bhat* as their registrar and separate barbers and Brahmins.[125]

Describing Balahis as 'one of the least attractive groups of the peoples of India',[126] Fuchs makes a serious attempt to predict their future. He regards their rituals and ceremonies as mere imitations of the surrounding Hindu culture and their level of proficiency in their traditional occupation, i.e. weaving, as very low and describes their social degradation and economic distress as common problems of every untouchable caste. Fuchs argues that Gandhi's 'Harijan movement' was unrealistic in the sense that it sought to treat the problems of the depressed classes with mere goodwill and persuasion—emphasising the agency of the upper castes in eradicating untouchability through a change of heart and viewing the 'Harijans' or 'untouchables' as simply an adulating audience devoid of voice—even though the problem of untouchability was rooted in ancient ideologies and in religion and was resistant to all such solutions. Fuchs concludes with a warning to Hindu society about the dangers posed by the Western world in the form of materialism and industrialism; he calls for the protection of Indian culture.[127] Notwithstanding Fuchs' efforts, however, studies on the marginalised sections of Indian society were ignored for another two decades. It was only in the 1970s that caste again attracted the attention of scholars, but within a different paradigm altogether.[128]

In this connection, it is worth delving into Badri Narayan's argument that the national imagination that takes hold among a mass of people is powerfully affected by advancements in print culture.[129] Narayan substantiates this argument by referring to Benedict Anderson's *Imagined Communities: Reflections on the Origin and Spread of Nationalism*. He argues that reading stories in school and imbibing cultural narratives through texts help people imagine a larger community affiliation. Marginal societies imagine their nation in the biographies of national heroes, but their local heroes are not included in these narratives, resulting in disillusionment with mainstream nationalism among them. With the help of literacy and other factors such as employment in government services, Dalits too tried to connect with this mainstream nationalism, to initiate a dialogue with the nation by writing stories and novels for popular consumption.[130]

In this whole process, Badri Narayan identifies two important elements, viz. imagination and memory. Both elements have their roots in myth and history, for this is 'the foundational requirement for the identity, self-respect and social existence of the marginalized communities in an age of power, conflict and competition'.[131] The self-respect, pride, and glory of the Dalit communities can be sourced to the heroic images of their caste heroes cultivated by them. Heroes and the myths centred on them give rise to ideas of emancipation from Brahminical ideology, which is rooted in ancient Brahminical texts; the nurturing of collective memory and of an imagination of heroes is, thus, a form of cultural assertion that helps Dalits assert themselves within the political discourse. This was first used by the Bahujan Samaj Party (BSP) in Uttar Pradesh, which developed a political language based on oral traditions. Jhalkari Bai's heroic image among the Koris and Uda Devi's heroic image among the Pasis are examples of how Dalit communities politically assert and subvert cultural domination through myths.[132]

Scholars dealing with untouchable communities have focused on a wide range of issues. Initially, what was observable was an inclination to understand the origins and development of agrestic servitude in different parts of India. Scholars involved in such studies were interested in unearthing the specificities of the historical context in which the system of bondage emerged and developed some of its distinctive features.[133]

Against the backdrop of the construction by Hindu society of the Dalit subaltern as the 'other' and the observance of a policy of exclusion with regard to the voice of this subaltern 'other', marginalised histories/subaltern studies had a very important point to make about indigeneity as a criterion for inclusion in 'civilisation', different from the criteria imposed by the powerful. Discussing the history of the history-less, Sabyasachi Bhattacharya argues that 'history from below' originated not in Third World nations but in England, where the practitioners of 'history from below' derived their inspiration from diverse sources, but mainly from a Marxist orientation. In this context, he cites the mention by Eric Hobsbawm of a new approach to history developed in the intellectual interactions of a group of Marxist historians who first got together in 1946 to re-edit the celebrated *People's History of England* (1938) by A. R. Morton.[134] In Indian historiography, the term 'history of the people' is bandied about by the right, the left, and the centre. William Hunter in his first prefatory statement to *Annals of Rural Bengal* argued, 'My business is with the people,'[135] intending to underline the distinction between the conventional British Indian histories of his time and the kind of social history he proposed to write. In the writings of the nationalist intelligentsia in the late nineteenth and early twentieth centuries, 'history of the people' has a slightly different connotation from what Hunter had in mind. The aim was not merely the enlargement of the scope of history, but to foreground the opposition between the rulers and the ruled. Thus, for example, Bankim Chandra Chattopadhyay writes of the need for a *jatitya ithihas* of the Bengali people as distinct from a history of the political rulers of Bengal.[136] As Swaraj Basu notes, it was out of these discourses that, during the early twentieth century, a new ethnological discourse on caste ranking emerged, in which issues like racial origin or *varna* status assumed supreme importance in determining the social status of groups.[137] In this atmosphere, the Bengali word '*jati*' began to acquire different meanings for different social groups. Sekhar Bandopadhyay has discussed how, for the more prosperous Subarnabaniks, '*jatiya itihas*' (national history) remained as important as '*jatir ithihas*' (history of the caste)[138] while, in the mental world of the Namasudras and Rajbansis, 'caste' had decisively replaced the concept of 'nation'; rarely in their literature did the word 'nation' mean anything other than caste.[139] Also relevant here is Purnachandra Ray's discussion of the Paundra Kshatriyas, to whom '*jatiya unnati*' primarily meant the advancement of the caste, which could eventually lead to the advancement of the 'nation' as well.[140]

It can be argued that the dominant schools of history writing in India are yet to acknowledge scores of 'history-less' communities, as a result of which history remains severely elitist and unholistic. Nevertheless, individual (Dalit and non-Dalit) attempts at the reconstruction of the outcaste caste in recent decades have made valuable contributions in this direction: Sekhar Bandopadhyay and Swaraj Basu have elaborately discussed the Namasudras of eastern Bengal and the Rajbansis of north Bengal, the history of Dalits in north India has been discussed by Badri Narayan and Nandini Gooptu, and this was followed by Raj Sekhar Basu's more detailed work on the history of the Dalits of south India and Y. Chinna Rao's work on Dalit political consciousness and their struggle for identity in Andhra Pradesh.[141] However, it is also true that, notwithstanding the increased interest in the hierarchical systems of Hindu society that it represented and the new approach to understanding history that it promoted, the Subaltern School itself had very little to offer to socially oppressed, economically exploited, and politically marginalised landless agricultural labourers and Dalits. Significantly, these categories were left outside the ambit of the 'subaltern' construction. Rather, the 'subaltern' as a category comprised the rural gentry and impoverished landlords, who were the direct oppressors and exploiters of the Dalit masses. It is on this basis that the Dalitist or Dalit perspectives of Indian history can be distinguished from 'subaltern history.'[142]

V

The 1980s saw almost all the presumptions of the established development paradigm challenged by advanced scientific and social analysis and increased political activity. Movements of landless, unorganised labour in rural and urban areas, Adivasis, Dalits, displaced people, peasants, urban poor, small entrepreneurs, and unemployed youth took up the issues of livelihood, opportunities, dignity, and development.[143] The 1972 Conference on Environment and Development at Stockholm had set the stage for the entry of the concepts of environment and ecology into the mainstream of Indian discourses on development and social movements. While the Western representatives highlighted the issues of pollution and the depletion of non-renewable natural resources, the official Indian position was that poverty was the greatest pollutant.[144] One concern that took centre-stage at the 1972 conference was related to the different rates of consumption of natural resources by the West and by countries such as India; the debate settled at the level of an uneasy consensus which, while accommodating the demands of the conservationist lobbies for wildlife protection, reserved forests and national parks, green belts in the cities, restrictions on the setting up of industries (particularly polluting industries) in urban concentrations, etc., reflected its faith in the dominant views on economic progress based on the use of technology.

To treat 1972 as a watershed is not to argue that alternative views on the man–nature relationship were not part of the Indian discourse previously. The most prominent of course was the Gandhian view, which from the early years of the twentieth century had consistently argued for a model of state and society based on the village as the primary unit and the farmer/peasant as the key productive agent. In *Hind Swaraj*, published in 1908, Gandhi had formulated both a well-worked-out critique of the industrial vision and an alternative to it.

In the early 1970s, when environmental experts were debating their viewpoints in Stockholm and at other similar forums, another movement, now famous in development literature as the 'Chipko' movement, started making an impact in India. Drawing on the struggles of forest- and hill-based people that had begun in the early nineteenth century in the lower regions of the Himalayas against the intrusion of the colonial and native princely states, the current phase of the Chipko movement began as an effort to save local forest resources from commercial exploitation by outside contractors. The initial demands were mainly for local control of local resources; the new demands were for a complete ban on the felling of trees (a demand conceded in 1973), for a substantial step-up in afforestation efforts around tree species that were environmentally suitable and locally useful, and for handing over control of local forests to local village communities.[145]

By the 1980s, demands like these were becoming a matter of concern for donor governments and international lending agencies as well. Reflecting the neoliberal philosophies that were gaining credibility in the West, they advocated a more limited role for the state and greater scope for marketisation, and these were prescribed as part of the structural adjustment policies offered to countries in Asia and Africa.[146] By and large, Indian movements of the 1980s were responding to the internal logic of marginalisation/disempowerment within the nation state, heightened by the experience of the suspension of democratic rights and civil liberties during the Emergency. The Chipko movement was a classic example of non-violent resistance and struggle by thousands of ordinary hill folk, without the guidance and control of any centralised apparatus, recognised leadership, or full-time cadre. Over the course of a decade and a half, it not only spread across the Himalayas but also inspired similar struggles in other parts of India.

The ideas and principles that the new people's movements articulated can be illustrated by referring to the issues highlighted by some prominent movements like the Chhattisgarh Mukti Morcha (CMM), which adopted the slogan '*Sangharsh aur Nirman*' (Struggle and Rebuilding). The Mazdoor Kisan Shakti Sangathan (MKSS) in Rajasthan unearthed the potential of the right to information as a guarantor of food and livelihood security. The Narmada Bachao Andolan (NBA) was an important milestone among socio-political movements in India. Protesting against the Narmada Valley project, a gigantic scheme consisting of more than 3,000 major and minor dams and involving an outlay of over Rs 25,000 crore,[147] the NBA raised the issues of displacement, environmental, and economic destruction.[148] In the early 1990s, grassroots movements confronted an entirely new set of terms justifying the hegemony of the newly established post-Cold War global order. Earlier, until the end of the Cold War, a significant number of grassroots movements in India had actively protested against the exclusionary, elite-oriented development model that was conceived of by the post-Second World War Bretton Woods institutions and their sponsor countries, who sought to apply the model all over the world. These protests were, however, articulated largely in the context of the discourse developed by new social movements in the West, where the nuclear and environmental threats produced by the Cold War were more poignantly felt. It was through this process that the idea and the campaign for 'alternative development' grew in the West. Although this idea had been propagated and practised in India for a long time by Gandhian activists, it was marginalised within the development discourse by India's modernist ruling elite after Independence. The whole discourse of development suddenly changed, both globally and in India, when the notion of alternative development was analytically formulated and propagated by various global groups. This was the discourse of globalisation. In the mid-1990s, there were protests against globalisation led by a few movements that were against its adverse impacts and this revitalised the entire spectrum of grassroots movements in India, giving rise to a new discourse and politics aimed at countering the forces of hegemonic globalisation, which, in the view of the movements, were making issues of poverty and social deprivation in the peripheral countries of the world ever more unintelligible in the global discourse.[149]

Economic liberalisation has, predictably, had an adverse effect on the livelihoods of Dalit groups, as the downsizing of the public sector has diminished job opportunities for Dalits in state-owned enterprises. Further, globalisation and the entry of corporate giants have deprived a section of Dalits from exercising ownership rights over land, which in the past was assigned to them as '*panchama*'.[150] In the pre-globalisation period, the assignees were forced to sell these lands to other castes to survive the pangs of starvation. Yet, these lands continue to be recorded year after year as DC (conditional) lands in official revenue records. It is ironic that the assignees of DC lands themselves have no real understanding of the conditions that were laid down for the exercise of occupancy rights over such lands. Their inability to comprehend the intricacies of land transfer has been of great advantage to upper-caste landlords and land speculators. Significantly, Raj Sekhar Basu has argued that the caste system adds a specific economic dimension to the social scenario of rural Tamil Nadu. He notes the observation of R. Balakrishnan, the chairman of the Tamil Nadu Commission for Scheduled Castes and Scheduled Tribes, that

> The caste system is an economic order. It prevents someone from acquiring land or receiving an education. It is a vicious cycle and an exploitative economic arrangement. Land owning patterns and being a high caste member are coterminous. Also there is a nexus between (being) lower caste and landlessness… Caste is a tool to perpetuate exploitative economic arrangements.[151]

This clearly references the degraded state of Dalit agricultural labourers, most of whom happen to be landless. As Basu has pointed out, the lack of access to landed resources compounds the economic problems of the Dalit masses. This state of helplessness is exploited by upper-caste landlords and rich peasantry belonging to the intermediary caste groups.

The complexities of Dalit history and identity cannot really be understood without a meaningful discussion on social exclusion as it has been practised in the past and is being practised in contemporary India. As discussed by Y. Chinna Rao, the term 'social exclusion' is very difficult to define due to the fact that it is interpreted differently in different contexts at different times. In Europe, the term emerged in the late twentieth century as a key concept among analysts and policy makers seeking to formulate approaches to alleviating some of the negative social effects of economic restructuring. In India, exclusion is embedded in societal interrelations and institutions that discriminate against, isolate, and deprive some groups on the basis of markers of identity such as caste and ethnicity. Development approaches from the 1950s to the 1980s primarily viewed social and economic development as outcomes of the development process and were less concerned with civil and political rights. It was only in 1989 that the Scheduled Caste and Scheduled Tribes Act was passed, which stated that caste-based atrocities committed against the members of Scheduled Castes and Tribes were punishable by law.[152]

By the last years of the twentieth century, social scientists could obviously locate the connections between centuries of exploitation and discrimination suffered by Dalits and their contemporary economic status, which was far worse than that of other social groups. In many parts of India, past and present-day experiences seemed to coincide as the problem of landlessness continued to be too vast to ignore. At the turn of the present century, the proportion of Indian population categorised as being below the poverty line (BPL) seemed to consist disproportionately of Dalit communities at the pan-Indian level.[153] However, despite the wide range of changes on the economic and political fronts, the debates on the historical links between caste and occupation have by no means lost their relevance. In the 1990s, some sociologists tried to argue that the overlaps between caste and occupation in rural India were gradually losing importance because of increasing mobility. Sanskritisation was regarded as integral to the mobility, in a way that was also relevant to Dalit communities. However, while some sections of Dalits might have opted for Sanskritisation, there were substantial sections that re-asserted and reclaimed their Dalit identity and adopted belligerent postures towards the upper castes and caste-dominated society as a whole. Some scholars argued that, while the old links between caste and occupation had shown signs of breaking down in the post-Independence years, there were very few options for the majority of the rural members of Dalit communities who wanted to extricate themselves from the economic, political, and physical powers of the local land-owning upper castes.[154]

Interestingly, the last decades of the twentieth century witnessed a debate centred round the phrase 'culture of poverty', which resembled in some ways a return to the colonial epistemological constructions whereby only the poor were to be blamed for their poverty. The votaries of this point of view utilised the merit-based logic of social mobility in the First World and the culture model to argue that the Third World was unchanging and immune to modern values, and this debate impacted how the problems of Dalit communities in India were understood. Arun Kumar, in his seminal article on the Musahar community in Bihar, tried to understand how the members of a Dalit community interpret their situation of wretchedness, which is part of their everyday experience.[155] Kumar points out the irony of Musahars also being known as 'Bhuiyan', a term that denotes their status as denizens of the earth; the paradox lies in the fact that Musahars hardly have any land of their own. Historically, Musahars have been engaged in different kinds of occupations and socio-religious positions, from being hunters in jungles to rendering unfree labour and from worshipping nature to being 'untouchables' within the Hindu caste system. Presumably, their inclusion in the jati fold was originally influenced by the continual demand for labour in paddy fields owned by caste Hindus.[156]

A more interesting example of how Dalits perceive their lives comes from Manuela Ciotti's research on the Manupur Chamars, who live on the outskirts of the city of Benaras. With the passage of time, due to education and political mobilisation, they began to question the status of communities who were believed to have been traditionally endowed with the virtues of knowledge, like Brahmin ritual specialists. This transformation led educated members of the community to uphold the view that the prevailing model of development needed to be replaced by a notion of development that emphasised social awareness among individuals and communities, a notion that was expressed in terms such as '*buddhi ka vikas*'.[157]

Thus, in the absence of the interest of mainstream historians, studies on Dalits have struggled to question Brahminical traditions and write histories from below. The project of 'de-Brahminising' Indian history has found great traction among the Dalit intelligentsia writing about Indian history, culture, and philosophy,[158] but the emphasis on the lived experiences of Dalits imparts an inflammable emotional tone to the issue of the oppression of Dalits rather than promoting a rational approach and upholding the idea that scholars of liberal and progressive persuasions can make significant changes to society's perception of issues related to the social exclusion and discrimination faced by Dalits. In fact, this issue of 'lived experience' could be exploited by radical communitarian ideologies operating within the narrow confines of their imagined communities to impose different sets of identities from above, which could bring Dalits on a war path within the nation state. It is important to remember, in this context, that there have existed differences of opinion over issues related to the emancipation of Dalits in India. While doctrinaire Marxists try to understand the issue of Dalit identity in terms of class, more radical intellectuals seem to privilege caste as a determinant vis-à-vis all issues related to the liberation or bondage of Dalits.[159] In spite of all these fissures, Dalit history and literature will continue to have a special place in Indian historiography. This volume seeks to give voice to the Dalit cause at a time when India is looking at a future not defined by pluralism but by an '*akhanda*' identity characterised by the erasure of all existing differences in the process of imagining the 'nation'.

Notes and References

1. Much of this literature is loaded with sociological enquiries on how the term is used as an undifferentiated category. For details see, A. M. Shah,

'The Dalit Category and Its Differentiation', *Economic and Political Weekly* 37(14) (April 6–12, 2002): 1317–1318.

2. Paramjit S. Judge, 'Introduction,' in *Towards Sociology of Dalits,* ed. Paramjit S. Judge (New Delhi: Sage, 2013), p. xxiii.

3. *Ibid.*

4. *Ibid.*

5. Y. Chinna Rao, 'Communities on the Margins: Dalit Consciousness in Colonial South India,' in *Narratives of the Excluded: Caste Issues in Colonial India,* eds. Raj Sekhar Basu, Sanjukta Das Gupta (Kolkata: K.P. Bagchi and Company, 2006), p. 51.

6. *Ibid.*

7. In response to A. M. Shah's article 'The Dalit Category and Its Differentiation', Sunita Reddy opposes the use of the term 'sub-jatis' and instead argues for using 'Dalit' universally in order to address a larger audience. For details see Sunita Reddy Bharti, 'Dalit: A Term Asserting Unity', *Economic and Political Weekly* 37(42) (October 19–25, 2002): 4339–4340.

8. The term 'depressed classes' was used by the British to refer to the untouchable castes, and by Ambedkar in his speeches. Ambedkar attributes its first appearance in print to *Dalit Bandhu,* a Marathi newspaper, in the 1930s. For details see B. R. Ambedkar, *Who Were the Shudras?: How They Came to Be the Fourth Varna in the Indo-Aryan Society* (Bombay: Thacker and Co., 1946); *The Untouchables: Who Were They and Why They Became Untouchables* (Delhi: Amit Books, 1948); and Atul Chandra Pradhan, *The Emergence of the Depressed Classes* (Delhi: Bookland International, 1986).

9. Monier Monier-Williams, *A Sanskrit-English Dictionary* (Delhi: Motilal Banarasidass, 1963).

10. For details see Jotirao Govindrao Phule, 'Slavery', in *Collected Works of Mahatma Jotirao Phule,* trans. Prof. P. G. Patil (Bombay: Government of Maharashtra Press, 1991).

11. Dalit Panthers is a movement and organisation dedicated to combating caste discrimination started by a group of educated activists in the slums of Mumbai in 1972. Prominent figures associated with it include writers and poets such as Namdeo Dhasal, J. V. Pawar, Raja Dhale, and Arjun Dangle, known for their fiery and confrontational styles. Their manifesto defines Dalits as 'members of scheduled castes and tribes, neo-Buddhists, the working people, the landless and poor peasants, women and

all those who are being exploited politically, economically and in the name of religion.' For details see, 'Dalit Panthers Manifesto', in *Untouchable!: Voices of the Dalit Liberation Movement*, ed. Barbara R. Joshi (London: Zed Books, 1986), p. 145; and Dr. Gangadhar Pantawane, 'Evolving a New Identity: The Development of a Dalit Culture', in *ibid.*, p. 87.

12. *Ibid.*, p. 79.

13. Romila Thapar quoted in Gopal Guru and V. Geetha, 'New Phase of Dalit–Bahujan Intellectual Activity', *Economic and Political Weekly* 35(3) (January 15–21, 2001): 130–134.

14. *Ibid.*

15. Ramnarayan S. Rawat, *Reconsidering Untouchability: Chamars and Dalit History in North India* (Bloomington: Indiana University Press, 2011), p. 9.

16. Guru and Geetha, 'New Phase of Dalit–Bahujan Intellectual Activity', *op. cit.*

17. S. M. Dahiwale, 'Introduction', in *Understanding Indian Society: The Non-Brahmanic Perspective*, ed. S. M. Dahiwale (New Delhi: Rawat, 2005), p. 1.

18. An interpretive methodology and approach based on the historical analysis of Marx, Phule, and Ambedkar. For details see *ibid.*

19. For details see Swaraj Basu, 'Introduction', in *Readings on Dalit Identity: History, Literature and Religion*, ed. Swaraj Basu (New Delhi: Orient BlackSwan, 2016). For details on Lokayata, see K. Damodaran, *Man and Society in Indian Philosophy* (New Delhi: People Publishing, 1970), pp. 31, 39, 42. Also see Gail Omvedt, *Buddhism in India: Challenging Brahminism and Caste* (New Delhi: Sage, 2003).

20. For details see Kancha Ilaiah, *God as Political Philosopher: Buddha's Challenge to Brahminism* (Kolkata: Samya, 2000).

21. Cho Dharman and Venkat Swaminathan, 'What is said and what ought to have been said,' *Indian Literature* 43(5) (September–October 1999): 91–93.

22. Shalini Ramachandran, 'Poisoned Bread: Protest in Dalit Short Stories', in *Race & Class* 45(4) (2004): 27–44.

23. Manoranjan Byapari and Meenakshi Mukherjee, 'Is There Dalit Writing in Bangla?', *Economic and Political Weekly* 42(41) (October 13–19 2007): 4116–4120.

24. *Ibid.*, p. 35.

25. Hazari, *Untouchable: The Autobiography of an Indian Outcaste* (New York: Fredrick A. Praeger, 1969).

26. Daya Pawar, *Baluta*, trans. Jerry Pinto (New Delhi: Speaking Tiger, 2015).

27. Aravind Malagatti, *Government Brahmana* (New Delhi: Orient BlackSwan, 2007).

28. Arjun Dangle, ed. *Poisoned Bread: Translations from Modern Marathi Dalit Literature* (New Delhi: Orient BlackSwan, 2009 [1992], Revised Edition). For a discussion on this work see Ramachandran, 'Poisoned Bread', *op. cit.*

29. Laura R. Brueck, *Writing Resistance: The Rhetorical Imagination of Hindi Dalit Literature* (New York: Columbia University Press, 2014), p. 5.

30. *Mangalkavya* is a genre of medieval Bengali poetry, comprising long narrative poems and episodic fragments thereof, composed and written between 1300 and 1800 AD. During this long time interval, popular deities and characters were lifted from folklore and conventionalised. *Mangalkavya* presents an interesting synthesis of indigenous folk and puranic Brahminical traditions of rural Bengal. Traditions that challenged the Brahminical were seen as revolutionary. For details see T. W. Clark, 'Evolution of Hinduism in Medieval Bengali Literature: Siva, Candi, Manasa', *Bulletin of the School of Oriental and African Studies, University of London* 17(3) (1955): 503–518.

31. Hitesranjan Sanyal, 'Continuities of Social Mobility in Traditional and Modern Society in India: Two Case Studies of Caste Mobility in Bengal', *The Journal of Asian Studies* 30(2) (February 1971): 315–339.

32. Guru and Geetha, 'New Phase of Dalit–Bahujan Intellectual Activity', *op. cit.*

33. For details see Hitesranjan Sanyal, *Social Mobility in Bengal* (Calcutta: Papyrus, 1981).

34. For details see Braj Ranjan Mani, *Debrahmanising History: Dominance and Resistance in Indian Society* (New Delhi: Manohar, 2007).

35. The term 'perspective from below', used by T. K. Oommen, is derived from Marxism. Gail Omvedt has also used this term to analyse the anti-caste movement in India. For details see T. K. Oommen, 'Understanding Indian Society: The Relevance of the Perspective from Below', in *Understanding Indian Society: The Non-Brahminic Perspective*, ed. S. M. Dahiwale (New Delhi: Rawat, 2005), pp. 31–50; Gail Omvedt,

'Perspective of the Anti-Caste Movements: Subaltern Sociological Visions', in *ibid.*, pp. 104–120.

36. The difference between these approaches lies in the question of who is studying what. The *etic* approach is independent of the native's cultural judgement, while the *emic* approach is an insider's view. For details see Oommen, 'Understanding Indian Society', *op. cit.*, p. 39.

37. *Ibid.*

38. *Ibid.*, p. 40.

39. Omvedt, 'Perspectives of the Anti-Caste Movements', *op. cit.*, p. 104.

40. *Ibid.*

41. S. V. Ketkar, *History of Caste in India* (Jaipur: Rawat, 1979 [1909]), p. 4.

42. Romila Thapar, *From Lineage to State: Social Formations in the Mid-First Millennium B.C. in the Ganga Valley* (New Delhi: OUP, 1996), p. 18.

43. For more details, see Braj Ranjan Mani, *Debrahmanising History, op. cit.*

44. Herbert Risley, *The People of India* (Calcutta & Simla: Thacker, Spink & Co., 1915), p. 68.

45. S. V. Ketkar, *History of Caste in India, op. cit.*, p. 15.

46. G. S. Ghurye, *Caste and Race in India* (London: Routledge and Kegan, 1932).

47. Ambedkar, *The Untouchables, op. cit.*

48. *Ibid.*, p. i.

49. *Ibid.*, p. v.

50. Max Weber, *Economy and Society: An Outline of Interpretive Sociology* (Berkeley: University of California Press, 1968), p. 302.

51. Célestin Bouglé, *Essays on the Caste System* (London: Cambridge University Press, 1971).

52. Louis Dumont, *Homo Hierarchicus* (New Delhi: Oxford University Press, 1970). The caste system is evaluated by Dumont against the principles of individuality and equality, with Rousseau's and Tocqueville's ideas on equality serving as his two prime theoretical constructs. For details see *ibid.*, pp. 10–20.

53. *Ibid.*, p. 21.

54. The later Vedic society had a fourfold partition. The fourth category, known as Shudra, was an addition to the first three *varnas*: Brahmin, Kshatriya, and Vaishya. This fourth *varna* can be found in a later hymn

of the Rig Veda and no doubt symbolises the forcing of aborigines into servitude. The roles defined for each caste are the priesthood, kingship, trade, and unfree labour respectively. *Ibid.*, p. 68.

55. *Ibid.*, p. 73. Also see, Badri Narayan, *Women Heroes and Dalit Assertion in North India: Culture, Identity and Politics* (New Delhi: Sage, 2006), p. 34.

56. Nicholas B. Dirks, *Castes of Mind: Colonialism and the Making of Modern India* (New Jersey: Princeton University Press, 2001), p. 5.

57. *Ibid.*

58. *Ibid.*, pp. 188–227.

59. In medieval times, these social groupings were political assemblages. For details see Susan Bayly, *Caste, Society and Politics in India from the Eighteenth Century to the Modern Age* (Cambridge: CUP, 1999), p. 3.

60. Dirks, *Castes of Mind, op. cit.*, p. 70.

61. *Ibid.*

62. *Ibid.*, p. 75.

63. *Ibid.*

64. *Ibid.*

65. Dipankar Gupta, 'Introduction: The Certitudes of Caste: When Identity Trumps Hierarchy', in *Caste in Question: Identity or Hierarchy?*, ed. Dipankar Gupta (New Delhi: SAGE Publications, 2004), p. ix.

66. McKim Marriott, ed. *Village India: Studies in the Little Community* (Bombay: Asia Publishing House, 1961).

67. Robert Redfield, a professor of social anthropology at the University of Chicago and a pioneer in the study of civilisations, introduced the concepts of 'great tradition' and 'little tradition' to mark differences between civilisations in terms of 'folk' and 'urban' practices and also to formulate a folk–urban continuum. For him, a civilisation is a complex whole of little and great traditions; the former refers to a village society within the larger context of a civilisation and the latter refers to the literate tradition of a society. For details see Robert Redfield and Alfonso Villa Rojas, *Chan Kom: A Maya Village* (Chicago: University of Chicago Press, 1962); Robert Redfield, *Tepoztlan, a Mexican Village: A Study of Folk Life* (Chicago: University of Chicago Press, 1930).

68. M. N. Srinivas, 'The Social System of a Mysore Village', in *Village India: Studies in the Little Community*, ed. McKim Marriott (Bombay: Asia Publishing House, 1961), pp. 1–36.

69. M. N. Srinivas defines a caste as a dominant caste if 'it pre-pondarates numerically over the other castes, and when it also wields preponderant economic and political power. A large and powerful caste group can more easily be dominant if its position in the local caste hierarchy is not too low.' For details see *ibid*.

70. Gupta, 'Introduction: The Certitudes of Caste', *op. cit.*, p. ix.

71. M. N. Srinivas, 'Caste in Modern India', *The Journal of Asian Studies* 16(4) (August 1957): 529–548.

72. *Ibid.*

73. M. N. Srinivas, 'On Living in a Revolution', *Economic and Political Weekly* 26(13) (March 30, 1991): 833–895.

74. Kathleen Gough, 'The Social Structure of a Tanjore Village', in *Village India: Studies in the Little Community*, ed. McKim Marriott (Bombay: Asia Publishing House, 1961), pp. 37–53.

75. Bernard S. Cohn, 'Changing Status of a Depressed Caste', in *Village India: Studies in the Little Community*, ed. McKim Marriott (Bombay: Asia Publishing House, 1961), pp. 54–79.

76. *Ibid.*

77. Although Alan Beals only does not fully explain this, possible reasons for wartime prosperity could be the expansion of the labour market, rise in wages, increased demand for certain leather items, and the emergence of the military fiscalist state in some parts of south India.

78. Andre Béteille, *Caste, Class and Power: Changing Patterns of a Tanjore Village* (Berkeley: University of California Press, 1965), p. 45.

79. Gupta, 'Introduction: The Certitudes of Caste', *op. cit.*

80. *Ibid.*

81. *Ibid.*

82. Badri Narayan, *Multiple Marginalities: An Anthology of Identified Dalit Writings*, eds. Badri Narayan and A. R. Mishra (New Delhi: Manohar, 2004), p. 28.

83. Badri Narayan, 'Nationalist Past and Political Present', *Economic and Political Weekly* 39(31) (July 31–August 6, 2004): 3533–3540.

84. *Ibid.*

85. *Ibid.*

86. Narayan, *Multiple Marginalities*, *op. cit.*, p. 31.

87. Christopher A. Bayly, 'Moral Judgement: Empire, Nation and History', *European Review* 14(3) (July 2006): 385–391; Y. Chinna Rao,

'Dalits and History Writing in India: Some Historiographical Trends and Questions', in *Approaches to History: Essays in Indian Historiography*, ed. Sabyasachi Bhattacharya (New Delhi: Primus Books, 2011), p. 324.

88. Suvira Jaiswal, 'Studies in Early Indian Social History: Trends and Possibilities', in *Past of the Outcaste: Readings on Dalit History*, eds. Sabysachi Bhattacharya and Yagati Chinna Rao (New Delhi: Orient BlackSwan, 2017), p. 83.

89. *Ibid.*

90. Y. Chinna Rao, 'Dalits and History Writing in India', *op. cit.*

91. After the Second World War, there was a perceived need to focus on the histories of the people who had been neglected for so long: the 'subalterns', who included slaves, members of the working classes, women, landless rural agrarian labour, and marginal ethnic groups, among others. The history of this subaltern group came to be known in the 1970s as 'history from below'. During the 1980s, there emerged a series of publications under the series title 'Subaltern Studies', edited by Ranajit Guha. For details, see P. Peres, 'Subaltern Spaces in Brazil', *Dispositio/n (American Journal of Cultural Histories and Theories)* 19(46): 113–126.

92. See Ranajit Guha, 'On Some Aspects of the Historiography of Colonial India', in *Subaltern Studies I: Writings on South Asian History and Society*, ed. Ranajit Guha (Delhi: OUP, 1982), p. 8.

93. Christian Lee Novetzke, 'The Subaltern Numen: Making History in the Name of God', *History of Religions* 46(2) (November 2006): 99–108.

94. Guha, 'On Some Aspects of the Historiography of Colonial India', *op. cit.*, pp. 1–3.

95. *Ibid.*

96. Ramnarayan S. Rawat and K. Satyanarayana, 'Introduction', in *Dalit Studies: New Perspectives on Indian History and Society*, eds. Ramnarayan S. Rawat and K. Satyanarayana (Durham: Duke University Press, 2016), pp. 1–2.

97. Nicholas B. Dirks, 'Castes of Mind', *Representations* 37 (Special Issue) (Winter 1992), p. 76.

98. Yagati Chinna Rao, *Writing Dalit History and Other Essays* (New Delhi: Kaniska Publishers, 2007), p. 121.

99. Laura Dudley Jenkins, *Identity and Identification in India: Defining the Disadvantaged* (New York: RoutledgeCurzon, 2003), pp. 1–3.

100. *Ibid.*, p. 23.

101. Dirks, *Castes of Mind, op. cit.*, p. 60. Quoted in Jenkins, *Identity and Identification in India, op. cit.*, p. 49.

102. Jenkins, *Identity and Identification in* India, *op. cit.*, p. 40.

103. *Ibid.*

104. Jenkins cited the case of the then president K. R. Narayanan, whose caste was listed as a Scheduled Caste in Kerala but not in the national capital. For details see *ibid.*, p. 87.

105. *Ibid.*

106. Geo W. Briggs, *The Chamars* (Delhi: Low Price Publications, 1997 [1925]).

107. *Ibid.*, p. 12.

108. Members of the Karavara community were those who had a Nisada father—descended from a Brahmin father and a Shudra mother—and a Vaidehi mother—Vaishya father and Brahmin mother. For details, see *ibid.*, p. 15.

109. *Ibid.*, p. 13.

110. *Ibid.*, pp. 23–34.

111. *Ibid.*, p. 121.

112. *Ibid.*, p. 200.

113. Kabir, whose teachings or *bijaks* are still considered attacks on the caste system, was a disciple of Ramananda who propagated the Bhakti movement in north India. Ramananda was a disciple of Ramanuja, who started the movement in south India. Ramanuja conceives of god as a person who rewards the devotion or bhakti of a disciple. His preachings were a revolt against the caste system. Rae Das was another disciple of Ramananda and a worshipper of Ram and Janki. Guru Nanak, known as the founder of Sikhism, also revolted against the caste system and did not believe in ceremonial and social restrictions. For details see *ibid.*, pp. 201–202.

114. *Ibid.*, p. 202.

115. *Ibid.*, p. 247.

116. Stephen Fuchs, *The Children of Hari: A Study of the Nimar Balahis in Madhya Pradesh* (Vienna: Verag Herald, 1949).

117. *Ibid.*, p. vi.

118. *Ibid.*

119. *Ibid.*, p. vii.

120. *Ibid.*, p. 7.

121. *Ibid.*, p. 17.
122. *Ibid.*, pp. 18–20.
123. *Ibid.*, p. 57.
124. *Ibid.*
125. *Ibid.*, pp. 76–80.
126. *Ibid.*, p. 434.
127. *Ibid.*, p. 436.
128. Rao, 'Dalits and History Writing in India', *op. cit.*, pp. 325–326.
129. Badri Narayan, 'National Past and Political Present', *op. cit.*
130. *Ibid.*
131. Badri Narayan, *Women Heroes and Dalit Assertion in North India: Culture, Identity and Politics* (New Delhi: Sage, 2006), p. 14.
132. *Ibid.*
133. For details see Raj Sekhar Basu, *Exploring Dalit Experiences in Colonial and Post-Colonial India* (New Delhi: Rajat Publications, 2010).
134. Sabyasachi Bhattacharya, 'History from Below', *Social Scientist* 11(4) (April 1983): 3–20.
135. William Wilson Hunter, *The Annals of Rural Bengal* (London: Smith, Elder, and Co., 1883).
136. Bhattacharya, 'History from Below', *op. cit.*, p. 5.
137. Swaraj Basu, *Dynamics of a Caste Movement: The Rajbansis of North Bengal: 1910–1947* (New Delhi: Manohar, 2003), pp. 14, 36–37, 65, 68, 71.
138. Sekhar Bandopadhyay, *Caste, Politics and the Raj: Bengal, 1872–1937* (Kolkata: K. P. Bagchi and Company, 1990), pp. 163, 167.
139. *Ibid.*, pp. 162–163.
140. Purnachandra Ray, *Arya Paundra Kshatriya Samaj* (Calcutta, 1917).
141. Rao, 'Dalits and History Writing in India,' *op. cit.*, p. 330. Also see for details Raj Sekhar Basu, *Nandanar's Children: The Paraiyan's Tryst with Destiny, Tamil Nadu 1850–1956* (New Delhi: Sage, 2010); Y. Chinna Rao, *Dalits' Struggle for Identity: Andhra and Hyderabad, 1900–1950* (New Delhi: Kaniska Publishers, 2003); Badri Narayan Tiwari, *Documenting Dissent: Contesting Fables, Contested Memories and Dalit Discourse* (Shimla: IIAS, 2000); Nandini Gooptu, 'Caste and Labour: Untouchable Social Movements in Urban Uttar Pradesh in the Early Twentieth Century', in *Dalit Movements and Meanings of Labour in India*, ed. Peter Robb (Delhi: OUP, 1996).
142. Rao, 'Dalits and History Writing in India', *op. cit.*, pp. 329–330.

143. Sanjay Sangvai, 'The New People's Movements in India', *Economic and Political Weekly* 42(50) (December 15–21, 2007), pp. 111–117.

144. Indira Gandhi, Speech at UN conference, 14 June 1972, Stockholm.

145. Ponna Wignaraja, *New Social Movements in the South: Empowering the People* (New Delhi: Vistar Publications, 1993), pp. 126–127.

146. Sarah Joseph, 'State, Democracy and the Problem of Exclusions', *The Indian Journal of Political Science* 63(2/3) (June–September 2002), p. 138.

147. Wignaraja, *New Social Movements in the South, op. cit.*, p. 131.

148. Sangvai, 'The New People's Movements in India,' *op. cit.*, p. 112.

149. D. L. Sheth, 'Globalisation and New Politics of Micro-Movements', *Economic and Political Weekly* 39(1) (January 3, 2004): 45–58.

150. *Panchami* or *panchama* land is the land which was assigned and distributed to Dalits in Tamil Nadu during British rule in 1892, and could neither be sold nor re-classified. For details, see Mathur Sathya, 'Understanding the History of the Panchami Land Struggle', Dalit History Month, *Medium*, 4 April 2021, https://dalithistorymonth.medium.com/understanding-the-history-of-the-panchami-land-struggle-b56f6b950c7c (accessed August 2024).

151. Raj Sekhar Basu, 'Dalit Politics in Tamil Nadu' (paper presented at 'Dalit Perspectives: a Symposium on the Changing Contours of Dalit Politics', February 2006).

152. Y. Chinna Rao, 'Social Exclusion and the Dalits in India', in *Social Exclusion, Integration and Inclusive Policies*, eds. V. Subramanyam and K. Sekhar (New Delhi: Rawat Publications, 2010), pp. 37–42.

153. For more details see, Ghanshyam Shah, Harsh Mander, Sukhdeo Thorat, Satish Deshpande and Amita Baviskar, *Untouchability in Rural India* (New Delhi and London: SAGE Publications, 2006), p. 39.

154. For details see Raj Sekhar Basu, 'Recapturing the Moments of Dalit History and Politics: A Journey from the Colonial to Post Colonial' (Presidential Address at the 74th Indian History Congress, Section III: Modern India, Ravenshaw University, Cuttack, 2013).

155. Musahars as a community did not have a name of their own, and were essentially categorised as a community of 'rat-eaters'. In everyday discourse, untouchability is assigned to them because of their practice of trapping rats—an occupation which makes them a defiling community in the eyes of other castes. For details see Arun Kumar, 'Culture, Development

and Cultural Capital of Farce: The Musahar Community in Bihar', *Economic and Political Weekly* 41(40) (October 7–13, 2006): 4281–4283.

156. For more details, see Ranajit Guha, *Elementary Aspects of Peasant Insurgency in Colonial India* (Delhi: Oxford University Press, 1983), p. 9.

157. Manuela Ciotti, 'In the Past We Were a Bit "Chamar": Education as a Self- and Community-engineering Process in Northern India', *Journal of the Royal Anthropological Institute* 12(4) (October 2006), p. 901.

158. Rao, 'Dalits and History Writing in India', *op. cit.*, pp. 330–331.

159. See for details Basu, 'Recapturing the Moments of Dalit History and Politics', *op. cit.*

1

Dalits and Martial Traditions

Historical Antecedents from Andhra

B. Rama Chandra Reddy

The present chapter explores Dalit martial traditions in the Telugu-speaking regions of the Indian subcontinent from the twelfth century to the first half of the nineteenth century. The chapter is divided into three parts. The first part deals with the textual tradition of theorising about and describing army composition in India from the epic period (1,000–600 BC) to the middle of the eleventh century. The second part highlights the martial traditions of the Dalit communities of these regions (hereinafter Andhra unless otherwise specified) from the twelfth century to the early part of the eighteenth century, utilising a variety of sources, including palm leaf manuscripts which appeared in printed form later, local records, caste histories, oral traditions, and colonial ethnographic reports. The third part of the chapter covers the role of Andhra Dalit communities in the colonial army and also explores why Dalits were dropped from the active fighting force of the Madras Infantry and confined to the corps of 'Pioneers', 'Sappers', and 'Miners'.

I

Political thinkers of ancient India referred to seven essential organs or elements of state (*saptanga*),[1] among which the army was seen as essential to smooth administration. It was entrusted with the duties of protecting the people and the boundaries of the state from external aggression, launching wars against enemy rulers, and quelling internal disturbances if necessary. Hence, rulers took elaborate measures to recruit soldiers, arrange for proper military training facilities, and equip their armies with arms.

Categorisation of Troops in Ancient Times

Valmiki mentions in the Yuddhakanda[2] of the Ramayana—perhaps the first ever such reference—five contingents or *bala*s of an army: one supplied by friends (*mitra bala*), three consisting of inhabitants of the woods (*atavi bala*), hereditary warriors (*maula bala*), and paid servants (*britya bala*) respectively, and one consisting of deserters from enemy armies (*dvisad bala*).[3] But in the third century BC, the foremost political thinker of India, Kautilya, mentioned in his *Arthasastra* six categories or *bala*s of soldiers, giving details of their composition and nature, when to employ each, and the relative merits of each group. Kautilya listed, in descending order of importance, hereditary troops, hired/paid troops (*bhritaka/brita bala*), a corporation of soldiers (*sreni*), troops belonging to a friend (*mitra*), troops consisting of enemy deserters (*amitra bala*), and wild tribes (*atavi bala*).[4] This categorisation and ranking of troops seems to have remained widely accepted without modification up until the time of Kamandaka's *Nitisara* (500–700 AD), when a slight change in wording was introduced.[5]

The *maula bala* or hereditary troops were a standing army composed of soldiers who may have served the king's family for several generations.[6] The *bhritak bala/brita bala* or hired/paid troops were also referred to as local volunteers, auxiliaries, or mercenaries. By profession, they were either farmers or small traders who took part in campaigns and then returned to their professions.[7] The *sreni bala* or corporation of soldiers consisted of trained and equipped bodies of mercenaries organised under their own leaders.[8] The *mitra bala* were troops loaned for particular campaigns by allies or friends. The *amitra bala* or *dvisad bala*, comprising deserters from enemy armies and prisoners of war,[9] were not to be trusted but their employment was recommended if the eventual outcome of battle was of little consequence.[10] The *atavi bala* or wild tribes could be employed when the enemy army had to traverse paths inhabited by wild tribes, when a small enemy army had to be attacked, and when the enemy army consisted mostly of wild tribes, which invokes the technique of breaking a wood apple (*bilva*) with another wood apple.[11] Kamandaka warned that three kinds of troops, viz. the forest tribes, the weaned-over, and the *sreni*, could be induced to indulge in excessive drinking and thus rendered incapable of service.[12]

Kautilya also refers to the employment of labour forces for clearing up camps, roads, waterworks, mills and ponds, for carrying machines, weapons, armour, implements, and food and for removing weapons, armour, and wounded men from the battlefield. Similarly, Kamandaka refers in *Nitisara* to labour forces entrusted with purifications or repairs, the rebuilding of pits and marshes (on the track), the construction of roads, the pitching of tents, and other miscellaneous duties.[13]

Categorisation of Troops in South India

The categorisation of army troops into six types seems to have existed in south India too in the twelfth century, as attested by the *Abhilashitarthachintamani*, also known as *Manasollasa*, an encyclopaedic Sanskrit text written by King Someswara Deva of the Kalyani Chalukya dynasty. The second chapter of the book deals with the army. King Someswara declares that '*maula, bhritya, maitra, sraina, atavika* and *amitra* are six types of troops' and contends that three regiments, namely *maula, bhritya,* and *maitra* (*mitra*) are the best among these. The *sraina* (*sreni*) troops, formed by guilds (*samaya*) of the same caste or profession, are said to be mediocre (*madyamam*) whereas *atavika* troops, consisting of tribals like Nishadas and Mlecchas who lived in and around the mountains, are said to be of inferior grade (*adhamam*). The surrendered forces of enemies were known as *amitraja*, and this text warns that a king who is proficient in warfare should never trust *amitra* troops or allow them near him.[14]

Interestingly, Someswara altered the order of importance and the relative merits of the troops laid down by Kautilya and Kamandaka. The 'mediocre' troops of guilds were relegated from the third to the fourth position and the surrendered forces of enemies, labelled most unreliable, were dropped from the fifth to the sixth position. He elevated the troops of friends or allies from the fourth to the third position and the troops of tribals from the sixth to the fifth position. The precise reason for this shuffling is not clearly known; it could have been due to changes that occurred over time or due to differences in regional experience, as *Manasollasa* is a south Indian text whereas the other two texts were composed in the north. It should also be noted that Someswara had actual experience of warfare, unlike the other major subcontinental writers before him who wrote about military matters.

Social System and Martial Character

According to textual accounts, Indian society has been broadly divided, at least since Vedic times, into four hierarchical social groups known as *varnas*: Brahmins, Kshatriyas, Vaishyas, and Shudras; a fifth *varna* appeared at a much later date, whose members were treated as untouchables or outcastes. Tradition ascribed to Kshatriyas the duty of protecting people. Hence, most warriors belonged to the Kshatriya group, although there are a few references to Brahmin warriors in the epics. In almost all cases, the martial arts teachers and trainers mentioned in the epics are Brahmins, and there are instances in the epics of martial training being denied to the base-born.[15] Thus, it is clear that fighting forces were once composed almost entirely of Kshatriyas and some Brahmins, but things seem to have changed by the Mauryan period in the third and second centuries BC, by which time the army is reported to have begun to employ Vaishyas and Shudras. The teacher of Kautilya stated that armies were made up of Brahmins, Kshatriyas, Vaishyas, or Shudras and 'that which is mentioned first is, on account of bravery, better to be enlisted than the ones subsequently mentioned in the order of enumeration.'[16] Curiously, *Arthasastra* assigns the duties of guarding and keeping watch over the interior of the kingdom to trap-keepers (*vagurika*), archers (*sabara*), hunters (*pulinda*), outcastes (*chandala*), and wild tribes (*aranyachara*).[17] Someswara, on the other hand, is silent about the caste composition of the army, which can perhaps be attributed to the south Indian social system being different from that of the north.

From the above facts, it is clear that neither specific reference to nor mention of the employment of Dalits in the army has been found in any text dating back to the period between the epic age and the early part of the twelfth century. However, in texts from the latter half of the twelfth century, we begin to come across references to Dalit warriors engaging in battle.

II

The Dalits of Andhra

The outcaste groups as a whole were variously known as Avarna, Chandala, Anthyaja, Panchama and the like, while particular groups were referred to using regional *jati* names. These communities had a low social and ritual status. Until the twentieth century, European travellers and British colonial administrators often used the generic term 'Pariah' to refer to different outcaste social groups of the various linguistic regions of south India, clubbing together all the major untouchable groups like Pariyans, Chakkiliyans, Puliyans, Holeyas, Malas, and Madigas, without properly understanding the intricacies of the Indian social system. In the first half of the twentieth century, newer identification terms like 'Scheduled Castes' and 'Harijan' began to be used. In the post-colonial period, these communities have preferred to call themselves Dalits, signifying their oppressed identity as communities 'suppressed, ground, arrested or broken to pieces'. Hence, the word 'Pariah', as used by the Europeans before the twentieth century, should be understood in the same sense as the modern connotation of the word 'Dalit'.

The Telugu-speaking region of India, what was until recently undivided Andhra Pradesh, is the abode of two major Dalit communities, namely Malas and Madigas, and their dependent communities (as well as some other smaller 'outcaste' communities). They were treated as untouchables and subjected to a variety of discriminatory practices: they were denied entry into the sacred spaces and dwellings of the elite classes, access to water from public sources, and the services of servicing communities such as washermen and barbers, and were granted only restricted entry into villages. They were forced to dwell in separate hamlets outside the village; medieval Andhra sources refer to quarters exclusively set apart for Dalit habitation.[18] During the modern period, these Dalit habitations are known as Mala *palli*/Mala *vada* and Madiga *palli*.

Edgar Thurston, writing over a century ago, notes that 'the chief occupations of the Malas are weaving, and working as farm labourers for Sudras; a few cultivate their own land', and provides a vivid account of their looms and weaving practices.[19] Ironically, there is not even a single reference in medieval Andhra sources to Dalit (Mala) involvement in agricultural operations, although the bulk of their men and women remain involved in agriculture even in present-day Andhra.[20] Seventeenth-century Nellore district inscriptions refer to a person known as '*vetti*'[21] or '*vetti* of [a specified village]'.[22] In the area being referred to, the *vetti*, corresponding to '*yelodu*' (perhaps a corruption of '*velivadu*', which means 'outcaste') in what is now Telangana, was the lowest-ranked village servant and messenger and a person involved in disposing of the dead. *Vetti*s invariably belonged to the Mala community.

The Madiga community consisted more of artisans than of unskilled labourers, mainly engaged in making footwear and leather products useful in agriculture. They mastered the art of crafting shoes and sandals, especially *kirrucheppulu*—sandals said to produce music when their (affluent) wearers walked in them. *Athavanavyavaharatantram*, a document prepared in the late eighteenth century by an unknown author at the request of an officer of the East India Company who desired to understand the Vijayanagara administration, mentions that Madigas supplied (leather) ropes, buckets, sandals, etc. to cultivators, who paid an agreed-upon fee in grain during harvest time.[23] Madigas also served as village servants and conveyed public messages using tom-toms (*dopavadu*).

Impact of Socio-Religious Reform Movements on the Dalits of Andhra

Socio-religious reform movements that originated in neighbouring linguistic regions in the twelfth century had a deep impact on the lives and conditions of Andhra Dalits. Virasaivism, a militant form of Shiva worship introduced by Basava or Basavesvara (1106–1167), the prime minister of Bijjala, the Kalachuri[24] king of Kalyan in the Kannada-speaking region of south India, emerged in opposition to the hierarchised, ritualised, and institutionalised nature of Hinduism.[25] Intensely anti-Brahminical and committed to a vision of an egalitarian society,[26] the Virasaiva sect offered membership to untouchables and was attractive to them for obvious reasons: it allowed Dalits to carry the *linga* (a phallic symbol of Shiva), which they were earlier barred from touching, and it also disregarded the concept of untouchables having a 'polluting' effect on those within the caste system. There are many vehement declarations in Virasaiva literature of the greatness of devotees belonging to the lower orders. It even advocated inter-marriage between high-caste and low-caste groups.[27] Basava's Virasaivism quickly became a revolution against the political and religious orthodoxies of the day.[28] Meanwhile, Vaisnavism gained popularity under the influence of Ramanuja (1017–1137 AD), a saint from the Tamil region. He propagated the concept of Sri Vaisnavism even among Shudras and outcastes, revealing two different ways of practising it to two classes of people: *bhakti* (devotion) to the upper castes and *prapatti* (surrender) to the lower castes. It is believed that, during a period of exile in the Kannada region, Ramanuja retrieved an idol of Krishna that had been taken from Melkote by a Muslim ruler who destroyed the temple it had been housed in; Ramanuja re-installed the idol in the rebuilt temple, and two outcaste communities—the Thirukula and Jambavakula—that assisted Ramanuja in bringing back the Krishna idol were offered the privilege of entering the holy temples of Melkote, Srirangam, and Belur once a year to express their devotion.[29]

These two reformist sects—the Virasaivas and Vaishnavites—had a profound influence on the Dalits of Andhra, providing them with the opportunity to participate (with restrictions) in rituals. The preachings and activities of these socio-religious reformers boosted the morale of Dalits and instilled self-confidence in them. Moreover, the egalitarian principles of the two sects resulted in opportunities for the Dalits of Andhra, especially those from the dry ecoregions, to serve in the armed forces. Two such instances are described in the *Katamaraju Kadhalu* (ballad of Katamaraju) and the *Palnati Viracharitra* (epic of Palnadu), unbroken oral histories that have been sung since the period currently under consideration, i.e. for at least 800 years, and were also recorded and preserved in palm leaf manuscripts.

Dalit (Madiga) Martial Traditions as Depicted in the Ballad of Katamaraju

A sequence of events in Andhra culminated in a war between the armies of Nallasiddhi, the Telugu Choda ruler of the Nellore region, and the Gollas under Katamaraju over the issue of a grazing tax (*pullari*) in the twelfth century.[30] Nallasiddhi, the Golla heroes (including Katamaraju), and the Madiga warriors who supported the latter attained heroic deaths in the course of the war. The incidents of and around this war entered the bardic tradition as one of the world's longest ballad cycles: the *Katamaraju Kadhalu*,[31] which describes the remarkable bond between the Gollas and their formidable military allies, the Madigas.[32] The ballad cycle refers to two important battles: the battle of Ballikurava and the battle of Mangalipadu, both of which took place in the dry zones of what is today Prakasam district in Andhra Pradesh, and featured displays of Dalit valour. Two valiant Madiga leaders, namely Musalinidu and his son Biranidu, met heroic deaths after a fierce battle alongside their trusted Madiga warriors.

The Battle of Ballikurava

As per the story, after Poluraju (the youngest uncle of Katamaraju) was killed at Cherukuru in a battle against Mukkanti (a general of the Choda king of Sri Rangam), one Pallikonda (a minister of Poluraju) proceeded to Yalamanchi, the capital of the Gollas, with Poluraju's wives, sons, and cattle. When the grandsons of Mukkanti attacked the party at Ballikurava to kill the sons of Poluraju, Pallikonda requested Gosangi[33] Musalinidu, a Madiga leader, to protect them, revealing the bond between the Madigas and the Gollas. The passage runs as follows:

> Oh famed Matanga![34] Renowned and honoured for your impetuosity; noble, valiant and virtuous man! You belonged to the Irabattu dynasty famed even to command the waters of Ganges of Kasi to reveal an indubitable truth. Ours is a bond created by Lord Vishnu.[35] Customarily, you are the one who perform the (trusted) deeds. The ruler (Poluraju) had faith in your exceptional ability and do perform the same deed as he said while entrusting you the task of escorting the Jangamas to Sri Sailam. You are the brave one! Do now whatever you did for my uncle and kindly ensure our victory in the impending war. For we will care for your kin, as you yourself would, impartially for all ages to come and as long as this world exists as we are kinsmen (*dayadulu*). Our fate on the battlefield is dependent on you. Oh valiant one, do come with your Gosangi army.[36]

Responding to the invitation from Pallikonda, Musalinidu appealed to the Gosangi heroes to attack like 'roaring tigers' and 'uphold the fame of the Gosangi'.[37] They followed Musalinidu, wearing shawls, faded waistcloths tightened with sashes, caste marks, and (as armour) cheetah, tiger, and bear hides, holding lion banners, carrying spears, clubs, swords, cross-hilted daggers, bows, horns, shields, and black silk umbrellas on horseback, accompanied by the music of flutes, tom-toms, and string instruments called *tamburas*. Then they proceeded to the battlefield on elephants and horses like wrestlers.[38]

The valour and heroic deaths of the two Gosangis, Musalinidu and Bodavula Annepaku, in the battlefield are vividly described. Musalinidu is said to have attacked and killed the enemies with a blow each, slitting throats, slicing chests and bellies, cutting off ears and noses, extracting teeth, etc. The 500 Gosangi warriors are compared to Bhairavas (fierce manifestations of Siva), and the battlefield is depicted as being strewn with blood and mutilated corpses of humans and animals, with birds consuming scattered flesh. According to the ballad, when Virabhallani, the ruler of Vinukonda, marched up to face Musalinidu with one thousand cavalry and elephant corps, Musalinidu exterminated the elephants and ravaged the cavalry, but the valorous Virabhallani injured Musalinidu with his sword. Musalinidu pierced Virabhallani's body with his sword, the enraged Virabhallani broke Musalinidu's ribs, and finally Musalinidu decapitated his opponent, collapsed, and died. In the meantime, Bodavula Annepaku fought against Gajakanta, the ruler of Kancherla, and supposedly cut his horses and elephants into pieces. Finally, Annepaku killed Gajakanta and died in the war along with other Gosangis.[39] Maremma, the wife of Musalinidu, and Annamma, the wife of Annepaku, performed sati on the pyres of their dead husbands, leaving their respective infant sons Biranidu (Viranidu) and Chennamanidu (Chennayya) to the care of Siri Devi, the wife of Poluraju.[40]

Battle of Mangalipadu

Sixty years after the battle of Ballikurava,[41] another ghastly war took place at Erragaddapadu between the Gollas and Nallasiddhi, the Telugu Choda king of Nellore, over the grazing tax (*pullai*). When the impending war was in sight, Biranidu approached Katamaraju along with the Gosangi warriors and requested him for an opportunity to fight on behalf of the Gollas. Biranidu was hailed by his followers as 'the son of Musalinidu, Matanga *gotra,* the blessed child of Siva reared by Siri Devi, the son of Pasupathi[42] and the incarnation of

Virabhadra'.[43, 44] Katamaraju asked Biranidu and the Gosangis to take up positions at Mangalipadu.[45]

Biranidu and his followers entrenched themselves at Mangalipadu, erecting black silk tents. Biranidu summoned all the Gosangi warriors when he got wind of Nallasiddhi's armies approaching. Four thousand Gosangis came with their staffs and arms,[46] wearing short trousers, pink girdles, gem-studded anklets, crests of tassel, red handkerchiefs, unsheathed swords, and brass shields and bells around the waist, singing and dancing to the beats of tom-toms while twirling their moustaches and beating their thighs (as signs of valour), and assembled before Biranidu like 'elephants in a rut' (*mathebham*).[47] After receiving permission from Biranidu to wage war, they prayed to Lord Virabhadra, and Biranidu ceremonially cut a sal tree in two with a single stroke of his sword.

Nallasiddhi sent rows of elephants against Biranidu and the Gosangis. 'Like fish swimming against running waters', Biranidu made his way through them, cutting the trunks and heads of the elephants and finally grounding all the huge mammals. Meanwhile, the enraged Chennayya and Gosangi warriors went about killing enemy soldiers. When the cavalry was sent in, Biranidu cut the horses and the riders to pieces with his sword. The Gosangis' hounds wreaked havoc in the battlefield, attacking animals and humans alike. The valour of the Madiga heroes left piles of heads and corpses behind, but then came a fury of enemy arrows that rained down on the Gosangis. Finally, after a fierce battle, Biranidu breathed his last on the battlefield, surrounded by the corpses of Gosangi warriors and their trusted hounds.[48]

Dalit (Mala) Martial Traditions Depicted in the Epic of Palnadu

Palnati Viracharitra is the history of a fratricidal war that took place in the latter half of the twelfth century AD between two princes of the Haihaya family of Palnad, a part of present-day Guntur district.[49] Nalagama, one of the two brothers, was ruling Gurajala under the guidance of a widowed Saivite female minister, Nayakuralu Nagamma of the Reddy community, while Brahma Nayudu, a

Velama[50] and a staunch Vaishnavite, was the minister and guardian of young Malideva, Nalagama's half-brother, who was ruling from Macherla. Differences between the two factions culminated in the battle of Karampoodi, in which all the heroes of Palnadu perished. Later, the heroes of Palnadu were deified and worshipped annually, a tradition that continues even today. The army of Brahma Nayudu included people from all classes and castes, including Dalits. One of the Dalit (Mala) heroes was Kannamanidu, also referred to as Kannama and Kannamadasu in *Palnati Viracharitra*.

Kannamanidu

Kannamanidu was the son of Teppali Nayudu and Pemmasani, and was said to have been born with the blessings of Brahma Nayudu and Lord Chennakesava (Vishnu).[51] Brahma Nayudu adopted him as his son, perhaps due to the death of his parents, and made him a Vaishnavite. Though Kannama identified as 'a Mala caste devotee of Brahma Nayudu',[52] throughout the ballad he behaves like and considers himself Nayudu's eldest son. Brahma Nayudu always refers to Kannama as 'son, Vikramarka in the battle'.[53] The physical description of Kannama in the text lays out his warrior-like qualities,[54] as do descriptions of fights like the one between him and Ravelapatar, a Golla warrior:

> They fought like two bulls mauling, like rutting elephants churning the earth, like hills clashing together. They fought like Rama and Ravana, like Karna and Arjuna coming together. The grasped each other as a vine twists around a tree. Kannama Nidu caught Ravelapatar in a mighty grip and leaped into the middle of the assembly hall in Macerla.

However, the fight was stopped by Brahma Nayudu.[55]

It was stated that the 'lionhearted' Kannama marched to the Karampoodi battlefield flanked on both sides by *masti*s (Dalit wrestlers/gymnasts) who were holding straight Bhairava swords.[56] At Karampoodi, Brahma Nayudu sent Kannama out in the middle of the night to examine the battlefield, which was believed to be infested with malevolent spirits and demons. With a rosary of tulsi beads heaving on his chest, wearing a twinkling bracelet (*kadiyamu*), a small bell, peacock feathers, and a black girdle and holding a fearful Bhairava sword, the 'sharp-moustached', 'red-eyed', 'well-built', and 'fearsome' Kannama started towards the battlefield like 'a moving hill of collyrium'. When the ghosts appeared before him, Kannama unsheathed his sword angrily like Shiva ('Kalagni Rudra') and faced them with 'fearless eyes'.[57]

It is clear from the above descriptions that Kannamanidu was a great warrior, likely heading a Dalit (*masti*) warrior group in the battle. Ironically, the details of his last battle cannot be found in the available texts or ballads. But it is evident that he also died fighting heroically in the battle and was deified later along with the fallen heroes (*virulu*) of Palnadu. His huge sword, known as 'Bhairava *khadgam*', can be seen even today in the preserved armoury of the Palnadu heroes at Gurajala.

Gosangis in the Epic of Palnadu

The Palnadu tradition also mentions the Gosangis, the mighty Madiga warriors who were with Brahma Nayudu at the beginning. In his translation, Gene H. Roghair describes the Gosangis as follows: 'Simbuni *Muta*[58] wielding the double-edged sword; Bobbili *Muta* wielding the great sword; brave Tevula Potu Nedu; Gandham Oppi Nedu; Sugandi, the wrestler who fights what [he] sees. With hairlock, garland of flowers, cymbals, great drums and bells, there were 24000 Gosangi warriors.'[59] However, a few days before the war, a compromise was suggested that was acceptable to Brahma Nayudu, and the Gosangis, seeing no more reason for war, went back home even though Balachandra, Brahma Nayudu's son, wanted to fight because a close aide of his had been murdered by the enemy forces. Messengers were repeatedly sent asking the Gosangis to come back, but to no avail. Roghair states that, while the Gosangis were 'the first followers of the creed', it was the Malas who later became 'the followers of the [Palnadu, i.e. heroic Vaishnava] tradition.'[60]

Martial Tradition as Depicted in the Oral Narrations of Dalit Minstrels

The *Katamaraju Kadhalu* and *Palnati Viracharitra* historical traditions have been preserved for posterity in the oral narratives of two sects of minstrels: the Kommula Vandlu, a sect of the Madigas,[61] and the Vira Vidyavanthulu, a majority of whom are Malas,[62] respectively. These epics are recited on important occasions like festivals, marriages, and deaths of members of the two communities. It is believed that Bhaktiranna, the lone survivor of the battle of Erragaddapadu, authorised the descendants of the Gosangi warriors to recite and propagate the stories of the Gollas—the stories that constitute *Katamaraju Kadhalu*—and ordered the Gollas to patronise them. These descendants later came to be known as Kommula Vandlu as they used a musical instrument called the *kommu*, a kind of horn, during their recitations.[63] It has proved difficult to unearth details about the authorisation received by the Vira Vidyavanthulu that are more substantial than their claim that their families have been reciting the ballads 'since the time of their forefathers'.[64] It is reasonable to believe that Brahma Nayudu or the Velamas, the caste to which Nayudu belonged, might have authorised the Vira Vidyavanthulu to be the official reciters of the Palnadu tradition. Though the epics were meant to be used to eulogise their specific patron communities, namely the Gollas and the Velamas respectively, the minstrels also preserved the descriptions of Dalit martial traditions in the ballads.

While narrating the epic of Palnadu, the Vira Vidyavanthulu are supposed to wear traditional attire. Roghair describes it thus:

> In his right hand he wields an *ande katti* (a sabre with bells on the hilt); in his left hand is *dalu* (a small, round brass shield). On his right leg is a jangling anklet. Wound round his head is a turban with an ornament bearing a crescent moon and an *ummahupitta*. Around his neck there must be a garland. His forehead and the right side of his chest are marked with a *tirumani* (a Vaishnavite symbol). The left side of his chest is draped with a red and white sash decorated with bells and beads and hangs down to his thigh. His white cotton garment is tied with a distinctive knot.[65]

The Kommula Vandlu, too, hold a sword and a shield in their right and left hands respectively on occasion during performances, although this is not mandatory.[66] The attire of the performers depicts clearly the nostalgia of the communities for their martial traditions.

Masti Tradition

According to ethnographic reports from the nineteenth century, there existed two kinds of *masti*s: Mala *masti*s and Madiga *mastis*, who depended on their respective patrons—the Malas and the Madigas—for their livelihoods. John Cain, a Christian missionary working at Dummagudem, was perhaps the first to mention a group of people known as 'Mastilu', who 'beg from Gollas, Malalu and Madigalu only and are regarded as low in the social scale.'[67] Thurston states that the 'Mastigas' were 'known as Mala Mastigas. When engaged in begging, they perform various contortionist and acrobatic feats.'[68] Syed Siraj Ul Hassan clearly distinguished between the two kinds of Dalit *masti*s, writing that the 'Mashti Madiga are story tellers and beggars, occasionally exhibiting acrobatic feats before the public' and 'Mala Mashti are acrobats and earn their living by performing physical feats.'[69]

*Masti*s are roving acrobats for their respective castes. Mala *masti*s are present in both the Telugu states—Andhra Pradesh and Telangana—but have always been more populous in Andhra Pradesh,[70] whereas Madiga *masti*s can only be found in Telangana.[71] They visit the hamlets of their patrons periodically and entertain them with songs, dances, and physical displays, in return for which they are paid annual dues. They lift weights, perform somersaults, have rams charge into their chests, break stones with their bare hands, pull bullock carts with their hair, etc.[72] They also engage in swordplay and stick-play, as *masti*s are experts in those martial arts; it has been reported that Mala *masti*s stood by the Malas in many bloody conflicts with other castes.[73] Mala *masti*s even train Mala youth in stick-play (*karra sadhanam*).

A Telugu copper plate of 1515 AD, supposed to have been issued by Sri Krishnadevaraya, was recently found in the possession of one Kaki Rambabu, a Mala *masti,* in Farijallipeta in East Godavari district of Andhra Pradesh. The inscription states that a certain Mala *masti* challenged the residents of a village in Krishnadevaraya's kingdom to a wrestling bout, demanding the wives of all the villagers if he remained undefeated. The bout continued for three days and, finally, the Mala *masti* emerged victorious but, instead of claiming the reward agreed upon, he requested a citation from the emperor, which was readily given. It is strongly believed that Krishnadevaraya recruited men of the Mala *masti* and Madiga *masti* communities into his army for their sheer strength and endurance and even certified them as dedicated soldiers of his army.[74] It is worth noting in this connection that the *Palnati Viracharitra* mentions *masti*s 'holding straight Bhairava swords' and flanking 'the lionhearted Kanukula Kannama' on both sides as the latter marched to Karampoodi battlefield to face the spirits.[75]

Although it is argued that the waning of reformist zeal in Andhra after the thirteenth century was majorly responsible for the decline in the employment of *masti*s in the military, Thallapally Manohar contends that *masti*s stopped being employed as military personnel after the arrival of Europeans and later became bodyguards and musclemen of local merchants and traders, but lost those positions too as soon as trade went into the hands of the Europeans. It was then that they became entertainers and acrobats, using the skills passed down to them by their martial traditions to eke out a livelihood.[76]

Dalit Martial Character in Banditry

Banditry, involving the threat of unlawful force, is a phenomenon that offers glimpses into particular kinds of outlaw groups during the medieval period. Extreme poverty and hardships in earning a livelihood were often the reasons for becoming a bandit. In his seminal work *Bandits,* Eric Hobsbawm identifies social bandits as consisting mostly of peasants and landless labourers who were ruled and exploited by others and as 'representing a primitive form of rebellion'. In fact, banditry tended to become endemic in times of pauperisation and economic crisis. Hobsbawm identifies two important causal factors in the formation of bandit groups:

> The first and probably the most important source of bandits is in those forms of rural economy or rural environment which have relatively small labour demands or which are too poor to employ all their able bodied men; in other words in the rural surplus population. The second most important source of free men are those who for one reason or the another are not integrated into rural society and are therefore also forced to marginality or outlawry. Among such marginals, soldiers, deserters and ex-servicemen played a significant part.[77]

This helps put in context the Dalits who lost their jobs in the armies and, unable to be integrated properly into the rural agrarian society in the dry ecoregion of Rayalaseema, seem to have taken recourse to banditry. After the twelfth century, there are no references to the employment of Dalits or Dalit soldiers in Andhra except the above-mentioned inscription of doubtful authenticity from 1515 AD that refers to the employment of Mala and Madiga *mastis* in the Vijayanagara armies. Writing about the Vijayanagara period, historian Venkata Ramanayya also states that the

> peaceful occupations, however, had no attractions for the spirited and enterprising men of the [Mala] community. As they were debarred by their birth from entering into the civil and military service of the state, they took to highway robbery. An enterprising leader would gather round him a band of allied spirits and organize expeditions of robbery and dacoity, until the government moved its lethargic machinery to put him and his followers down.[78]

We come across no less than three important references from the Vijayanagara and post-Vijayanagara periods that mention Dalits either forming bandit groups or playing important roles in them as trusted and loyal members. All the references are from the local records or *kaifiyats* of villages in the Rayalaseema region of Andhra.

Racherla Kaifiyat and Tupakula Chennama Nayudu

The *kaifiyat* of Racherla village in Kurnool district of Andhra Pradesh provides details about a Mala bandit chief called Tupakula Chennama Nayudu. During Krishnadevaraya's reign, Chennama formed a band of robbers and, from his headquarters in the Racherla hills, began to plunder the surrounding villages. When the villagers complained about this to the emperor, the latter commanded Vengala Reddy, one of the three sons of Budda Reddy,[79] to put an end to the career of the 'Mala Nayudu'. Having learnt that Chennama and his gang were encamped in a palmyra grove in the forest, Vengala Reddy, his brothers, and their retainers stealthily marched to the camp and fell upon the intoxicated bandits. Even though they were intoxicated and caught by surprise, the bandits fought so valiantly that Vengala Reddy lost both his brothers in the fight. But Reddy ultimately prevailed against the robbers and slew Chennama Nayudu.[80]

Venkata Ramanayya suspects that Tupakula Chennama Nayudu was the original name of the Mala robber chief Kakasmasru, whom Krishnadevaraya describes graphically in his book *Amuktamalyada*.[81] This reputed literary work is notable for, among other things, detailing the modus operandi of the bandits. According to Krishnadevaraya, the bandit leader and some of his followers would first join the targeted travellers and enquire about their destination. After a day or two, the bandit leader would misdirect the travellers into a dense forest. Upon reaching a particular spot marked for the robbery, he would whistle, and his followers, hidden in the forest, would immediately pounce on the travellers.

> The thieves did not chase to attack the men with bows but attacked and stabbed those in front of them; did not severely injure the misers holding their money bags, but only caused small bruises to create fear in them; did not grab every possession of those who were fleeing, but grabbed whatever they could from anyone they came across; did not leave anyone who had no coins in their hands, but checked them thoroughly by taking them aside. They whipped their swords around the bushes and dragged out men hiding inside them; they ... [took everything]

from them, but left a small piece of cloth as loin cloth. They took out small leaf-like knives and sliced open everyone's slippers to look for coins. In this manner, the thieves stole everything from everyone according to their own will and wish.[82]

Settigunta Kaifiyat and Dalit Valour

The *kaifiyat* of Settigunta village of Kadapa district vividly describes the valour and loyalty of two Dalits—one Mala and one Madiga—in the second quarter of the eighteenth century. One Manneti Timmi Nayudu, a highwayman of the Muttaracha community, was known to loot pilgrims on their way to Tirupathi during the reign of Tiruvengalanadha Raja, who ruled over Siddhavatam assisted by his brother Ananta Raju. After Timmi Nayudu's death, his son Manneti Venkata gained even more notoriety than his father, gathering more followers, terrorising and looting towns in Puligulanadu, Pottipinadu, and Chandragiri, and killing travellers. As he had become a menace in the countryside, the rulers decided to curb his activities. At the behest of the king, Ananta Raju set out with his army and one Rama Raju, a well-known warrior, to nab Venkata. Getting wind of this, Venkata sent one of his Mala followers to ascertain the strength of the enemy's army. Noticing that Venkata was hesitant about attacking, the said Mala told him that he would hold off the enemy troops for half a day (*'pagalu madhyanamu paryantamu'*), and Venkata accepted the proposal to buy time to prepare for a pitched battle. The Mala fought the army of Ananta Raju while his wife was filling the matchlocks with gunpowder. He halted the army for two *'jhamus'* (or six hours), as promised, by killing ten and wounding twenty during his valiant resistance.[83] The next day, Venkata killed Rama Raju, wounded Ananta Raju in battle, and forced the army to retreat due to heavy losses.

After some time, the menace of Venkata came to the notice of Sadatullah Khan, the Nawab of Arcot. He entrusted Poluri Varadappa Pantulu, a Brahmin merchant from Golconda and a trusted servant of the Nawab's, to deal with Venkata. Varadappa slew Manneti Venkata by treachery in 1732–1733 AD.[84] Sometime later, when Varadappa Pantulu was travelling from Tirupathi to Yerraguntla in his palanquin, a Madiga follower of Venkata who had been waiting for an opportune time to avenge his master's deceitful killing murdered Varadappa by piercing him with a spear, making it a point to inform his victim that he was a follower (*koluvugadu*) of Manneti Venkata.[85] This episode makes it amply clear that a number of Dalits were actively associated with the bandit gang of Manneti Venkata and served him valiantly and loyally.

The Talari

The *talari* (village watchman) was one of the servants (*ayagar*) in a traditional village administration during the medieval and early modern periods. In most villages of Andhra, the post of *talari* was held by a member of the Dalit community, whose duties consisted purely of policing or patrolling and, hence, the *Athavanavyavaharatantram* refers to him as the 'village *kotwal*'.[86] He was the guardian of the village, protecting the lives and properties of the villagers from thieves and brigands. He had to watch closely the movements of vagabonds and strangers and was held responsible for any property stolen from the village. In such cases, he had to track down the thieves and restore the stolen property.[87] Literally following the footsteps of offenders seems to have been the most common way of discovering offenders. If the *talari* was unable to trace the offenders, he was liable to be punished with a fine, imprisonment, or removal from office.[88]

III

As is evident from the material covered in the previous section, there are references to the martial traditions of Dalit communities throughout the medieval and early modern periods of Andhra history. They are characterised as valiant, trusted, and loyal soldiers in the twelfth century and this characterisation persisted in various forms—through the recitation of ballads by minstrels or through displays of their martial skills as *mastis*. When the option of military employment disappeared, they took recourse to brigandage and continued to display their heroism and loyalty. Furthermore, they discharged police duties as village watchmen in the traditional village administrative system.

The English military was completely different from the armed forces mentioned in the classical tradition and the armies of succeeding kingdoms during the medieval period. In the eighteenth century, European companies recruited natives into their army as sepoys to protect their settlements, a practice started by the French in south India, but vigorously followed by the English in the making of the Madras Army. Lending substance to the notion that 'the Indian army was 'the iron fist in the velvet glove of Victorian expansionism', the Madras Army accomplished the task of conquering south India for the British in no time, displaying valour and loyalty during all the wars 'of Clive, of Lawrence, of Smith, and of Coote'.[89]

Castes and Classes of the Madras Army

The foundations of the British Indian Empire lay in south India and rested exclusively on the military might and achievements of the coastal native army that was later known as the Madras Army. According to James Welsh writing in 1793, this army was 'composed of five distinct castes or classes of men differing most essentially in manners, in religion and in customs, who never unite, even at a meal or in marriage .... [T]he discipline and harmony which have ever distinguished those native forces are truly wonderful.' The 'five distinct castes or classes' mentioned by Welsh are:

1. The 'Mussulman', who were 'generally brave, enterprising and intelligent', constituted one-third of the army.
2. The 'Rajahpoot or descendants of the ancient Rajahs, the highest caste of Hindoos', who were 'the bravest and most devoted soldiers, far surpassing all other natives, in a romantic but sometimes mistaken notion of honour.'
3. The 'Telinga or Gentoo, a race of [Telugu] Hindoos' who were 'obedient and faithful but not very intelligent or enterprising soldiers.'

4. The 'Tamoul or Malabar', who were similar to the 'Telinga or Gentoo', and
5. The 'Pariah or Dhere', who were 'brave, active and attached ... to their officers and service, with a few European failings, such as dram drinking and eating unclean meats &c'. The corps was 'composed almost entirely of this degraded class, than whom there [existed] ... not in all India, a braver, more efficient or zealous body of troops.'[90]

In this connection, it is worth noting certain observations made by Raj Sekhar Basu. Firstly, he equates Pariyans (Pariahs) with the Dalit communities of only the Tamil regions and contends that they were recruited into the Madras Army due to the non-availability of 'proper castes', the low wages of the sepoys, and the high price of rice. Secondly, Basu notes that the infantry of the Madras Army was composed of a substantial number of Pariahs in the eighteenth century and 'until the middle of the nineteenth century they had been the most numerous in the British Indian Army's regiments, such as the Queen's Own Sappers and Miners.' Thirdly, Basu reinforces the argument that the

> the impact of 1857, as the Dalit writers have argued, was felt towards the end of the nineteenth century. The abolition of the old presidency armies as well as the increased recruitment of north Indian 'martial races' denied the Pariyans the opportunity of future recruitment in the army.[91]

These observations need to be re-examined using available sources.

Dalits and the Madras Army

One report on the Madras Native Infantry states that, when it was established, it was composed of Muslims and Hindus of 'good caste' and none were enlisted but men of 'high military tribes'.[92] However, over time natives of every description came to be enrolled in the military due to the need to wage major wars in south India. During the British wars against Hyder Ali and Tipu Sultan in 1782–1784, infantry recruits were drawn from amongst the 'Moormen,

Rajahpoots, Gentoos, Malabars and Pariahs' (Muslims, Rajputs, Telugus, Tamilians and Malayalis, and Dalits respectively).[93] As noted by Basu, the English are said to have recruited 'short-statured' men and those of low castes, i.e. 'low in size and low in caste', due to the non-availability of members belonging to 'good castes'/'proper castes',[94] as they were already in the service of the native rulers, and unlikely to be attracted by the paltry payments offered to the sepoys.[95] Hence, it was said that the composition of various Madras Army sepoy battalions depended entirely upon 'the accidental caste of recruits who presented themselves for enlistment in various regiments'.[96] Although it was considered injudicious to admit the 'Pariah' group into battalions with 'men of reputable castes', it was admitted, in typical colonial 'divide and rule' fashion, that the mixture was extremely beneficial, as 'it ... restrained all dangerous confederacies, which could not escape the jealousy of contending sects.'[97] Another reason for the recruitment of 'low caste men' into the military service was that they 'volunteered for foreign service with greater alacrity than those more restrained by prejudice'.[98]

In contrast, escaping from caste oppression and economic misery and receiving attractive pay by their standards, an assured means of livelihood, and a decent and respectable life were said to be the attractions of the profession for Dalits. Recruiting officers are said to have wooed Dalits by evoking the utopia of not only the status that affinity with the imperial army promised but the possibility of transgressing caste taboos through access to pure and superior spaces and bodily comportment in thus far unimaginable ways.[99] Through employment in the army, Dalits obtained 'economic emancipation and social redemption.'[100]

Ironically, the martial traditions of Dalit communities have largely been ignored by colonial and post-colonial discourses, barring a few statements like those of Welsh. Whatever be the reasons for the recruitment of 'Pariahs' by the army, the material surveyed in this chapter suggests quite strongly that one of the forces that drove Dalits to enrol themselves in the Madras Infantry was the martial tradition displayed by members of Dalit communities from at least as far back as the twelfth century (as far as the Andhra Dalits are concerned). Further, the British used the word 'Pariah' as a generic term to denote all the outcaste populations of south India, if not India. A military record from 1859 provides the following details:

> Of ['lower castes, or ... unrecognised castes'/Dalits] ... we have eighty and they consist of sixty-seven Pariahs [or Dhairs], eight Pullars [a slave tribe in the Madura districts], and five Chucklers [Chumbars or leather workers]. The Pariahs are not really in the caste scale at all; still they will not eat with, or take water from the hands of a Chuckler or Pullar. There is a marked difference between the Carnatic [i.e. southern], and the Telinga [i.e. northern] Pariah.[101]

Further substantiating the argument is an entry of Hobson-Jobson that traces the usage of the word:

> [Pariah is t]he name of a low caste of Hindus in Southern India, constituting one of the most numerous castes, if not the most numerous, in the Tamil country. The mistaken use of Pariah, as synonymous with out-caste, has spread in English parlance over all India. The name first became generally known in Europe through *Sonnerat's Travels*. In this work the Pariahs figure as the lowest of castes. Pariah has come to be regarded as applicable to the whole body of the lowest castes, or even to denote outcastes or people without any caste.[102]

Hence, it is reasonable to argue that the term 'Pariah' was used by the British to denote the erstwhile untouchable/Dalit communities of both Tamil and Telugu linguistic regions.

Telugus and the Madras Army

The Telugu people increasingly joined the Madras Army and, in fact, the Northern Circars, roughly corresponding to present-day coastal Andhra Pradesh, was described in the military recruitment manuals as a good recruiting area. An official record from 1859 clearly mentions that the Madras Army recruited only Shudras and Dalits from the Telugu regions: 'There are, among the Telingas, all classes of Hindoos, viz., Brahmins, Kshatriyahs, Vaisyahs and

Soodras. The men we enlist, and indeed the only class who will enlist, are the Soodras. We also get a few Pariahs from this part of the country.'[103] Between 1798 and 1804, twenty-one new battalions were raised in the Madras Army—eight in the districts south of Coleroon (four in Trichinopoly, one in Tanjore, one in Madurai, and two in Tinnevelly), four in the Carnatic (one in Vellore, one in *Nellore,* one in Walajabad, and one in Madras), five in the Northern Circars (one in *Masulipatam,* one in *Guntur,* one in *Ellore,* and two in *Chicacole*), and four in Mysore and the Ceded Districts (one in Seringapatam, one in Bangalore, one in Erode, and one in *Cuddapah*).[104] In other words, twelve were raised from the Tamil region, seven from predominantly Telugu-speaking districts, and two from the Kannada region.

It should be remembered that many Telugu people, including Dalits, migrated to the Tamil region as soldiers, cultivators, weavers, and menials during the Vijayanagara period and later. Hence, it may be presumed that a number of Telugu people were also recruited from the Tamil region. Referring to the percentage of the people recruited from each region in the nineteenth century, Henry H. Dodwell states that 'the Northern Circars ... provided over 35 per cent of the 6500 men enumerated in the regimental registers' and 'next came Trichinopoly and the southern districts with over 30 per cent, the Carnatic provided 16 per cent, Mysore and Ceded Districts 11 per cent, Hyderabad and North India only 6 per cent.'[105] Further, it was stated that 'Mohammadens and Telingas' supplied three-quarters of the whole of the Madras Army in roughly the proportion 4:3. The Tamils on the whole provided not a third of the numbers provided by the Telingas.[106]

Sometime after 1839, it was resolved by the military department of Madras 'to recruit in equal proportions from four main classes—Tamils, Telugus, Mussalmans and men of lower castes; but even so, it was not intended to group any of these in any particular regiment, but divide them equally through the whole.'[107] Further, a military record from 1859 noted that there was a marked difference between the Carnatic (southern/of the Tamil region) and the Telinga (northern/of the Telugu region) Pariah. The former was 'forward and self-possessed, by no means abashed or ashamed of the position he holds, most thoroughly independent of his purer fellow creatures, uninfluenced by their assumption of superiority', while the latter was 'timid, subdued and subservient' and would 'obey whatever instructions they got'.[108] Though there are references to Dalits of the Telugu region in military records, it is difficult to ascertain either the actual number or the percentage of Telugu Dalits in the Madras Army, but it may be assumed that they constituted a substantial portion of it.

However, by the beginning of the nineteenth century, the strength of the Dalits in the actual fighting force began to dwindle due to the increased recruitment of the 'clean castes'. Though Dalits continued to be employed in the army, they were put to work constructing field fortifications, digging trenches, erecting military camps, repairing bridges and roads, and performing other menial jobs as 'Pioneers' from 1780 and as 'Sappers' and 'Miners' from 1831. One report of 1817 states that

> A considerable number of Pariahs and other low caste men were serving in the Madras infantry battalions between the years 1776 and 1817, from which it would appear that the sepoys who fought through the Mysore and Mahratta wars, and gained the series of victories from Chengamah in 1767 to Mahidpur in 1817, were largely recruited from the classes now found in considerable numbers in the Sappers and Miners.[109]

The British apprehended the ire and disgust of the 'higher classes' and 'good castes' at the equal treatment of the Dalits in the army, at the 'considerable reputation' of the Dalits as soldiers, and at their promotions in the rank and file as this meant that the higher-caste soldiers would have to work under Dalits. Perhaps the earliest references in this regard appeared in 1793. James Welsh in his reminiscences expresses such concerns, noting that Pariahs

> have [of] late years been excluded from the line, in order the more fully to conciliate the higher classes, who however they may differ from each other in many points, are all united in considering any

> mixture with these as contamination. They are now enlisted only in the Pioneers and as artillery and tent Lascars.[110]

A similar statement appeared in 1817:

> The native infantry of Madras is generally composed of Mahomedans and Hindoos of good caste; at its first establishment none were enlisted but men of high military tribes. In the progress of time a considerable change took place, and natives of every description were enrolled in the service. Though some corps, that were almost entirely formed of the lowest and most despised races of men, obtained considerable reputation, it was feared their encouragement might produce disgust, and particularly when they gained, as they frequently did, the rank of officers. Orders were, in consequence, given to recruit from none but the most respectable classes of society; and many consider the regular and orderly behaviour of these men as one of the benefits which have resulted from this system.[111]

Thus, it is presumed that the colonial authorities at Madras discouraged the enlistment of men belonging to Dalit communities with a view to conciliating the 'higher classes' in the native ranks. Consequently, 'the former excellent class was gradually diminished and recourse had to be the fairer, taller and more cleanly men of higher caste'.[112] In fact, it may, firstly, be argued that it was the prevailing caste prejudice of the 'proper castes' that was responsible for ejecting Dalits from the active field force. Secondly, at almost the same time, Lord Wellesley introduced the subsidiary alliance system, which the south Indian native states readily accepted. The native armies were disbanded and armed personnel belonging to the 'proper castes' too lost military employment. Perhaps they sought employment with the British, assuring a regular supply of 'clean castes' in the Madras Native Infantry, thereby hampering the employment opportunities of South Indian Dalits in the military. Thirdly, south India had become comparatively peaceful after the extermination of the Mysore and Maratha powers by the early nineteenth century, as is revealed by a statement of Lt. Gen. Burton, writing in 1888:

> If the Madras sepoy is now of less worth than he was in the days of our first struggles for empire in India, it is because of disuse of war and of enforced inactivity, to which the dominant policy of the Supreme Government has of late condemned him.[113]

George F. MacMunn also expressed a similar opinion in 1933:

> One of the sorrowful things that the years have brought forth, the years of the Pax Britannica that have prevailed for over a century in Southern India, is the elimination of the men of the Madras Presidency from the fighting forces of the Crown. So much has this been the case that there now remains but the 1st Madras Pioneers, and the Queen's Own Corps of Sappers and Miners.[114]

Hence, it is argued by many that British military officers discouraged the enlistment of men belonging to the Dalit communities around the second decade of the eighteenth century, if not earlier. British commanders are supposed to have favoured the recruitment of upper-caste groups and to have been influenced in this regard by the 'martial race' theory, according to which certain ethnic, religious, caste, or social groups were regarded as possessing a more masculine character, being loyal, and therefore especially suited to military service. Basu opines that

> Undoubtedly, such moves stalled much of the employment opportunities for the 'lower caste' groups in the military establishment. The Tamil Paraiyans were the worst affected, and their presence rapidly dwindled in the military departments other than the Miners and Sappers Unit of the Madras army.[115]

However, it is to be noted that the Madras Army did not fulfil British expectations in Burma in 1885, perhaps due to their long period of inactivity in peaceful south India. Shortly after, a number of its units were reconstituted with north Indians, and this was to be the practice thereafter. Contrary to the then-widespread view, MacMunn, in *The Martial Races of India*, was of the opinion that 'Pariahs or sturdy outcaste tribes soon proved, with a tot of rum in their stomachs and a Brown Bess on their shoulders, to be no mean opponent to the Rajwara troops, and dacoits who might be opposed to them.'[116] Further, MacMunn identified 'Indian Christians, Pariahs and other depressed classes (chiefly for special technical corps), Tamils (cultivators), Moslems, descendants of foreigners as in Western India (a very few)' from south India as castes that retained their martial proclivities and ways of enterprise and courage—in other words, as 'martial races'.[117] He also opined that the Madras soldiers were 'smart, well-drilled, alert, obedient, apt to handle arms, and good shots' and had 'many of the qualifications that make good soldiers.'[118]

Conclusion

The army, indispensable in the exercise of coercive power and in protecting the state from external aggression and internal disturbances, has been considered one of the seven essential elements of the state in the Indian subcontinent since ancient times. Five different categories of soldiers began to appear from the time of the Ramayana, namely hereditary warriors, mercenaries, troops supplied by friends, forest tribes, and deserters from enemy armies, and the corporation of soldiers was added to the list by the time of *Arthasastra*. Indian rulers continued to employ these six classes of soldiers until the beginning of the twelfth century, though the relative merits of the categories changed from time to time, as attested by classical texts. Ancient Indian political thinkers were unanimous in declaring that the members of the Kshatriya community were well-suited to military purposes, followed by those belonging to the Vaishya, Shudra, and Brahmin communities, in that order of preference. No references have been found to the employment or participation of Dalits in the Indian armed forces until the twelfth century AD.

It was the egalitarian socio-religious reformist movements of south India—Virasaivism and Vaisnavism—that provided the outcastes some opportunities for participation in rituals and in the armed forces, a historical development that is particularly true of the Dalits in the dry ecoregions of the Telugu-speaking areas, whose valour and loyalty in times of war were memorialised in the oral traditions of the *Katamaraju Kadhalu* and the *Palnati Viracharitra*. After the waning of the reformist spirit, employment opportunities in the armed forces for Dalits seem to have dwindled, but the martial traditions persisted in various forms—public displays of acrobatic and gladiatorial skills, banditry, roles as village watchmen in the traditional village administration of Andhra from the medieval times onwards. In all these capacities, Andhra Dalits effectively discharged their duties, earning a reputation for being valiant, trustworthy, and loyal.

The Madras Army raised by the British during the modern period recruited a sizable number of south Indian Dalits in its famed Madras Native Infantry. It is worth noting in this context that, while it was believed that the term 'Pariah' was a reference to the lower castes among the Tamil people, research has shown that, rather than confining it to a particular linguistic region, the British used the word as a generic term—similar to the modern term 'Dalit'—to denote all the erstwhile 'outcaste' and 'untouchable' populations of south India. Though the officially pronounced reasons for Dalit recruitment in the army were the non-availability of 'proper castes', paltry payment, and the high price of rice, the martial traditions of members of the outcaste communities of south India, like those represented by Musalinidu, Biranidu, Kannamanidu, and Chennama Nayudu from the Telugu region, played no mean role. Though there are no exact figures, it is known that Andhra Dalits constituted a substantial portion of the Madras Army and played an important role in conquering south India for the British. Joining the army allowed Dalits to escape caste oppression and economic misery; however, after south India was conquered, they were soon removed from active field forces for reasons that were perhaps not as simple as those suggested by established historiography. Contrary to the belief that south Indian Dalits stopped being employed in the military due to the Revolt of 1857 and the British reliance on the 'martial race theory' after 1870, it may be argued that Dalits were removed from active field forces and enlisted in allied military activities as 'pioneers', 'sappers', and 'miners' due to the caste prejudices of the 'clean castes' in the army. Subsequently, the comparative peace prevailing in south India might have rendered the Madras Army inactive, leading to the disbanding of battalions or the recruitment of soldiers from 'up country'. In reality, the martial race theory had nothing to do with this process and, indeed, MacMunn identified the 'Pariahs and other depressed classes' of south India as martial races. Moreover, they continued to excel in the work assigned to them, as E. G. Phythian-Adams has stated explicitly: 'No corps in the Indian Army has a higher reputation than the Madras Sappers and the Madras Pioneers also were admittedly first class troops.'[119]

Notes and References

1. According to Kautilya, a sovereign state has seven elements, namely the king (*swamin*), the minister (*amatya*), the country (*janapada*), the fort (*durga*), the treasury (*kosha*), the army (*danda*), and the friend (*mitra*). R. Shamasastry, trans. *Kautilya's Arthasastra*, 3rd edition (Mysore: Wesleyan Mission Press, 1929), p. 287. (Henceforth *Arthasastra*.)

2. Yuddhakanda or Book of War is the sixth book of the *Valmiki Ramayana*, in which the war between the armies of Rama and Ravana is described.

3. *Valmiki Ramayana*, Book VI, Yuddhakanda, Chapter 17, Verse 24. https://www.valmikiramayan.net/utf8/yuddha/sarga17/yuddhaitrans17.htm (accessed August 2024).

4. *Arthasastra*, Book IX: The Work of An Invader, Chapter 2: The Time of Recruiting the Army, p. 370.

5. Upinder Singh, 'Politics, Violence and War in Kamandaka's Nitisara', *The Indian Economic and Social History Review* 47(1) (January 2010): 32. The only noticeable change was the use of the word *dvisad* in the Ramayana and *Nitisara* in place of *amitra* used by Kautilya. Manmatha Nath Dutt, *Kamandakiya Nitisara or The Elements of Polity* (Calcutta: H. C. Dass, 1896), p. 241. (Henceforth *Kamandakiya Nitisara*.)

6. The *maula* troops were 'famous for their attachment' to the king as their contingent's existence depended on that of its master, and hence considered very reliable. Mark McClish and Patrick Olivelle, ed. and

trans. *The Arthasastra: Selections from the Classic Indian Work on Statecraft* (Indianapolis: Hackett Publishing Company, 2012), p. 131; Harjeet Singh, 'The Kautilya Arthasastra: A Military Perspective', *Manekshaw Paper* 38 (2013): 13 (New Delhi: Centre for Land Warfare Studies and KW Publishers).

7. Harjeet Singh, 'The Kautilya Arthasastra', *op. cit.*, pp. 13–14; *Arthasastra*, p. 371.

8. *Arthasastra*, p. 376. These soldiers were natives actuated by feelings of rivalry and anger and expectations of success and gain similar to those of the king, and who had the same goal in view. But Kaushik Roy opines that the *sreni bala* comprised 'mercenary soldiers belonging to the private guilds and trading corporations; in general, the duty of the *sreni* was to protect the trading centres, commercial routes, and caravans. But during emergencies, the rulers also hired them.' Kaushik Roy, *Hinduism and the Ethics of Warfare in South Asia: From Antiquity to the Present* (New York: Cambridge University Press, 2012), p. xvii.

9. Kamandaka says they comprised enemy troops who had changed sides or been weaned over. *Kamandakiya Nitisara*, p. 241.

10. Harjeet Singh, 'The Kautilya Arthasastra', *op. cit.*, p. 14.

11. *Arthasastra*, p. 372.

12. *Kamandakiya Nitisara*, p. 243.

13. McClish and Olivelle, *op. cit.*, p. 131; *Kamandakiya Nitisara*, pp. 249–250.

14. R. Shamasastry, ed. *Abhilashitarthachintamani of Someswara Deva, Part I* (Mysore: Government Branch Press, 1926), p. 97, verses 559–564. I thank Dr. Avadhanam Umamaheswara Sastry for the translation of the Sanskrit verses.

15. In the Mahabharata, Drona refused to teach archery and provide martial training to Ekalavya, a Nishada, and Karna, who was brought up by a charioteer (*suta*). In another episode, Arjuna, a Kshatriya, refused to fight a duel with Karna as the latter was considered base-born. See J. A. B. van Buitenen, trans. and ed. *The Mahabharata, Volume I: The Book of the Beginning* (Chicago: The University of Chicago Press, 1973), pp. 275–283.

16. *Arthasastra*, p. 373. But Kautilya ruled out the employment of Brahmins in the army, as the enemy could put Brahmin troops out of action simply by prostrating before them. By law, prostrating persons could not be

killed, and it appears that Brahmins were known to strictly follow this law. Hence, Kautilya categorically stated that an 'army of Kshatriyas trained in the art of wielding weapons' was the best, while allowing the employment of Vaishyas and Shudras in the army for 'great numerical strength'.

17. *Ibid.*, p. 45.

18. The earliest inscriptional reference to a Dalit hamlet—'*chandalavatike*'—appears in 1378 AD; see 'Anavema Reddy Pedapalakaluru Tamra Sasanamu', in B. N. Sastri, *Reddy Rajya Sarvaswamu* (Hyderabad: Vignana Sarovara Prachuranalu, 1998), pp. 506–513. A fifteenth-century Telugu text written by the poet Srinadha refers to it as *velivada*; see Srinadha, *Sivaratri Mahatyamu (Sukumara Charitramu)* (Kakinada: Andhra Sahitya Parishad, 1930). *Kridabhiramam*, another fifteenth-century text, mentions the Dalit neighbourhood of Orugallu (Warangal) city as *velipalem*; see Veturi Prabhakara Sastri, ed. *Srinadhuni Vidhinataka (Prabandha) mu Kridabhiramamu anu Pera Vinukonda Vallabharaya Kruthi ga Rachitamu* (Hyderabad: Manimanjari Prachuranalu), p. 19; and Vinukonda Vallabharaya, *A Lover's Guide to Warangal: The Kridabhiramamu*, trans. Velcheru Narayana Rao and David Shulman (Delhi: Permanent Black, 2002), p. 42. The *kaifiyat* of Gandikota Durgam mention that the Dalit quarters (*Mala-Madiga palyalu*) were outside the fort walls; see N. Venkataramanayya, ed. *Cuddapah Inscriptions: Cuddapah Silasasanamulu Vagaira* (Madras: Tamil Nadu Government Oriental Series CLIX, Government of Tamil Nadu, 1972), p. 6. Foreign travellers like William Methwold and Thomas Bowrey have also remarked that the Dalits dwelt in separate hamlets; see W. H. Moreland, ed. *Relations of Golconda in the Early Seventeenth Century* (London: The Hakluyt Society, 1930), p. 19; and Richard Carnac Temple, ed. *A Geographical Account of Countries Round the Bay of Bengal, 1669–1679 by Thomas Bowrey* (New Delhi, Madras: Asian Educational Services, 1993 [1905]), p. 41.

19. Edgar Thurston and K. Rangachari, *Castes and Tribes of Southern India*, Vol. IV (New Delhi: Asian Educational Services, 1990 [1909]), pp. 350–351. Inscriptional sources, especially those of Draksharamam (1117 AD), Dharmavaram (1600 AD), and the Gandikota Durgam *kaifiyat* also attest that Malas were involved in weaving. *South Indian Inscriptions*, Vol. IV, No. 1384; and *Ibid.*, Vol. X, No. 753; and Venkataramanayya, ed. *Cuddapah Inscriptions*, *op. cit.*, p. 7.

20. However, 'the Mala, the Holeya or the Pariah constituted the bulk of agricultural labourers in south India. Spinning and weaving served them as important by-industries.' N. Venkata Ramanayya, *Studies in the History of the Third Dynasty of Vijayanagara* (Madras: University of Madras, 1935), p. 361.

21. Alan Butterworth and V. Venugopaul Chetty, eds. *A Collection of the Inscriptions on Copper-Plates and Stones in the Nellore District*, Part II (New Delhi: Asian Educational Services, 1990 [1905]), Kandukuru 47 and 48; Kavali 46; Nellore 3, 24, 26, and 114; and Part III, Rapur 40.

22. *Ibid.*, Part II, Nellore 1, 6, 11, and 116; Rapur 3, 26, 28, 30, 43, 44, 50, 51, 53, and 63.

23. M. P. R. Reddy, ed. *Athavanavyavaharatantram: A Mackenzie Manuscript (April 1802)*, Mackenzie Records Vol. 154 (Fl. 22–28), (preserved in the Government Oriental Manuscript Library, Madras, Centre for Historical Studies, Kavali, Undated), pp. 7–12; (henceforth *Athavanavyavaharatantram*). H. H. Wilson, *A Glossary of Judicial and Revenue Terms and of Words Occurring in Official Documents Relating to the Administration of the Government of British India* (London: H. Allen and Co, 1855), pp. 211–345.

24. The Kalachuris of Kalyan were a dynasty that ruled over parts of present-day Karnataka and Maharashtra in the twelfth century AD.

25. Velcheru Narayana Rao and Gene H. Roghair, trans. *Siva's Warriors: The Basava Purana of Palkuriki Somanatha* (New Jersey: Princeton University Press, 1990), pp. 8–11. (Henceforth *Siva's Warriors.*)

26. Atluri Murali, 'The *Basava Puranam*: Its Social and Ideological Context', in *Proceedings of the Indian History Congress, 56th Session* (Calcutta, 1996): 262–270.

27. For details, see *Siva's Warriors, op. cit.*; Veturi Prabhakara Sastri, ed. *Basavapuranamu—Palkuriki Somanadhudu* (Telugu) (Tirupathi: Sri Veturi Prabhakara Sastri Vangmaya Pitam and Tirumala Tirupathi Devastanamulu, 2013); and Peddamatam Rachavira Devara, ed. *Piduparti Somanadhuni Basava Puranamu* (Hyderabad: Virasaiva Dharma Granthamala, 1994).

28. 'Basava inspired and even led the lower-castes and untouchables in an insurrection against regional overlords.' Dunkin Jalki, '*Vachanas* as Caste Critiques: Orientalist Expression of Native Experience' (Ph.D. diss., Manipal University, September 2009), p. 98.

29. B. Lewis Rice, *Mysore: A Gazetteer Compiled for Government*, Vol. II (Westminster: Archibald Constable and Company, 1897), pp. 272–273; Alkondaville Govindacharya, *Ramanujacharya: The Exponent of the Visishtadvaita Philosophy* (Madras: S. Murthy & Co., 1906), pp. 189–190.

30. The date of the battle is contested; for a discussion on this, see P. Sadanandam, *Art and Culture of Marginalised Nomadic Tribes in Andhra Pradesh* (New Delhi: Gyan Publishing House, 2008), pp. 130–143.

31. For a printed version of the oral tradition, see T. V. S. Rao, ed. *Katamaraju Kadhalu*, Vol. I and Vol. II (Hyderabad: Andhra Pradesh Sahitya Academy, 1976 and 1978) (henceforth *Katamaraju Kadhalu*.) The ballad cycle comprises thirty-two stories. *Katamaraju Kadhalu*, Vol. II, pp. v–vii; M. Nagabhushana Sarma, *Folk Performing Arts of Andhra Pradesh* (Hyderabad: Telugu University, 1995), pp. 37–38; and Sadanandam, *Art and Culture, op. cit.*, pp. 55–64.

32. Priyadarshini Vijaisri, 'Outcaste Pasts: Rethinking the Boundaries', in *The Past of the Outcaste: Readings in Dalit History*, eds. Sabyasachi Bhattacharya and Yagati Chinna Rao (Hyderabad: Orient BlackSwan, 2017), p. 191. Vijaisri rightly states that 'the Madiga memory of "*dakshinadi veerulu*"—heroes of the south—has interesting allusions in the *Yadava Purana*.'

33. 'Gosangi' is another name for the Madiga community.

34. 'Matanga' is a refined word for Madiga.

35. This is perhaps an interpolation, as Poluraju and Musalinidu were ardent Saivites.

36. *Katamaraju Kadhalu*, Vol. I, pp. 405–406; Vijaisri, 'Outcaste Pasts', *op. cit.* Vijaisri's translation has been slightly modified by the author to bring it closer in meaning to the original.

37. The names of the Gosangi followers of Musalinidu mentioned in the ballad are Uridhadii Sekharu, Urugallu Naga, Gangapenti Ganga, Gajjela Ranga, Hanumantha Lingana, Alugula Basuva, Palapaku Singana, Bondadi Siddu, Kalinga Rudrappa, Gadikoti Bhadra, Ippapuvula Thati, Isapaku Bondu, Kuppela Koneru, Konikipaku Marri, Tabeti Dhadineda, Tamera Marraya, Abothu Lakkana, Arigela Kanakana, Gummadi Govindu, Kovelala Chandu, Dommimukala Vairu, Duddipaku Parasu, Valapusa Vannayya, Vavilla Jangayya, Chilakkamukku Shankamu, Chikapaku Ankayya, Chetudumu Singana, Chekathi Mangu, Potura Papayya, Palaki Tatti, Charuvakatti Challaya, Sompu Balayya, Korusa Muppati Jakkana,

Kundetti Dandi, Arupalli Achana, Alugu Bachanna, Taruvadi Dharmanna, Dalamu Kambanna, Bodavula Annepaku, and Burugala Sakshi.

38. *Katamaraju Kadhalu*, Vol. I, pp. 411–412.

39. *Ibid.*, pp. 413–415.

40. *Ibid.*, pp. 424–426.

41. After Biranidu's death at Mangalipadu, Bhaktiranna remembers the heroic death of Musalinidu at Ballikurava sixty years previously. *Katamaraju Kadhalu*, Vol. II, p. 558.

42. 'Pasupati' or 'Pashupati' is another name for Shiva.

43. Virabhadra is a fierce form of Shiva, created by him in a state of rage and vengefulness.

44. Biranidu's Saivite affiliation is explicitly depicted in the ballad: 'In his tent, a tiger skin was spread on a rug and he kept a phallus of Mukkanteswara (Siva) on it. Biranidu gave a sacred bath to the linga with water and the milk of sacred cows. Amidst the ringing of five sacred bells and the uttering of "om" (*pranavam*), Biranidu worshipped the sacred linga with a variety of flowers.' *Katamaraju Kadhalu*, Vol. II, p. 370.

45. *Ibid.*, pp. 689–695.

46. *Ibid.*, p. 371. The names of the Gosangi followers of Biranidu mentioned in the ballad are Bodduganta Rangana, Bodepati Singana, Bididampu Vuramana, Pidugu Marenedu, Addagatti Kanchinedu, Adidem Kachu, Merupukatti Sandinedu, Medapagu Lanku, Vairigeda Musalinedu, Birudula Balenedu, Rompi Gaddam Naginedu, Rudrasagu Lingana, Kempula Komminedu, Ketapagu Konda, Pattugatti Papenedu, Bakula Bemminedu, Gogulanka Surenedu, Gallapagu Boddu, Kanchutarigala Polu, Gandham Abbinedu, Nichakayyam Lemmu, Nelavari Bampu, Peddakatti Vesana, Chepoli Madhavu, Sadana Sandenedu, Samideka Pakubomma, Arigela Kanchenu, Andela Paguyerru, Gudipettu Gundanna, Gummadi Parenedu, Tarubotula Sominedu, and Karchichu Tamminedu.

47. *Ibid.*, p. 372.

48. *Ibid.*, pp. 379–383.

49. The causes of the battle were stated to be 'Aruvelli Nayakuralu's (Nagamma's) evil counsel, cock fight (*kodiporu*) and inter-caste dining (*chapakoodu kudupu*)'. Vallabharaya, *A Lover's Guide to Warangal, op. cit.*, p. 52; Sastri, ed. *Srinadhuni Vidhinataka, op. cit.*, pp. 33–34; and Gene H. Roghair, *The Epic of Palnadu: A Study and Translation of Palnati Virula*

Katha, A Telugu Oral Tradition from Andhra Pradesh, India (Oxford: Clarendon Press, 1982), p. 81.

50. Velama is the name of a high caste found mainly in Telangana and Andhra Pradesh.

51. Umakantha Vidyasekharulu, ed. *Srinadha Bhatta Kruti: Palnati Viracharitra,* 2nd edition (Chennapuri: Sri Rama Press, 1911), p. 10. (Henceforth *Palnati Viracharitra.*)

52. Roghair, *The Epic of Palnadu, op. cit.,* p. 246.

53. 'Vikramarka' means 'valorous like the Sun'. The use of this name indicates that Brahma Nayudu thought Kannamanidu was a great warrior.

54. 'Kannama was fully accoutred for war with a sharp broad sword and a sharp moustache. He wore a warrior girth.... As he marched along, he carried a six-cubit broadsword in his left hand and a twelve-cubit sword in his right hand.' *Ibid.,* p. 179. Elsewhere, he is described as 'shining with valour', grasping his weapon firmly in hand, and impressively attired: 'trussed-up truss, the truss of Hanuman; a lower cloth with knot tied on knot; folds, garlands, badges, and..., a turban like the moon wound round his head; ... rings in his ears; large sapphire; fine chest ornaments, a black truss tied in style.' *Ibid.,* p. 262. Alaracamallu (Alaraju), the ambassador of Brahma Nayudu who was sent to Nalagama Raju of Gurajala, stated that in valour, Kannamanidu alone was a match for 19,00,000 proud war elephants. At Kannama's 'display of his power, Nalagama Raju's elephants fled away to Nalgonda. At Kannama's display of valour, Nalagama Raju's horses stamped the earth with all four feet and went galloping and stampeding away. At Kannama's display of might, Nayakuralu's footsoldiers...went running scattered in all directions. The throne in the court trembled and quaked and shook.' *Ibid.,* p. 284. Later on the same day the maidservants told Nagamma, 'The fort of Gurajala is the mortar of the oil-press; Kannama Nidu is the bullock that drives the press; the weapon in his hand is the roller; all the people of Gurajala are the sesame seeds. He will press out the sesame, separating it into oil and cake. By nightfall, he will complete his work and return to Medapi.' *Ibid.,* p. 286. Though the passages seem hyperbolic, Kannama was clearly depicted as a great hero.

55. Roghair, *The Epic of Palnadu,* p. 230.

56. *Ibid.,* p. 5.

57. *Ibid.,* pp. 9–11.

58. *Muta* means 'band'.

59. *Ibid.*, p. 349.

60. *Ibid.*

61. For more details, see Thallapally Manohar and Battula Srinivas, 'Eulogizing the Patrons: The Kommus and the Epic of Katamaraju', in *Proceedings of Annual Conference on Management and Social Sciences, 5th Session* (Kuala Lumpur, 2015): 64–74.

62. Roghair, *The Epic of Palnadu*, p. 34.

63. *Katamaraju Kadhalu*, Vol. I, pp. ccii–cciv.

64. Roghair, *The Epic of Palnadu*, p. 34.

65. *Ibid.*, p. 33. It is unclear, even to Roghair, what the word '*ummahupitta*' means.

66. Personal correspondence with Prof. Thallapally Manohar, Warangal.

67. John Cain, 'The Bhadrachellam and Rekapalli Taluqas', *The Indian Antiquary: A Journal of Oriental Research*, Vol. VIII, 1879 (Delhi, 1984): 218.

68. Thurston and Rangachari, *Castes and Tribes of Southern India, op. cit.*, Vol. V, p. 49.

69. Syed Siraj Ul Hassan, *The Castes and Tribes of H. E. H. The Nizam's Dominions*, Vol. I (Bombay: The Times Press, 1920), pp. 412, 430.

70. P. D. Satya Pal Kumar and K. E. Rajpramukh, 'Nuances of Nomadism with Reference to a Satellite Dalit Community in Andhra Pradesh', in *Practices and Approaches in Empowering Nomads*, ed. B. Vasudeva Rao (Andhra University Press, 2010), pp. 91–97.

71. Thallapally Manohar, ed. *Madigala Sankshipta Charitra* (Hyderabad: Pragma Publications, 2016), pp. 87–93.

72. *Ibid.*; Kumar and Rajpramukh, 'Nuances of Nomadism', *op. cit.*; J. Chalapathi Rao, 'Social and Economic Profile of Mala Mastis of Andhra Pradesh: A Select Study', *International Journal of Innovative Science and Technology* 8(4) (April 2023): 61–66.

73. Kumar and Rajpramukh, 'Nuances of Nomadism', *op. cit.*

74. Rao, 'Social and Economic Profile of Mala Mastis of Andhra Pradesh—A Select Study', *op. cit.*

75. *Palnati Viracharitra*, p. 5.

76. Manohar, ed. *Madigala Sankshipta Charitra, op. cit.*, pp. 87–93.

77. Eric J. Hobsbawm, *Bandits*, revised edition (New York: Pantheon Books, 1981), pp. 31–33.

78. Ramanayya, *Studies in the History, op. cit*, p. 361.

79. As per the *kaifiyat*, Kauluri Budda Reddy was a leader of 400 armed personnel who had been gifted some villages by Sri Krishnadevaraya on the condition that Budda Reddy would keep the route through those villages free of wild animals and highwaymen.

80. *Mackenzie Manuscripts*, Vol. 120, No. 298, *Racherla Kaifiyat*, MSS, pp. 30–33. I thank Prof. R. Chandrasekhara Reddy, School of History, Culture and Archaeology, P. S. Telugu University, and Sri Sailam for providing me a photocopy of the *Kaifiyat*. See also Ramanayya, *Studies in the History*, *op. cit.* pp. 260–261.

81. Ramanayya, *Studies in the History*, *op. cit.*, p. 260.

82. Srinivas Sistla, trans. *Sri Krishna Deva Raya Amuktamalyada* (Vishakhapatnam: Drusya Kala Deepika, 2010), pp. 424–427.

83. *Settigunta Kaifiyat*, *Mackenzie Kaifiyattulu*, *Kadapa Jilla* (Telugu), Vol. I (Kadapa: C. P. Brown Bhasha Parisodhana Kendram and Yogi Vemana Viswavidyalam, 2007), pp. 79–81.

84. *Chitvel Kaifiyat*, *Mackenzie Kaifiyatullu*, *op. cit.*, Vol. IV, p. 217.

85. *Settigunta Kaifiyat*, *Mackenzie Kaifiyatullu*, *op. cit.*, Vol. I, p. 84.

86. *Athavanavyavaharatantram*, *op. cit.*, p. 6.

87. *Ibid.*; Ramanayya, *Studies in the History*, *op. cit.*, pp. 253–254.

88. B. John Robert, 'Country Police System, 1550–1857 AD: A Study in Ceded Districts of Rayalaseema Region of Andhra Pradesh' (Ph.D. diss., Sri Krishnadevaraya University, Ananthapur, December 2006), p. 115.

89. David Washbrook, 'South Asia, the World System and World Capitalism', *The Journal of Asian Studies* 49(3) (August 1990): 481.

90. James Welsh, *Military Reminiscences: Extracted from a Journal of Nearly Forty Years' Active Service in the East Indies*, Vol. I (London: Smith, Elder and Co., 1833), pp. 14–15.

91. Raj Sekhar Basu, 'Ideas, Memories and Meanings: Adi Dravida Interpretations of the Impact of the 1857 Rebellion', in *The Great Rebellion of 1857 in India: Exploring Transgressions, Contests and Diversities*, ed. Biswamoy Pati (London and New York: Routledge, 2010), pp. 161–178.

92. R. P. Jackson, comp., *Historical Records of the XIII Madras Infantry* (London: W. Thacker & Co., 1898), p. 172.

93. *Ibid.*, p. 164.

94. The earliest definition for 'proper caste' in south India seems to be that of 'Rajputs, Mussalmans and three Telugu castes—the Kammavaru, the Razu and the Velama varu.' Henry H. Dodwell, *Sepoy Recruitment in*

the Old Madras Army (Calcutta: Superintendent Government Printing, 1922), p. 14.

95. E. G. Phythian-Adams, *Madras Infantry 1748–1943* (Madras: Government Press, 1943), pp. 109–110; Dodwell, *Sepoy Recruitment, op. cit.*, p. 20; Basu, 'Ideas, Memories and Meanings', *op. cit.*, pp. 168–169.

96. Dodwell, *Sepoy Recruitment, op. cit.*, p. 15.

97. *Ibid.*

98. *Ibid.*, p. 171.

99. Wearing the imperial military uniform, it was said, Dalits could walk through Brahmin localities and spit anywhere. L. M. Swarnalatha, 'The Madras Army, 1746 to 1861 AD: A Study' (Ph.D. diss., Bharathiar University, Coimbatore, December 2005), pp. 50–51.

100. *Ibid.*, pp. 50–51 and 196.

101. 'The Madras Native Army', *The Calcutta Review Vol. XXXVIII*, July–December 1859 (Serampore: 'Friend of India' Press, 1859), p. 139.

102. Henry Yule and A. C. Burnell, *Hobson-Jobson: Being a Glossary of Anglo-Indian Colloquial Words and Phrases, and of Kindred Terms; Etymological, Historical, Geographical, and Discursive* (New Delhi: Rupa, 1986 [1896]), p. 679.

103. 'The Madras Native Army', *op. cit.*

104. Dodwell, *Sepoy Recruitment, op. cit.*, p. 31. Italics are mine, indicating the Telugu districts.

105. *Ibid.*, p. 47.

106. *Ibid.*, pp. 45–46.

107. *Ibid.*, p. 16.

108. 'The Madras Native Army', *op. cit.*

109. Jackson, *Historical Records, op. cit.*, p. 171.

110. Welsh, *Military Reminiscences, op. cit.*, p. 15.

111. Jackson, *Historical Records, op. cit.*, p. 172. The same is quoted in Alexander Macleod, *On India* (London: Longmans, Green and Co., 1872), pp. 61–62. Macleod reproduced an entire article in his book, and expressed sincere thanks to Mr Murray for allowing him to reproduce it from the *Quarterly Review* of 1817, p. 111.

112. Jackson, *Historical Records, op. cit.*, p. 173.

113. Lt. Gen. Burton, quoted in Phythian-Adams, *Madras Infantry 1748–1943, op. cit.*, p. 112.

114. George Fletcher MacMunn, *The Martial Races of India* (London: Sampson Low, Marston & Co., 1933), p. 290.

115. Basu, 'Ideas, Memories and Meanings', *op. cit.*, p. 170.

116. MacMunn, *The Martial Races of India, op. cit.*, p. 169.

117. *Ibid.*, p. 237.

118. *Ibid.*, p. 291.

119. Phythian-Adams, *Madras Infantry 1748–1943, op. cit.*, p. 114.

2

Problematising Dalit History

Slavery in South India

P. Sanal Mohan

This chapter raises specific issues related to the writing of Dalit history that need to be addressed in order to arrive at a more engaged, critical understanding of Dalit identity and the processes that have shaped it. While it is impossible to write histories of Dalit communities that treat them as isolated from other social groups, attempting something that resembles an isolated and focused history helps reveal several unique challenges that the historian has to navigate in framing questions and dealing with Dalit history or Dalit sociology. Through a consideration of these challenges, I argue that the perspective of Dalit history makes possible the exploration of new questions that much of the dominant discourse fails to articulate.

Some of the questions pursued in this chapter came up when I was working on my book, *Modernity of Slavery: Struggles Against Caste Inequality in Colonial Kerala*. An important component of my study was an analysis of discourses of equality as they had developed in Kerala from the mid-nineteenth century onwards, initiated by Christian missionaries and carried forward by social movements of enslaved castes in the twentieth century. There is a rich literature on the work of missionary organisations, their interactions with oppressed and enslaved castes, and the resultant transformation of such social groups across south India.[1] Numerous works deal with particular communities and their transformations.[2] Some of them look at long-term changes in oppressed castes, adopting an ethnographic framework that focuses on the unfolding life histories of individuals,[3] and thereby convey a sense of the transformation of both individual lives and of the community.

The lifeworld of oppressed castes is, of course, influenced by dominant castes, and the nature and diverse aspects of this influence in different parts of India have been studied by scholars across disciplines within the social sciences and humanities. In the field of economic history, the oppressed castes have been studied as part of the agrarian social structure, providing the necessary labour power for production, but without rights to property or any resources other than what was considered essential to their survival and the physical reproduction of their labour. They were exploited by various regimes of labour control that could all be generalised as 'slavery'—a word I use fully aware of the discussions and debates it has generated on labour control regimes in India.[4] In the last few decades, the central debates among scholars studying slavery as a labour control regime in agricultural production in south India have revolved around the importance of slave labour in pre-colonial/pre-capitalist production and its eventual abolition, marking the coming of capitalist production based on free wage labour. Meanwhile, another group of scholars has been concerned with the causative factors behind the abolition of slavery, such as the humanitarian concerns of the abolitionists, including missionaries, and their efforts to speed up the march towards freedom, and the eventual transformation of the slave castes into full members of humanity. Three different perspectives related to the abolition of slavery emerge from these debates, which focus respectively on the humanitarian ideology of missionary organisations,[5] free wage labour for capitalist economic production,[6] and the argument that the idea of synergy between abolition and capitalist economic production was far-fetched and that the plantations did not offer any freedom to plantation labourers of enslaved-caste origin.[7]

Experiential Aspects of Slavery

While the above-mentioned studies are important and the information they generated on enslaved castes laid the foundation for a critical understanding of the economic and social aspects of slavery, all of them suffered from a substantial lack of engagement with slavery's experiential dimension. A different history of slavery can perhaps be conceptualised through a reverse ethnographic reading of the sources used in the histories of slavery that are in circulation, with a view to locating in the source narratives the emergence of the bodies, souls, names, feelings, emotions, and relationships of the slaves as well as their past, present, and future.

An engagement with the lifeworld of enslaved castes is crucial to understanding their experience of modernity. Some sources[8] speak of aspects of slavery, captured in the narratives of enslaved people, which privilege their experiences as human beings with emotions. Enslaved people provide testimonies of their oppression and suffering and their resolve to understand their structural position in society. The experiences recollected by them are often drawn from their social memory of slavery, and engaging with these narratives points to ways in which the historiography of slavery can be productively re-thought. This is undertaken not merely to lament past sufferings, but also as a strategy that allows for a critical revisiting of the past.[9]

Social Memory

In contemporary social theory and historiography, there is significant emphasis on social memory, an extremely important source in research on enslaved social groups. Recollection is a valuable historical method of accounting for past experiences of trauma, such as genocide/ethnic cleansing or the social sufferings of a people. In the case of enslaved castes, memories of social suffering and oppression are prominent when they recollect their past.

However, while memory is constitutive of history, it is not history as such—it can be loaded with meanings and allusions that go beyond the remit of history. And yet memory, specifically secondary memory or memory that has been recorded for purposes different from those of the historian, is the material with which the Dalit historian has to work; it is the historian's decision to reflect on the past and make use of memory that governs what happens to the many meanings attached to it. The peculiar nature of memory—and its continuous, simultaneous construction in the course of its recollection and narration—makes it a unique source whose value cannot be replicated by other sources.

Dominick LaCapra argues that memory—despite all its lapses and tricks—poses questions to history, pointing to problems that are still alive or invested with emotion and value. LaCapra observes that, ideally, history critically tests memory and prepares it for a more extensive attempt to work through a past that has not passed but remains, persists, and is accessible. At the same time, it is necessary for historians working on the material of memory to understand the 'false memory syndrome', which, according to LaCapra, is one of the more socially consequential forms that the tricks of memory can take.[10] This caution is significant, as historians often work with secondary memory. It is possible to create and sustain memories through discursive practices that privilege, for example, the experience of suffering. With an awareness of this broad context, one can use social memory to analyse slavery and its various manifestations across south India. While it is difficult to retrieve slave memory without active rememoration of slavery, this does not preclude us from using secondary memory to analyse the lifeworld of enslaved castes.

The Religion of Enslaved Castes and a Critique of its Historiography

Central to the discussion of the experience of slavery is the question of the religion of enslaved castes, a question that is historically grounded in the mobilisation of support by Christian missionaries for the abolition of slavery. During their interactions with enslaved castes in south India under British rule, the missionaries realised that slavery was embedded in the power structures of these regions, and rooted in the Hindu caste system. This led them to believe that only if these castes could sever themselves from the Hindu religion would their members be able to evolve as independent human beings.[11] Although the historiography of this particular aspect of south Indian history deals with a range of issues, it is possible to pursue two significant questions in this connection without delving into the motives for joining new and different religions, whether Christianity, Islam, Buddhism, or others.

The first and foremost question concerns the relationship that different Dalit communities had with Brahminism as it was practised in different regions; as contemporary debates reveal, this relationship was a complex one. It may be argued that castes such as Pulaya and Paraiyar (similar to other castes in south India), that together form a majority of Dalit Christians in Kerala today, had no historic links with Hinduism although they were very much a part of the hierarchical structure of economic production as slave labourers. It is equally important to note that such hierarchies were never extrinsic to the Hindu religion, whether in its textual or practical aspects. One historian of Dalit movements in Kerala has observed that the enslaved castes never had any religion,[12] although this does not mean that they did not have rituals and related worldviews. The religion of enslaved castes has remained elusive despite ethnographic efforts; much of colonial ethnography treated it as a residual category. The segmented nature of the caste society that allowed these castes to have their own gods and rituals is the major factor to be considered here. The relevant literature establishes that, although these castes were part of village society due to their involvement in economic production, they were kept outside the ritual world of the dominant castes. In other words, perhaps until categories such as 'religion' were enumerated for governmentality, there was no reason to believe that the enslaved castes were part of the exclusive world of the dominant upper-caste religion, even for definitional purposes.

However, the religiosity of the enslaved castes needs to be treated as authentic in its own right to explore their lifeworld and to understand the symbolic world they developed in different regions of south India. The reformist agenda of the twentieth century, with its denunciation of ancestral worship and sorcery/witchcraft, ended up negating the validity of the religious practices of the enslaved castes. But there is data in the ethnographic writings and the still-living practices of formerly enslaved castes that can be used to study their symbolic world in a diachronic manner, using the tools of historical ethnography; I include among such practices 'black magic' and other categories of prevalent rituals that give us an entry point into that symbolic world.

The second important question is related to what is generally labelled 'conversion.' It has already been established that enslaved castes were hardly part of the Hindu religion, but with the arrival of Catholic and Protestant missionaries in south India, they became members of Christianity, an organised religion, and began to adopt the worldview associated with it. However, they were also open to negotiations, as contemporary analyses of popular Christianity in south India show. In other words, some recent writings, following the social anthropology tradition, suggest the liminality of such practices, referring to how several aspects of the lifeworld of enslaved castes were used to convey Christian concepts, such as that of God Almighty.[13] This, in my opinion, is an area that needs further study.

The historiographic debate around the adoption of Christianity by enslaved castes tends to be overpowered by a concern with the 'motives' of 'conversion', one of the prominent positions being that, since their conversions were primarily motivated by social and economic considerations, their belief system fell short of being authentically 'religious'. In his book on conversion and social equality, Dick Kooiman makes an interesting observation: the lower castes were more eager 'to better their worldly conditions, to emancipate themselves from their social misery, to be freed from the tyranny of the higher castes' than to pursue the more privileged ideal of the salvation of the soul.[14] Similarly, writing about the politics of funerals among the Ezhavas of south India who converted to Christianity, Olga Nieuwenhuys explicitly states that 'rather than by conviction of sin or a strong desire to be saved, Christian converts were inspired by a desire ... to better ... [their] worldly conditions ....'[15] In his book on the Paraiyars of Tamil Nadu, Robert Deliege addresses the same question, and concludes rather absurdly that the Paraiyars prayed 'to obtain something from the gods'[16]—as if the upper castes, or *anyone* who prays to God, did not!

Without venturing in search of more examples, I would like to discuss the problems with such historical and sociological constructions. Let us begin with Kooiman, in whose observations one can hear echoes of some foreign missionaries who perhaps felt disgusted or disillusioned with their mandate to proselytise and who questioned the motives behind it. In fact, even before the mass conversions began, similar observations were made by Christian missionaries working across south India. But are not these observations about motives, these tropes used by Kooiman—the desire of enslaved castes to liberate and emancipate themselves from their slavery, social misery and upper-caste tyranny, all of which have been referred to in other scholarly writings and historical sources I have mentioned here—evocative of the very situation that compelled Jehovah to send Moses to lead the Israelites out of Egypt? The archives of the Church Missionary Society, London Missionary Society, and similar missionary organisations are eloquent on this issue—the enslaved people of Travancore on many occasions compared their situation with that of the Israelites under Egyptian captivity when referring to the conditions obtaining under the domination of Nairs and Syrian Christians, and the liberation that they felt when Church Missionary Society missionaries worked among them. This implies that so-called 'worldly' conditions have always been constitutive of spiritual motivations.

It may be reiterated here that the 'worldly conditions' to which Kooiman refers completely dehumanised the people of the enslaved castes, as has been clearly established by contemporary research on slavery; some narratives speak of the emancipation that these castes experienced and their reflections on their accumulated social suffering. Conventional historiography has failed to grapple with the multiple meanings of 'emancipation', including its spiritual connotations, and the very nature of the social suffering of castes enslaved under upper-caste tyranny. This calls for efforts to arrive at a deeper understanding of the experiential aspect of slavery.

A related question to address is whether it is problematic to desire food or other worldly goods. Studies on converts to Christianity from the lower castes reveal that, in many areas of south India that saw mass conversion movements, the economic conditions of the converts have not significantly improved since their conversion; in fact, a large majority have continued under various forms of servitude that involved extra-economic coercion. I would agree with the view that material pursuits invalidate claims to religiosity if other communities, particularly the upper castes in Kerala or south India, were known to undertake forms of self-mortification for the salvation of their souls with no regard for the accumulation of wealth. Nieuwenhuys' work on the Ezhavas was based on field research in a south Kerala village, but the instrumental rationality that influenced her perception of lower-caste religiosity prevented her from undertaking further research on these questions, and she provides her opinion as a substitute for that research.

In the context of religion, it is pertinent to consider the concepts of sin, repentance, and salvation and the worldviews that derive from them, which were extremely significant for the enslaved castes. Contrary to the arguments of Kooiman and a host of other scholars, the journals of missionaries who worked among these castes provide substantial evidence that the notion of sin was not only deeply ingrained in the minds of these people but indeed powerful enough to 'discipline' them.[17] Moreover, contemporary social science recognises the centrality of the concept of sin to the worldviews of indigenous peoples around the world who joined Christian missions.[18] One of the main themes of missionary speeches was the necessity of avoiding sin and the impending punishment that awaited sinners in hell. Those who joined the mission congregations were made to understand the theological classification of sins, such as original sin, mortal sin, and minor sin, and the differences between them.

Based on ethnographic and archival sources, I would argue that those who listened to these sermons and catechisms began to evaluate their lives and actions in a new light. The numerous instances of people confessing their sins to missionaries and taking the decision to avoid habits and situations leading to sin, including drinking,[19] should be regarded as authentic responses to being instructed about rightful conduct anchored in righteous words and deeds, and a well-ordered life built around the practice of attending church services and catechisms. Missionary letters and other documents speak of the effectiveness of their efforts to reform the people.[20] Non-attendance of Sabbath service and working on Sabbath were considered big sins. Observance of prayer time was considered extremely important; missionaries have noted that slave-caste Christians, who would have spent their time on other activities, including quarrels at night, were serious about their evening prayers and the reading of the scriptures. One missionary in Travancore observed that 'among this people not only drunkenness, adultery, thieving and other vices, formerly very common, were almost banished but also evil spirits were obliged to run away from the place, there being scarcely any instance of demonical propitiation, real or imaginary.'[21] Rev. Koshi Koshi, another missionary, refers to a Syrian Christian observing that 'in the stillness of the night, he could daily hear in his home the united voices of men, women, and children from their different huts, praying and praising God most fervently'.[22] Interestingly, in Dornakal in Andhra Pradesh, we come across examples of lower-caste (Mala and Madiga) Christian converts reforming their marriage practices—among others—in response to missionary interventions.[23]

Upper-caste members of the neighbourhoods, too, noted the changes in the habits of their enslaved/semi-slave workers, whom they had previously thought of as unruly. I argue that all of this indicates a change in the attitudes of the people and their conduct, which underwent a process of disciplining, and that a critical history of Dalits must account for this phenomenon. Another line of questioning that needs to be emphasised with a view to understanding the enslaved-caste mentality in their interactions with Christian missionaries concerns the prayers used and the language in which they became popular. Here, what is important is not whether the Paraiyars' prayer is just a plea for worldly goods,[24] as even the Lord's Prayer includes the plea 'give us this day our daily bread,' which is followed by a prayer to be forgiven for one's sins. My concern is a different one: to understand the language in which these prayers were made available to enslaved castes, language that had the potential to create a different culture and worldview.[25] The stories, sermons, and speeches of the missionaries were oral performances that had a decisive impact on enslaved-caste people, as evidenced especially by the life histories of those among the latter who were very well-versed in prayers and their performative rendering. This makes it pertinent to consider the varieties of speech, the 'codes' and 'registers' of missionary linguistic practices—'code' being the language spoken by a particular social group, while 'register' is the way a language is spoken in a particular situation[26]—and, furthermore, to consider the question of literacy and the new tastes that developed among enslaved castes and their significance in shaping the cultures of these social groups. Research in these areas will deepen our understanding of the relationship between enslaved-caste/Dalit literacy and institutions such as the church, family, community, and state.

Writing a Dalit History Centred on Dalit Experience

The extensive work by sociologists on the religion of enslaved castes in south India actively engages with 'idioms of subordination and styles of protest'. In the writings of scholars such as David Mosse, we find lower-caste interaction with Christianity being treated as a significant social experience that should be viewed as important on its own terms. Mosse examines the enslaved castes' experience of being dominated by looking at their manipulation of the institutions and symbols that define their subordination to forge new social relations based on honour, respect, and autonomy.[27] This deviates from interpretations of earlier scholars such as Michael Moffatt, who speaks of the reproduction of hierarchy among the lower castes, and contemporary scholars like Deliege, who views the authenticity of lower-caste religiosity with suspicion.[28]

Serious consideration of the social experiences of different lower-caste communities in south India demands a close look at religion within the context of modernity and emancipatory politics. It is necessary to accept the oppressed castes as political agents, i.e. 'Dalits' as a political category, and to work towards a critical understanding of how the symbolic and cultural resources of enslaved-caste communities have been reinterpreted for political purposes. In some studies on Dalit cultural and social practices, we come across the explicit use of the Dalit worldview and symbols to reimagine emancipatory politics. Kancha Ilaiah has reinterpreted the religious traditions of Dalits, such as the Yellamma/Pochamma cult, as resources for egalitarian mobilisation and expressions of the need to reconstitute society on different, egalitarian lines; he refers to this process as 'Dalitization'.[29] Similarly, in Tamil Nadu, S. Clarke explores the symbolic world of the Paraiyars as a theological source for conceiving of an emancipatory theology that he develops from the primeval symbol of the drum, which has a decisive role in their lived experience. Here, the drum is elevated to a symbolic realm where it communicates with the people in a distinct language and assumes a different ontology. Meanwhile, the identification with Buddhist theological and religious practices by Dalits in Tamil Nadu is G. Aloysius' main concern. All these are major efforts to explore Dalit cultural resources in the context of discussions on religion and the agency of oppressed people.[30]

Another realm in which we find the social imagination of lower-caste/Dalit communities articulated strongly is the literary. I am considering here in particular works of the colonial period, although contemporary literary expressions are equally important. Some recent works of Malayalam literature explore experiences of slavery to unpack strategies of textual representation and the social context of slavery.[31] For instance, slavery has been studied from a critical Dalit/feminist perspective that focuses on the social dimension of desire in the discussion on N. Kumaran Asan's *Duravastha*.[32] Studies on literary figures and their contributions to social change among Dalit communities, the genres introduced by them, and the literary sensibility and taste of such interventions have offered invaluable insights into specific aspects of the Dalit experience.[33] I would also include in the category of literary works the folk songs and prayer songs of lower castes, Hindus, and Christians of various denominations, including those that have existed as liminal entities.[34] These literary expressions also form part of what is famous today as Dalit literature, a site that is crucial to understanding the social imaginaries at work in the construction of Dalit identity, history, and politics.

Another phenomenon that needs to be studied is the emergence of new family forms among different Dalit communities, with due attention to the contexts of their emergence. A study of this can be based on late-nineteenth- and twentieth-century debates. In Kerala, there were debates about family, property, and inheritance among enslaved castes in the Sri Mulam Praja Sabha of Travancore, and these debates took place against the larger backdrop of social movements demanding the recasting of the social structure. Family was considered an important site by lower-caste movements in general and enslaved-caste movements in particular, as it was generally impossible for members of these castes to achieve stable family life, given the practice among landlords of selling men, women, and children of enslaved-caste families separately. These practices only began to decline towards the end of the nineteenth century, which was also when the notion of the Christian family began to take root among the enslaved castes that joined the missionary churches. In the twentieth century, when social movements emerged among the oppressed castes, questions began to be articulated about the institution of family in the Dalit context and the interventions that would be required to modernise it.

Conclusion

One of the main concerns of this chapter was the historiographic construction of the socio-religious world of enslaved castes in

Kerala and other parts of south India, a project hitherto dominated by interpretations and assumptions that reveal a lack of engagement with the experiential aspects of Dalit history. Enslaved castes emerged as social agents in their interactions with missionary Christianity and later social movements. Considering its political significance and the agential action it entails in the Dalit context, religion, thus, requires special attention, as does the gradual transformation of the Dalit lifeworld. Revisiting some of the debates around issues related to enslaved castes' relationship with religion and its role in transforming their lifeworld, I have tried to highlight the scope for reconsiderations and further research that will help challenge the dominant genres of history and push the boundaries of the discipline by engaging critically with the problems of social memory, religion, and the experiential aspects of slavery.

Notes and References

1. Robert Eric Frykenberg, 'On the Study of Conversion Movements: A Review Article and a Theoretical Note', *The Indian Economic and Social History Review* 17(1) (January 1980): 121–138; John Wilson Gladstone, *Protestant Christianity and People's Movements in Kerala: A Study of Christian Mass Movements in Relation to Neo-Hindu Socio-religious Movements in Kerala, 1850–1936* (Trivandrum: Seminary Publications, 1984); Dick Kooiman, *Conversion and Social Equality in India: The London Missionary Society in South Travancore in the 19th Century* (New Delhi: Manohar, 1989); Geoffrey A. Oddie, ed. *Religion in South Asia: Religious Conversion and Revival Movements in South Asia in Medieval and Modern Times* (London: Curzon Press, 1977).

2. K. G. Daniel, *Let the Hills Rejoice: The Conversion of Hill Arrians of Kerala and Its Effects on Evangelism* (New Delhi: Indian Society for Promoting Christian Knowledge, 1998); Robert Deliège, *The World of the 'Untouchables': Paraiyars of Tamil Nadu*, trans. David Philips (Delhi: Oxford University Press, 1997); David Mosse, 'Idioms of Subordination and Styles of Protest among Christian and Hindu Harijan Castes in Tamil Nadu', *Contributions to Indian Sociology* 28(1) (January 1994): 67–106; George Oommen, 'Strength of Tradition and Weakness of

Communication: Central Kerala Dalit Conversion', in *Religious Conversion Movements in South Asia: Continuities and Change, 1800-1900*, ed. Geoffery A. Oddie (Surrey: Curzon Press, 1997).

3. Josiane Racine and Jean Luc Racine, *Viramma: Life of an Untouchable*, trans. Will Hobson (London: Verso, 1997).

4. Gyan Prakash, *Bonded Histories: Genealogies of Labour Servitude in Colonial India* (Cambridge: Cambridge University Press, 1997).

5. Benedicte Hjejle, 'Slavery and agricultural bondage in South India in the nineteenth century', *Scandinavian Economic History Review* 15(1–2) (1967): 71–126; Robin Jeffrey, *The Decline of Nair Dominance: Society and Politics in Travancore, 1847–1908* (New Delhi: Vikas Publishing House, 1976); Kalathilparambil Kumaran Kusuman, *Slavery in Travancore* (Trivandrum: Kerala Historical Society, 1973); Sundararaj Manickam, *The Social Setting of Christian Conversion in South India: The Impact of the Wesleyan Methodist Missionaries on the Trichy–Tanjore Diocese with Special Reference to the Harijan Communities of the Mass Movement Area, 1820–1947* (Wiesbaden: Franz Steiner Verlag, 1977); Kunjulekshmi Saradamoni, *Emergence of a Slave Caste: Pulayas of Kerala* (New Delhi: People's Publishing House, 1980).

6. Paul E. Baak, 'About Enslaved Ex-slaves, Uncaptured Contract Coolies and Unfreed Freedmen: Some Notes about "Free" and "Unfree" Labour in the Context of Plantation Development in South West India, Early Sixteenth Century–Mid 1990s', *Modern Asian Studies* 33(1) (January 1999): 121–157; K. K. N. Kurup, 'The Colonial Investment and the Abolition of Slavery in South India: A Case Study of Kerala', *Journal of Kerala Studies* 2(I–IV) (1984): 187–199; Kooiman, *Conversion and Social Equality in India, op. cit.*

7. K. Ravi Raman, 'Bondage in Freedom: Colonial Plantations in Southern India, c. 1797–1947' (Working Paper No. 327) (Trivandrum: Centre for Development Studies, 2002).

8. Extant writings of Church Missionary Society (CMS) missionaries based in the Travancore region of Kerala provide substantial information about the lives of enslaved people. For example, see the *Journals of Rev. George Mathan, 1846–69* (CMS Archives, University of Birmingham).

9. Saidiya Hartman, *Lose Your Mother: A Journey Along the Atlantic Slave Route* (New York: Farrar, Straus and Giroux, 2008).

10. Dominick LaCapra, *History and Memory after Auschwitz* (New York: Cornell University Press, 1998).

11. Rev. Richard Collins, *Missionary Enterprise in the East: With Special Reference to the Syrian Christians of Malabar and the Results of Modern Missions* (London: Henry S. King and Co.,1873), pp. 216–227.

12. T. H. P. Chentharasseri, *Ayyankali* (Trivandrum: Prabhat book House, 1979).

13. Selva J. Raj. 'Transgressing Boundaries, Transcending Turner: The Pilgrimage Tradition at the Shrine of St. John de Britto', in *Popular Christianity in India: Riting Between the Lines,* eds. Selva J. Raj and Corinne G. Dempsey (New York: State University of New York Press, 2002), pp. 85–111.

14. Kooiman, *Conversion and Social Equality in India, op. cit.*

15. Olga Nieuwenhuys, 'Mourning Amma: Funerals as Politics among South Indian Ezhavas', *Mortality* 9(2) (2004): 97–113.

16. Deliege, *The World of the 'Untouchables', op. cit.*

17. P. Sanal Mohan, *Modernity of Slavery: Struggles Against Caste Inequality in Colonial Kerala* (New Delhi, Oxford University Press, 2015), pp. 92–102.

18. Joel Robbins, *Becoming Sinners: Christianity and Moral Torment in Papua New Guinea Society* (Berkeley: University of California Press, 2004).

19. See Rev. George Matthan, entry dated 20 April 1856, *Journal for the Quarter ending 30 June, 1856* (CMS Archives, University of Birmingham).

20. See Rev. Koshi Koshi, annual letter dated 2 January 1857 (CMS Archives, University of Birmingham).

21. Letter of Rev. George Matthan to Rev. J. H. Osmaston dated 22 January 1857 (CMS Archives, University of Birmingham).

22. Rev. Koshi Koshi, annual letter, *op. cit.*

23. S. B. Harper, 'The Dornakal Church on the Cultural Frontier', in *Christians, Cultural Interactions, and India's Religious Traditions,* eds. Judith M. Brown and Robert Eric Frykenberg (London: Routledge Curzon, 2002).

24. Deliège, *The World of the 'Untouchables', op. cit.*

25. Peter Burke, *The Historical Anthropology of Early Modern Italy: Essays on Perception and Communication* (Cambridge: Cambridge University Press, 1987); Peter Burke and Roy Porter, eds. *The Social History of Language* (Cambridge: Cambridge University Press, 1987).

26. Quoted in Burke, *The Historical Anthropology of Early Modern Italy, op. cit*, p. 83.

27. Mosse, 'Idioms of Subordination and Styles of Protest among Christian and Hindu Harijan Castes in Tamil Nadu', *op. cit.*

28. Michael Moffatt, *An Untouchable Community in South India: Structure and Consensus* (Princeton: Princeton University Press, 1979).

29. Kancha Ilaiah, 'Productive Labour, Consciousness and History: The Dalitbahujan Alternative', in *Subaltern Studies, Vol. IX*, eds. Shahid Amin and Dipesh Chakrabarty (New Delhi: Oxford University Press, 1999), pp. 165–200.

30. G. Aloysius, *Religion as Emancipatory Identity: A Buddhist Movement Among the Tamil Under Colonialism* (New Delhi: New Age International, 2000); Sathianathan Clarke, *Dalits and Christianity: Subaltern Religion and Liberation Theology in India* (New Delhi: Oxford University Press, 1998).

31. Dilip M. Menon, 'Caste and Colonial Modernity: Reading *Saraswativijayam*', *Studies in History* 13(2) (August 1997): 291–312. https://doi.org/10.1177/025764309701300205 (accessed September 2024).

32. T. M. Yesudasan, 'Caste, Gender and Knowledge: Towards a Dalit Feminist Perspective', in *Dalits and Peasants: Emerging Caste–Class Dynamics*, ed. Ashish Ghosh (New Delhi: Gyan Sagar Publications, 1999); and 'The Poetics of Integration and Politics of Representation, an Ambedkarian Reflection on Fiction in Kerala' (Unpublished paper presented to Dept. of Politics and Public Administration, University of Madras, 2000).

33. K. Satyanarayan and Susie Tharu, *No Alphabet in Sight: New Dalit Writings from South India, Dossier I: Tamil and Malayalam* (New Delhi: Penguin, 2011).

34. Zoe C. Sherinian, 'Dalit Theology in Tamil Christian Folk Music: A Transformative Liturgy by James Theophilus Appavoo', in *Popular Christianity in India: Riting Between the Lines*, eds. Selva J. Raj and Corinne G. Dempsey (New York: State University of New York Press, 2002); Margaret Trawick, 'Spirits and Voices in Tamil Songs', *American Ethnologist* 15(2) (May 1988): 193–215.

3

On the Nature of Caste Violence

Pollution, Territoriality, and Madness

Priyadarshini Vijaisri

'There would come a time when your untouchability would vanish and you will be received with warmth as one of us.'

A Madiga genealogist on the moment in the future when Jambavamuni would be absolved of the curse of untouchability for the sin of sacrificing his son, Chapalamuni[1]

'The kingdom where Shudras are very numerous, which is infested by atheists and destitute of twice born (inhabitants), soon entirely perishes, afflicted by famine and disease.'

Manusmriti[2]

The apocalyptic epigraphs above together represent a fundamental contradiction within the culture/nation that is India, related to the conceptions of self and other in caste society and the notion of territoriality inherent to those conceptions. The making of a nation is a violent process shaped by cultural and historical factors. While perspectives on patriarchy and communalism have furthered our understanding of the complex nature of violence in the Indian context, the distinctiveness of caste violence remains a nebulous matter. This chapter explores the nature of caste violence, foregrounding cultural conceptions of territoriality. It argues firstly that the nation as a referent provided a new locus for reflexivity in engaging with caste during the later colonial period. This historical transition is examined through an analysis of the positions of cult figures who decisively shaped modern Indian consciousness: Vinayak Damodar Savarkar, Mahatma Gandhi, and Babasaheb Bhimrao Ambedkar. The impasse resulting from the contestation among these and other positions on caste found radical rearticulation in terms of territoriality, with its ultimate consummation in the idea of Dalitstan. Secondly, this chapter argues that the persistence and manifestation of inner conflict within culture/nation is akin to a state of madness, drawing for this analysis on classical texts and archival sources to trace the conceptions and structures underlying caste consciousness and grasp its uniqueness and extreme potential.

Caste, Territoriality, and Conflicts

A grim feature of post-colonial history has been the persistence of caste violence manifesting as conflicts over claims to public spaces, eruptions over breaches of norms governing traditional occupations and bodily dispositions, and resentment against the changing status and legal privileges of ex-untouchables. Underlying these conflagrations is the communal dimension of caste violence that finds expression in the destruction of symbols, which is preceded by defilement rituals. Achieving any understanding of caste violence necessitates excavating the distinctive conceptions and correlations between the body, cultural notions of purity/pollution, and spatiality.

This chapter explores the conception of spatiality in the limited sense of territoriality that is inherent to caste and as an attribute of sovereignty dense with expressions of power. Space, access to 'material and emotive power' expressed through imagined demarcations and boundaries, is entrenched in perceptions of self and other.[3] Territorial practices indicate the centrality of territoriality to the coalescing flows between ideational and collective identities/events; territory idealised as homogeneous space is an attribute of the modern nation state, in contrast to the heterogeneous spaces of pre-modern societies. An attempt to identify the basic conceptual elements of caste-based notions of territory may enable us to grasp the meanings of customary practices and the ways in which these notions of territory shape consciousness.

Earlier theorisations of caste in terms of territoriality contra tribe are encapsulated in Max Weber's assumption that a formative feature of caste is its distinctiveness as a non- or trans-'territorial corporate body'.[4] The essence of caste, according to Weber, lies in its social 'fixity', defined by restrictions on ownership of land. Contrary perspectives recognise the correlation between 'a system of territorial segmentation' and hierarchy, promoting

> localized interdependent relations between castes, especially at the village level, by limiting the spatial range of inter-caste relations for all castes and ... support[ing] the hierarchical order of castes by permitting greater mobility and a greater spatial range of intra-caste relations for those at the top of the scale than for those at the bottom. The larger and more inclusive the territorial unit in which members of a caste can move, the higher the rank of that caste.[5]

Such alignment, Eric J. Miller argues, precludes the 'growth of caste solidarity over a wider area'; only when 'its force is lost' do castes at the same or similar hierarchical levels 'develop internal bonds of solidarity at the expense of their local complementary interdependence'. The systematic regulation of caste behaviour in ritualised patterns, orienting everyday interactions between castes, is an aspect of the caste system that is reiterated in most studies. Yet, the distinctive universalism caste opens up indicates that territoriality is radically reconfigured by cosmologies of caste. Here, Mircea Eliade's postulation of sacred space as 'non-homogeneous', revealing 'the central axis for all future orientation', offers a way of understanding how the whole is ordered and enacted for the religious being, especially the tremendous appeal of the 'symbolism of the center as the formative principle' of all spatial units when juxtaposed with the profane, homogeneous, and disordered world that symbolises chaos.[6]

Two broad trajectories can be identified here—the mystical and the caste cosmology—as shaped by sectarian systems that converge in different degrees. The point of convergence in every case is the basic idea of pollution as a state of danger, with the latent potential of violence threatening being/order. The collapse of the boundaries between the pure and impure is a moment with infinite possibilities, both creative and destructive. This cultural notion is the central grid around which two different conceptions of pollution are anchored. One is the metaphysical idea of the commission of sin or violation of dharma as defilement and the other relates to bodily cleanliness as a desired state of ritual purity. While the former conception of defilement is common to Vedic, Buddhist, and Jain metaphysics, the latter is specifically associated with the ritual system. Often, the distinction between the two conceptions is blurred, with the latter connected to the law of predetermination and certain signifiers marked on the corporeal body. The nature of the interplay between these two conceptual schemes in specific cultural contexts shapes regional caste systems.

The Vedic texts enunciate a natural relationship between territory, law, and a hierarchised collective. The gods created the sacred land Brahmavrata as the centre of the world and a model to be emulated. From this purest land issued a larger territorial unit, Aryavrata, 'the land fit for sacrifice' and 'beyond', and this 'land of the foreigner' was and is recognised as a distinct cultural, geographic, and linguistic entity.[7] Manu prophesised that the blurring of the boundaries between the two spaces and the eventual overflow of the impure into the pure space would spell the demise of the sacred order, and it is this notion of the degree to which the contamination of one space by the other (evil forces/beings) can be contained on which the hierarchisation of spaces according to communities is based. Upon this conception of pollution is superimposed the organic notion that bodily substances and effluvia are agents of contagion.

The totalitarian tendencies within the *varna* ideology, based on this transfigured notion, reached their fullest expression during the rule of the Peshwas. The untouchable occurs as a source of danger to pure society, with restrictions on the bodily movements and dispositions of the former enforced in grisly regimental ways.[8] Paradoxically, the aversion and dread that the presence of the untouchable caused was paralleled by the sheer indispensability of the untouchable to the very preservation of the caste Hindu self and the Brahminical order. This dyad of aversion and interdependence was to render the 'pure' self fragile, assailed as it was by an internal tension and an external threat.

Parts of the southern region where the right- and left-handed model of caste were practised—whereby the right-handed faction was made up of castes involved in agricultural labour while the left-handed faction consisted of those involved in manufacturing and trade—defied the concept of a singular hierarchy, and the role of the sovereign in the arbitration of conflicts was an important variation that offers us an understanding of differing regional processes. Linked to territoriality was a pattern of alliances between the oppositional castes and honorific entitlements: separate settlements for different communities being the custom, settlement in the habitations of oppositional castes required official permission subject to conditions affirming the pre-eminence of the original settlers and the forfeiture of any prior honorific privileges. Several communities petitioned the colonial authorities seeking permission to access privileges that were contested by the opposite block. For instance, during the seventeenth century, the trading communities in Pondicherry petitioned the French government to obtain concessions from the right-handed castes to settle in their streets and forfeited rights to any kind of ceremonial treatment while crossing the streets. Breaches of the same were sufficient provocation for riots. Petitions to use flags bearing specific emblems and the prohibition in 1824 on displaying eighty-five flags of different communities caused contestation and arson. Petitions were submitted to the government requesting the right to honorific privileges like the use of palanquins, horses, and music en route to cremation grounds or during festivals, the setting up of *pandals*,[9] and the use of specific kinds of footwear (closed or open)—most often, decisions favouring any community resulted in public riots. Severe conflicts forced communities to seek shelter in British territories.[10] The rights to cross streets and take out processions animated constant public disorder and bloody feuds between the communities.[11]

The left-handed castes of merchants, traders, artisans, leather workers, oil pressers, and peasants and the right-handed castes of dominant landed communities, ritual specialists were all implicated in this conflict, as were the communities of weavers and labourers who were aligned with one or the other block; while Brahmins (whose position within this order is unclear) were not involved in such conflicts, they too were affected and sought government protection. Occasionally, the authority of the government was challenged—the residential quarters of the French government were attacked when officials were thought to be deviating from custom—with dire consequences. These crises were also times for forming newer alliances with communities that would otherwise have remained neutral. The temporary suspension of all processions and public ceremonies in the French territories during the last decade of the eighteenth century is indicative of the flux in the region caused by the dualistic order. By the later decades of the nineteenth century, conflicts around such disputes were no more a factor causing grave public disorder.

Similarly, in British territories, accounts record such animosities spiralling into bloody riots, inciting such passion that the 'rioters stand up against several discharges of artillery without exhibiting any sign of submission'.[12] It is noted that such sentiments were losing their grip on the superior castes and that the outcastes and lowly castes were the ones involved in such bloody feuds. These disturbances are curiously attributed to the lack of fixed privileges and the animosity that persisted between the 'lower castes'.

The religious space, revealing the ideational model, is found to be fraught with conflicts centred around varied conceptions of order and disorder, *kula* (community or tribe) and sovereignty. The loci of power in religious spaces were reconfigured by the nature of priesthood, sovereignty, and inter-caste relations and acquired a distinctive quality that found expression in communal rituals. The dominant understanding of priesthood, recognising Brahminical priesthood as normative, devaluated ritual systems centred around non-Brahminical and outcaste priesthoods. The latter systems envisaged a distinctive caste ethic for the sustenance of the caste order, rejecting an order that demeaned communities whose very existence was crucial to the sustenance of the moral economy. Here, the meanings and values of bodily substances are contrary to those premised on the *varna* model. Much of this invisibilised history is available in fragments and points to customs and alliances that depart from the normative;[13] intimacy between the touchable and untouchable castes and contrary conceptions of purity and pollution have shaped regional traditions and brought them closer to mystical traditions.

Thus, the multitude of competing caste and sectarian worldviews that decentred religious and cultural power positively precluded the realisation of totalitarian tendencies within caste, except in brief historical periods and in limited contexts.[14] Far from being rigid, the porosity of spaces was facilitated by ritual breaks and enactments wherein desired differentiations were worked out harmoniously for the well-being of the whole. Only over the last century have such ritual systems been gradually delinked from sovereignty (of any recognised traditional authority), leading to the reorganisation of the caste system based on according pre-eminence to Brahminical authority and the shrinking of religious power/spaces, a phenomenon that has impacted the historical imagination of diverse pasts.

Cartographers of the Nation: Savarkar, Gandhi and Ambedkar

Nationalist and revivalist/reformist narratives, based on a specific historical understanding, converged in reproducing the master motif of the outcaste as external to the pure space whose reclamation was contingent on purification. Occluded out of this imagination were diverse historical processes, regional distinctions, and, most importantly, spaces that illustrated inter-caste affinities and had produced an apocalyptic imagination prophesising a time when untouchables would be liberated from the transient state of untouchability. Inspiration for change was offered by the modern notion of territoriality with a fixed centre: the state. From the late nineteenth century onwards, reforms and demands to facilitate untouchables' access to public institutions and spaces were regarded as contraventions of traditional caste privileges. It was the emergence of the nation as a new referent that heralded a discursive shift; various conflicting ideological influences shaped the collective consciousness of the relationship between caste and nation and this is indicative of the distinctive value the untouchable signified during this period. The moral and political challenge posed by the caste system initiated internal churning and generated newer ideals and movements. These catalysing factors shaped the imagination of caste and promises unfulfilled and later, during the post-colonial period, produced a contradiction—one form that contradiction assumed was violence of an absolutely degraded nature.

The imagination of caste and the position of the untouchable in the emergent nation were distinctively shaped by Savarkar, Gandhi, and Ambedkar. Caste and territoriality were transfigured from porous and dynamic conceptions to fixed, centred ones. This envisioning of a homogeneous space was illustrated by the many metaphors signifying the transfigured figure of the outcaste. In the journey from the 'purified untouchable' and 'rebellious untouchable' to the merger of the pure and the impure in the motif of the Bhangi can be traced an imagination of nationhood informed by very distinctive conceptions of territory.

Savarkar's ideological formulations and agenda afford us a familiarity with the Hindu mind, the inner conflicts of Hindu identity and nationhood in his imagination. Though he was influenced by Lokmanya Bal Gangadhar Tilak, his radical social ideas mark a definitive shift and their emergence coincided with Tilak's death in 1920. Tilak, a staunch proponent of the caste system, which he saw as promoting virtue and the fundamental reason for the survival of the Hindu nation, advocated non-interference in religious matters. Tilak was critical of both the colonial government and reformers whose proposals breached caste etiquette.[15] Though Savarkar might seem like Tilak's protégé, he established himself as a formidable force in his own right, his ideology infusing his political and social endeavours with radicalism. In 1924, during his internment at Ratnagiri, Savarkar was actively involved in caste reform for almost thirteen years (almost a decade prior to the commencement of Gandhi's reformist activities).[16]

The Indian National Congress and Gandhi in particular were deeply suspicious of the underlying motives of Savarkar's endeavours,[17] but the ideas and activities initiated by the latter were remarkable, both in terms of their radical departure from the extremist Hindu/Brahminical line of nationalists like Tilak on the issue of social reform and for introducing innovative ways of breaking caste taboos.[18] Savarkar was responsible for an epistemic shift in the reimagination of caste, postulating as he did a new locus for the untouchable within the Hindu religion and nation. An agnostic with aggressive cultural pride, he expressed seemingly a will to break, with the ideal of the Hindu nation and Hindutva as the referent, the 'shackles' imposed by tradition.[19] Underlying this foundational shift was the perceived threat to the Hindu majority and the advocacy of a militant Hindu identity in the 'struggle for existence'.

The influence of social evolutionary theory permeates Savarkar's critique of caste, which is characterised by rationalism and utilitarianism. Paradoxically, even though he was an atheist, his political ideology is saturated with religiosity rooted in Vedic philosophy. Departing from the colonial racial theory of caste and the non-Brahminical historical narrative of subordination, he acknowledged the positive role caste played in the 'survival of the Hindu race' and simultaneously denounced the evils associated with caste that had led to the enslavement of the Hindu race. He denounced critics of caste for their 'ingratitude' in not recognising its role in the 'preservation', 'stability', and 'interests of the Hindu nation', debunking their positions by ingeniously arguing that the 'human race' ought to be 'grateful' for this grand experiment, inspired by 'scientific outlook and thought, sheer guts and amazing diligence', and the ambition to 'find out the extent to which natural laws of heredity may possibly benefit the human race.'[20] It is important to note that this social Darwinist exposition of caste centred on human groups deviates from and thereby, in a way, discredits the divine origin theory of caste.

Savarkar identified the origin of the casteist impulse in 'competition and struggle for survival' and the emergence of human organisation. The spiritual universalism of the Hindus was supremely pre-eminent, but it was 'dimmed to keep the radiance of the banner in full view', for the 'world was too young' and the rule of 'the iron command' of 'the law of evolution' was an 'imminent threat to such universality'.[21] Thus, the 'banner of nationality' symbolised but a stage in the struggle between nations, wherein the possibilities of the vigorous Hindu race were enmeshed in an almost imperialistic enterprise beheld thus by Savarkar, quoting Tukaram: 'the limits of the Universe—there the frontiers of my country lie'. This vision does not contradict his conception of Hindu *jati*, which is a 'testimony of the common flow of blood from a Brahman to a chandala, all of one jati, of a brotherhood'. The 'Panchamas' too, as Hindus racially 'bound together by the dearest ties of blood', had 'suffered and triumphed' in the ghastly 'conflict of life and death' against the 'common foe', the iconoclastic and rapacious Mohammedan invaders.[22] By introducing a singular past, Savarkar weaned that past towards a pan-Hindu communal identity with the nation as its new centre.

Through this utilitarian approach to religion and morality, treating untouchability as suicidal to the nation, Savarkar brings an urgency to reformist mobilising. He advances the position that the Panchamas, rather than being seen as a threat to the Hindu religion, were to be brought within the fold of Hindu society, and that this was nothing less than a sacred duty. Premising his movement against untouchability on a high ethical plane, he instituted a discourse that drew concepts and principles from traditional moral codes and statecraft. This quest is described as motivated not by *apaddharma* (law during crisis or political expediency) but by a real sense of dharma (eternal/moral law), for it conformed to principles of truth and righteousness. Thus, the movement itself was dedicated to the expiation of the touchables for the sins committed by them against the untouchables. This radical stance on caste reforms and legitimation of pleas for opening up public spaces, temples, and schools rested on Savarkar's ideological position that the untouchables are Hindus, belonging to the Hindu *jati*, bound by ties of blood over centuries of castes intermixing despite the strong injunctions to maintain pure blood ties. Here, he sustained a distinction between a harmless notion of ritual impurity and the social malaise of ritual impurity, i.e. untouchability. Customs originating from notions of ritual impurity resulted in 'social and national decline' and, by causing great suffering, had alienated the Hindus from their dharma. The 'expiation of sins committed ... [and] rectification of past blunders'[23] against untouchables, and thus the abolition movement itself, was for the purification and 'the salvation of misguided orthodox touchables.' Paradoxically, it was Savarkar's adversary Gandhi whose penitential approach to the question of untouchability later gained greater credence.

Savarkar's anti-untouchability movement, it is said, was generously acknowledged by Ambedkar.[24] It worked towards opening up public spaces, institutions, and new modes of associationality, critiquing the practice of untouchability both among touchables and untouchables, delinking the idea of 'profession' from that of hereditary occupation, campaigning for mixed schools, engineering a new pan-Indian religious community, and introducing the cultivation of a new ethical self/*swadharma* founded on the pledge to personally act on the spirit of 'touchability' by opening up private spaces, wells, etc. Taboos around food were disavowed and presented as a matter of 'individual preference' and as a 'medical issue'.[25] Inter-dining was posited as 'the magic sorcerer that will bury the demon of caste distinction.' It was seen as setting into motion violations of several prohibitions that were detrimental to the interests of the Hindus, such as the aforementioned 'shackles' of tradition—'prohibitions of touch, sea faring, re-conversion', etc.[26] The Hindu Mahasabha organised 'all-caste dinners' and undertook the opening up of temples to the untouchables while introducing a novel model of religious association for the pan-Hindu/Indian community in the form of the 'Patit Pavan' temple and experimenting with priesthood and inter-dining. Visiting the hamlets of untouchables to support their cause, Savarkar motivated them to fight and be prepared to suffer in their struggle for rights, while censuring them for their feebleness, which he felt was 'worse than the wickedness' of the caste Hindus. His determination and efforts to emancipate the untouchables were heroic and unprecedented in Indian political life, due to which he was subject to condemnation and resentment in his personal and public life.

For a brief period, these efforts infused the community of untouchables with a radical spirit, but this soon fizzled out. In the grandiose engineering of a Hindu *jati* that demanded absolute loyalty to the *pitrubhumi*/fatherland and *punyabhumi*/holy land, the untouchables were mobilised to consolidate the strength of Hindus. The reforms rested on the premise that untouchables were Hindus and implied that the rights being fought for were forfeited once they ceased to be Hindus. Untouchables appear in this construction as an alienated mass whose presence in history is overshadowed by the epochal history of the Hindus. Accounts of the origin of caste system that cast the Aryan as a catalyst, an 'ennobling influence on the assimilated', in the glorious history of the Hindu civilisation and glorified the Peshwas as heroic liberators of the Hindu nation were far from appealing to untouchables, given the bitter memories of their debasement and the tyranny of caste during Peshwa rule. What makes Savarkar's account particularly fallacious is his rendering of caste and religion as immutable, expressed in his tongue-in-cheek comment that it is 'insane to believe that caste changes forever' as a result of sitting in physical proximity and inter-dining.[27] Related to this is his critique of the Gandhian principle of *ahimsa*, which Savarkar interpreted as 'monomaniacal senselessness', an immoral absurdity that lacked wisdom and was not even in accordance with the Jain principle, which did not advocate absolute non-violence. Considering it 'especially detrimental to Hindu interests', Savarkar proposes 'relative non-violence', which is indispensable to survive in both the 'brute world' and the social world.[28]

While the aggression and virility of the Hindu was glorified with a view to strengthening Hindus against internal and external threats and campaigns for the militarisation of Hindu males remained central to his ideas and the activities of the Hindu Mahasabha, such militancy in matters of social reform was dissuaded. It was 'the command of dharma' that impelled the sacred duty; it had to be by 'persuasion of the Hindus'. With regard to inter-dining and inter-marriage, Savarkar cautioned that force in such matters was undesirable while 'warning' the 'extremist leaders of untouchables' that demands for 'compulsory marriages' were entirely 'mistaken, extravagant and unjustifiable',[29] for inter-marriage could be promoted not by actively encouraging such marriages but by adopting a more passive, tolerant approach that mandated refraining from expressing disapproval of such unions. The imagined nation was to be engineered by abjuring force in the restructuring of the space within, even as the use of violence against the enemy and the militarisation of Hindus were advocated. Moreover, the historical validation of violence was delinked from any sense of guilt for, in consonance with Manu and Jain scriptures, Savarkar argued that 'the sin of killing in such cases recoils on the murderer himself whose act was responsible for the reaction.'[30]

The invocation of Manu and the accommodation without any moral compunctions of the possibility of Hindu aggression against minorities who failed to conform to the ways of the Hindu majority within the imagined nation space only validated the fear of the prospect of Hindu consolidation bereft of any genuine empathy for the untouchables. Fear of what Hindu consolidation entailed is betrayed in Ambedkar's explicit rejection of the Hindu Mahasabha, on which Savarkar had great influence, as unfit to 'address problems of untouchables ... [as its] sole aim was to conserve everything that is Hindu'.[31] This aggressive assimilationist policy saw no great progress in spite of the launch of Savarkar's 'untouchability uplift program'. Over the following years, the indispensability of the untouchables to the consolidation of Hindu majoritarianism was observed by passing resolutions for the 'removal of disabilities on the untouchables', but Ambedkar held that such 'social resolutions were facile as [the Hindu Mahasabha] was basically a political organization whose sole ambition was to combat [the] Muslim League' and that the only way the organisation could maintain its 'social stability was by not talking about caste and untouchability'.[32] The Mahasabha's programmes lacked the early Savarkarite radicalism, evading 'issues of power, control and exploitation'[33] and remaining confined to the agenda of the *shuddhi* movement, which produced an oxymoronic category of 'purified untouchables', expressive of resentful inclusion and the paradoxical nature of assimilation. Real reform remained no more than a delusion; 'intimidation and occasional physical violence typified the upper caste resistance when the purified untouchables asserted the claims of the newly claimed status'.[34]

It is true that untouchables were indispensable to the consolidation of Hindu identity, given the palpable threat posed by proselytising religions during the 1930s. However, antagonism within the orthodoxy was already surfacing in response to proposals for the removal of caste-based disabilities. The Sanatanists, who were unhappy with the Arya Samajists' anti-untouchability programme, which was seen as weakening Hindu feelings of nationalism by deviating from 'shastric injunctions', called for the protection of 'varna ashrama dharma' and the 'defence of Hinduism from both within and outside.'[35]

Thus, while the reformist zeal was directed towards the recognition of untouchables' religious rights as 'natural Hindus' to acquire 'religious instruction' that would enable them to perform their duties as 'useful members of Hindu society', the simultaneous objectification of the untouchable as a savage who was filthy, ignorant of tradition and religion due to centuries of separation from the cultured and superior castes, was gaining popular currency. This contradictory tendency was beset with hostility, as the assimilation of untouchables imperilled the Hindu notion of being, even as Hindus were seen as agents through whose 'ennobling influence' the fallen were taught the 'tradition and customs of the Hindu society.'[36] Untouchables were desired as allies, even if only as inferior allies, in the struggle against the enemy; yet, it did not necessarily imply that, for the Hindu, the untouchable was not a lurking threat, an 'enemy within' who had to be coerced by force and without remorse, if need be, to consolidate the strength of the Hindus.

Savarkar's radical innovations and religious scepticism vis-à-vis untouchability and his rejection of notions of sanctity according to which gods could be polluted by the mere glimpse of an untouchable, are crucial to understanding the impulse that generated radicalism in the face of orthodox opposition. The threat to orthodoxy was voiced in the orthodoxy's disapproval of such notions and reformist actions as 'sacrilegious', as imperilling religion and polluting sacred places and the gods.[37] However, these contradictions produced conflicts and turmoil within families, and Savarkar's remarkable epistemic shift from Brahmavarta to Hindu Rashtra, not devoid of a creative imagination of an aggressive territorial nation state, failed to make for an enduring consensus that would recreate the 'Hindu *jati*', instead producing ambiguous subjects and convulsed spaces.

The notoriety attributed to Gandhi in anti-caste discourse has to do with a moment in history that renders him either as a 'cunning' and 'shrewd' politician or as a 'Mahatma' who is credited with having averted a colossal threat to Hinduism while being seen as simultaneously emasculating Hindus. Gandhi's thought and approach cannot be reduced to any bounded categories. Gandhi, who considered himself a Sanatani Hindu, proposed a most remarkable reinvention: the secularisation of tradition undergirded by an unflinching conviction in the wisdom and purity of the sacred scriptures. This is reflected in his 'quirky' reflections and experiments on the repositioned figure of the Bhangi, which, with its inversion of the meaning of purity, becomes a signifier for a desired ethic and cultivation of self. In a way, the excessive emphasis on the Bhangi as the new ideal of purification betrays Gandhi's inability to expand the scope of the anti-untouchability campaign; only by spiritualising it could he offer it as an alternative to Hindus.

Gandhi's approach was that of an ascetic who sourced the impulse for change to mystical traditions, abstracting from those traditions core ethical values and postulating them as the principles by which to reform and revive the original spirit of Hindu society. From the glorification of caste to its abandonment by the revival of *varnashrama*, Gandhi's ideas are beset with contradictions and ambiguity. His early writings on caste and untouchability express his inclination to be regarded less as an enemy of the Hindus than as an upholder of the rights of untouchables; only in the later phase of his political career was there a departure from this. In the 1920s, Gandhi stood with the orthodoxy in defending *varna* dharma as eternal law.[38] He defended prohibitions against inter-dining and inter-marriage in almost ludicrous terms—he viewed eating as a private and dirty act, akin to defecation, and caste-based marriage restrictions as expressing a general spirit of restraint for the spiritual welfare of Hindus. Similarly, the destruction of caste meant for Gandhi turmoil, as the abandonment of hereditary occupations 'would create a chaos in everyday life' and establish a society 'under constant flux.'[39] Later, he departed from his earlier stance and proposed a disjunction between inter-dining and *varna* dharma on the grounds that restrictions on commensality were solely a matter of hygiene.[40] Gandhi's concerted efforts were directed at addressing the 'root of the problem', i.e. untouchability, an evil and a sin that degraded untouchables and touchables alike.

The Poona Pact in 1932 marks a significant moment, as it led to the foundation by Gandhi of the All India Anti-Untouchability League (Harijan Sevak Sangh), which was primarily conceived of as an exclusivist caste Hindu organisation of 'penitent debtors' (caste Hindus/sinners). The inaugural issue of the journal *Harijan* begins with a poem titled 'The Cleanser', on the divine and maternalistic nature of the service rendered by the manual scavenger in expelling filth;[41] the cleanser is one who, in a very basic and fundamental sense, upholds the primary order of life. In three years, Gandhi changed his position by introducing a distinction between caste (social) and *varna* (spiritual/pristine and validating caste-based occupations/ *jatidharma*); the excrescence of untouchability had to be rooted out to purify and revive the *varna* system.

Like Savarkar, Gandhi's discourse was premised on concepts like sin/*paap* and penitence/*prayaschitta,* which resonated with both the folk moral consciousness and the code of moral injunctions in the Dharma Sutras. Possessing the power to cleanse sins, penance entered the vocabulary of modern political discourse in service of the purification of Hindu society and Hinduism. This stance remained constant, though eventually the semantic field of the motif of the scavenger was expanded to encompass proximate states and eventually collapse the binary of the touchable and the untouchable. That Gandhi's obstinacy and conviction resulted in the introduction of a new work ethic in his ashram based on this idealisation is proof that it was no mere gimmick.[42]

The larger programme was beset with deeper complexities as Gandhi sought to garner greater consensus. Working with the Hindu Mahasabha on this issue, Gandhi sought shastric legitimacy for rehabilitating the untouchables within the Hindu fold. Thus, he proposed a conditional acceptance of untouchables, who were to shed impurity by 'receiving *diksha*, daily bathing, and reciting mantras before meals' and 'giving up beef and eating of carrion and leavings of dishes along with avoidance of liquor'. The assumption underlying these conditions was that morally repulsive habits had caused untouchables to degenerate into a dirty and irreligious people and that they would benefit from the opportunity to interact with cultured Hindus.

Yet, Gandhi's departure from orthodoxy is evidenced by the Hindu Mahasabha's rejection of his simplistic view of untouchability as simply a matter of cleanliness unrelated to ritual practices, occupation, and birth. Responding to the possibility of his undertaking a fast in the cause of the anti-untouchability campaign, the organisation ordered Gandhi to exercise caution, for 'pride of *tapasya* could not only corrupt' him but 'would have harmful consequences'; solutions to religious issues were to be arrived at through 'peaceful persuasion alone'. Notwithstanding the Hindu Mahasabha's grip over Gandhi, it is useful to see how the latter's position helped shape the anti-untouchability movement. By divesting the concept of pollution of religious connotations and linking it instead to the very innocuous notion of uncleanliness, Gandhi postulated untouchability as a universal rule of sanitation practised in various degrees by all religions, a temporary state that endangered any person ('a paid [B]hangi or an unpaid mother') who happened to come into contact with dirt (while for instance 'attending to scavenging'). Once uncleanliness was shed, the person was no longer untouchable, and such a state was achieved 'immediately after cleansing'.

However, as mentioned, this postulation also reinforced the idea, shared by the Theosophists and caste Hindus, that it was the lack of contact with 'decent society' that had resulted in the abject degeneration of the untouchables. Thus, the notion that the untouchable existence was similar to that of 'caged wild animals', that untouchables were 'treated worse than the most uncared for village dogs', though intended to evoke the sympathy of Hindus, contributed to naturalising the inferiority of the untouchables. The consequence of this perception was seen in programmes designed to facilitate the assimilation of untouchables into Hindu society by 'cleaning' the dirt they had accrued over the ages.[43] The conjuring up of such imagery was not exclusive to Gandhi; what was perhaps uniquely problematic was his characterisation of the untouchables as 'a burden upon society', '40 million human beings' who not only brought discredit to Hinduism but also threatened to flood the rest of Hindu society with their 'depression'. It was to combat these negative repercussions that they had to be 'made honorable and equal members of society.'

Underlying Gandhi's avoidance of a confrontationist stance against the orthodoxy was a discernible concern with hurting 'Hindu sentiments'—a euphemism that may be understood to denote caste privileges and the structural foundations of caste. The flaccidity of the proposed reforms, the appeals to the individual moral consciousness, Gandhi's aversion to use any 'force or compulsion' (both brute and moral force, including *ahimsa* or non-violence) being exercised on the Hindu public, and the constriction of modern avenues of redress like legal mechanisms securing the rights of untouchables foreclosed concrete change. Ambedkar made it a point to observe that the Mahatma never once used his weapon of *satyagraha* (civil disobedience and non-violent resistance, including fasting, it literally means 'holding fast to truth') in service of the untouchable cause.

Within a severely limiting context, a distinctive secular ethic emerged from Gandhi's revisionist traditionalism, which found expression in a constructive programme. The untouchable body itself became the locus of reform. As mentioned earlier, the semantic field of the motif of the Bhangi itself was expanded (into the notion of the 'ideal Bhangi') to allow for greater reflexivity and self-engagement among Hindus. What is crucial here is that, while aversion to dirt was recognised as the cause of resentment towards the untouchable, the proposed mode of change called for a positive engagement with dirt itself, thus collapsing the pure/impure binary and departing from orthodoxy. It is here that the potency of madness inherent in unmediated chaos is channelled to create a new Hindu space, for, in a philosophical turn similar to that embraced by tantrics/*sadhakas*, a newer consciousness and order were predicated on creative re-engagement with the self. Scavenging itself was transfigured into a spiritual act, one that cleansed the soul, purged it of its fetters, and disciplined the body and mind as it brought into view newer modes of associationality and morality. The impulse for this sensibility and spirit of self-cultivation was seen to lie in the dharmic conception of the primacy of duty over rights. Gandhi, then, proposed an entity not unlike the 'purified untouchable' of the Sanatanists/Arya Samajists; his entity, proximate to the Bhangi or 'Bhangi by adoption', was powered by moral conviction and the willingness to overcome resentment and conduct the self in such a manner as to dissolve the distinction between the pure and impure by embodying the purifying force. He shifted the focus of the anti-untouchability movement from the 'purification of the untouchable' to engagement with the abhorrence of dirt itself as self-redemption and the overcoming of this abhorrence as a restoration of pristine order; thus would the reformist and the 'Bhangi by adoption', like the mystic, be led to the threshold of a newer consciousness and rescued from the utter loss of self that was threatened by the prospect of the collapse of the pure/impure order.

What Gandhi offered was not without contradictions, at times seeming to deny the very possibility of actualising what he regarded as the common rights of Hindus. With the dawn of the era of India's independent nationhood, Gandhi's position on claims to public places and means of change were to have an important bearing on the national consciousness. In 1948, he expressed deep suspicion regarding the use of satyagraha by untouchables to claim the right to temple entry. Though '[they are] a part of the Hindu society', Gandhi failed to understand the 'importunity' of the Harijan satyagrahis 'squatting in front of the temple' when the temple gates were closed: 'in my opinion such dharna carries no merit—it is irreligious, sinful and fit only to be eschewed.' Doubting the religious sincerity of the satyagrahis, he advised them to wait patiently for the time when Hindus would receive them with honour and suggested that, 'pending such consummation', the Harijans 'stay in their homes, sanctify them by the purifying waters of Ganga of their devotion.'[44] Gandhi had very real concerns about the possibility of clashes between the defenders of the restrictions on temple entry and the protestors, but he was also guided by far more idealistic notions: that such changes, if they were to endure, could not be based on any form of coercion by either side and that it was far more honourable for untouchables to not subject themselves to a situation in which coercion was practised in any form. Gandhi held that legal recourse was a 'passive form of brute force' and that it was wrong to 'give effect to law by force' in democracy; though his disapproval of all prohibitions against untouchables in public places and institutions remained unaffected, he simultaneously maintained that the 'law cannot be enforced in the teeth of public opinion.'

Gandhi's objections could also be attributed to his disapproval of the impunity with which 'every community from the untouchables to the priests' was turning to satyagraha to assert its rights. He reflectively noted his own scepticism regarding the technique of *ahimsa* that had been shaped by conditions of powerlessness under British rule, which he regarded as passive resistance and not an authentic form of non-violent struggle; he was yet to discover the non-violent technique of the strong. The preconditions of satyagraha required an awareness of the stages involved and the inculcation of virtuous qualities. It called for a recognition of one's duty, non-cooperation in the spirit of love, *brahmacharya*; the satyagrahi was to be like a sanyasi, with the former's performance of satyagraha akin to the latter's performance of '*tapasyacharya*'. Gandhi's appeals and rhetoric were not anchored in a radically contrary element but in the invocation of the general pre-modern spirit of relatedness, austerity, and moral consciousness, all of which were to constitute the selfhood of a generation of Indians,[45] and meant that, in independent India, the Harijan Sevaks and especially the ex-untouchables were disarmed of moral techniques of persuasion as well as legal methods of change, while the caste Hindus were no longer impelled by the very force that had mobilised them against the colonisers prior to Independence.

No attempt to read Gandhi can sidestep the criticisms levelled against him by Ambedkar, who saw him almost as a trickster whom untouchables had to be wary of. Ambedkar condemned Gandhi's reluctance to use the 'soul force' of the satyagrahi, deployed in the anti-colonial struggle, against his own caste Hindus, and his choice to envision social change as a change of heart on the part of the oppressor, and as expiation inspired by limited kinds of persuasion. It is likely that Gandhi's scepticism about the use of passive force was partly shaped by the unprecedented chaos and bloodbath of communal violence that marred the anti-colonial struggle and Partition, during which he was accused of appeasing Muslims. Gandhi's image as the champion of Hindus at stake, he may have realised that any further demands made of caste Hindus to assimilate untouchables would only be taken as portentous of the impending doom of Hindus, and his calls for restraint in advocating any serious anti-untouchability programmes were thus designed to avoid provoking already agitated Hindus into violent reprisals against untouchables, thereby igniting caste violence. However, in Ambedkar's view, Gandhi's failing could be attributed to the ascetic and philosophical mode that the Mahatma espoused in dealing with the pursuits of worldly life, undergirded by the law of *matsyanyaya* (i.e. 'might is right'). The collective moral consciousness of caste society, now constituted of free citizens with stakes in the emergent nation, was thus sought to be appeased by the notional idea of equality contained in the proposal to abolish untouchability.

Ambedkar's ideas and his analytical, discursive approach were strongly characterised by his impatience with chicanery and mystification. His diagnosis of the socio-political turmoil of the 1940s was anchored in his understanding of what he termed the 'tragic relationship' between Hindus and untouchables.[46] His discerning critique deflated the discourses of the orthodoxy and Gandhi that valorised the Hindu past. Ambedkar saw nothing sagacious in Gandhi's distinction between caste and *varna*, labelling it rather an infantile deception that was made all the more ludicrous by Gandhi's decision to forsake his own ancestral calling. The lackadaisical approach of reformers to caste was laid bare in 'puerile measures' like *shuddhi* and their half-hearted (and later aborted) efforts to promote inter-dining, temple entry, and the purification of untouchables. The stigmatisation of the untouchable, whose identity as the bearer of the stain of pollution continued to threaten Hindu/pure spaces, persisted. Ambedkar's final response—his announcement that he would leave Hinduism—came with a sense of utter hopelessness, expressing as it did his despair of any possibility of reordering the religious and social life of Hindus by making foundational changes to the religion.

Critiquing its foundations as fallacious and unpragmatic, Ambedkar debunked the very idea of 'Hindu society' and its evolution into a duplicitous idea of a nation. In an inversion of Savarkar's social evolutionist theory and his vision of a 'Hindu Rashtra', and against the grain of Hindu opinion, Ambedkar argued that Hinduism was a confederation of atomistic, self-enclosed castes that represented 'survival in self-defeat' rather than the 'fitness of survival' and that had in fact 'emasculated the Hindu' majority, as seen in the struggles between Hindus and Muslims. The sole motive that impelled the system was that of preserving one's own caste, which flew in the face of the idea of a unified Hindu society. The timidity of Hindus was thus attributed by him to a lack of solidarity and that of the untouchables was linked to prohibitions against owning weapons. He saw nothing honourable in the glorified Peshwa rule under which caste had flourished; rather, for Ambedkar it was the Mauryan period, when caste was annihilated and Shudras ruled, that was more deserving of glorification. Caste being a 'pathology', a nation could not be built on its 'crumbling foundations'; for Ambedkar, caste was incompatible with the very idea of nation and 'what the Hindus call[ed] ... nationalism' was 'just militant Hinduism masquerading as Indian nationalism.'

Ambedkar's penetrative understanding grasps the essence of the cartography of caste, its logic of territoriality, and the impending perils for the stigmatised in the imminent nation. Hinduism was a 'veritable chamber of horrors' for the untouchables, who were not part of Hindu society 'but a part apart.' The lack of social spirit among Hindus, the hostility to opening up public spaces, and the extreme, religiously sanctioned degradation of and brutality practised against untouchables subjected the latter to a terror that had acquired the nature of a totalitarian order. With the opening up of public spaces and newer opportunities, the convulsed colonial space had produced a singularly predominant pattern of boycott, terror, and violent repression. Deeply distrustful of Hindu organisations and the Congress due to their vacillations on satyagraha and the tendency to concede to Hindu political pressures, Ambedkar's belief in the unbridgeable separation between untouchables and Hindu society lingered through all the alternatives he envisaged. His rebellious stance and aspiration for liberation from Hindu society were shaped by his repugnance at the moral corruption of caste Hindus and caste ideology. He knew that campaigns for the conferring of 'civil rights' on untouchables in villages were bound to meet with the backlash of orthodox Hindus, for his conception of the Indian village was in complete contrast to Gandhi's.

In his most striking enunciation of the location of untouchables, Ambedkar wrote, 'Factually the Hindus and Untouchables are divided by a fence made of barbed wire. Notionally, it is a cordon sanitaire which the untouchables never have been allowed to cross and can never hope to cross.'[47] Ambedkar was categorical about this: freedom for the untouchable within Hinduism and caste society is an illusion; liberation is possible only when 'the link is broken' and through 'a complete divorce from the Hindus'. He proposed a 'separate settlement' for untouchables as a part of a 'new life movement': the only way to create a new space untouched by stigma and all its marks was to group untouchables into separate villages.

This idea was to inspire radical followers like B. Shyam Sunder in the Deccan region and, for brief moments in the 1960s, inflame the desire for complete autonomy in 'Dalitstan'.[48] The basic condition for emancipation was deterritorialisation—breaking the traditional boundaries, erasing the surroundings and the memories of centuries of 'feelings of bitterness, revenge, hatred, nurtured in their hearts'. To avoid the 'eruption' of a 'volcano', it was necessary to erase collective memory, which would be possible only in a space that was in a real sense free from caste oppression.[49] Ironically, though Ambedkar postulated caste as incompatible with the idea of nation, his solution to the contradiction within Hinduism finds its most powerful expression in the idea of Dalitstan, hinting at the latent sovereignty within atomistic, self-enclosed caste communities that could be triggered in specific circumstances. The ideal of Brahmavarta was to logically culminate in Dalitstan, seeded by a man who had committed the sacrilegious act of burning the Manusmriti.

Years after the formation of the Indian nation state, the enthusiasm of the Gandhian Harijan Sevak Sanghs had fizzled out and the various skewed socialist reclamation projects had been abandoned. The abolition or reinvention of the caste order had been substituted by the abolition of untouchability and the consigning of caste to the private realm, introducing a deep strain in the collective consciousness.

Pollution, Chaos and Madness

The caste system entails a total enactment, whereby one's own being unfolds in synchrony with others as a whole. The security within the system emanates from the acceptance of mental and physical dispositions guided by codes that define action and being. The ex-untouchable continues to be indispensable to the Hindu and yet lurks as a menacing threat of contagion not due to proximity or engagement with impurity but by representing the possibility of the loss of being of the touchable and traumatic suffering due to the inability to deal with the loss, to confront confidently the chaos within and outside. It is with 'brute force' that the caste Hindu strives to reclaim his being, for the touchable and untouchable live in a nebulous state of unfreedom, premised as it is on a state of dependence, and any breach of caste deluges Hindus with existential angst as they stare into an abyss of absent or perhaps transvalued cultural or secular ethics or codes laying out modes of relating to the self and the other. The tension between the secular principle of equality on the one hand and cultural dictums on the other has resulted in the consistent perpetration of violations against untouchables,[50] presented through the extreme forms of violence unleashed by caste. The convergence of brute force and the banality of the notion of purity has spectacularly reproduced the polluted subject and shaped caste violence into a distinctive form analogous to a state of madness, elements of which can be detected by returning to particular ingrained notions of purity and pollution. Here, the mystical space offers prototypes of the relationship between order and disorder, the potentiality of violence, and the perils that befall the self upon the blurring of boundaries. The disruption of the pure/impure order and the violence it entails themselves constitute a state akin to madness in which inhere dense potentialities of destruction and further regression—or creation, by way of marking a threshold at which the imagination of a newer self/order begins.

Multivalent notions of purity/pollution and auspiciousness/inauspiciousness underlying different orders of caste affiliation shaped by diverse religious traditions are not malleable to any singular ideology or structure. The pre-colonial space was deeply porous, with body and space regarded as being animated by continuous flows of conflicting substances and elements. Purity of caste was acquired through dependence on a retinue of service providers and specialists who broke the flow of impurity into spaces and persons. Temporary phases of untouchability—as in the cases of menstruating women and excommunicated caste members—and permanent impurity were both regulated by prescribed rules of conduct.

Within the caste system, the Chandala symbolises evil and is abhorred and degraded for being the violator of taboos. While occupations like scavenging heighten the dread of impurity, which is integral to the Brahminical ritual system that is predicated on an organic notion of pollution, it is the innocuous notion of pollution as bodily uncleanliness, superimposed on a profound philosophical and ethical notion of pollution (common to the Indian metaphysical systems propagated in the Upanishads and in Buddhism and Jainism) as violation of dharma and thus productive of stigma, that has rendered the cultural notion of purity banal and paralysed the ethical consciousness of Hindus. The Chandala is, to the deluded Hindu, Janus-faced, symbolising the colossal dread of the intimate subsummation of the pure by the polluted, and yet is indispensable for sustaining that very banalised order. The mergers of these two contrary conceptions in different degrees with ritual systems and their valuations have evoked different historical responses.

Tantric rituals serve as ideal windows of insight into the inherent nature of the violence contained in the organic notion of pollution. Mystics of both the Bhakti and Tantric traditions recognised the severe impediments imposed upon the spiritual consciousness by the excessive fetishisation of purity and aversion to impurity in the cultivation of the self and its relationship with the other/world. The performance of one's duty to the self—by regulating the body in accordance with Brahminical notions of purity and pollution—instils an aversion to sources of pollution. Thus, the emphasis is on constant strife, on reinstating purity by effecting breaks with polluting flows and substances. According to the mystical traditions, such aversion/negativity, connoting as it does a mental state of unfreedom, can be overcome through radical breaks with Brahminical conceptions, each one a moment that opens up a new threshold of consciousness. Remarkably, the collapse of the mental structure of the pure/impure order is followed by a period of transition, akin to a state of divine madness, which gravitates towards a mystical zeal to reclaim oneself from within deep chaos. In the face of the threat of the loss of self, this mystical state seeks suspension in the deep recesses of the mind so as to explore the depths of being and harness thereby the power to withstand the oppressive seizure of aversion to pollution and the dread of its menacing overflow unto one's being. It is this state of flux—bodily suspension in a state that is pregnant with chaotic flows—that can lend itself either to destructive or creative potencies. The body itself is harnessed to shed the fear and aversion ensnarling the soul and keeping it cordoned off from a wholesome state of consciousness.

The state described above is poignantly exemplified by the angst of Ramakrishna Paramahansa, an angst that unleashed an uncontrollable condition prior to his search for self and for divine revelation. B. R. Kishore described this angst as a state of 'abnormal behaviour and fits of unconsciousness' that distressed Ramakrishna's mother Chandra Devi, as did his tendency to spend time in 'solitary place[s]' including 'nearby cremation grounds', where he 'sat stark naked absorbed in contemplation' and 'offered sweets to the jackals, demigods, ghosts and ghouls'. The 'symptoms' of such 'godly madness' also include burning sensations 'all over the body', sleeplessness, and 'complete loss of control over his body and limbs.' Consequently, writes Kishore, in order to overcome his sense of aversion to dirty things as a 'Tantra sadhaka', Ramakrishna consumed 'the remnants of food eaten by dogs, jackals, and cats without any tinge of aversion, repulsion or hesitation. Later he took a piece of human excreta on his palm and touched it with the tip of his tongue.'[51]

Such was the mystical state of Ramakrishna, who is regarded as having inspired the most crucial phase of religious reform, cultural introspection, and scepticism in Bengal and having had an indelible influence outside Bengal Presidency as well. The collapse of the pure/impure structure ordering both the inner consciousness and the external world is characterised as an event that foreshadows the release of disarrayed forces and imagined and unimagined perils. So also the boundaries of ordered space blur and merge with zones of danger, wilderness, death and everything that unleashes disorder. Such transitions are marked by violence, a force that may not always be malleable to free will. It is here that the parallel between the individual body and the social body becomes relevant, whereby there is a collective recognition of some forms of violence as morally reprehensible and thus evil or demonic.

Conversely, in the secularised modern space, another form of madness persists, but one that is exteriorised and relayed or inscribed on the bodies of others, those who are regarded as polluted, as marks of abomination for acting against the eternal prescriptions of caste. These manifestations of horrifying impulses of aggression signify the threat contained in the notion of the collapse of the pure/impure order, entailing virtual chaos with real consequences for both the oppressor and the oppressed—the restoration of order entails gory, unimaginable violations and indulgence in the forbidden. A few cases illustrate the extreme nature of caste madness.

Pollution violence finds mention as the first offence in the SC and ST (Prevention of Atrocities) Act, 1989, indicating recognition of the fact of its occurrence across regions. While the criminalisation of '[w]hoever ... forces a member of SC or ST to drink or eat inedible or obnoxious substance' does not detail *what* constitutes the 'inedible or obnoxious substance', the clause dealing with acts of injury or insult not directly affecting the body is more forthcoming: 'excreta, waste matter, carcass or any other obnoxious substance'.[52] Certain atrocities reported from the northern and eastern states of India exhibit patterns of behaviour centred on precisely these substances. For instance, a case in 2008 from a village in Dhanbad involved two Dalit widows, accused as responsible for the outbreak of chicken pox, being forced to ingest human excreta by villagers.[53] In Uttar Pradesh in April 2014, a youth was assaulted, made to ingest excreta, forcibly tonsured, and paraded with a garland of footwear in the village; it was alleged by the villagers that he had been caught stealing from the house of the perpetrator of the assault.[54] In another case from Uttar Pradesh later that same year, in Khaira village in Jhansi district, a Dalit man was 'forced to consume faeces and drink urine' and had 'a stick wrapped with cloth and doused in petrol [inserted] into his rectum'.[55]

Moments that threaten the dissolution of caste identity signify to the caste Hindu the danger of being subsumed by the menacing threat of dirt, the effacement of the essence of being—that very danger is enacted in a spectacle whereby the idea of the threat is played out or relayed on the body and is heightened to accomplish the final act—the symbiosis of idea and action, whereby objects of pollution are subsumed within the corporeal body of the agent of pollution. The human being is transformed into an abominable creature, no longer belonging to normal spaces, transformed into human refuse itself. Each time such an abomination occurs, it implicates all those who are consigned as polluted and instils within them the dread of the imminent, inescapable violation of their own self/being, a fear that perpetuates the dominance of those who claim purity of status. In such cases, humiliation is indelibly marked and complete; any fuzziness surrounding 'intentions' and consequences is vacuous.

The spectacle of caste violence hinges on the ways in which it implicates the spectator as a vicarious subject in the frenzied, ecstatic, aggressive act. The frenzy and madness of caste violence indicates the failure to generate a consensus against envisioning and building a nation on the socio-religious foundations of caste. Increasingly, contemporary manifestations of caste violence are motivated by a primal aggressive instinct directed towards the preservation of self/community, as espoused by the Shastras and appositely diagnosed by Ambedkar, with a propensity for destructive madness, as Gandhi bemoaned. And both Ambedkar and Gandhi would have been in agreement about the predicament of Hindus: that caste Hindus and ex-untouchables, deluded by a specious notion of freedom, still largely live in a state of unfreedom.

Notes and References

1. Jambavapurana, Clan purana of the Madigas (Narrated by Sri. Venkateshu, Timmarajapalli).

2. George Buhler, *The Laws of Manu* (Delhi: Motilal Banarasidas, 1993), p. 256.

3. Jan Penrose, 'Nations, states and homelands: territory and territoriality in nationalist thought', *Nations and Nationalism* 8(3) (July 2002): 277–297.

4. Max Weber, *From Max Weber: Essays in Sociology*, trans. Hans Heinrich Gerth and Charles Wright Mills (London: Routledge, 2009), p. 398.

5. Eric J. Miller, 'Caste and Territory in Malabar', *American Anthropologist* 56(3) (June 1954): 410–420, p. 410.

6. Mircea Eliade, *The Scared and the Profane: The Nature of Religion*, trans. Willard R. Trask (New York: Harvest Books, 1957), pp. 21, 29.

7. Patrick Olivelle, *Manu's Code of Law: A Critical Edition and Translation of the Manava-Dharmashastra* (Delhi: OUP, 2006), p. 95.

8. Barbara R. Joshi, *Untouchable! Voices of the Dalit Liberation Movement* (London: Zed Books, 1986), pp. 16–17.

9. A *pandal* is a large, open-sided pavilion used for public events.

10. Jacques Weber, 'Les établissements français en Inde au XIXé siècle (1816-1914)' (Ph.D. diss., University of Provence Aix-Marseille), p. 535. Also see Niels Brimnes, *Constructing the Colonial Encounter: Right and Left Hand Castes in Early Colonial South India* (Richmond, Surrey: Curzon Press, 1999).

11. Weber, 'Les établissements français en Inde au XIXé siècle (1816-1914)', *op. cit.*

12. Jean-Antoine Dubois, *Hindu Manners, Customs and Ceremonies*, trans. Henry K. Beauchamp (Oxford: Clarendon Press, 1906), p. 25.

13. Emma Rauschenbusch-Clough, *While Sewing Sandals: Tales of a Telugu Pariah Tribe* (New York: F. H. Revell, 1899), p. 67.

14. Jean Luc Chambard notes this totalitarian nature of the caste system in 'The Violence of a Hindu village, the Suicide of a Young Woman: "Legitimate Violence" and Dominant Castes in Central India', in *Violence/Non-Violence: Some Hindu Perspectives*, eds. Denis Vidal, Gilles Tarabout and Eric Meyer (Delhi: Manohar, 2003), p. 190.

15. Parimala V. Rao, *Foundations of Tilak's Nationalism: Discrimination, Education and Hindutva* (New Delhi: Orient BlackSwan, 2010).

16. Dhananjay Keer, *Veer Savarkar* (Bombay: Popular Prakashan, 1950), p. 193.

17. Dhanajay Keer notes that, though Gandhi did not 'object' to his followers participating in Savarkar's untouchability abolition movement, he 'added that untouchables were shrewd enough to know who was their real benefactor.' *Ibid.*, p. 171.

18. *Ibid.*

19. According to Savarkar the shackles that bound Hindu society were prohibition of touch, inter-dining, inter-caste marriage, the pursuit of certain occupations, seafaring, observance of rites and modes of worship sanctioned by Vedas, and reconversion (*shuddhi*). Vinayak Damodar Savarkar, 'Six Glorious Epochs of Indian History', in *Selected Works of Veer Savarkar*, Vol. 3 (Chandigarh: Abhishek Publications, 2007), p. 138.

20. *Ibid.*, p. 139.

21. The 'iron command' of the 'law of evolution' is reduced to the following dictum by Savarkar: 'immobile forces are the easy prey of the mobile ones; those with no teeth fall prey to those with deadly fangs; those without hands succumb to those with hands, and the cowards to the brave'. Vinayak Damodar Savarkar, *Hindutva: Who is a Hindu?* (Delhi: Hindi Sahitya Sadan, 2012 [1923]), p. 48.

22. *Ibid.*

23. Keer, *Veer Savarkar, op. cit.*, p. 181.

24. *Ibid.*, p. 195.

25. Vinayak Damodar Savarkar, *My Transportation for Life* (1927). https://savarkar.org/en/pdfs/my-Transportation-for-Life-Veer-Savarkar.pdf (accessed August 2024).

26. Savarkar, 'Six Glorious Epochs of Indian History', *op. cit.*, p. 138.

27. Savarkar wrote this in 1931, after years of active engagement in social reform and experiments in the assimilation of untouchables. See Vinayak Damodar Savarkar, *Essay on Abolition of Caste* (1931). https://savarkar.org/en/encyc/2017/5/22/Abolition-of-caste.html (accessed August 2024).

28. Vinayak Damodar Savarkar, *Hindu Rashtra Darshan: A Collection of the Presidential Speeches Delivered from the Hindu Mahasabha Platform* (Bombay: Laxman Ganesh Khare, 1949). https://savarkar.org/en/pdfs/hindu-rashtra-darshan-en-v002.pdf (accessed August 2024), pp. 83, 84.

29. Dhananjay Keer, *Savarkar and His Times* (Bombay: India Printing Works, 1950), p. 189.

30. *Ibid.*

31. Bhimrao Ramji Ambedkar, *What Congress and Gandhi Have Done to the Untouchables* (Bombay: Thacker & Co., 1945), p. 23.

32. *Ibid.*, p. 23.

33. Prabhu Bapu, *Hindu Mahasabha in Colonial North India, 1915–1930: Constructing Nation and History* (London: Routledge, 2013), p. 54. Bapu mentions that Chamars 'were allowed to draw water from the village wells and after the symbolic gesture the wells were purified with Ganges water.'

34. *Ibid.*

35. *Ibid.*, p. 55.

36. *Ibid.*, p. 57.

37. *Ibid.*

38. M. K. Gandhi, *The Removal of Untouchability*, compiled and edited by Bharatan Kumarappa (Ahmedabad: Navajivan Publishing House, 1954), pp. 33–37.

39. It would mean that 'everyday a Brahman is to be changed into a Shudra' and vice versa. See Ambedkar, *What Congress and Gandhi Have Done to the Untouchables, op. cit.*, p. 286.

40. M. K. Gandhi, 'A Practical Solution', *Harijan* 5(1) (February 1937).

41. Satyendranath Dutta, 'The Cleanser', trans. Rabindranath Tagore, *Harijan* 1 (February 1933).

42. Ashis Nandy's narration, in the course of a personal interaction with me, of an experience his relative had at Gandhi's ashram helps substantiate this point. According to Nandy, his relative, having come from abroad to serve the nation, met Gandhi and expressed his wish to stay in the ashram and offer his services. Gandhi asked him to begin by cleaning the ashram toilets. After a few days, Gandhi asked him how he was faring at his work, to which the man responded by confessing that the sight of filth was unbearable to him. A few days later, Gandhi asked him the same question and received a similar response expressing resentment at having to deal with the stench of filth. Nandy's relative was asked to continue with the work. A few more days passed by and Gandhi asked him once again about his work. This time, he stated with disaffection that it didn't bother him anymore. At that moment, Gandhi asked him to the stop cleaning toilets and entrusted him with other work.

43. In *What Congress and Gandhi Have Done to the Untouchables*, Ambedkar describes the hostility of the Theosophists towards any attempts to promote the opening up of schools to untouchable children.

44. M. K. Gandhi, 'Harijans and Temple Entry', *Harijan* 12(1) (February 1948).

45. Narendra Bastar, commenting on the resonance of Gandhi's ideas, offered in Hindi a fine rendering of this selfhood: *'Mere liye Gandhi woh hai jisse mera main bana hai'* ('Gandhi is for me that which has forged my selfhood'), https://www.facebook.com/JholawalaFilms/videos/1623049864412323/ (accessed 26 August 2024).

46. The following analysis and extracts quoted on pp. 118–119 are based on Bhimrao Ramji Ambedkar, *Annihilation of Caste, with a Reply to Mahatma Gandhi* (Bombay: B.R. Kadrekar, 1937); Ambedkar, *What Congress and Gandhi Have Done to the Untouchables, op. cit.*, p. 198; and Ambedkar, 'Yeola Declaration on Caste and Conversion' (1 January 1926), https://berkleycenter.georgetown.edu/quotes/b-r-ambedkar-yeola-declaration-on-caste-and-conversion (accessed 26 August 2024).

47. Ambedkar, *What Congress and Gandhi Have Done to the Untouchables, op. cit.*, p. 187.

48. N. D. Kamble mentions that, in the context of increasing violence against members of the Scheduled Castes and the inability of the government to restore order or protect their lives and dignity, a demand for separate statehood for the Scheduled Castes was made by a delegation led by Nicholas Roy to Delhi in 1966. N. D. Kamble, *Atrocities on Scheduled Castes in Post-Independent India: 15th August 1957 to 15th August 1979* (Delhi: Ashish Publishing House, 1981).

49. B. Shyam Sunder, *They Burn: The 160,000,000 Untouchables of India* (Hyderabad: Samantra Book House, 2009), pp. 19–20.

50. Details of these violations can be found in the annual reports of the National Commission for Scheduled Castes, reports of the National Commission on Dalit Human Rights since 1998, in various human rights reports prepared by Dalit organisations, and in Ghanshyam Shah, Harsh Mander, Sukhadeo Thorat, Satish Deshpande, and Amita Baviskar, *Untouchability in Rural India* (Delhi: Sage Publications, 2006).

51. B. R. Kishore, *Ramakrishna Paramhansa* (Delhi: Diamond Books, 2004), pp. 25–30.

52. The Scheduled Caste and Scheduled Tribe (Prevention of Atrocities) Act, 1989.

53. Law Kumar Mishra, 'Dalit women forced to swallow excreta', *The Times of India* (7 April 2008), https://timesofindia.indiatimes.com/india/dalit-women-forced-to-swallow-excreta/articleshow/2931328.cms (accessed 22 October 2024).

54. NCDHR fact-finding report from a village in Uttar Pradesh, received via personal communication in 2015.

55. Arindam Ghosh, 'Dalit tortured, forced to eat human faeces', *The Times of India* (20 September 2014), https://timesofindia.indiatimes.com/india/dalit-tortured-forced-to-eat-human-faeces/articleshow/42945561.cms (accessed 22 October 2024).

4

The Political Economy of *Theyyam*

A History of Use and Appropriation

Rajesh Komath

This chapter argues that *theyyam*, a Dalit folk ritual dance practised widely in the northern part of Kerala, has been subjected to varied uses and appropriations by many entities—*tharavadus* (joint families of upper castes), local committees, and political parties—that have interpreted the meaning of the dance to suit their needs and ideologies. Patronage of *theyyam* was a way for Nair *tharavadus* to routinely reinforce their social status as a dominant caste in north Malabar, but the economic decline of the Nairs in the 1950s brought a halt to *theyyam* festivities until the Thiyyas of the same region revived the festivals with a view to establishing their social status as a newly empowered intermediate caste, even as Sri Narayana Guru, a spiritual leader, advised them to avoid primitive practices like *theyyam* worship. Soon, local people's committees began to revive historically silenced places of *theyyam* worship—*kaavus*—to muster popular support for political parties who viewed these as sites of political mobilisation.

In this process, *theyyam kettu*, the process of tying the headgear and costumes of the performers to their bodies and dancing in a frenzied mood before the villagers of north Malabar, has not been accorded dignity as a religious ritual—rather, it has been used for political purposes, with the (untouchable) dancer's body, labour, and pain being appropriated for micro-politics centred around the *kaavus*, dominant upper-caste families, and local committees. Looking at the diverse social discourse around the dance form, I, as a performer of this ritual since my childhood, find that it is a performative tradition that has transformed over a period of time according to the many different appropriative modes of larger hegemonic social groups in society.

The *Theyyam* Ritual: A Dalit Performance

Theyyam has traditionally been performed by (ex-)untouchable castes, primarily in the northern part of Kerala, as part of their duties within the context of village life. Dalit castes such as the Malayans (hill people), Vannan (washers of clothes), and Velan (exorcists) perform this ritual for the benefit of superior castes and landlord *tharavadus*. It is, in other words, a caste-based occupation, one assigned by superior castes and landlords to the Dalit castes and for the performance of which certain social spaces called *cherujanmam* were demarcated. Dalits perform many kinds of caste-based jobs in Indian villages—Mahars (the caste into which Dr Ambedkar was born) in Maharashtra serve as village guards and dispose of dead animals while Chamars in Uttar Pradesh are leather workers—but the uniqueness of *theyyam* dancers lies in the fact that theirs is a religious performance in which they play the parts of gods, and they are treated as gods and goddesses, at least for a day or two, by all the villagers. As soon as the dance ends or the costumes of the gods are taken off the bodies of the dancers, they revert to being untouchables. The rewards for these services have never been fixed; they have always been decided by the upper castes and most rewards have been in the form of kind. Dominant feudal *tharavadus* maintain a kind of patron–client relationship with the dancing castes, through which they confer upon the latter, in return for their services, the right to a portion of the produce belonging to other castes.

Theyyam is a Dalit performance because it is performed by members of Dalit castes and portrays the feelings and experiences of the lower castes. Moreover, *theyyam* is based on a myth about the killing by upper castes of a lower-caste character who was deified later as a response to caste-based atrocities. Some *theyyams* directly question the caste system and the practice of untouchability. The songs of *pottan theyyam*—a type of *theyyam*—ask, 'When our body is cut what gushes out is blood and when your body is cut what comes out is blood. Then why do you talk of differences?' Since the coconut is one of the major agricultural products of Kerala and a principal item of rituals, *theyyam* uses the metaphor of the coconut to pose the same question: 'When we break the coconut, what comes out is coconut, the same as when you do it.' *Theyyam*, in other words, narrativises injustices inflicted upon the lower castes by the upper castes, and many forms of *theyyam* are reactions against caste-based untouchability practised in Malayali society.

Theoretical and Methodological Premises

Theyyam is dedicated to multiple gods and performed by hereditary specialist performers who assume the imagined forms of those gods and, thus transformed, communicate directly with devotees, resolving their problems. Once a devotional practice and a form of worship, it is now regarded as a performing art, an aesthetic practice meant to gratify spectators, and hence a commodity. The factors determining this shift have not only been economic but also the social processes that accompany economic change. Thus, *theyyam* cannot be precisely defined as a cult, a ritual, a festival, a dance, a performance, or an art form—it is defined and perceived according to the time and space in which it is performed. Space here is understood as a social construct, for the 'social' itself is spatially moulded. Human activities and interactions are situated in social spaces, which produce a variety of social meanings and are determined by the time period under consideration.

Social scientists from a diverse range of disciplines have found *theyyam* a fertile terrain of study. In order to understand a tradition like this, however, the usual disciplinary perspective is inadequate. It has to be looked at in a way very different from that of conventional discipline-based studies, which enable only pinhole visibility. What needs to be undertaken is an interdisciplinary study, by which I do not mean attempting to surround the object of study by multiple disciplines, but instead propose that it must be extricated into an open field of investigation affiliated with none of the established disciplines. It is a trans-disciplinary exercise. The heuristic justification for this is that the object of study does not belong to any of the disciplines and none of them exhausts the study of any of its aspects in isolation. In other words, this is an attempt to study all aspects of *theyyam* not as independent facets but as parts of the whole, with a view to achieving what may be called total visibility. Therefore, I will look at *theyyam* from multiple angles to transcend the simplistic, unidimensional level of seeing it as a ritual or a cult or a performance. Combining personal narratives, biographies, local history, and ethnographic insights, I try to explain the relationship of *theyyam* with space, culture, and economy and the shifts witnessed therein through the twentieth century; some of the information presented is based on my own lifelong experience as a *theyyam* performer. I seek to avoid even the inadvertent privileging of any one aspect of it and to start instead with the proposition that it must be visibilised in terms of its ontology, spatiality, caste/class structures, community relations, institutionalisation, patronage, and diversified contexts to facilitate a better understanding of it in its entirety than has hitherto been achieved.

The Location of *Theyyam*

People's participation in this *kaavu*-centred festival is governed by the caste-based duties and obligations that they are required to uphold. Each caste plays a specific role that facilitates the organisation and mobilisation of resources essential to the festival; for instance, the Thiyyas are responsible for offering toddy and tender coconut leaves, while the Malayans contribute an embodied participation by performing *theyyam*. The conduct of the festival, using as it does local resources and patronage, either of committees or of families, establishes patron–client relationships within the framework of worship, thereby forming a moral community centred on a performance of veneration that is seen and valued as a ritual rather than as entertainment. The context is predominantly devotional and its ideology is embedded in ritual. Though the form has been undergoing transformation as its costumes, rhythms, and oral texts have been standardised, it remains very difficult to differentiate, in the process of change, the artistic elements of *theyyam* from its ritual context.

What also needs to be considered, of course, when discussing *theyyam* is that it is a caste-based occupation, for the social structure of caste was the base on which it was ritualised. When viewed as a ritual that is performed to release the tensions that are built into the inequality and contradictions of a caste-ridden society, *theyyam* can be seen as trying to create the ambience of a carnival. As a dramatised performance of ritually intensified social remorse, in effect it functions as a catharsis, too. Its myths and narrative lore-texts (*thottampattukal*), such as *kadavangottu makkam* and *pottan theyyam* (two genres of *theyyam*), manifest in their forms a deep sorrow that society is unable to bear. The wrath of the deity or fear of the same is at work in the collective consciousness of the rural folk. *Pottan theyyam*, for example, reveals how the ritualisation of protest against caste inequities in the social hierarchy served as a safety valve, a strategy of containment, by providing occasional inclusion to the oppressed sections at the cult-site, temporary freedom to scathingly criticise and openly protest against the atrocities of the caste system; a caste protest enacted through the language of ritual. On the other hand, when it is viewed against the backdrop of political and economic changes, especially those of the 1930s, its meanings and definitions alter: new forms of social order have reconstructed this tradition and the economy of the *theyyam* festival is not reliant on the agrarian rental surplus of the dominant *tharavadus*.

The context of *theyyam* has consistently undergone changes throughout its history, with the arrival of the colonial powers bringing the rituals and customs of the people into direct conflict with the values of the colonial administration. This was further sharpened by the proselytising zeal of the Christian missionaries, who were contemptuous of 'pagan' practices. However, through much of the second half of the twentieth century (1970–2000), no significant changes occurred at the local level in terms of patronage apart from new forms of local committees coming into being to conduct the festival in the eventuality of the *tharavadus* being unable to finance the rituals. The changes in the post-2000 period emerged from shifting political ideologies, the commodification of culture, and the government's policy on preserving the symbols of Indian tradition. The establishment of academies, councils, universities, and international cultural exchange programmes put in place a national and international context that endowed *theyyam* with an academic halo and created the need to nurture it as a cultural product native to India.

Theyyam has thus been transformed from a participatory ritual of a locality into an ethnic community ritual and gradually been integrated with the market economy, transcending boundaries of the village community, and assuming a new role in the context of the nation and the market-driven globalised environment. Under the patronage of the state and other modern agencies, it is now performed in its traditional sites—*kaavus*—as well as in new spaces—e.g. grand international cultural festivals—where it is venerated as a cultural commodity. Like the category of 'folk' was ideologically deployed in the service of nation-building by invoking the folk elements embedded among the people and the land—in Nazi Germany and Soviet Russia, for example—*theyyam* has also been used in the micro- and macro-politics of public discourses that build the notion of togetherness, especially in the society and culture of north Malabar.

Scholars have employed conceptual renderings like the *theyyattam* (*theyyam* dance) community to make sense of community relations within the larger tradition.[1] This label refers to all the castes that perform *theyyam* as their traditional occupation, prescribed by the *jati* (caste) system in north Malabar, a grouping that is justified because these castes share many distinct socio-cultural characteristics, beliefs, and common sources of livelihood, often mediated by the performance of *theyyam*. The word '*theyyam*' is a derivative of the word '*daivam*', meaning 'god', and *theyyam* dancers are understood to perform in 'possessed' states in the sacred groves or shrines of north Malabar, admonishing devotees, predicting the future, recalling past events, and receiving adulation and worship from villagers, primarily in Kannur and Kasargod districts. Such traditions do exist in southern Malabar, too, and in the border areas of south Kanara and Coorg (districts of neighbouring Karnataka). There are also regional terminological differences: for example, it is known as '*thira*' in south Malabar. It invokes lineage ancestors, local heroes, and Puranic deities who are collectively worshipped through a whole orchestra of performing modes—drumming, singing, possession, feasting, and entertainment.[2]

The castes that perform *theyyam* also perform other folk arts to earn their livelihoods. Traditionally, *theyyam* is performed in a shrine called a *kaavukal* (but it is sometimes also performed in the compounds of houses). In the past, most such shrines were controlled by upper-caste *tharavadus*, and *theyyam* was used to establish the authority of such *tharavadus* over the whole village. Landless agricultural labourers belonging to the Pulaya caste widely believed that the *theyyam* deities would punish them with disease and other calamities if they did not work hard for their landlords, a belief that represents the superior castes' success in creating mental servitude among subaltern communities and thereby expropriating the economic surplus produced by them. In this process, *theyyam*, which was the art form and cult of the 'inferior' or the depressed classes, seems to have been converted into a means of subjugation by the classes in power.[3] Some of the disputes between Nairs are still settled before a *theyyam* deity, with implicated parties accepting the solution decreed by him, and intra- and inter-caste disputes and land disputes between neighbours are also settled by the deity. However, the decisions of the deity are not completely uninfluenced by the patrons of the shrines, who were upper-caste *tharavadus*.

Earlier, *theyyam* used to be performed for a range of different purposes, although they were generally purposes common to all members of society. It was sometimes performed in paddy fields to ensure agricultural productivity and protect the village from diseases like cholera and small pox, which were feared in the late nineteenth century all over the Madras Presidency.[4] The procreative aspect of femininity was also worshipped, as can be seen in cults of the mother goddess; the Vasurimala *theyyam*, invoking the female deity Vasurimala, was performed to ward off small pox and for soil fertility.

Historically, performing castes have been service castes, servicing the whole village society, and, as mentioned earlier, the position of the performing castes was contextualised within a kind of patron–client relationship in the village economy. Therefore, their social condition was rooted in a subsistence-moral economy (Scot 1985: 9–15);[5] the people of the villages in general and the patrons of shrines in particular were morally concerned with the subsistence of the performers, a concern that arose from a kind of reciprocity (the performers were, after all, servicing the interests of the villagers). Traditional forms of patron–client relationships, reciprocity, and redistributive mechanisms can be seen in this process. Dilip Menon has described this community as a 'moral community' built on the myth of the *theyyam*,[6] as it is the duty—*janmavakasam* (right to perform rites)—of the performing families of the area or *cherujanmam* under the jurisdiction of a *tharavadu*, taken as a unit, to perform *theyyam* for the well-being of the whole village community. Also implicated through similar rights and privileges in the obligation to be involved in the performance are different groups of artisans and other occupational groups under the sway of the *tharavadus*, like the previously mentioned Malayans, Vannans, and Velans as well as Kanisans (astrologers), Asaris (carpenters), Tattans (goldsmiths), Kollans (blacksmiths), Veluthedans (washers of the clothes of deities), and Vilakkathalavans (barbers).[7] The services of all these castes are crucial to the performance of *theyyam* and common village activities. Malayans, Vannans, Velans, and some Adivasi groups like Chingathans have been involved in the performance of *theyyam* since medieval times, and communities like the Nalkathayars, Mavilars, and Pulayars have also participated but in more limited ways. All these castes belong to the lowest strata of the society of north Malabar—they have been included in the lists of Scheduled Castes and Scheduled Tribes of Kerala—and participate in different capacities, including as assistants and singers of *thottam* (the ballad sung before the *theyyam* performance).

Theyyam is performed annually or on festive occasions as an expression of the local people's faith in the divine force and as the artistic expression of their collective social consciousness. It has a significant place in the daily life of the ordinary people of north Malabar, as *theyyam*-related rituals are closely connected to their forms of worship, life ceremonies, culture of sorcery, and tradition of *bhakti* or devotion. The performance of *theyyam* can also be understood as a philosophy of the performing community, for it is an artistic reaction against their oppression;[8] the performer is possessed by the deity and criticises the upper castes for their misdeeds and for their acts of commission and omission towards their servants or labourers as well as for their bloated egos. Members of the upper castes, well above the performers in the social hierarchy, watch such performances and obediently listen to the words recited by the performer. The myths, legends, and stories related to *theyyam* tend to question the *jati* system and the practice of untouchability. This is particularly evident in the myths and *thottams* of *pottan theyyam*.

Theyyam can also be read as a social mechanism to deflect and to invert—for a day—the authority and hierarchy under which the performers have to live and work. This helps generate self-esteem among the lower castes and untouchables in a world otherwise loaded against them.[9] The upper castes do not mind it, as it does not last long and their social upper hand is not seriously challenged. Similar examples can be found in studies of carnivals in other societies and even in other traditions in Kerala, like *chakiar koothu* (another folk dance) and *thullal* (another ritual tradition).

The *theyyam* performer enjoys social respect during the performance, with even members of the higher castes coming forward to pay obeisance to the performer. It is unknown why the right to enact *theyyam* was conferred on those communities alone whose socio-economic status is low. While these aspects demand further research, it is a fact that the untold miseries internalised by these castes find expression in the performance of *theyyam*; it serves as a manifestation of the depressed consciousness of a whole community. Visualising the deity as performed not only provides an occasion for devotees to make physical contact with divinity but also imposes on the members of the lineage and village community moral and economic responsibilities towards one another.[10] It is the general belief among local people, members of the *tharavadus*, and the community of performers that, during the annual performance of *theyyam*, their ancestors appear in the form of the god or deity to bless them and that the celebration is, thus, for the welfare of society at large. But in the course of social change, the moral economy of *theyyattam* has disappeared; patrons have been able to diversify their obligations into wage payments and other facets of modern employer–employee relationships, but clients or performers are still trying to find a new place in the changing social hierarchy. Though reciprocal relationships between performing castes and patrons are on the wane, the attitudes of the performers towards their lives have not changed. Early initiation into the traditional ambit of *theyyam* meant that many pursued their traditional job, i.e. performing *theyyam*. Some studies mention that traditional performers have been able to secure modern employment, allowing them to break out of their traditional way of life,[11] but they return to their caste-based occupation in the seasons of *theyyam* performance from October to April every year. Meanwhile, the majority of them are still trapped in their traditional occupation and culture and are therefore socially immobile. In an empirical study comparing the dynamics of father–son and mother–daughter intergenerational occupational and educational mobility of a *theyyam*-performing group and a non-*theyyam*-performing group, I have argued that the traditional barriers of caste and culture prevented the former from gaining access to other realms of social and economic activity.[12]

Changing Social Discourses in Time and Space

A sequence of events that can be traced back to the implementation of the Malabar matriliny act of 1933 has had significant socio-political effects on the community of *theyyattam*. The act precipitated the fragmentation of *tharavadus*, the sale of properties, the fragmentation of holdings and the eviction of labourers, and subsequently led to the decline of Nair dominance as patrons of the shrines and festivals due to a lack of finances.[13] The 1960s may be regarded as the end of the old order of shrine festivals; the decline of *theyyam* festivals had been underway for around three decades. But then, a dynamic transformation occurred in the early 1970s, by which time the shrines had been taken over by Thiyyas (traditional toddy tappers). Various factors made it possible for the Thiyyas to assume control over the cultural/religious institutions of north Malabar. One of them was the Kerala Land Reforms Act, 1969, which was widely and effectively implemented in north Malabar.[14] Though based on the motto 'Land to the Tiller', promoted by the communist movement that spearheaded the land reforms, this act resulted in the transfer of land to the tenants, including even the minor tenants.[15] As a result of this, they were able to control land and, through land, the *kaavus*. They were thereby able to begin enjoying the social privileges that Nairs had enjoyed earlier. One important method used by Thiyyas to assume a higher social position was that of enforcing their customary *theyyam*-related practices upon groups of lower status like the Pulayas and Malayans, requiring such groups to recognise their subordinate position; this was practised all over the region. The Sri Narayana Movement (SNM), the communist movement,[16] and other social and political movements that had had a significant impact on the region found extreme adherents and also direct beneficiaries from among the Thiyyas.

The most important legislation that directly benefited the Thiyyas was enacted when the communist movement, sweeping through north Malabar, tried to do away with all kinds of ritual-related practices, prior to which the SNM had weakened the folkloric aspects of *theyyam* performances, attacking *bhuttakriya* (sorcery) with particular severity. The communist movement that followed also took up a position of opposition to *theyyam* and related ritual cultures, for the communists believed that *theyyam* was an offshoot of feudal practices and was instrumental in habituating working people to an acceptance of feudal suppression. Between the 1940s and the 1970s, communists tried to 'liberate' *theyyam* performances from the *kaavus* while at the same time using local mythology to mobilise peasants and other sections of the working people. In the course of the latter, they managed to use *theyyam*, recreated in a form devoid of its religious roots, on theatrical stages and even in political demonstrations.[17] Being of folk and cult origin, *theyyam* lore was constituted of several experiences of oppressed and backward people's solidarity, rebellion, and militancy that fitted in with Marxist ideology.

Both the SNM, which tried to upgrade and Sanskritise the wide spectrum of 'religious' practices of backward castes, and the communist movement, which used the artistic dimensions of the folk or cult practices associated with *theyyam* in their efforts to mobilise working people and backward castes, ended up demolishing the folk/cult aspects of this traditional culture. Meanwhile, the *theyyam* performances held in *kaavus* during festivals gave the identity-building of the Thhiyas who controlled them a major fillip. With gains from land reforms, minimum wage legislation, and the public distribution of essential commodities, all of which were showily ascribed to the influence of the communist movement in Malayali society,[18] the Thiyyas formed an economic group that replaced the Nairs in conducting *theyyam* festivals in *kaavus*, turning the *kaavus* and the festivals into rallying points for a resurgent Thiyya community. Interestingly, even in the non-cult, non-folk, ritualised *theyyam*, traditional performers who belonged to castes and groups considered lower than the Thiyyas could not be replaced. In fact, the resurgent Thiyya community, notwithstanding its baptism in communist ideology, required an inferior social group in relation to which its newfound superior social identity could be asserted. The traditional performers of *theyyam*, who had limited faith in the capacity of the communist movement to upgrade their quality of life, did not benefit much from the social-change-related legislations like land reforms largely due to their abject initial condition of assetlessness; to use the language of Pierre Bourdieu,[19] they were unable to trade their symbolic capital as performers for other kinds of capital. Meanwhile, the Thiyyas, who traditionally provided rural labour as toddy tappers, coir manufacturers, garden land cultivators, artisans, and petty landholders, were in a much better bargaining position to corner benefits accruing from the legislations, not least because they happened to be the ideal targets, in terms of their socio-economic position, of the communist strategy of mobilising the proletariat.

Sri Narayana Guru, who Sanskritised Thiyya worship, was outspoken in his opposition to *bhuttakriya* and other practices associated with *theyyam*.[20] At Palakunnu in Kannur district, he proclaimed that 'the temple is not a toddy shop; the temple is not a butcher shop',[21] referring to the use of toddy and animal sacrifice in the worship of the goddesses in *theyyam* culture. In fact, the SNM was trying to 'upgrade' the modes of worship and ritual practices of all the backward castes. As part of this process, several *kaavu*s were transformed into temples, and the original deities were replaced with Sanskritised idols. Instead of venerating local heroes through the worship of their swords, Vedic idols of deities such as Shiva and Vishnu were installed. Local myths associated with these deities were reimagined and aligned with narratives from Puranic texts such as the Ramayana and Mahabharata. Local priests were replaced by Brahmins, who entered the sacred groves and reinterpreted the original myths in terms of verses rooted in the Sanskritic tradition.

What seems to have happened is that, while the reform movement—both communist reforms and social reforms in general—largely bypassed the community of *theyyam* dancers, the Thiyyas who gained from the social and economic reforms used their newfound control of *kaavu*s to accumulate social capital. Their assertion in this particular respect turned them, as a community, into a site of contestation for competing ideologies too. The main contenders for the control of temples and festivals in north Malabar were the left-wing CPI(M) (Communist Party of India [Marxist]) and the right-wing Rashtriya Swayamsevak Sangh (RSS). *Theyyam* performers formed an integral part of the contested terrain, as all sections of society in the region believed in the exclusive traditional right of the performing castes to perform *theyyam* in a *cherujanmam*. However, the role of these castes in the contestation has been a subsidiary one, as the sponsors of the festivals are mainly Thiyyas and Vanias (another intermediate caste). In feudal times, which can perhaps be said to have ended by the 1960s, the castes that performed *theyyam* were subjugated by the upper castes, but in today's modernised, post-feudal society, and with a ritualised *theyyam*, they are subjugated by the resurgent lower middle castes.

As times and spaces have changed, the social conditions of the *theyyam* performing groups have also changed, but their position in the social hierarchy has not. The culture of the *theyyam* tradition has been appropriated by the intermediate castes in order to gain the kind of social and cultural capital that used to be enjoyed by the upper castes. The symbolic value of *theyyam* has been appropriated by the castes just above the social order of the *theyyam* dancers, such that what has resulted is a kind of subordinated inclusion of the *theyyam* performing castes to make visible the social privileges of the intermediate castes. Social power relations have not yielded any heightened social status to the *theyyam* dancers but the images of *theyyam* have continued to be mobilised in service of the social superiority of higher castes.

Globalisation, Intangible Heritage, and Culture

In the globalised era, the 'commodification' of cultural traditions is common. This is a new arena of the market that has brought within its fold all kinds of art and culture.[22] In recent years, there has been a concerted effort to preserve culture, especially languages, folk arts, and other aspects of many cultures that are feared to be dying. One such initiative is the UNESCO Proclamation of Masterpieces of the Oral and Intangible Heritage of Humanity, as part of which *kudiyattam* (an ancient form of dance-theatre that was originally performed in temples) of Kerala was awarded the title of 'Masterpiece'. This kind of preservation, an important part of the process of commoditisation, impacted almost every traditional art of India, and *theyyam*, too, entered the national and international markets as a cultural tourism product or as a product of the cultural heritage of Kerala.

Through a continuation of the same process that displaced it from cult to ritual and then to the theatre, the commodification of *theyyam* has involved converting it into an image and icon. Striking images of *theyyam* performers in their traditional costumes and make-up have been used in various contexts by various kinds of stakeholders, including local scholars and students of folklore. It is not uncommon for performers of *theyyam* to earn extra money by dancing in their costumes at political functions or posing as attractions during tourism festivals. The tourist guidebook of Kerala published by the Kerala Tourism Development Corporation contains images of *theyyam* on its cover.[23] Such photos are frequently taken by authors writing about *theyyam* and are used in annual calendars by the many local cooperative banks in northern Malabar, while studios and theatre groups commercially use a range of *theyyam*-related media. The *thottam* of *theyyam* is available in digital CDs and cassettes, but the singers and custodians of the form do not hold the copyright to their own songs. Foreign tourists visiting often take photographs and videos of *theyyam* performances, paying fees to the owners of the *kaavus*. These owners, in turn, pressure performers to pose for the photographs, as the payment is directed to them rather than the performers. All of this reflects a broader devaluation of *theyyam* as it is commodified into a tourism product, and rarely is an acknowledgment to be found of the performers or the labour involved in creating the costumes, applying facial makeup, or other aspects of the ritual performance.

Indigenous performers who have participated in the annual Republic Day parades and folk dance festivals held in New Delhi and elsewhere have stated that, due to their lack of knowledge of the English language, they were not able to understand the terms and conditions of the agencies that organised the events and were, as a result, highly exploited by intermediaries. For instance, Mr Ramaperumalayan from Kannur, who has performed *theyyam* in New Delhi (on Republic Day) and abroad, filed a suit in the Kerala High Court against intermediaries for not paying him the remuneration that was agreed upon before an event.

In the 1950s, *theyyam* was showcased in the Republic Day parade as a powerful symbol of 'unity in diversity'. It was again honoured in 2016 when a *theyyam* performance was organised as part of a ceremonial reception at Rashtrapati Bhavan.[24] Under the auspices of the Ford Foundation, American cultural elite and bureaucrats have provided money and guidance for the documentation and preservation of *theyyam* and to re-legitimise 'tradition'.[25] There have also been attempts to institutionalise the folklore associated with *theyyam*. Wayne Ashley has pointed out that five institutes were established for *theyyam* cultural studies, all funded by foreign donors.[26] The state-funded Kerala Folklore Academy in Kannur was another addition to this list, established in 1996. The University of Calicut, too, has a separate school for folklore studies that exhibited the 'cultural heritage of Kerala' in four large-scale 'folk festivals', organised with the financial and ideological support of the Ford Foundation.[27] As part of a project concerned with 'important performing arts forms connected with mother worship and nature worship in Kerala' under the supervision of the late Prof. G. Sankara Pillai (former director of the School of Drama, University of Calicut), university personnel documented—450 colour prints, 563 slides, and 42:45 hours of video and audio recordings—120 cultural forms.[28]

On another front, the Kerala Tourism Development Corporation is appropriating *theyyam* as an iconic folk ritual for marketing and product development strategies aimed at promoting tourism development. It has been performed since then at folk festivals held in many parts of the country and the world in the name of preservation. This aggressive commodification of regional cultural heritage suggests that new modes of patronage for *theyyam* may be emerging as a consequence of state-sponsored efforts to re-contextualise the ritual art form within more profitable and productive capitalist relations. If these efforts had been able to protect the common property of the community and to preserve indigenous cultural heritage, which is what most such schemes in developed countries achieved,[29] they would provide hope to the community of *theyyam* dancers. But their failure to do so raises the question—what is the state of culture in this age of globalisation? Who determines the modes and routes of cultural exchange and at whose expense? Can the *theyyam* performing community and spaces survive the replacement of the traditional patron–client relationship by the anonymity of the market and the patriarchy of the state? What kind of impact will these global processes have on the performing community and who will determine the copyrights of the art form that has been preserved over centuries by that community? There has been an increasing cognisance among culturally conscious people of the imbalance between the traditional knowledge, folklore, and genetic materials that are flowing freely out of Third World countries, unprotected by intellectual property rights (IPR), and the cultural products from developed countries that are flowing in, well-protected by IPR agreements—an imbalance that is backed by the threat of trade sanctions. These are some of the political and economic questions that concern the ownership of an intangible property like *theyyam*.

In various international fora, governments of developing countries have increasingly taken the view that traditional knowledge and folklore need to be protected legally and that the formal IPR system legitimises their misappropriation. In order to address the issue of misappropriation, researchers presented a range of proposed systems and measures to protect traditional knowledge and folklore in the light of ongoing international negotiations taking place at the World Trade Organization (WTO) and World Intellectual Property Organization (WIPO). In such a context, is it possible for a developing country like India to protect its rich cultural heritage and popular folk cultures before they are drained out to developed countries? If so, is it possible to introduce common community property rights into the frameworks set up for the protection of these forms?

Conclusion

It is a fact that the society that institutionalised *theyyam* years ago only takes from performing communities and gives them practically nothing in return. The rehabilitation of the economically weak members of the *theyyam*-performing families also remains unaddressed. Workshops are held and leaders grow eloquent in praise of the folk arts of Kerala and the hoary past of the *theyyam* tradition but are reluctant to do anything concrete about the social and economic development of these communities. Bereft of the ability to identify with either the socio-religious movements on caste questions or with the leftist ideologies or rightist forces on the political front, these communities of traditional performers are struggling to find a space in the changing social and economic order.

The younger generation is reluctant to perform *theyyam* due to caste-based inhibitions and feelings of alienation from village society. The youth, occupying a social position that interfaces tradition with modernity, want to receive the benefits of modernity without being burdened by considerations of their old, hoary tradition and culture. But this is an effect, not a cause, of the process of change to which *theyyam* performers have been subjected; no proposal for the propagation of *theyyam* has ever emerged from the civil society of Kerala that favours the real custodians of the form. Ultimately, the form itself has been preserved by the community that performs, and not through the crusaders of the global culture market, and the community has done so while dealing with thousands of conflicting village forces and the always-looming question of livelihood that emanate from a highly stratified *jati* system.

Notes and References

1. Rajesh Komath, 'Social and Economic Mobility of a Traditional Social Group: A Case of the Theyyam Performing Communities in North Kerala' (M.Phil diss., Jawaharlal Nehru University, 2003); Rajesh Komath, 'Political Economy of the "Theyyam"—A Study of the Time–Space

Homology' (Ph.D. diss., Mahatma Gandhi University, Kottayam, 2013); John Richardson Freeman, Jr., 'Purity and Violence: Sacred Power in the Teyyam Worship of Malabar' (Ph.D. diss., University of Pennsylvania, 1991).

2. Wayne Ashley, 'Recodings: Rituals, Theatre, and Political Display in Kerala State, South India' (Ph.D. diss., New York University, 1993), p. 5.

3. K. K. N. Kurup, *The Cult of Teyyam and Hero Worship in Kerala* (Kolkata: Indian Publications, 1973); Komath, 'Political Economy of the "Theyyam"', *op. cit.*

4. David Arnold, 'Cholera and Colonialism in British India', *Past and Present* 113(1) (November 1986): 125.

5. James C. Scott, *The Moral Economy of the Peasant: Rebellion and Subsistence in Southeast Asia* (London: Yale University Press, 1976), pp. 1–13.

6. Dilip Menon, 'The Moral Community of the *Teyyattam*: Popular Culture in Late Colonial Malabar', *Studies in History* 9(2) (August 1993): 209–217.

7. K. K. N. Kurup, *A Study in the Agrarian Relations of Malabar* (Calicut: Sandhya Publications, 1981).

8. Komath, 'Social and Economic Mobility of a Traditional Social Group', *op. cit.*

9. Menon, 'The Moral Community of the *Teyyattam*', *op. cit.*, p. 192.

10. Ashley, 'Recodings', *op. cit.*, p. 5.

11. Wayne Ashley and Regina E. Holloman, 'Caste and Cult in Kerala', *South Asian Anthropologist* 4(2) (1983): 93–104.

12. Rajesh Komath, 'Intergenerational Occupational and Educational Mobility: Case of Village Social Structure of North Malabar, Kerala', *Calicut University Research Journal* 5(1) (2005): 29–30; 'The Living Cult of the Theyyam and Social Behavior: Certain Anthropological Observations' (Draft paper presented at the Regional Seminar on the Socio-economic Conditions of the Tribal Society in Malabar, organised by Nirmalagiri College, Kuthuparamba, under the auspices of the Institute for Research in Social Sciences and Humanities, in association with the Anthropological Survey of India, Kolkata, March 11–12, 2004).

13. Menon, 'The Moral Community of the *Teyyattam*', *op. cit.*, p. 216.

14. Kakkadan Nandanath Raj and Michael Tharakan, 'Agrarian Reform in Kerala and Its Impact on the Rural Economy: A Preliminary Assessment',

in *Agrarian Reform in Contemporary Developing Countries*, ed. Ajit Kumar Ghose (New York: St. Martin's Press, 1983).

15. Ronald J. Herring, *Land to the Tiller: The Political Economy of Agrarian Reform in South Asia* (Delhi: Oxford University Press, 1983).

16. Menon, 'The Moral Community of the *Teyyattam*', *op. cit.*

17. Wayne Ashley and Regina E. Holloman, 'From Ritual to Theatre in Kerala', *The Drama Review* 26(2) (Summer 1982): 72–101.

18. V. K. Ramachandran, 'On Kerala's Development Achievements', in *Indian Development: Selected Regional Perspectives*, eds. Jean Dreze and Amartya Sen (Delhi: Oxford University Press, 1997).

19. Pierre Bourdieu, *Outline of a Theory of Practice* (Cambridge: Cambridge University Press, 1977).

20. A. Aiyappan, 'Iravas and Culture Change', *Bulletin of the Madras Government Museum* 5(1) (1943): 99.

21. Ashley and Holloman, 'From Ritual to Theatre in Kerala', *op. cit.*, p. 101.

22. Rustom Bharucha, *The Politics of Cultural Practice: Thinking through Theatre in an Age of Globalization* (Delhi: Oxford University Press, 2001).

23. Shrihari Nair, *Theyyam Charisma* (Kannur: AUM Communications, 2002).

24. Thaniya Kaliyanthil Leela, *Goddesses of North Malabar: An Anthropological Study on Kinship and Ritual in North Malabar* (M.Phil diss., University of Bergen, 2016), p. 48.

25. Ashley, 'Recodings', *op. cit.*, p. 28.

26. *Ibid.*, p. 246.

27. *Ibid.*, p. 305.

28. *Ibid.*, p. 322.

29. Anthony McCann, 'All that is Not Given is Lost: Irish Traditional Music, Copyright, and Common Property', *Ethnomusicology* 45(1) (December 2001): 89–106.

5

Education and Exclusion

Historically Situating the Marginalised in Kerala

Roshni Padmanabhan

The development process that led to the formation of the 'Kerala model'[1] as a consequence of redistributive policy measures,[2] operative as early as the beginning of the second half of the nineteenth century and promoted by 'public action',[3] is well-documented.[4] However, it is also well known among students of development that gains from the development process were unevenly distributed among various social groups, barely trickling down to the traditionally disadvantaged;[5] the 'systematic marginalization' of disadvantaged communities in the state is understood to be an inadequacy of the Kerala model.[6] Consequently, in the literature on Kerala's development experience, Dalits, Adivasis, and traditional fisherfolk have been identified as 'outliers' with relatively poor access to social development.[7] Their persistent exclusion has resulted in the creation of impoverished colonies and the deterioration of skills, knowledge, and resources of lower-caste groups.[8]

Since the introduction of modern education in Kerala in the nineteenth century, different social groups in the state have gained access to it in different degrees and at different times. However, the educational backwardness of Dalits, which has remained a matter of concern[9] since then, is not the outcome of a lack of demand in the early stages;[10] indeed, education was demanded by Dalits precisely as a way out of traditional caste oppression. While we have some scholarly literature that explores the dimensions of this backwardness, there is little work available that probes the broader contexts which have shaped the situation and the precise manner in which this disadvantage continues to be reproduced despite a considerable number of interventions by the government and other agencies.

This chapter does not present a full-fledged empirical investigation into the question mentioned above. Rather, it offers a historical narrative of the evolution of Dalit demands for education in the princely states comprising present-day Kerala in the late-nineteenth and twentieth centuries and the responses of the princely states. The historical data used here pertain largely to the princely state of Travancore in south Kerala, where demands for education and government efforts to supply it were both already being made in the late-nineteenth and early-twentieth centuries. The proceedings of the Travancore Sri Mulam Praja Sabha, Cochin Legislative Council, and Travancore Cochin Legislative Assembly and various Administrative Reports have been used extensively to construct the narrative. The Assembly debates provide both quantitative and qualitative information that sheds light on the developmental aspirations of different social groups.

The Context of Lower-Caste Assertion in the Late-Nineteenth and Twentieth Centuries

Through the nineteenth century and until the formation of Kerala in 1956, three regions in the modern-day territory of the state were marked by distinct state policies with respect to education, land tenancy, and administrative reforms: Malabar, a district of the Madras Presidency in British India, and Travancore and Cochin, both princely states formed in the mid- and late eighteenth century respectively that came under indirect British political control[11] through a residency system whereby a British 'Resident' served as adviser to the native ruler.[12] This was in keeping with British colonial policy; the East India Company tended to cite corruption and poor administration as pretexts for the annexation of territories from princes.[13] In 1811, Colonel John Munro, the Resident of Travancore, undertook a series of administrative reforms, 'reducing the power of local court officials, abolishing various taxes, dividing the principality into districts and subdistricts along the lines of British administration in India, and setting up a modern administration at these various levels'.[14] In other words, over the course of the nineteenth century, the government machineries of Travancore and Cochin were gradually altered under British pressure in ways that enabled colonial penetration of the economy.

Between the twelfth and the nineteenth centuries, the economies of Kerala's princely states were based on slave labour,[15] which was used to cultivate large tracts of rice fields. Agricultural surplus was the most important source of revenue for the state. '*Sirkar* slaves' were slaves who were attached to government ('*sirkar*') lands and were leased out with those lands to private individuals; the annual revenue derived from their labour was Rs 4,041. In Malabar, too, the labour of slaves was a significant source of government revenue.[16] Although it may seem like the lenient attitude of the princely governments towards colonial powers expanding their trade in the kingdom had a positive impact on traditional labour relations—by the Proclamation of 1853, the Travancore *sirkar* emancipated the children of *sirkar* slaves who were born after September 15, 1853, and a similar proclamation was issued in Cochin on February 16, 1854—slavery continued to be practised in both princely states even after its abolition.

The onset of British rule (rather than mere expansion of trade), however, had complex results: weakening the power of the upper castes, it shook the foundations of the caste order that the traditional rulers of Kerala were duty-bound to protect. Several measures undertaken by the British Resident and, later, by missionaries—especially of the London Missionary Society (LMS)—struck at the roots of upper-caste control over the lower castes, especially over their labour. These developments probably accentuated tensions around upper-caste control that already existed in Malayali society—there is evidence to suggest that these tensions and lower-caste resistance to upper-caste control pre-dated the advent of the missionaries or the British.[17] Such tensions escalated from the 1820s onwards into full-fledged social confrontations, commonly referred to as the 'breast-cloth' disturbances,[18] over the role of the traditional monarchies in Travancore and Cochin as defenders of caste. In response to such pressures from below and equally powerful pressures from above—from the British Resident—the governments of Travancore and Cochin began to seek modern foundations for state power.

Modernisation of state power in Travancore and Cochin included reforms in land tenure and the expansion of education and healthcare in the mid-nineteenth century,[19] which helped improve literacy rates, weaken landlordism, and create a large working population for factories and plantations set up by the British. While these reforms were in general significantly fuelled by fear of annexation by the British, the key factor that triggered education reform in Travancore was missionary activity. The European missionaries who came to Travancore were primarily interested, of course, in conversion, but their work had other political and cultural consequences, both intended and unintended. In the beginning, they tried to convert the upper castes but were spurned. The Church Missionary Society (CMS) reported in 1857 that there were no more than ten Nairs among the 5,000–6,000 believers in Travancore.[20] The situation of the LMS in the south was similar: the majority of its converts were from the lower castes. From the late 1860s onwards, there were large-scale conversions to Christianity; the census report of 1901 states that 1,38,862 persons in Travancore converted to Christianity during the preceding decade alone.

The demand for education among the lower castes was voiced quite early in the history of missionary intervention in Kerala, and this demand grew after 1860. Following the success of the anti-slavery campaign by missionaries, a significant number of Pulayas from different parts of Central Travancore requested CMS missionaries to provide them with Christian instruction and schools for slaves, and the missionaries complied, opening several such schools, and focusing on primary education and literacy programmes as Dalits began to flock to the Anglican Church. Missionaries also campaigned for the civil rights of Dalits. For instance, CMS and LMS missionaries fought for the establishment of government schools for the lower castes in the 1870s.[21]

The Pulaya Charity School, set up in Trivandrum in 1861 by the LMS, was maintained with an annual grant of rice from the Travancore government, meant to cover the noonday meal of the students, and with the interest from an endowment fund established by Dr Waring, a missionary and educator of the London Missionary Society who was influential in advancing several education initiatives, particularly in Travancore. Students from this school were trained to be mission agents, gardeners, and domestic servants. Some of them were employed as government vaccinators in charge of their caste and some were sent to Nagercoil Seminary for education in English, with the prospect of future employment as teachers in the mission. In 1830, there were 100 LMS schools in Travancore; this number had tripled by 1860, when approximately 14,000 students, most of whom came from Dalit families, were enrolled in these schools. Since public schools were not open to Dalits then, conversion to Christianity was the only option available to those among them who wanted their children educated. During the same period, the state spent considerable sums of money on spreading Western education in Travancore. However, the impact of caste on these efforts is stark; according to an 1875 report on the Travancore census that provides the literacy rates of different castes and communities in the princely state, only 0.09 per cent of Pulayas and 0.31 per cent of Parayas were literate.

Madhava Rao, the Dewan of Travancore, placed great value on education, clearly spelling out his position in an 1866 speech:

> Education would be the chief passport to honour and preferment, and so far as *sirkar* was concerned, all important posts under it would be filled by educated men and educated men alone, as soon as they become available.[22]

Table 5.1: Literacy rates among different castes/communities in Travancore in 1875

Castes	Literacy Rate
European	83.90
Eurasian	34.49
Brahmins	27.13
Ambalavasi	16.35
Nayars	11.12
Ezhavas	1.57
Kammala	4.49
Pulaya (Cheramar Hindu only)	0.09
Paraya (Sambavar Hindu only)	0.31

Source: Report on the Census of Travancore taken on May 18, 1875.

Madhava Rao thus linked education to government employment. On the one hand, the number of vernacular schools, both government and aided, showed a tremendous increase from 12 in 1865–1866 to 1,606 in 1894–1895[23] and, correspondingly, expenditure on education had increased from a few hundred rupees to lakhs annually. On the other hand, *sirkar* schools were open only to the high castes. Foreseeing the danger of driving the low castes to missionaries, Madhava Rao initiated a discussion with missionaries on starting separate schools for depressed castes, but the proposal was rejected by the British Resident and the Madras government; *sirkar* schools remained exclusively for the high castes and Syrian Christians. And yet, the *sirkar*'s emphasis on education and the link drawn between education and government employment aroused hopes in the lower castes too.

Development of a modern state is actualised through inclusive governance and redistribution of developmental resources, with education and literacy providing the tools with which this transformation is navigated. This process was initiated under British guidance in the princely state of Travancore: the traditional elites were restructured and incorporated to enact this process, either as state officials or as other agents of developmental governance. Needless to say, the process was largely exclusionary, and, in response, the lower strata of society launched different kinds of public activism, seeking inclusive developmental reformism. At this juncture, it would be appropriate to understand the social conditions of the depressed castes/Dalits during this period. As has been established, Dalit education had not received the attention of Travancore state, but those who joined the Christian missions were imparted basic literacy. George Oommen quotes CMS archival documents to suggest that missionaries were pressurised by Pulaya converts to establish schools rather than churches.[24] During the second half of the nineteenth century, Christian missionaries were the most important non-governmental providers of education to the lower castes, starting separate schools for Dalit children and also admitting them to regular schools. The first CMS missionary in Kerala, Thomas Norton, was a pioneer in spreading education among the downtrodden. Due to great opposition from Catholic priests, a school started by Norton in Alleppey was destroyed, but in 1818 he started another school in Alleppey, at Great Bazaar. In 1835, he was asked to start a school by Arayas from the northern side of Alleppey, which he did; around fifty children took admission in the school. Another missionary, Sr. Rev. Mead, started a school for Pulayas and gave monetary incentives to teachers who brought lower-caste children to the school: one *fanam*[25] for each slave boy and half a *fanam* for each slave girl.[26]

In 1830, there were 100 LMS schools in Travancore; the number of schools had tripled by 1860, with approximately 14,000 students. Most of the students came from the depressed castes, whose educational demands were ignored by the Travancore government. The Travancore state continued to function like an orthodox, upper-caste Hindu cultural edifice. By the mid-nineteenth century, the demand from the depressed castes for education had reached a pitch that could not be completely ignored by the state. In 1865, Madhava Rao proposed the idea of a school for Shanars and other lower castes in Southern Travancore through Circular No. 2965.

There were mixed reactions to this proposal, one of them being that such a school would be a failure because Shanars did not freely mix with Shudras,[27] and, predictably, it was rejected by the government. Dalit children remained excluded from government schools. In a letter to the Government of Madras in April 1870, Resident G. A. Ballard wrote that the exclusion of lower-caste children from government schools was one of the main disabilities the lower castes faced in Travancore. The *sirkar* schools continued for some time to be accessed almost exclusively by elite castes; as noted by Koji Kawashima (1998), 'In 1891–92, Ezhavas were only 2.1 per cent of all pupils in government schools, while they constituted 16 per cent of the population.'

Noting the aspirations of the lower castes and their demands for education, in 1895, the Maharaja of Travancore reminded the state that all castes had the right to access public schools,[28] and subsequently, the Travancore government opened fifteen schools for the backward classes: four schools for Muslims, seven for Ezhavas, two for Pulayas, one for Marakkans (fishermen), and one for Kani (tribes). Another fifteen schools were added the following year. However, persistent discrimination against the depressed castes by the state in subtle ways meant that the former still had to rely more or less completely on missionary schools.

Statistics compiled by A. W. Painter in 1882 establish that CMS schools for Pulayas existed in major parts of Travancore by then.[29] By 1890, 12,000 Dalit convert students, both girls and boys, were being taught in CMS vernacular schools. In 1891, there were 322 boys and 83 girls in the fourteen Pulaya schools in Kottayam.[30]

The increase in the number of Pulaya schools is itself proof of the desire for education in the community. Their insistence compelled missionaries to open schools before constructing churches, and the process was expedited by the Pulayas' willingness to contribute to the construction of schools in new locations.[31] The Pulayas even offered to contribute economically to support teachers. As the efforts of missionaries spread, the primary request they encountered among Dalits was for schools,[32] a fact that is important because it establishes that, while Christian missionaries contributed greatly to the education of Dalits, the latter's own efforts also constituted a significant force in the history of education in Kerala.

When the number of students increased, and with it the number of schools and the related expenses, LMS and CMS missionaries requested financial support from the Travancore government. As a result, the government began to provide grants-in-aid to missionary schools, which they too benefited from, since untouchable students did not go to the government schools that were effectively only for the upper castes.[33] The effect of the educational policies enacted in Travancore and Cochin was an improvement in literacy levels among all communities. However, while illiteracy was fast reducing among the upper castes, the rate of reduction among Dalits was not proceeding apace. Improvements in Ezhava literacy came about only after the 1930s. And meanwhile, in the case of Malabar, the literacy levels of all castes remained low and Dalits remained illiterate.

Table 5.2: Pulaya schools in Travancore

Pastorates	Number of Converts	Number of Schools
Trichur	117	1
Mavelikkara	733	12
Thiruvalla	1,599	3
Alleppey	233	6
Kottayam Pallam	886	5
Thalavadi	643	8
Changanassery	892	4
Erikatt	1,109	4
Olesha	1,617	6
Mullappalli	594	2
Total	**8,424**	**51**

Source: George Oommen, 'Education, Self-Perception, and Identity: The Experience of the Pulaya Christians of Kerala (1860–1930)', in *Education and Social Change in South Asia*, eds. Krishna Kumar and Joachim Oesterheld (New Delhi: Orient Longman, 2007), p. 107.

Table 5.3: Expenditure on education as a percentage of total expenditure of the Travancore state, 1864–1945

Year	Percentage
1864–65	1.4
1874–75	2.8
1884–85	3.3
1894–95	4.7
1904–05	6.2
1914–15	11.4
1924–25	14.6
1934–35	20.4
1944–45	16.2

Source: Bright Singh, 'Financial Developments in Travancore: 1800–1941 AD' (Ph.D. diss., Travancore University, Trivandrum); and Manali Desai, 'Indirect British Rule, State Formation, and Welfarism in Kerala, India, 1860–1957', *Social Science History* 29(3) (Fall 2005): 457–488.

Table 5.4: Literacy levels of select communities during the pre-Independence period

Communities	Travancore			Cochin			Malabar		
	1911	*1931*	*1941*	*1911*	*1931*	*1941*	*1911*	*1931*	*1941*
Pulaya	0.8	3.3	17.0	0.5	5.3	9.8		1.2	1.9
SC (as a whole)	3.0	5.0	18.0			9.6			1.0
Muslim	9.4	14.8	30.1	7.4	13.7	23.2	5.7	6.2	7.5
Ezhava/Thiyya	10.1	21.3	46.5	8.2	26.2	34.7	10.6	21.9	
Syrian Christians	18.4	35.7	55.6	21.5	40.1	55.4	32.4	37.3	40.5
Nair	23.0	35.5	61.7	27.1	55.7	63.2	26.1	28.0	37.7
Malayali Brahmins	45.2	50.9	73.9	42.5	68.0	73.7	42.8	44.7	57.0

Source: P. Sivanandan, 'Caste and Economic Opportunity' (Ph.D. diss., University of Kerala, 1989); Census Reports: Travancore, Cochin, Malabar for 1911, 1931, and 1941.

Community Formation and the Competition for Education

The history of early-twentieth-century Malayali society is characterised by the formation of powerful modernising communities fashioned from the caste groups of traditional society. The process was fired by a combination of several elements of social change: the opening up of Kerala's economy in the mid-nineteenth century, which provided economic opportunities to important social groups such as the lower-caste Ezhavas and the upper-caste Syrian Christians; land reform in Travancore and Kochi, which strengthened tenants and created a land market; the expansion of modern education through state initiatives; and the weakening of traditional forms of caste power through the self-assertion of the lower castes, which was aided by the missionaries. Modern education was widely viewed as the key to the future, and communities competed for access to it.

In the early 1880s, two associations were formed in Travancore: Syrian Christian Jathiyayikya Sangham and Nair Malayali Sabha. Though neither lasted long, they can be seen as symbolising the proliferation of caste-based and communal associations in Travancore over the next half-century, a large number of which sprang up between 1900 and 1910, like Sree Narayana Dharma Paripalana Yogam (SNDP) and Nair Service Society (NSS). The leaders of these associations, who had at least some exposure to Western education and the wider world, encouraged the spread of education, especially among women, and pressed for social and religious reforms. The low-caste associations focused mainly on being guaranteed basic civil rights, which included access to public places and schools and subsequently to all branches of government service and centres of worship. Better representation in government services was, in particular, a concern of the Ezhava elite, since they were the only lower-caste group that boasted a significant number of English-literate members.

The activities of the associations created a community consciousness that came to overlay, and in some cases even subsume, the diversity of sub-castes among Nairs, Ezhavas, and the Christian sects.[34] After 1890, which was when Ezhava assertion began, these three consolidated communities began competing for larger shares of state power and resources.

At the beginning of the twentieth century, 927 out of every 1,000 Ezhavas in Travancore were illiterate; despite the removal of legal hindrances, Ezhava students were excluded from schools. Even if they were educated, employment opportunities were hard to come by, as they were not recruited into government service.[35] A powerful political awakening had been spurred in Travancore by the 1891 G. P. Pillai-led agitation against the autocratic administration of the state and the denial to native communities of their due share in government jobs. The agitation, which adopted 'Travancore for Travancoreans' as its slogan, finally led to the drawing up of the Travancore Memorial (Malayali Memorial), a petition to the Maharaja signed by Nairs, Ezhavas, and Christians. However, the primary interest underlying the petition was that of the Nair community, and its major grievance was that the native upper castes were not being given adequate representation in the bureaucracy; the discrimination suffered by Ezhavas was only superficially touched on. The reply from the *sirkar* pointed out that 'Ezhavas were a [contented] lot and if the government was to adopt a deliberate policy to give them a share in education and administration it would be unproductive and would create tension and strain communal harmony'.[36]

Realising that the Malayali Memorial was a failure from their point of view, the Ezhava community, under the leadership of Dr Palpu, submitted in 1895 a lengthy petition, composed in English, to Sankara Subaiyer, the Dewan of Travancore, enlisting the disabilities suffered by them. Another memorandum was submitted to the Maharaja in 1896. Both of these, known as the Ezhava Memorials, demanded entry into government schools and government employment. In response, the Dewan assured the Ezhavas that they would be granted special schools, but this assurance proved insubstantial; only two primary schools were opened for them. Dr Palpu's disappointment with the Dewan's response gave birth to the Ezhava Mahajana Sabha in 1896,[37] but the organisation was unable to gather any significant momentum. It was only with the formation of SNDP in 1903 under the spiritual leadership of Sri Narayana Guru that the Ezhava struggles and demands received a meaningful boost.

The first objective of SNDP was to remove the obstacles in the way of Ezhava admission to government and government-aided schools. Later, the Yogam shifted its focus to establishing its own schools and colleges. Narayan Guru's motto was 'Strengthen through organisation, liberate by education,' and this inspired the Ezhava community; under his guidance, SNDP attracted Ezhavas not only in Travancore but also in Cochin and Malabar.[38]

This does not mean that other communities were not seeking similar possibilities. They, too, organised themselves and began attempting to climb the social ladder, but their role was marginal in this game of power. English education, control over land, and access to government offices were the three variables that affected the status and power of every community at the time. By the 1930s, education had become a majorly contested political issue; while the lower castes that demanded education were often seeking escape from various forms of elite oppression, upper-caste interest in modern schooling was clearly linked to new opportunities for employment in the rapidly modernising states, the expanding bureaucracy and welfare network, and the economic opportunities emerging in the wake of Kerala's economic integration with the world-system. The access enjoyed by different communities across the social spectrum to education, land, and employment was neither even nor characterised by the same calculations of advantage, but education was perceived by everyone as the door to economic upward mobility and the emerging political field.[39] Inevitably, the powerful communities—those with economic clout and/or caste clout—triumphed.

Apart from Protestant missionaries, Syrian Christians also invested a lot in education. By the end of the nineteenth century, we see the Syrian Orthodox Church registering a society to manage and coordinate its educational activities.[40] From the 1880s, Indian Catholics started establishing schools, and they quickly made outstanding progress in this field: between 1882 and 1887, the number of schools under Catholic management increased from around 10 to over 1,000. A famous Syrian Christian leader of this time period, Father Immanuel Nidhiry, is reported to have said in a speech that an English school would be 'a more prized asset than the golden crosses of churches', which could be stolen.[41] Clearly, the church accorded great importance to the matter of investing in education. It is important to note in this regard that Syrian Christians also received assistance in their efforts from the government in the form of liberal grants-in-aid.

The experience of the less powerful communities, however, appears to have been different. The coastal Arayas also initiated efforts at modernisation between the late nineteenth and early twentieth centuries but did not succeed significantly. Despite its early efforts, the Araya reform movement failed to establish an adequate and sustainable network of secular community institutions to promote education and other skills needed for modern political and economic life. A large number of institutions sprang up, but they were short-lived, mainly due to financial constraints.[42]

Meanwhile, Southern Travancore was seized by a different kind of politics. Under the leadership of Ayyankali (1863–1941), Dalits started laying claim to public spaces, including schools. In 1898, Ayyankali, who later became the first Dalit nominated member in Sri Mulam Praja Sabha,[43] broke caste rules by riding his *villuvandi* (ox cart) from Venganoor to Aralamudu market in Balaramapuram, heralding in a sense a more forceful era of Dalit assertion. In 1907, Ayyankali established the Sadhujana Paripalana Sangham, a movement that targeted the retrograde practice of keeping the Pulaya away from public roads and marketplaces. Several other Dalit organisations sprang up around the same time: Prathyaksha Raksha Sabha (under Poykayil Yohannan, later known as Kumara Guru Devan), Thiruvathamkoor Paraya Maha Sabha, Sidhanar Service Society, Sambavar Mahasabha, Cheramar Sangathana, and Sathya Vilasini Sangham.[44]

In 1904, the Pulayas under the leadership of Ayyankali set up a school in Venganoor, which came to be considered a milestone in Dalit education,[45] but this school was destroyed by the higher classes. Similarly, a 1910 government order calling for Dalits to be permitted entry into schools was sabotaged by the upper castes in the administration. School authorities, who were landowners, refused to comply with the decision. A March 2, 1910 editorial in *Swadeshabhimani* likened teaching pupils from both upper and lower castes in the same class to yoking a horse and a buffalo to the same plough.[46]

Ayyankali took a stand against the continuing discrimination, proclaiming, 'If our children are not allowed into schools, we shall henceforth refuse to work in the field.'[47] Kerala's very first farm labour agitation, a landmark struggle led by Ayyankali, was a fight not for livelihood but to learn the alphabet, built around the threat that, if their children were denied education, farmworkers would cut off the supply of grain. Consequent to this, the government not only permitted school entry to children who came from the suppressed classes but also the opening of schools for these children. However, the collusion of school owners, officials, and certain authorities effectively prevented the implementation of this decision.

The Demand for Education from the Lower Castes

The persistent demands raised by Dalit representatives in Sri Mulam Praja Sabha primarily express their urge to acquire access to three resources: education, land, and employment. Discussions around these demands reveal that they were aware of the advancement that different communities had been able to achieve through access to these resources and of the institutional structures that determined that access and the chances of advancement.[48] They wanted to improve their lives by changing institutional structures and tried to do so by highlighting problems with the registration of *puduval* land,[49] school admission, the provision of noon meals, books, clothes, and scholarships, fee exemptions, minimum pass marks in examination, and securing government employment.

Noting in a speech[50] on February 29, 1916, that Paraya children were refused admission in government schools and had to plead for it, a Paraya representative named Kandan Kumaran suggested that one Paraya boy from each *taluk* be granted a scholarship for a certain number of years. A similar issue was taken up by Ayyankali,[51] who debunked the fear that the dissemination of knowledge among Pulayas would negatively affect the supply of field labour, citing the industrial and agricultural prosperity that had closely followed the abolition of slavery. He argued that scholarships would assist the Pulayas considerably in their pursuit of higher education, pointing out that if rich communities like the Mohammedans could get fee concessions of up to 50 per cent, it was not too much for the Pulayas to ask to be entirely exempted from fee payments. A similar demand was raised by Ayyankali again in the Assembly on February 26, 1918,[52] when he made the following demands:

1. That all schools admit Pulaya boys with total fee exemption up to Class 7 and at least 10 per cent of them be awarded scholarships to pursue further education.
2. That the government order in respect of Pulaya admission be enforced rigorously, as, although a large number of schools had been thrown open to Pulayas, most were still not admitting them.
3. That a line of huts be built for Pulayas in Venganoor or some other central locality, along with a school for primary education and vocational training and provisions for noontime meals.
4. That a separate amount be earmarked for the education of Pulayas in the state budget.

On March 10, 1921, Ratnaswami, a nominated member of the Sambava community, submitted a memorandum[53] to the government containing proposals for the grant of scholarships to boys and girls of the Sambava community. He proposed two Rs 7 scholarships per *taluk* for children studying in English schools, and two Rs 15 scholarships per *taluk* for those who pursued college studies. On the same day, in the Assembly, Ayyankali[54] observed that even though the government was trying to promote welfare activities for the depressed castes, the number of Pulaya students had fallen by 295 in 1920. On another occasion, Ayyankali drew attention to the fact that, while the Pulayas of the country now numbered about three lakh, the number of those who attended school was only 12,381, and of this the number that persisted beyond Class 5 was only 136; extreme poverty prevented most of them from going further. Apart from providing insights into the conditions of Dalits at this time, these statistics are also indicative of the Dalit representatives' vigilance vis-à-vis the issues they were raising. Kurumban Daivathan[55] also requested total fee concession and noonday meals for the backward classes and that twenty-five boys and twenty-five girls be provided a full school education at the government's expense. He also suggested that primary education be made compulsory for the backward classes, that all schools be thrown open to them, and that scholarships be granted continuously regardless of whether the concerned pupils actually passed the annual examination.

Ayyankali's speeches frequently featured demands for meals at noon for schoolchildren from the depressed classes at the government's expense. He recommended the continuation of this provision for fifteen years.[56] On March 15, 1930, he added the demand that every Pulaya be allotted one *chakram*[57] and one 'cash' (*kaasu*)[58] per day for the purpose of noon meal. Describing the subtle ways in which the government hindered the efforts of Pulayas, K. P. Karuppan, a Member of the Cochin Legislative Council regarded by many as the voice of all the depressed castes in Cochin, complained in the council about a school built by Pulayas in Mualavukadu having been destroyed by the higher castes, who had started a toddy shop there. In another instance, Karuppan said, the government, having granted *puramboke* land (land that was unlisted in the revenue records) to the Pulayas for the construction of a school, transferred the same piece of land to a British individual who had requested it.[59]

The depressed castes were, to an extent, able to translate their demands into government policies. As a result, students from the lower castes started enrolling in schools and a few were even able to access higher education: as per the Administrative Report of 1932–33,[60] one Paraya and two Pulaya students were attending classes in college in Travancore that year, out of a total of 15,726 Pulayas, 5,218 Parayas, and 3,031 Kurava pupils during the period covered by the report. The Administrative Report of 1935–36 reports that 31,259 students from the Pulaya, Parayar, and Kurava communities and hill tribes, 9,711 of them girls, were enrolled in colleges, English schools, and vernacular schools. The 1938–39 report[61] reveals that attempts were also being made to address other demands: textbooks were supplied free of cost to the backward class pupils of Classes 3 and 4 and thirty Dalit schools were provided grants that year. By this time, Dalit representatives, not satisfied with merely elementary education, had brought higher education within the purview of their demands. In course of a discussion on March 7, 1928, Cheramar representative Paradi Abraham Isaac made the following demands:

1. That five Cheramar candidates who had passed the Senior School Leaving Certificate examination be selected from each of the three divisions of Kottayam, Quilon, and Trivandrum and be given a special scholarship of Rs 15 each by the government to pursue a Bachelor's degree, and
2. That government services give precedence to applications from Cheramar candidates over all others and the maximum age of applicants be raised from 25 to 28.

A speech by Kandan Kumaran[62] on March 7, 1928, showcases the eagerness of Parayas to invest in educational assets during the twentieth century. Referring to an orphanage housing fifteen children and maintained by the community in Peruvinvha, Sivagiri, Kunnathurtaluk, Kumaran suggested that the government contribute to the construction of a school attached to the orphanage and provide it a grant-in-aid. He also informed the Assembly that in Kunnathur, Chengannur, Thiruvalla, Changanassery, Peerumedu, Mavelikkara, Karunagappali, and Ambalappuzha *taluks*, the Paraya community had fifty-two schools in which forty-six teachers were Parayas, three were Ezhavas, two were Nairs, and one was Christian.

He urged the government to provide sufficient grants to these schools.[63]

In March 1931, Poykayil Yohannan informed the assembly[64] that members of the Paraya community proposed to start a private English school and, additionally, requested timber free of cost from the government for the conversion of a school into a high school. Similarly, the Sambava community requested liberal grants and the free supply of books, newspapers, etc. for libraries and reading rooms opened by them and suggested that boarding schools be started for the benefit of Sambava boys and girls in Central Travancore.[65]

On the other hand, an observation made by N. G. Parameswaran Pillai on the desirability of reforms to elevate the lower castes reflects the hostility and the negative attitude of the upper castes towards the reforms:

> It was an admitted fact that, during the past ten years, vast progress had been made in the spread of education at considerable cost for which people were grateful to the government, but the question was whether the benefit reaped was proportionate to the large expenditure already met. There was poverty in the country and it had to be seriously considered whether that poverty was on the increase or decrease with spread of so much education. Another feature of that education was the growing number of school children from the depressed classes such as Pulayas, Parayas and the working or artisan classes. One positive evil was that the children of those classes abandoned their ancestral trade and thought it inferior to follow it and did not equip themselves with that kind of education and training which could maintain them in life.[66]

The demands of Dalits and the resultant educational policies in Travancore led to a marginal increase in literacy rates among the lower castes, but their investments in education were not sustainable for too long, as, unlike the dominant communities, their revenue sources were scanty. In response to a question raised by K. C. Chandi in 1946,[67] the number of recognised private primary schools and their respective student strengths in the *taluks* of Tovala and Agasteeswaram and within the municipal limits of Nagarcoil and Trivandrum, grouped according to the demographic profile of the management, were placed before the Assembly. The data revealed (see Table 5.5) that all the schools managed by LMS, Salvation Army, Zenana Mission, Kerala Hindu Mission, Harijan Sevak Sangh, Brahmin, Nair, Nadar, Muslim, Ezhava, Vellala and several other Hindu castes had been surrendered to the government.

Table 5.5: Number of schools in Tovala, Agasteeswaram, Nagarcoil, and Trivandrum, sorted by management composition and student strength in 1945

	Management	**Number of Schools**	**Student Strength**
		Hindu	
1	Brahmin	2	532
2	Nair	9	2,146
3	Vellala	2	476
4	K.H. Mission	8	747
5	Harijan	5	186
6	Nadir	6	1,143
7	Ezhava	3	726
8	Others	10	1,540
		Christian	
1	SIUC	49	7,168
2	Roman Catholic	33	6,264
3	Salvation Army	6	900
4	Belgium Mission	1	242
5	Zenana Mission	1	332
6	Lutheran Mission	10	1,015
		Muslim	
1	Muslim	1	232
	Total	**146**	**23,649**

Source: Proceedings of the Travancore Sri Chitra State Council, Fourth Session, 15 August 1946, p. 559.

Table 5.6: Role of the Christian community in education, 1943–1944

Category of Education	Total	Management and Control		
		Government	Private other than Christians	Christians
Colleges	6	2		4
English high schools	111	26	17	68
English high schools for girls	25	3		22
English middle schools	162	18		144
English middle schools for girls	26	4	1	21
Malayalam and Tamil schools including primary	3,283	978	237	2,068

Source: George Mathew, *Communal Road to a Secular Kerala* (New Delhi: Concept Publishing Company, 1989).

In the 1930s, relations between the government of Travancore and the managements of community-run schools took a turn for the worse, especially after Sir C. P. Ramaswamy Iyer became the Dewan of Travancore in 1936. The 1940s saw an exacerbation of this conflict when the government decided to assume control of primary education with the definite objective of making it both free and compulsory. The Dewan's attempts to 'regulate' private schools and redo the foundations of the 'Hindu state' of Travancore played out against the backdrop of a massive confrontation between Sir C. P. and the powerful Christian community, which, according to Catholic sources, ran about 80 per cent of private schools in Travancore.

Unemployment was another pressing problem that the depressed castes faced. Representatives from various Dalit communities knew that representation in the government would change their communities' destinies and therefore vehemently argued for it. Ayyankali even demanded guarantees of employment in government departments for Pulayas. He suggested:

1. The upgradation of Pulayas employed as piece workers in the government press to permanent service.
2. The appointment of Pulayas as
    a. *maistries*, much like they were employed as coolies in the Public Works Department;
    b. warders in hospital wards meant for Pulayas;
    c. watchers and guards in the Forest Department.

On February 27, 1926, Ayyankali[68] demanded that young men who belonged to Pulaya and similar communities but did not possess examination qualifications be recruited as peons, such that every government department have at least one peon from these communities, particularly in *taluk* cutcherries, and that subordinate appointments, especially in the Forest Department, be more liberally conferred upon them. A similar demand was raised by Ayyankali again on March 15, 1930, during which he explained the process by which Pulayas were excluded from government jobs:

> Pulayas who applied for appointments were, in the first instance, made to understand by heads of departments that though, for want of vacancies, they could not be immediately provided with jobs, preference would be shown to them when vacancies arose. But when those men again approached the officers and pointed out vacancies, they were told that, ... [until those currently working were relieved of their duties], no new hands could be entertained. That excuse, however, could not be advanced in respect of the appointments to newly created departments, like the waterworks and census departments. Early orders should be issued for the appointment of Pulayas in those departments.[69]

The response from the authorities was that 'the complaint that applicants for appointments are not given jobs as soon as they present their applications is true. It is not possible to provide appointments always. The applicants must wait till vacancies arise.'

On March 11, 1931, Ayyankali complained that the applications of qualified Pulayas for appointment as teachers in the Education Department were not being favourably considered and demanded that orders be issued to appoint Pulayas to all the peon vacancies arising across all the departments. As a response to this concern, the Dewan of Travancore replied that, '... qualified members of the community will be appointed to government service as far as possible, but it is not to the advantage of the community that all qualified men should look up to government service alone.'[70]

These discussions illustrate that Dalit representatives were efficiently using political spaces to articulate vexing problems related to land, education, and employment. The ensuing debates help us understand the nature of the Dalit struggle to acquire access to those resources. Today, it remains important to acknowledge how those struggles shaped the Kerala development experience by eventually compelling the state to implement welfare policies.

Conclusion

All communities in Kerala perceived education as the most valuable social asset. Some discovered it earlier, some later. The dominant communities realised early that acquiring modern education, ownership of educational institutions, and the access they offered to government employment would determine their social and economic status; starting schools on modern lines brought them prestige, economic power, and social influence. Christians had an initial advantage, but slowly other communities also started entering the arena.

As has been seen, the backward classes wanted to acquire the fruits of education and had been demanding it from both the missionaries and the government since the advent of modern education in Kerala. However, in the early-twentieth-century context of heightened communal politics, Dalits were no match for organised, powerful communities with greater resource endowments. Asset formation within Dalit communities proceeded at a slow pace and the number of Dalits gaining positions as teachers within the existing network of community-run educational institutions remained limited. But the expansion of public schooling yielded gains in terms of improved access to modern schooling for Dalits. Education in Kerala has become universal, with enrolment and attendance remaining at high levels. At the same time, the continued deepening and broadening of inequality in education suggests that, despite the serious efforts to refurbish public education with resources and fresh ideas in the past decade, results in terms of improved competitive capacities among underprivileged lower-caste learners are yet to be seen.

Notes and References

1. Scholarship on Kerala suggests that Kerala is a relatively poor state in India when judged by conventional norms of per capita income. Despite this, it has been possible for the state to make fairly impressive advances in the spheres of education and health, and hence to bring about a perceptible difference in the quality of life. See CDS/UN, *Poverty, Unemployment and Development Policy: A Case Study of Selected Issues with Reference to Kerala* (Centre for Development Studies, 1975); P. K. Michael Tharakan, *When the Kerala Model of Development is Historicised: A Chronological Perspective* (Centre for Socio-Economic & Environmental Studies, 2008); Patrick Heller, 'From class struggle to class compromise: redistribution and growth in a South Indian state', *Journal of Development Studies* 31(5) (June 1995): 645–672; Govindan Parayil, 'The "Kerala model" of development: development and sustainability in the Third World', *Third World Quarterly* 17(5) (December 1996): 941–958; Patricia Justino, 'The impact of collective action on economic development: empirical evidence from Kerala, India', *World Development* 34(7) (February 2006): 1254–1270.

2. CDS/UN, *Poverty, Unemployment and Development Policy*, *op. cit.*

3. Jean Drèze and Amartya Sen, eds. *Indian Development: Selected Regional Perspectives* (New Delhi: Oxford University Press, 1997).

4. *Ibid.*; K. P. Kannan, 'Public intervention and poverty alleviation: A study of the declining incidence of rural poverty in Kerala, India', *Development and Change* 26(4) (October 1995): 701–728.

5. P. Sivanandan, 'Caste and Economic Opportunity' (Ph.D. diss., University of Kerala, 1989), http://hdl.handle.net/10603/421552 (accessed September 2024).

6. M. Kunhaman, *Globalisation: A Subaltern Perspective* (Thiruvananthapuram: Centre for Subaltern Studies, 2002).

7. John Kurien and Antonyto Paul, 'Nets for Social Safety: An Analysis of the Growth and Changing Composition of Social Security Programmes in the Fisheries Sector of Kerala State, India' (International Collective in Support of Fishworkers, 2000).

8. J. Devika, 'Egalitarian Developmentalism, Communist Mobilization, and the Question of Caste in Kerala State, India', *The Journal of Asian Studies* 69(3) (August 2010): 799–820.

9. P. Sivanandan, 'Economic backwardness of Harijans in Kerala', *Social Scientist* 4(10) (May 1976): 3–28.

10. George Oommen, 'Education, Self-Perception, and Identity: The Experience of the Pulaya Christians of Kerala (1860–1930)', in *Education and Social Change in South Asia*, eds. Krishna Kumar and Joachim Oesterheld (New Delhi: Orient Longman, 2007), pp. 101–128.

11. Dick Kooiman, *Conversion and Social Equality in India: The London Missionary Society in South Travancore in the 19th Century* (New Delhi: Manohar, 1989).

12. C. A. Bayly, *Indian Society and the Making of the British Empire* (Cambridge: Cambridge University Press, 1988).

13. Koji Kawashima, *Missionaries and a Hindu State: Travancore, 1858–1936* (New York: Oxford University Press, 1998).

14. Manali Desai, 'Indirect British Rule, State Formation, and Welfarism in Kerala, India, 1860–1957', *Social Science History* 29(3) (2005): 457–488.

15. P. Sanal Mohan, *Modernity of Slavery: Struggles against Caste Inequality in Colonial Kerala* (New Delhi: Oxford University Press, 2015).

16. Robin Jeffrey, 'Monitoring Newspapers and Understanding the Indian State', *Asian Survey* 34(8) (1994): 748–763; Sivanandan, 'Caste and Economic Opportunity', *op. cit.*

17. Desai, 'Indirect British Rule, State Formation, and Welfarism in Kerala, India, 1860–1957', *op. cit.*

18. R. N. Yesudas, *British Policy in Travancore 1805–1849* (Trivandrum: Kerala Historical Society, 1977).

19. Desai, 'Indirect British Rule, State Formation, and Welfarism in Kerala, India, 1860–1957', *op. cit.*

20. Robin Jeffrey, *The Decline of Nair Dominance: Society and Politics in Travancore, 1847–1908* (New Delhi: Manohar Publishers, 1994), p. 35.

21. Kawashima, *Missionaries and a Hindu State, op. cit.*; Oommen, 'Education, Self-Perception, and Identity,' *op. cit.*

22. Jeffrey, *The Decline of Nair Dominance, op. cit.*

23. *Ibid.*

24. Oommen, 'Education, Self-Perception, and Identity', *op. cit.*

25. A *fanam* was a silver coin from Travancore that was worth 1/8th of a rupee until India's independence in 1947.

26. P. K. Michael Tharakan, 'Socio-Economic Factors in Educational Development: Case of Nineteenth Century Travancore', *Economic and Political Weekly* 19(45) (1984): 1913–1928.

27. *Ibid.*

28. *Ibid.*

29. Oommen, 'Education, Self-Perception, and Identity', *op. cit.*

30. Report of the CMS Mission in Travancore and Cochin for the year 1907, G215/01890/41.

31. *Ibid.*

32. *Ibid.*

33. Kooiman, *Conversion and Social Equality in India, op. cit.*

34. James Chiriyankandath, '"Communities at the Polls": Electoral Politics and the Mobilization of Communal Groups in Travancore', *Modern Asian Studies* 27(3) (July 1993): 643–665.

35. Jeffrey, *The Decline of Nair Dominance, op. cit.*

36. George Mathew, *Communal Road to a Secular Kerala* (New Delhi: Concept Publishing Company, 1989), p. 53.

37. Jeffrey, *The Decline of Nair Dominance, op. cit.*

38. M. K. Sanoo, *Narayana Guru Swamy* (Irinjalakkuda: Vivekodayam Publication, 1976), p. 269.

39. Dilip M. Menon, *Caste, Nationalism and Communism in South India* (Cambridge: Cambridge University Press, 1994).

40. Tharakan, 'Socio-Economic Factors in Educational Development', *op. cit.*

41. *Ibid.*

42. K. M. Udhayabhanu, 'The Dheevara Community and Social Change in Kerala' (Ph.D. dissertation, University of Kerala, 1990).

43. The Sri Mulam Popular Assembly (SMPA) was established in 1904. It had no legislative powers and was intended purely to allow landholders and merchants to bring their concerns to the government. Modelled on the Mysore Representative Assembly, it was initially a wholly appointed body, but the right to hold elections was granted to it in 1905 and, from 1914 onwards, 43 of the 100 members were directly elected from the 33 *taluks* in the state.

44. Tharakan, *When the Kerala Model of Development is Historicised, op. cit.*, p. 16.

45. C. Abhimanyu, *Ayyankali* (Thiruvananthapuram: Department of Cultural Publications, 1990).

46. Cherayi Ramdas, *Ayyankalikku Aadarathode* (Ernakulam: Uparodham Books, 2009), p. 70.

47. Abhimanyu, *Ayyankali, op. cit.*

48. Sanal Mohan, 'Narrativizing Oppression and Suffering: Theorizing Slavery', *South Asia Research* 26(1) (February 2006): 5–40; Mohan, *Modernity of Slavery, op. cit.*

49. *Puduval* land was land not registered under any individual in the accounts of the *sirkar* and therefore considered the property of the *sirkar*. In his first speech in the Sri Mulam Popular Assembly (SMPA) on 27 February 1912, Ayyankali highlighted the urgent need among Dalits for land:

> ... many petitions were put in for the registration of certain *puduvals* in the Neyyatinkara, Vilavancode, Trivandrum and Nedumangadutaluks, but no purpose. Many obstacles were thrown in their way by the inhabitants of the locality, assisted by some subordinate revenue officials. The effect of which was that the *puduvals*, which were hitherto unknown to the people but sought and found out by the Pulayas, were obtained by the rich higher classes and the Pulayas were persecuted and driven out from the habitations, and even the little they had before was lost to them now.

Proceedings of Sri Mulam Popular Assembly of Travancore, Library Archives, Kerala Legislative Assembly, p. 19.

50. Kandan Kumaran's speech on February 29, 1916. Proceedings of Sri Mulam Popular Assembly of Travancore, Library Archives, Kerala Legislative Assembly, pp. 104–105.

51. Ayyankali's speech on February 29, 1916. Proceedings of Sri Mulam Popular Assembly of Travancore, Library Archives, Kerala Legislative Assembly, p. 105.

52. Ayyankali's speech on February 26, 1918. Proceedings of SMPA of Travancore, Library Archives, Kerala Legislative Assembly, p. 105.

53. March 10, 1921. Proceedings of SMPA of Travancore, Library Archives, Kerala Legislative Assembly, p. 126.

54. Ayyankali's speech on March 10, 1921. Proceedings of SMPA of Travancore, Library Archives, Kerala Legislative Assembly, p. 127.

55. Kurumban Daivathan's speech on February 10, 1922. Proceedings of SMPA of Travancore, Library Archives, Kerala Legislative Assembly, p. 174.

56. Ayyankali's speech on February 27, 1926. Proceedings of SMPA of Travancore, Library Archives, Kerala Legislative Assembly, p. 94; Ayyankali's speech on March 7, 1928. Proceedings of SMPA of Travancore, Library Archives, Kerala Legislative Assembly, p. 146.

57. A *chakram* was worth a quarter of a *fanam*.

58. One 'cash' or *kaasu* was worth a sixteenth of a *chakram*.

59. K. P. Karuppan's speech on August 7, 1925. Proceedings of Cochin State Legislative Council, Library Archives, Kerala Legislative Assembly.

60. Administrative Report of Travancore for the year 1932–33, Government Press, 1934, p. 225

61. Administrative Report of Travancore for the year 1938–39, Government Press, 1940, pp. 190–191.

62. Kandan Kumaran's speech on March 7, 1928. Proceedings of SMPA of Travancore, Library Archives, Kerala Legislative Assembly, p. 147.

63. *Ibid.*

64. Poykayil Yohannan's speech on March 11, 1931. Proceedings of SMPA of Travancore, Library Archives, Kerala Legislative Assembly, p. 291.

65. N. M. Markose's speech on March 18, 1932. Proceedings of SMPA of Travancore, Library Archives, Kerala Legislative Assembly, p. 230.

66. N. G. Parameswaran's speech on February 18, 1919. Proceedings of SMPA of Travancore, Library Archives, Kerala Legislative Assembly, p. 69.

67. Proceedings of the Travancore Sri Chitra State Council (Fourth Session), August 15, 1946, p. 559.

68. Ayyankali's speech on February 27, 1926. Proceedings of SMPA of Travancore, Library Archives, Kerala Legislative Assembly, p. 94.

69. Ayyankali's speech on March 15, 1930. Proceedings of SMPA of Travancore, Library Archives, Kerala Legislative Assembly, p. 365.

70. Response of the Dewan of Travancore to Ayyankali's speech on March 1931. Proceedings of Sri Mulam Popular Assembly of Travancore, Library Archives, Kerala Legislative Assembly.

6

From Derogation to Dignity

The Construction of Dalit Identity by Mala Mahanadu and Madiga Dandora in Andhra Pradesh

S. Victor Babu

Identity is viewed as part of an individual's self-conception.[1] Discourses of identity in the West have evolved through different phases; for instance, the Eurocentric discourse on identity devalues African Americans, and the response over time to this 'other-defined' identity discourse has been the discovery and glorification of African heritage—a 'self-defined' identity. The 'Black is beautiful' cultural movement in the United States tried to counter the racist ideological construction of Blackness as ugly, and the Black identity that has emerged from this counter-construction is characterised by ideological flexibility, psychological openness, and self-confidence about one's Blackness.[2]

Historically, in the Indian subcontinent, caste identity has discredited and discounted Dalits in India, resulting after centuries of oppression in people of lower-caste origin seeing themselves as inferior and uncritically accepting as natural their caste identities and the system of social stratification based on birth that was introduced and reinforced by Brahminical religious sanctions.[3] Nonetheless, the emergence of social reform movements influenced by the Western ideological framework of equality, fraternity, and liberty as well as the democratic institutions introduced by British rule in India during the eighteenth and nineteenth centuries have together contributed to self-awakening and self-assertion among Dalits.[4]

This chapter looks at how Dalits of Andhra Pradesh tried to turn the tables against caste oppression. With improved economic conditions, and growing social and political awareness and empowerment, Dalits chose to define themselves with the same caste tags that had been used for centuries by the so-called 'caste Hindus' to degrade, insult, and demonise them. Much literature is available on the demands for sub-categorisation within reservations for Scheduled Castes in Andhra Pradesh, but one of the particularly noteworthy social by-products of this movement was the emergence of a remarkable trend: suffixing sub-caste names to their names in the public sphere, which forced others to use the same caste name that, until years ago, had evoked contempt, degradation, and filth. What previously could not be uttered in public became respectable. This proved transformative, giving Dalits an identity constructed by them and not by others.

While sociologists have tended to view caste as a form of social stratification, others have treated it in terms of pure/impure binaries. Some have viewed it as a construct of colonialism. However, the *varna* system described in classical Sanskrit literature—a four-fold division of society into Brahmin, Kshatriya, Vaishya, and Shudra—bears little resemblance to the complex realities of modern Andhra society. Whether the *varna* system was ever an accurate description of social divisions in India is a debatable point; the caste identities of specific groups have been ambiguous for over a millennium, and some regard the *varna* scheme as an idealised paradigm of the social.[5]

Understanding the emergence of Dalit identity during the colonial and post-colonial period requires an understanding of the transformations that they experienced over a long historical period. The social structure of ancient and medieval Andhradesa was extremely complex. Brahminism was at its height in coastal Andhra during the period of the kingdom of Vengi (642–1075 AD).

The proliferation of castes was a marked feature of medieval Andhra society. Even Brahmins were no exception to this; an inscription in Simhachalam Temple dating back to 1393 AD bears testimony to the existence of sub-castes among Brahmins. On the one hand, they were divided into two major sub-castes based on profession: the Vaidiki Brahmins were those who followed *vaidikavritti* or the ways of priesthood and the Niyogi Brahmins were those who followed *lavkikiavritti* or the secular way. Another differentiating factor was the religious sect they belonged to, like Jain Brahmins and Vaishnava Brahmins. And yet another set of Brahmin sub-castes came to be named after the regions in which they resided, like Velanati Brahmins, Venginati Brahmins, Kammanati Brahmins, and Pakanati Brahmins.

Brahmadeyas—tax-free lands donated to Brahmins that essentially functioned as agricultural villages—became nerve centres of remarkable socio-economic developments as the demands of expanding agriculture warranted changes in the *varna* system. The expansion of agriculture increasingly brought many aboriginal communities from neighbouring forests and hill tracts into intimate contact with centres of civilised life.[6] These were gradually absorbed into different *varnas*/*jatis* of society according to their positions in tribal society, which is made clear by the fact that many of the names of Brahmins found in inscriptions from the time sound non-Sanskritic and aboriginal.[7] Social assimilation of this nature was even allowed by law,[8] and it led to the rapid growth of the Brahmin population, compelling them to pursue professions other than learning and teaching.

Similarly, as many aboriginal tribes were assimilated into the peasant class, the ranks of Shudras swelled as well. The Boyas are believed to have been one such community; Eastern Chalukya records suggest that they were acculturated through economic and religious developments and that Boya priests started emulating their counterparts in Brahminical society by mastering Vedic learning and performing Vedic rituals.[9] Ketana, a poet of the thirteenth century, wrote that Brahmins became the teachers of Boyas. To consolidate their frontiers and to win the support of Boyas, the Eastern Chalukyas employed them as officials; an inscription attributed to the Chola king Rajendra Chola mentions that a Boya chief called Mahamandaleswara Gunda Boya was the lord of 480 villages and that he owed his allegiance to the Chola king.[10] It was not only expanding agriculture but also the military requirements of constant warfare that drove this process of assimilation; this was how the Boya Kottams of Pakanadu and Telugu Codas, Banas, and Vaidumbas—all aboriginal communities—emerged as political forces in response to the exigencies of the time.[11] Under these circumstances, it is not surprising that the hardworking peasant class was converted into a fertile recruiting ground from which the bulk of the army was sourced. These recruits attended to agricultural activities during peacetime but fought the wars of their kings and lords whenever they were called for. Such soldiers abounded even during the Kakatiya period (twelfth to fourteenth centuries AD) and were known as *ekkatlu* or *ontarlu*. They were economically supported by the *arthasiri* system, operational on brahmadeya lands, of dividing the produce of the land between the landlord and the tenant.

Improved economic conditions together with secure employment in the army and court gave rise to a strong peasant-warrior class.[12] From about the middle of the Vengi Chalukyan period, the names of assimilated tribal families began to appear in connection with responsible administrative and military positions. The Matsyas, Durjayas, and Pattavardhanis are some of them. Even the Kakatiyas in Telangana had a similar origin. The Banas, Vaidumbas, and Telugu Codas emerged into political prominence during the period of the Pallava–Rashtrakuta conflict. The Recherlas, subordinates of the Kakatiyas who were Shudras like most of the royal families, disregarded their origins to claim membership of the Kshatriya Raghuvamsa community. Having improved their positions economically and politically, these Shudras naturally aspired to a correspondingly improved social status.

Panchamas, Bhakti Sects and Political Alliances in the Medieval Period

The denunciation of the caste system and the ritual concepts of purity and pollution in the twelfth century by Basava or Basavanna, the social reformer, philosopher and poet who revived the Lingayat tradition of Shiva *bhakti*, paved the way for the betterment of the lower castes. Inspired by his teachings, people of all castes joined the Lingayat sect revived by him and found respect, including even the Panchamas, who occupied the lowest rung of the *varna* system. In works left behind by Lingayats, we come across mentions of *panchamasali*, which literally means 'a weaver of the Panchama community'.[13] Many other devotees referred to in these works belonged to the 'Kata Kota' (Golla), 'Machayya' (Chakali or clothes-washer), and 'Gundayya' (Kumaris or potter) communities. The emphasis on social equality within the Lingayat movement was so strong that, at Golaki Matha, an inn in Malkapura, food was offered by Brahmins to Panchamas.[14]

Panchamas and the Epic of Palnadu

The war of Palnadu[15] (1178–1182 AD) is a unique example of the kind of feudal warfare that characterised the history of Andhra before the rise of the Kakatiyas. This war was fought between two branches of the Haihayas of Palnadu, who were feudatories of the Cholas through the Durjayas of Velanadu. It may seem like any other battle in history, but is in fact suggestive of far-reaching social and religious changes. The main source of information about the war is *Palnati Viracharitra*, a ballad attributed to the famous Telugu poet Srinatha, who lived in the first half of the fifteenth century in the Reddi court of Kondavidu;[16] the ballad subsequently went into the possession of the Malas (Panchamas), who made a living by singing it on important occasions. Mala performers of the *Palnati Viracharitra* are called Viravidyavantulu or Palnativaru (people of

Palnadu). Every year, people from different caste backgrounds and places gather in Karempudi to honour the fallen heroes of the battle of Palnadu.[17]

Brahma Nayudu, the minister of the Haihaya king of Macherla, was a staunch supporter of Sri Vaisnavism. He is described as being so radical in his outlook that he began to denounce the caste system. Tradition has it that Brahma Nayudu married girls from all four castes and adopted Kannamadasa, a Dalit, as his son. Kannamadasa was later made commander-in-chief of Brahma Nayudu's army.[18] Brahma Nayudu is also said to have opened the gates of Chennakesava Temple in Macherla to Panchamas and insisted on *chapakudu* or inter-caste dining; in fact, it was this insistence on inter-caste dining that is believed to have caused the battle of Palnadu. Brahma Nayudu's radical approach—he offered initiation into Vaisnavism (Vaisnava *diksha*) by making prospective converts eat his leftovers (*uchchista*), and change their names to 'Dasa'[19]—distinguished his sect and the belief system espoused by them came to be known as Viravaisnavism.

Srikrishnadevaraya, the king hailed by his contemporaries as '*Sahiti-samaranganasarvabhauma*' (one equally skilled in literary craftsmanship and warfare), mentions in his famous epic poem *Amuktamalyada* that all the castes and tribal communities in his kingdom started following Sri Vaisnavism. The main theme of the poem is the devotion of two *alvars*, mystic Vaisnavite poet-saints in what is today Tamil Nadu, although the poem is in Telugu and weaves together the cultural strands of the Tamil-, Kannada-, and Telugu-speaking regions of south India. This poem is considered very important because of its reference to the Mala-Dasari myth, which highlights the *bhakti* (devotion) of an untouchable saint. Thus, efforts were made by caste-Hindu society at different times in history to construct the identity of Panchamas. However, in spite of these efforts by different Bhakti sects during medieval times, Panchamas continued to be discriminated against and excluded.

Construction of the Adi Andhra Identity During the Colonial Period

But all this was to change remarkably under colonial modernity. Marginalised and excluded from social, economic, political and cultural spheres, Dalits had to negotiate different levels of inequality and exclusion. In the 1930s, Dalits in colonial Andhra did not accept the use of epithets like 'Panchama' and made attempts to constitute themselves as 'Adi Andhra'. The discourse on marginality shifted, under the influence of the Aryan migration theory and the caste inequality and disabilities associated with it, from a focus on the purity/pollution binaries to a concern with the question of 'original' inhabitants ('sons of the soil'). Dalit leaders wanted their communities to have access to natural resources, dignity, and respect.

The Dalit movement, according to Y. Chinna Rao, can be seen in two ways. First, it is an ideological movement for an egalitarian social order that necessitates rejection of the existing Hindu social order, whose sanctioning and glorification of inequalities and oppression is exemplified most clearly in the inhuman practice of untouchability. Second, it is a radical movement which set in motion the visualisation of the reconstruction of Dalit 'self'-identity while deconstructing the pejorative identities imposed on Dalits by non-Dalits.[20] In this context, it is worth mentioning Madari Bhagya Reddy Varma (1888–1939), who founded an organisation called Jagan Mitra Mandali in Hyderabad to work on the awakening of social consciousness among untouchables. He arranged regular Harikatha *kalakshepams* during which he propounded the Adi ideology, eloquently expounding the idea that Dalits were the real and original inhabitants of the country, that the others had migrated from central Asia for their livelihood, and that the main cause of Dalit backwardness was their ignorance and illiteracy.[21]

Rejection of the 'Panchama' Identity

Prior to the year 1935, when the Government of India Act was enacted, communities suffering from the stigma of untouchability were referred to as untouchables, exterior castes, depressed classes, Panchamas, or by various caste names, most of which were derogatory. The census superintendent in 1931 used the term 'exterior castes' as an alternative to the term 'depressed classes'. As part of the social and political changes that were to be introduced in 1935, the castes that suffered social disabilities were listed in a schedule and from that time onwards they were collectively described as 'Scheduled Castes', a term that was neutral in its connotations, encompassing within itself a number of communities suffering from the social disability of untouchability.

In 1922, the legislative council of the composite Madras State passed a resolution recommending to the government that the term 'Panchama' or 'Paraya', used to refer to the ancient Dravidian community in southern India, be deleted from government records and the terms 'Adi Dravida' and 'Adi Andhra' be used instead in the Tamil and Telugu districts respectively. While the government made it clear that it would not be possible to edit old records, it had no objection to the new terms proposed and accordingly issued directions for the terms Adi Dravida and Adi Andhra to be used in Tamil and Telugu districts respectively—and the term 'Dravida' to be used if any member of the Dalit community preferred to be called that—in place of Panchama or Paraya.

Reconstruction of Sub-Caste Identities with Dignity

However, this Adi Andhra identity could not subsume sub-caste identities; various Dalit sub-castes continued to use their identities along with the Adi Andhra identity in the post-colonial period. They continued to live in separate, caste-specific localities that had names like Mala *palli* and Madiga *palli*.[22] In the post-Independence period, in spite of land reforms, the landed castes continued to wield hegemony in the economic, political, and cultural spheres.[23] Despite constitutional safeguards for the protection of Dalits, caste violence against them in Andhra Pradesh also continued. Dalits no longer wanted to take the Sanskritic route to social mobility; they wanted to define themselves in a non-Sanskritic mode.

There are fifty-nine castes listed in the Andra Pradesh Scheduled Caste order, of which the Mala and the Madiga communities are 'by far the largest[,] ... making up about 80 per cent of the Scheduled Caste population of the state.'[24] and they became increasingly concerned with the self-construction of their identities, forming powerful organisations to represent their interests. In 1995, the Madiga Reservation Porata Samiti (MRPS), also known as Madiga Dandora, began raising demands for sub-categorisation within the reservations meant for Scheduled Castes in Andhra Pradesh. These demands were countered by the Mala Mahanadu, which argued against the sub-categorisation of reservations.

But what the movement has achieved on the social front has been immeasurable, especially insofar as Madiga identity and self-respect are concerned. Earlier, the term 'Madiga' was used in an abusive and derogatory manner;[25] non-Dalits using it to address Dalits could attract the Scheduled Castes and the Scheduled Tribes (Prevention of Atrocities) Act, 1989. But this very term, associated with filth, became a symbol of identity and self-respect after Manda Krishna and others of the Dandora movement began to suffix 'Madiga' to their given names. The name was prefixed to the movement and all related activities as well—e.g. the Madiga Dandora Rally.[26] Since then, the other Dalit castes have also taken to adding their caste names to their names, just like the upper castes—Reddy, Rao, and Chaudhury—do. This is a symbolic achievement of the self-respect movement,[27] causing great discomfort in a society used to addressing Krishna Shastris and Krishna Reddys respectfully but suddenly confronted by the prospect of having to address Krishna Madigas in the same manner.

> And when people confessed to themselves that they found it embarrassingly absurd to think of someone as Krishna Madiga,

> they were forced to ask themselves why they did not find it absurd to think of someone as Krishna Shastri, Krishna Reddy or Krishna Naidu.
>
> Since true victory over an oppressor lies not in putting a bullet through his head but in making him turn a self-critical eye towards his own pretensions to superiority, it must be said that this deliberately chosen tactic of the Madiga movement did as much as anything has ever done to puncture upper caste arrogance.[28]

Thus, Dalit identity in Andhra Pradesh had evolved over the centuries. The upper-caste construction of Dalits as Panchamas was rejected by them in favour of an Adi Andhra identity for all Dalit communities, but this too proved untenable as the Adi Andhra identity was not a homogeneous one. Under the 'Scheduled Castes' administrative category, many sub-castes continued to live with their own separate caste identities. They also lived in separate residential areas, and the movement for sub-categorisation of reservations is, therefore, in a sense a natural corollary to the continued heterogeneity within the general term 'Dalit'. While the positive and respectable way in which caste identity has been constructed through these efforts is remarkable, it remains to be seen to what extent this will help in forging Dalit unity against caste oppression.

Notes and References

1. Justin P. Jose, 'Identity and Social Exclusion of Dalit Women: A Psychosocial Perspective', *Contemporary Voice of Dalit* 8(2) (November 2016): 136–152.
2. Stephanie M. H. Camp, 'Black Is Beautiful: An American History', *The Journal of Southern History* 81(3) (August 2015): 675–690.
3. Vinod Chakkittakudiyil Varghese, 'Dalit Christian Life in the Interactional Milieu: A Social Dominance Perspective', *Contemporary Voice of Dalit* 8(2) (November 2016): 220–238.
4. *Ibid.*

5. Cynthia Talbot, *Pre-Colonial India in Practice: Society Region and Identity in Medieval Andhra* (New York: Oxford University Press, 2001).

6. *Ibid.*

7. 'Goginaja', Kondamudi plates, *Epigraphia Indica* V, p. 186; 'Ganamadija', Mayidavolu record, *Epigraphia Indica*, pp. 84–89; and 'Vilasarma', Pikira plates, *Epigraphia Indica* VIII, p. 159 are some of the names.

8. Georg Buhler, *The Sacred Laws of the Aryas* (Oxford: Oxford University Press, 1882).

9. Burton Stein, *Peasant State and Society in Medieval South India* (New Delhi: Oxford University Press, 1980).

10. *South Indian Inscriptions*, Vol. X (Telugu inscription from Madras Presidency, 1947), p. 90.

11. B. S. L. Hanumantha Rao, *Social Mobility in Medieval Andhra* (Hyderabad: Telugu University, 1995).

12. *Ibid.*

13. *Ibid.*

14. *Ibid.*

15. A part of what is currently the district of Guntur in Andhra Pradesh.

16. Rao, *Social Mobility in Medieval Andhra, op. cit.*

17. Tangirala Venkata Subbarao, *Ballad Poetry in Telugu* (Bangalore: Sri Rasa, 2000).

18. Srinatha Bhatta, *Palnati Veera Charitra*, ed. Umakantha Vidyasekharulu (Madras: Sriramamudrakshara Shala, 1955).

19. Palkuriki Somanatha, *Panditaradhya Charitra*, ed. N. R. Chilukuri (Hyderabad: Telugu University, 1990).

20. Yagati Chinna Rao, 'Dalit Movement in Andhra Pradesh: A Historical Outline of a Hundred Years', *Indian Historical Review* 42(1) (June 2015): 113–139.

21. *Ibid.*

22. Clarinda Still, 'The State in the Palli: Dalit Perspectives on the State in Andhra Pradesh', *Contemporary South Asia* 19(3) (2011): 315–329.

23. Dalel Benbabaali, 'Caste Dominance and Territory in South India: Understanding Kammas' Socio-Spatial Mobility', *Modern Asian Studies* 52(6) (July 2018): 1938– 1976.

24. K. Balagopal, 'A Tangled Web: Subdivision of SC Reservations in AP'. *Economic and Political Weekly* 35(13) (March 25–31 2000): 1075–1081.

25. Sam Gundimeda, 'Madiga Dandora: A Social Movement for Rationalization of Dalit Reservations', In *Dividing Dalits: Writing on Sub-Categorisation of Scheduled Castes*, ed. Yagati Chinna Rao (New Delhi: Rawat Publications, 2009).

26. Yagati Chinna Rao, *Dividing Dalits: Writings on Sub-Categorisation of Scheduled Castes* (New Delhi: Rawat Publications, 2009).

27. K. Purushotham, 'Evolution of Telugu Dalit Literature', *Economic and Political Weekly* 45(22) (May 2010), https://epw.in/journal/2010/22/special-articles/evolution-telugu-dalit-literature.html (accessed 21 August 2024); K. Satyanarayana, 'Dalit Reconfiguration of Caste: Representation, Identity and Politics', *Critical Quarterly* 56(3) (October 2014): 46–61.

28. Balagopal, 'A Tangled Web', *op. cit.*

7

Popular Culture and Social Mobility among the Lower Orders of Colonial Bengal

Sudarshana Bhaumik

The study of popular culture—understood to include both 'folk' and 'popular' beliefs and practices—has, since the nineteenth century onwards, more or less consistently been treated as worthy of serious scholarly attention, but developments in anthropology, history, communication, American studies, and literary criticism in the twentieth century have given this field of study new analytical tools and legitimacy. The Annales school of French historians was instrumental in initiating this change, promoting a new form of history by replacing the study of leaders and the literature of the elite with the study of the lives of ordinary people and replacing the examination of politics, diplomacy, and wars with inquiries into climate, demography, agriculture, commerce, technology, transportation, and communication. To quote Chandra Mukerji and Michael Schudson:

> Marc Bloch argued that this approach was particularly necessary for the medieval period, for which written records are scarce. Others found this method of writing history equally useful for the early modern period, when the literate elite was still small and written documents presented information primarily about

> the social worlds of the elite. Fernand Braudel was among the historians who began to approach the history of the early modern era with this new perspective and produced a new understanding of popular culture in that period.[1]

Based on the above authors' arguments, this chapter, focusing on the history of popular culture in Bengal, suggests a number of interpretative strategies for retrieving the multiple Hinduisms of the past, which include an increased emphasis on non-scriptural sources and regional traditions. The cultural products and the activities of the lower orders of nineteenth-century Bengal in general, and Calcutta in particular, developed in large measure from the traditional folk culture of the countryside. Fifteenth-century Bengal saw the efflorescence of a vigorous plebeian culture bursting with song-filled dramatic performances (*jatras*) and collective rituals, mainly under the influence of Vaishnavism. From this time onwards, all the way to the beginning of the eighteenth century, religious myths in Bengali folk culture were characterised by an undercurrent of secularisation. Rural bards used stories and characters from mythology to express contemporary social concerns and depicted gods and goddesses as ordinary villagers, vulnerable and fallible like human beings. The series of *Mangalkavyas* or narrative poems composed during the sixteenth and seventeenth centuries often offered realistic replicas of daily life in rural Bengali society. In the communal songs sung during religious rituals, the audience could comfortably recognise a hard-working Bengali bride and her poor indolent hemp-smoking husband—familiar characters in a rural community—as goddess Durga and her consort Shiva. Later, in the devotional hymns of Ramprasad Sen, a mid-eighteenth-century mystic poet, goddess Kali frequently resembled typical female characters of Bengali households.[2]

In this context, it is pertinent to refer to Emmanuel Le Roy Ladurie's *Carnival in Romans* (1980), in which the French historian describes the moment when a medieval carnival celebration in the city of Romans turned into a peasant revolt and explains how disrespect for the elites, made legitimate in the carnival, turned into a serious political event. Also relevant is Natalie Davis' *Society and*

Culture in Early Modern France (1965), in which Davis counters political arguments about the culture of the people in this early era as being too simple, describing how popular culture was enriched by the Reformation and the invention of printing, and how these larger cultural patterns grew powerful through their translation into the world of popular culture. However, while these historians provide new insights into popular culture in the early modern period, they do not discuss its character and importance directly; for that, we must turn to such works as Peter Burke's *Popular Culture in Early Modern Europe* (1978), in which the English historian suggests that the increased urbanisation and wealth in the early modern period allowed the traditional foci of European popular culture (such as Saint's Days or street performances in cities) to reach new levels of aesthetic development and cultural elaboration.[3]

It is this very aspect of the popular culture of Bengal that has been elaborately dealt with by Sumanta Banerjee and Jawhar Sircar. Banerjee has discussed the extraordinary degree of autonomy demonstrated by traditional folk culture between the fifteenth and eighteenth centuries, which was carried into the nineteenth century by migrants from villages who arrived in the new metropolis, Calcutta, in search of jobs. The street literature of nineteenth-century Calcutta—songs, dances, and theatrical performances—became a melting pot of tradition and topicality.[4] Among the folk elements that dominated urban life were the Kartabhajas who attracted the poor, recently-migrated labouring classes. Like the wandering minstrels of the Baul tradition with whom they shared many close ties, the Kartabhajas conveyed their mystical teachings through a genre of song known as *bhaver gita*; Sudhir Chakraborty points out that these songs represented an odd fusion of rural and urban forms, wedding the simple language of folk songs like those of the Bauls with the more complicated styles of the '*baithaki*' or parlour songs of nineteenth-century Calcutta.[5]

Jawhar Sircar has discussed the importance of the festival of Gajan—similar to Taiposam in Tamil country and celebrated on the last day of Chaitra (mid-April to mid-May, the last month of the Bengali calendar) in most parts of rural Bengal—as a community festival completely lacking in the observance of caste distinctions:[6] on Gajan, the so-called 'untouchables' offer their devotion to Lord Shiva, the supreme god of the Gajan tradition. The month of Chaitra has always belonged to Shiva, Shitala, Annapurna, and Dharmathakur, who happen to be the deities of the *Mangalkavya* narratives. Throughout the month, people dressed up as Shiva and Parvati wander the streets of villages, singing and dancing and invoking Mahadev. Dharmathakur rises to great prominence as a deity during this month, and the Gajan rituals practised in the temples dedicated to him are marked by a strong sense of caste interdependence and by interactions among residents of all economic strata and occupational streams.[7]

Another tradition that has been very popular among the marginalised sections of the Bengali community is Shitala *pala* or Shitalar *gaan*, a part of the *Mangalkavya* tradition that is still performed during the month of Baisakh (April–May) in many localities of Kolkata, especially the College Street area, Doctor Lane (between Moulali and Taltala), and Kalighat. The importance of Shitala *pala* lies in its evocation of the demographic organisation of early Calcutta; for instance, Doctor Lane was earlier called Hadipara after the members of the low-caste Hadi community who lived there, and Kalighat was called Patuapara after its primary residents, the potters of the Patua community.[8]

In Bengal, what could be regarded as popular culture/religion was marked by two kinds of overriding influences: the beliefs and practices of the indigenous population on the one hand, and the influence of popular Vaishnavism, Shaivism, and Islam on the other.[9] Here, 'popular religion' may be defined, through 'a process of exclusion', as the 'other' religion which the elite did not subscribe to or discarded as being too plebeian or typical of the subordinate classes.[10] It could be directly linked to the general accommodation of the upward mobility of lower castes through 'peasantisation', as described in the *Mangalkavya* narratives.[11]

This paper tries to explore the relationship between popular culture and social mobility among the lower orders of colonial Bengal. Social mobility was not a rare phenomenon in pre-colonial

Bengal; known cases of mobility involving what Sircar has described as 'lower labour and new peasants' date back to the seventeenth century,[12] and the use of the *Chandimangalkavya*, an important genre of the *Mangalkavya* tradition, as a historical source reveals links between such mobility on the one hand and the processes of land reclamation, and the development of settled agriculture in the deltaic plain on the other.[13]

Settled Agriculture and Upward Mobility

From the seventh or eighth centuries AD onwards, Bengal witnessed the predominance of local chieftains whose livelihoods were based on an agrarian economy. The ruling classes or factions in villages were drawn from either a single dominant caste or a few influential agricultural castes that employed and controlled the 'untouchables' and tribals living in separate parts of the villages. In the villages of Midnapur, the dominant group would likely have consisted of Kaibartas; in Burdwan—Sadgops and Aghuris; in Rangpur and Dinajpur—Muslims; in Cooch Bihar—Rajbansis; in Jessore, Faridpur, and Backerganj—Muslims and Namasudras; in Bishnupur—Brahmins.[14]

The reclamation of forest lands and temple-building activities had provided the pastoral Gops (Sadgops) in south-western Bengal, the tribal Bhumij families in southern Purulia and adjacent areas of Singhbhum, and the Chasi Kaibartas (Mahisyas) in eastern and southern Midnapur with opportunities for social mobility. Trade and moneylending, on the other hand, became sources of mobility for the Tilis, Subarnabaniks, Gandabaniks, and Tambulibaniks. There were two stages in the development of such movements: in the first phase, they aimed to acquire symbols of high status; in the second phase—during the colonial period—the emphasis shifted to more material sources of high status, i.e. education, employment, and political power.[15]

Historian B. B. Chaudhuri has discussed two different processes by which Hinduism and Islam transformed the lives of the rural peasantry in the western and eastern parts of Bengal respectively. In the case of the former, state patronage of a community stimulated an increase in cultivation, mainly through the reclamation of wasteland, and also helped broaden the popular base of the religion itself. In the case of the latter, agricultural success preceded the conversion of the entrepreneurs and their followers to Islam. The sense of belonging to a new religion strengthened their identity as self-confident economic entities. This influence also had a role in consolidating the agriculturalists into a 'community'.[16]

Hitesranjan Sanyal states that it is not possible to determine the exact nature and character of the relationship that existed between the new settlements of the Gops and the larger Hindu society in Bengal. Certain indications, however, seem to suggest the seclusion of the former from the latter. The hereditary priests of Dandesvara Siva and Mahamaya—deities of the local rajas—at Karangarh were Madhyasreni Brahmins, who were originally barely literate agriculturists and were considered unclean. More evidence of the influence of caste on this relationship has been found in a local custom of Gopbhum: while the Brahmins of Gopbhum did not object to dining on the same floor as Sadgops, the two communities were to be seated in different rows.[17]

The Gops also achieved remarkable heights in the fields of religion and culture. Syamnanda, one of the main preachers and organisers of Gauriya Vaishnavism, was born in a dissident Gop family. His efforts led to Gauriya Vaishnavism spreading all over western and south-western Midnapore and the adjoining tracts of Mayurbhanj (Orissa) and Singbhum (Bihar). The Kartabhaja religious sect, which blurred caste-based and religious distinctions and exerted considerable influence on peasants and artisans in the district of Nadia and adjoining areas, was founded by a dissident Gop called Ramsaran Pal. Gops appear to have played an important role in spreading the cult of Shiva as well: the *anadi linga* or the temples of Shiva in Bengal, including the famous shrine of Taraknath at Tarakeshwar (Hooghly), have mostly been found where Sadgops reside in larger numbers, from Murshidabad and Nadia in the east to the south-western peripheral tracts in the west. The legends around the *anadi linga* indicate that the Gops spread the cult of Shiva in the places they reclaimed. The combination of material status with political power and cultural ascendancy enabled the dissident Gops to claim superior status by adopting the generic name 'Sadgop'.[18]

During the nineteenth century, temples were no longer built chiefly by kings and their wives or hereditary chiefs; they were also built by successful businessmen, often in the process of setting up their *zamindaris*. A considerable section of the new aspirants to higher caste status came from the castes of traders, artisans, and cultivators (also known as the Nabasakh castes), who sustained themselves on a localised market economy and contributed greatly to the building of temples;[19] the dissident Gops began doing so—and offering *brahmottara* grants (rent-free land grants) and other ancillary benefits to Brahmins—as early as the end of the sixteenth century, acquiring popular recognition for these activities. Interestingly, the upper castes often responded to the architecture of the new temples with attempts to reinforce their hierarchical superiority through the performance of rituals. While upper-caste landlords preferred the *chala* style (curved or sloping roofs and cornices) of temple architecture that had originated in Bengal in the fifteenth century, the Nabasakh or Sadgop castes were found to be discarding this style in favour of the *ratna* (smaller towers or pinnacles above a curved roof), *shikhara* (larger towers rising from the temple), and the ordinary *dalan* (flat roofs) motifs in their architecture.[20]

Popular Religion Challenges the Hierarchical Ideology of Caste

While noting that 'popular religion' and 'popular culture' provide the 'lower orders' of Bengal with an autonomous space where they can challenge the hegemony of the Vedic–Brahminical dharma and caste hierarchy, Partha Chatterjee has concluded that the ultimate 'failure [of these castes] to construct an alternative universal to the dominant dharma' is 'the mark of their subalternity'.[21] An interrogation of this failure, however, reveals causative links with hegemonic cultural processes. Examining the roots and transformation of popular Bengali rituals that were still current in the early 1940s, the renowned painter Abanindranath Tagore theorised that Hindu theologians had first tried to impose Vedic gods and their grand ceremonial style of worship on the indigenous population, 'by crushing the freedom and spontaneity of their efforts and thoughts.' Later, these theologians accepted some of the indigenous deities and rituals but transformed them so as to 'pass them off as scriptural' in order to 'preach the greatness of Hindu divinities.'[22] This theoretical proposition, formulated in the 1940s, anticipates in large measure Jacques Le Goff's theory, propounded in the 1980s, about the suppression of folkloric elements in popular religion by the dominating classes in medieval Europe.

Popular religion and institutionalised theology in India had interacted over centuries, borrowing from each other and exchanging ideas and practices, and this process had not remained untouched by Brahminical practices. The transformation of the Vaishnavite movement in Bengal is illustrative of this—the upper-caste and upper-class institutionalisation of what had been initiated by Chaitanya in the sixteenth century as an egalitarian and flexible system turned it into a hierarchical replica of the caste-based Brahminical order.[23] The radicalism of the Gauriya Vaishnav Sampradaya, of earlier liberal trends that had had a significant influence on the lower orders of society, was overshadowed as the sect evolved into an institution that was more a part of the established religious order of Bengali Hindu society than an exception to it; it was more attractive to the upwardly-mobile, middle-ranking peasant and trading castes, like the Sadgops or Tilis, who saw in it a convenient way to legitimise their newly acquired social status and wealth.[24] Gradually, this orthodox trend became dominant as Brahmin gurus, threatened by the ever-growing number of low-caste converts, surrounded themselves with privileges and introduced caste-based rules and differentiation.[25] While the mainstream Gauriya Vaishnava order was thus appropriated, the more radical Sahajiya Vaishnava tradition, whose origins lay in Tantric Buddhism, continued to interrogate the ideology of *varnashram dharma* and the rituals of Vedic Brahminism.[26] Thus, Shudra Sahajiya gurus, most of whom had no links with the orthodox Gauriya Vaishnava order, attracted thousands of lower-caste devotees who flocked to them in search of social emancipation. Kunal Chakraborty has argued that the rise of various deviant orders or Sahajiya cults under non-Brahmin gurus represented a successful interrogation of the ideology of hierarchy, and this was perhaps best exemplified by the fact that the casteless Vaishnavs, the 'unclean' Shudras as well as some tribals became devotees of the Sahajiya cult.[27] These processes must be regarded as significant, representing as they do the gradual dissociation of Hindu religiosity from processes of Sanskritisation that have been instrumental in bringing about a gradual decline in the concern for the ritual hierarchy of castes—according to Srinivas, one of the major changes in the caste system in modern India. The different Sahajiya sects that emerged also represented a higher level of Sanskritic culture.[28]

In the context of the present study, it is important to engage with the emergence during the early nineteenth century of certain syncretic sects/orders, like the Balaramis, Kartabhajas, and Matuas, who derived their heritage from a tantric tradition and, inspired by non-Brahmin gurus, persistently interrogated the caste system.[29] Among these sects, the Balarami order, founded sometime around 1780 by Balaram Hari of the so-called untouchable community of Meherpur in Nadia, was distinguished by its lack of Sahajiya leanings and total rejection of the Brahminical caste order;[30] in the list of twelve of Balaram Hari's disciplies provided by Sudhir Chakraborty, all were low-caste (Munchi, Namasudra, Jugi, Hadi, Mahishya) or Muslim, and three of whom were women described as 'earning their livelihood by begging'. Jogendranath Bhattacharya reported in 1890 that the Balaramis had a following of about 20,000 people. Chatterjee, turning his gaze away from educated leaders of the depressed classes and instead focusing on the consciousness of people at the grassroots in his article 'Caste and Subaltern Consciousness', notes that, unlike the Sahajiya Vaishnava sects, the Balaramis did not have a guru–disciple structure in their order, but he also acknowledges the triviality or the 'very marginality' of the sect's insubordination, which ultimately failed to affect or alter the system.[31]

The Kartabhajas, whose *bhaver gita* songs exhibit a unique and esoteric language that is drawn in large part from the older traditions of Indian tantra, represent both the most important branch of the extant Sahajiya tradition and also a fascinating transformation of the older Sahajiya tradition under the new conditions of colonial rule.[32] This sect exerts tremendous influence among the peasant community and was founded by Ramsaran Pal, a dissident Gop.[33] Another sect, the Matuas, emerged among the Namasudras of Faridpur around the 1870s, and their doctrine reflected the emotional needs of an upwardly mobile community, rejecting all Brahminical rituals and prescribing for its devotees a simple religion of personal devotion.[34]

With the decline of Buddhism and its consequent degeneration into Tantricism during the ninth and tenth centuries AD, Islam became one of the most powerful rival forces that Brahminism in Bengal confronted. Besides the political advantage enjoyed by Islam, its liberalism, as opposed to the rigid Brahminical caste system, had a natural social appeal for diverse social groups across Bengal. Some of the Baul orders like the Aul, Baul, Gharpagla, Kartabhaja, and Sahebdhani were profoundly influenced by Sufi mysticism, flourishing during the seventeenth and eighteenth centuries in the regions of Pandua, Dhaka, 24 Parganas (Magra), and Mymensingh.[35] Some of the most significant similarities between Vaishnavism and Islam from the point of view of social anthropology are to be found in the parallels between some of the religious roles that were embraced by devotees of each; perhaps the most important of these pairs, in terms of its propensity to attract outsiders, was the *bairagi*-fakir pair. Hardly a day went by in the village without a visit from a Muslim or Vaishnava mendicant begging for a little food. The merging of the *bairagi* and fakir roles is virtually complete in the Baul, a religious mendicant whose attire, song, and speech all consciously mixed symbols from Vaishnavism and Islam.[36]

The pantheistic mysticism of the Upanishads and the devotional mysticism of the Vaishnavite and Sahajiya movements offered Sufism a ready field for its speedy growth and spread in India. In fact, Sufism entered Bengal as a natural consequence rather as an overflow from north India.[37] The Madariya Sufi Silsila, which originated in north India during the fifteenth century, greatly influenced the folk culture of rural Bengal and became a significant force in Sylhet during the latter part of the sixteenth century. Francis Buchanan-Hamilton and R. M. Martin, in their surveys of various districts of north Bengal and Bihar, mentioned the existence of 1,600 Madariya families in Purnea in the early nineteenth century. The appeal of the Madaris, who settled in Basta in Dhaka district, was such that they were able to attract devotees from such distant places as Mymensingh and Faridpur, and this can be attributed to the many legends, folk tales, and ballads that celebrated pirs and their supernatural powers. Those who flocked to the *silsila* as devotees were no doubt illiterate and low-born. As the Madaris had adopted some un-Islamic practices, they did not hesitate to incorporate these poorer classes, engaged primarily in agricultural activities and unlikely to take to rigorous Islam, into their order.[38]

Finally, out of the popular need to adjust to emerging social and religious changes in the early modern age emerged the Satya Pir cult.[39] Satya Pir was the most prominent figure among the middle and lower classes of both Hindus and Muslims in Bengal and Orissa in the fifteenth century, and he remained one of the most popular pirs of Bengal for nearly five centuries. Literature about him begins to appear with regularity in the late sixteenth century, following the first-known works of Phakir Rama (a Muslim saint), Ghanaram Chakrabarty (the most important contributor to the *Dharmamangalkavya* tradition), and Rameswara Chakrabarty (author of the Shivayan genre of the *Mangalkavya*). As a Muslim moral exemplar, Satya Pir challenged the hubris and exclusivity of conservative Brahminical authority, but this did not stop him from being conferred with a Vaishnava identity as an incarnation (avatar) of Vishnu or Narayana, descended to earth to right the dharmic balance in the Kali Yuga or age of Kali. He was worshipped by Muslims and Hindus (including Hindu women) alike.[40]

The veneration of Satya Pir in the early modern folklore of Bengal as an incarnation of a familiar god brought into being the Satyanarayana cult, which flourished during the reign of Sultan Alauddin Hussain Shah in Bengal in the late fifteenth century. Shah and his successors preceded Akbar in encouraging the growth of an eclectic culture based on traditional indigenous religious beliefs and rituals as well as the Islamic ideas and legends that had arrived on the scene more recently.[41] The widespread acceptance of Satyanarayana as a deity can be seen as a manifestation of a consistent popular craving for a divine protector and benefactor. In oral narratives, Satya Pir is characterised as helping the poor (Brahmins) become rich and protecting the enterprising (merchants) from adversities.[42] After the end of Muslim rule in Bengal, however, when the Brahmin orthodoxy reasserted their supremacy over Bengali Hindu society and attempted to devise different systems of religious norms and behaviours to restore Hinduism to its past glory, the ubiquity of Satyanarayana within respectable Bengali Hindu middle-class spaces was dealt with by stripping the deity of Muslim traces, bringing into view the pure Satyanarayana. Instead of the Persian term *shirni*, the offering made to the deity started being described using the Sanskrit word *naibedya*. It is in this style that the deity is worshipped in Bengali Hindu middle-class homes even today.[43]

Conclusion

Local faiths were in many ways linked with the occupational patterns of the lower castes and their beliefs and practices and thus clearly defined by a particular cultural identity, which was very different from the Aryan heartland. It becomes pertinent to ask, in this context, to what extent the ritual behaviours of the 'great tradition' practised by the literate few were accommodative of the features of unlettered folks' 'little traditions', and to what extent the so-called segregated communities were able to retain their own rituals beyond the frontiers of caste-based Puranic Brahminism.[44]

The lower orders of Bengal, comprising Kaibartas, Bagdis, Gops, Cochs, and Rajbansis, identified strongly with local festivals and local deities, the most important among them being popular Shaivism and the festival of Gajan because Shiva was worshipped as a local harvest god by the people at large. Therefore, Shiva, according to popular conceptions, was firstly a peasant.

In the rural parts of Bengal, south Bihar, and Odisha, it is necessary for every shrine of Dharma or Shiva to perform the annual Gajan, which is known in different places by different names such as Charak and Nil Puja. The last ritual of this festival is the hook-swinging ceremony, which was borrowed from a popular sun festival that had nothing to do with the Puranic Shiva and included animal sacrifice as an essential feature. However, due to the continued influence of Puranic Shaivism, animal sacrifice was abandoned in the celebration of Gajan and in shrines with which the image of Shiva was associated.[45]

Structural studies of Gajan rituals suggest that its rites of transition connote the crossing of social boundaries. This time-bound ritual programme brings a sense of tragic relief to members of the 'unclean' castes, who are debarred from approaching their beloved god Shiva throughout the year. While the primary deity of Gajan is not necessarily Shiva everywhere (due to the festival's connection with Buddhism, which had spread among the lower castes of Bengal by the time Islam arrived in the region in the thirteenth century AD), this Bengali year-ending festival is held in honour of Shiva and, although the psychic relief that the ritual affords devotees is more important than the deity selected, by arbitrary selection devotees have established a preference for Shiva—the highest god in the Hindu pantheon. This superimposition of Shiva is certainly meaningful, for the choice of the highest deity of the great tradition by the unclean masses is suggestive of the latter's unhappiness with this liberal god remaining in the custody of 'clean' caste devotees. However, at the same time, this superimposition also implied allegiance to the great tradition, even if this implication was unintended.[46] Sanyal states that the legends of *anadi* Shiva tended to project the Gops as the vanguard of Puranic Brahmanism in the newly settled tribal areas. Dissident Gop kings also promoted the Shakti cult, which involved some of the most rigorous conventional Brahminical rituals, alongside the worship of Shiva. Sivakshya was the family deity of the Raja of Arambagh. Dugdhesvara Siva is another important deity of Arambagh. The Karangarh Rajas were devotees of Mahamaya and Dandesvara Siva. Brahmani is the family deity of the Rajas of Narayangarh.[47]

The worship of goddess Manasa is widespread among Gops in Gopbhum (Howrah), which was more pastoral than agricultural in the sixteenth and seventeenth centuries. Owing to the possibility of being bitten by snakes, the *goala* or cattle grazers used to worship Manasa as Rakhal Manasa.[48] Serpent worship is also practised by the Rajbansis, who constitute the main population of Rangpur, Jalpaiguri, and Cooch Behar districts. This was, as noted by the late-nineteenth-century writer W. W. Hunter, particularly interesting in the case of Cooch Behar, where snakes were neither very numerous nor particularly deadly.[49]

Social divisions on the basis of class and caste have been visible in the society of Bengal since the time of the Guptas (third to sixth centuries AD). While the upper castes—the Brahmins, Kayasthas, and Baidyas—controlled the land, the physical labour required to cultivate it was provided by the lower castes. Nirmal Kumar Bose argues that the constant interaction between the two strata resulted in the 'Hinduisation' of the tribes. Information found in the various census reports and District Gazetteers of the colonial period attests to the predominance of the indigenous population in the western part of the Ganga delta, which constituted the Rarh. Jawhar Sircar has argued that, in Rarh (or western Bengal), the autochthonous followers of Dharma and its sister cults began to play a vital socio-religious role in the wake of the composition of the *Mangalkavyas* and the spread of the Bhakti tradition by moving closer and closer to the Hindu mainstream from the late fifteenth century to the mid-sixteenth century.[50]

B. B. Chaudhuri has, however, refuted Bose's theory, being of the opinion that the so-called absorption was an economic process. In many cases, it has been found that petty local chieftains saw improvements in their social standing after acquiring land. This can be directly related to Mukundaram's *Chandimangal*, in which Kalketu is blessed with land by the goddess Chandi and becomes a landlord who controls his subjects. This kind of upward social mobility was prevalent in Bengal among the Malla Rajas of Birbhum, Rajbansis of north Bengal, Sadgops of Gopbhum, and Bhumij Kshatriyas of Purulia. It can, therefore, be argued that social mobility was a pre-colonial phenomenon and was first noticed in the Rarh region of Bengal.[51] Sanyal has argued that the caste system was able to survive for such a long time because of this inner dynamism or ability to accommodate upward social mobility, which allowed it to absorb tensions from below.[52]

British colonial ethnographers, however, overlooked this social pattern that was prevalent in Bengal; instead, they discovered two central contradictions in the pluralist society of Bengal: one between Hindus and Muslims, and the other between the advanced high-caste *bhadralok* (civilised folk) at one end and the underprivileged lower castes, eventually known as the 'depressed classes', at the other.[53]

Notes and References

1. Chandra Mukerji and Michael Schudson, 'Popular Culture', *Annual Review of Sociology* 12 (1986): 47–66.

2. Sumanta Banerjee, 'Bogey of the Bawdy—Changing Concept of Obscenity in 19th Century Bengali Culture', *Economic and Political Weekly* 22(29) (July 1987): 1197–1206. Also see David Gordon White, 'Digging Wells while Houses Burn? Writing Histories of Hinduism in a Time of Identity Politics', *History and Theory* 45(4) (December 2006): 104–131.

3. Mukerji and Schudson, 'Popular Culture', *op. cit.*

4. Banerjee, 'Bogey of the Bawdy', *op. cit.*

5. Hugh B. Urban, 'Songs of Ecstasy: Mystics, Minstrels and Merchants in Colonial Bengal', *Journal of the American Oriental Society* 123(3) (July–September 2003): 493–519.

6. Akos Ostor, *The Play of the Gods: Locality, Ideology, Structure and Time in the Festivals of a Bengali Town* (Chicago: University of Chicago, 1980), pp. 98–102.

7. Frank Korom, '"To Be Happy": Ritual, Play and Puja in the Bengali Dharmaraj Puja', *International Journal of Hindu Studies* 3(2) (August 1999): 113–164.

8. Information gathered during field surveys in different parts of Kolkata, dated March 2018.

9. For details see Hitesranjan Sanyal, 'Temple Building in Bengal from the 15th to 19th Century', in *Perspectives in Social Sciences: Historical Dimensions*, ed. Barun De (Calcutta: Centre for Studies in Social Sciences, 1977).

10. David Hall, 'Introduction', in *Understanding Popular Culture: Europe from the Middle Ages to the Nineteenth Century*, ed. S. K. Kaplan (Berlin: De Gruyter, 1984), p. 6.

11. For details see Sanyal, 'Temple Building in Bengal', *op. cit.*

12. For details see Sekhar Bandyopadhyay, *Caste, Politics and the Raj: Bengal, 1872–1937* (Calcutta: K. P. Bagchi & Co., 1990); Jawhar Sircar, 'The Construction of the Hindu Identity in Medieval Western Bengal? The Role of Popular Cults' (Occasional Paper 8, Institute of Development Studies Kolkata, 2005).

13. See Kabikankan Mukundaram Chakrabarty, *Chandimangal*, ed. Sukumar Sen (Kolkata: Sahitya Akademi, 1986).

14. Ratnalekha Ray, *Change in Bengal Agrarian Society, 1760-1850* (New Delhi: Manohar, 1979), pp. 52–53.

15. Hitesranjan Sanyal, *Social Mobility in Bengal* (Calcutta: Papyrus, 1981).

16. Binay Bhushan Chaudhuri, *Peasant History of the Late Pre-Colonial and Colonial India* (Delhi: Pearson Longman, 2008), pp. 130–131.

17. Gopal Chandra Mukhopadhyay, *Bangye Vaisya Nirnay* (Calcutta, 1885), p. 143.

18. Sanyal, *Social Mobility*, *op. cit.*, pp. 45–46, 75, 86–92.

19. For details see David McCutchion, *The Temples of Bankura District* (Calcutta: Writers Workshop, 1972).

20. Sanyal, 'Temple Building in Bengal', *op. cit.*, pp. 134–135.

21. Partha Chatterjee, 'Caste and Subaltern Consciousness', in *Subaltern Studies VI: Writings on South Asian History and Society*, ed. Ranajit Guha (New Delhi: Oxford University Press, 1989), p. 185.

22. Abanindranath Tagore, *Banglar Brata* (Calcutta: Visva-Bharati, 1995 [1943]), pp. 8, 18. See also Dineshchandra Sen, *Bangabhasa O Sahitya*

(Calcutta: Paschimbanga Rajya Pustak Parishad, 1986 [1896]); Damodar Dharmananda Kosambi, *Myth and Reality: Studies in the Formation of Indian Culture* (Bombay: Popular Prakashan, 1962).

23. For details see Ramakanta Chakravarti, *Vaisnavism in Bengal* (Calcutta: Sanskrit Pustak Bhandar, 1985); and Chakravarti, 'Chaitanyer Dharmandolan', in *Baromash* (Calcutta, 1986).

24. For details see Sanyal, '*Social Mobility in Bengal*', *op. cit.* Also see Sanyal, *Trends of Change in the Bhakti Movement in Bengal* (Calcutta: Centre for Studies in Social Sciences, 1985).

25. Chakravarti, *Vaisnavism in Bengal, op. cit.*, pp. 321–322, 333.

26. Shashibhushan Dasgupta, *Obscure Religious Cults as Background of Bengali Literature* (Calcutta: K.L. Mukhopadhyay, 1969), pp. 51–53, 166.

27. Chakravarti, *Vaisnavism in Bengal, op. cit.*, pp. 321, 325–340, 351.

28. A. M. Shah, 'Sanskritisation Revisited', *Sociological Bulletin* 54(2) (May 2005): 238–249.

29. Edward C. Dimock, Jr., *The Place of the Hidden Moon: Erotic Mysticism in the Vaisnava-Sahajiya Cult of Bengal* (Chicago: University of Chicago Press, 2005), pp. 70–71, 82–83.

30. Sudhir Chakraborty, *Balahari Sampraday ar Tader Gaan* (Kolkata: Pustak Bipani Kolkata, 1986), pp. 21, 23.

31. Chatterjee, 'Caste and Subaltern Consciousness', *op. cit.*, pp. 180–181, 194–199.

32. For details, see Hugh B. Urban, *Songs of Ecstasy: Tantric and Devotional Songs from Colonial Bengal* (New York: Oxford University Press, 2001).

33. Sanyal, '*Social Mobility in Bengal*', *op. cit.*, p. 46.

34. For details, see Sekhar Bandyopadhyay, *Caste, Culture and Hegemony: Social Domination in Colonial Bengal* (New Delhi: Sage Publications, 2004).

35. Momtazur Rahman Tarafdar, *Husain Shahi Bengal, 1494–1538 AD: A Socio-Political Study* (Dacca: Asiatic Society of Pakistan, 1965), pp. 165, 188–190.

36. David Kopf, ed. *Bengal Regional Identity* (East Lansing: Asian Studies Centre, Michigan State University, 1969), p. 40.

37. Dasgupta, *Obscure Religious Cults, op. cit.*, pp. 167–168.

38. Ananda Bhattacharya, 'Madariya Community in the Perspective of Folk Culture in 18th and 19th Century Bengal', *Annals of Bhandarkar Research Institute* 87 (2006): 241–258.

39. Sumanta Banerjee, 'From Aulchand to Sati Ma: The Institutionalization of the Syncretist Karta-bhaja Sect in Nineteenth Century Bengal', *Calcutta Historical Journal* 16(2) (1995): 76.

40. David Gilmartin and Bruce B. Lawrence, eds. *Beyond Turk & Hindu: Rethinking Religious Identities in Islamicate South Asia* (New Delhi: India Research Press, 2002), pp. 21–49.

41. Banerjee, 'From Aulchand to Sati Ma', *op. cit.*, pp. 61–62.

42. See Munshi Abdul Karim's introduction to Ballav's *Satyanarayaner Punthi* (Bengali) in *Bangiya Sahitya Parisat Patrika*, 1322 B.S. (1915), quoted in Girindranath Das, *Bangla Pir Sahityer Katha* (in Bengali) (Barasat, 1976), p. 447.

43. Banerjee, 'From Aulchand to Sati Ma', *op. cit.*, pp. 72, 75.

44. For details see Tushar K. Niyogi, *Aspects of Folk Cults in South Bengal* (Kolkata: Anthropological Survey of India, 1987).

45. Asutosh Bhattacharya, *The Sun & the Serpent Lore of Bengal* (Calcutta: Firma KLM, Pvt., 1997), pp. 8–17, 19–21, 46–53, 57, 59, 65, 67–68.

46. For details see Niyogi, *Aspects of Folk Cults, op. cit.*

47. Sanyal, *Social Mobility in Bengal, op. cit.*, pp. 45–46, 86–92.

48. L. S. S. O'Malley, *Bengal District Gazetteers Howrah,* Vol. 18 (Calcutta: Bengal Secretariat Book Depot, 1909), p. 44.

49. William Wilson Hunter, *A Statistical Account of Bengal,* Vol. V (Calcutta, 1875), p. 196.

50. For details, see Jawhar Sircar, 'The Construction of the Hindu Identity', *op. cit.*

51. Bandyopadhyay, *Caste, Culture and Hegemony, op. cit.*, pp. 46–49.

52. For details, see Sanyal, *Social Mobility in Bengal, op. cit.*

53. Bandyopadhay, *Caste, Politics and the Raj, op. cit.*, pp. 200, 202, 261.

8

Leather-working Communities and their Dependent Castes

Patron–Client Relations in Telugu-Speaking Regions of South India

THALLAPALLY MANOHAR

Various sources attest that tanning and leather work were specialised crafts in ancient India; the terms 'tanners' and 'leather' occur even in Vedic literature.[1] However, tanners, manufacturers of leather articles, and makers of shoes in the subcontinent have predominantly belonged to communities regarded as untouchable precisely because of their occupation. In south India, the leather-working communities have long been recognised by their regional *jati* names, as is evident from the ethnographic data of the colonial period: they are called Madigas in erstwhile Andhra Pradesh, Chakkiliyans and Vettiyans in Tamil Nadu, Madigas, Mochis, and Samagaras/Chumagaras in Karnataka, and Tolkollans in Kerala.

Madigas are considered the lowest of the low in the social hierarchy of the Telugu-speaking regions, as their occupation is particularly stigmatised by the caste-Hindu society of these regions. They have traditionally been deemed unclean and untouchable on account of the inclusion of beef in their diet, the fact that they work with leather, which was forbidden, and their lifestyle, which was considered unhygienic, and have been forced to live in hamlets outside villages, at a distance from the so-called caste Hindus. What is particularly interesting about them, however, is their highly sophisticated social structure: Madigas are divided into specific professional groups along with their dependent communities, like the Madiga Jangam, the Chindu, the Dakkali, the Masti, the Mastiga, the Baindla, the Kommu Madiga, and the Gosangi communities. This paper explores the nuances and dynamics of the patron–client relationship between the leather-working Madiga community and its dependent castes.

Madigas: A General Overview

Scarcely clothed, tall, dark, and well-built, Madigas are the largest Telugu-speaking community considered untouchables in south India. They have lived for most of their known history on the eastern outskirts of villages,[2] close to water bodies, cleansing animal skins and using them to make gardening equipment, primarily eating the meat of the animals they skin, consuming locally available liquor, and remaining unburdened by any considerations of hygiene. They have also traditionally played the drum (*dappu*) on both auspicious and inauspicious village occasions and have been engaged as bonded and agricultural labourers.

Somewhat curiously, a large number of other castes are defined by the services they provide Madigas. Madiga Jangams or Nulaka Chandayyas are the Madigas' priests; Bainollus or Baindlavarus preserve the sacred lore of the Madigas—the legends generally known as Gamata Puranam and Matangi or Mathamma Katha—and perform traditional rites on both auspicious and inauspicious events, including ritualistic *pooja*s called '*koluvu*' for the goddesses Ellamma and Matamma; Madiga Mastis perform adventurous jugglery and craft wooden items; Chindu Madigas entertain Madigas by melodiously reciting the Ramayana, Mahabharata, and Jamba Purana, an oral epic that tells the origin myth of the

Madigas and is narrated with the help of illustrated scrolls painted by Dakkalis. Thus, the Madiga community is the patron caste of a large number—larger than that of any other caste in the country—of dependent castes with varied occupations.

Although Madigas attribute divinity to all aspects of nature, their principal deity is Ellamma, a manifestation of Adishakti.[3] Their devotion to a feminine deity manifests itself in their treatment of their womenfolk as equals of their menfolk; Madiga women work and eat alongside and enjoy the same rights as Madiga men. However, superstitious beliefs that continue to hold sway within the community force some of the women to become *joginis*[4] and *matangis*.[5] While monogamy is the most common form of marriage among Madigas, there are instances of polygamy, with child marriage and widow remarriage also being practised.

Sub-classifications among Madigas

Those excluded from the *varna* system have traditionally been classified as Chandalas, Panchamas, Antyahas, and untouchables, and this is the classification to which Madigas have always belonged; they have also been derogatorily called Dhers or Dedh (half) to emphasise the lowliness of their status. As noted, however, there are several sub-classifications based on occupation within the Madiga community. Those working as bonded labourers are known as Begaris; those working with animal hide are called Chambars, which is a corrupted form of the Sanskrit term '*charmakar*' (cobbler or leather-worker); those toiling as menials are termed Kamatis. Similarly, Madigas who play the drums are known as Dappu Madigas, or as Peddinti Varu based on their reverence for Ellamma who is also known as Pedda Devara. Moreover, being the descendants of the progeny of Matangi—the reincarnation of Ellamma—they are sometimes called Matangis; as they are *go hamsakas* (killers of cows), they are also known as Gosangis or, because of their participation in battles, as Gosangi soldiers.[6]

The Dependent Castes

Of the castes that are dependent on Madigas, the most prominent based on their occupations are the Madiga Jangams (Nulaka Chandayyas), Baindlas, Dakkalis, Madiga Mastis, Chindu Madigas or Bhogam Madigas, and Kommu Madigas, who are unique in that they are equally dependent on the Gollas, a community of Shudras. The people belonging to all these castes are balladeers by profession, eking out a livelihood by seeking patron families and narrating the Kula Puranas, which explain the origins of all the castes that make up the caste system. It is important to note in this connection that the act of narrating the Kula Puranas is in itself an effort to project superior social status, to propagate the notion that the caste of the narrator and the occupations associated with it are respectable, sacred, and honourable. Notwithstanding their status as members of dependent castes, the narrators have to be acknowledged as belonging to a lineage that has, for generations, preserved the literature that reflects their culture. They are literate and artistically skilled, which they exhibit with great pride; while Nulaka Chandayyas inscribed the Jamba Purana on rolls of paper, Dakkalis, Kommus, and Baindlas wrote the Jamba Purana, the ballad of Katamaraju, and the stories of Ellamma respectively on palm leaves. Ironically, Madigas, despite their status as a patron caste to these communities, have no knowledge of the Telugu script.

The unwritten agreement between the patron and dependent castes is known as *tyagam*, which literally means 'sacrifice', but it is more a remuneration paid by the patron castes to the dependent castes for the balladeering performed by the latter through the year. This agreement between artisan castes and their dependent castes is prevalent even to this day in the villages of Andhra Pradesh and Telangana.

Nulaka Chandayyas

Madiga Jangams or Nulaka Chandayyas are family priests and preceptors. They lead austere lives as absolute vegetarians and teetotalers and dress just like Brahmin purohits, wearing red silk *dhotis*, *rudrakshas* around the necks, the sacred thread (*jandhyam* or *yagnopaveetam*) with the *lingam* (a symbol of Shiva) attached to it slung across the left-shoulder, and the three *vibhuti* lines across the forehead, arms, and chest. Thus attired, they visit Madiga ghettos to narrate the Jamba Purana, fix auspicious times for events, give advice after inauspicious events, and accept remunerations. for their services. Although lower in the *varna* hierarchy than Madigas, and dependent on them, Nulaka Chandayyas are only dependent economically; in matters of ritual, religion, and decision-making, it is Madigas who are dependent on Nulaka Chandayyas. Moreover, Nulaka Chandayyas do not dine with Madigas and, while Nulaka Chandayya men marry Madiga women, they do not marry their daughters to Madiga men.

Mythological Origin

The Jamba Purana that Nulaka Chandayyas narrate traces their origin to Shiva asking Jambavan to provide Vishwakarma with the tools he needed to make the *puste* and toe rings (*tali*) for Shiva and Parvati's marriage. Jambavan complies with this request by cutting up his son Yugamuni and using the different parts to make the different tools Vishwakarma needs: the *dakali* (anvil), *eligaram* (borax), the lens, the balance, the mould, the rasp, the bellows, the fire pot, the hammer, the anvil, etc. Shiva blesses him for this act, and simultaneously a young boy manifests out of Shiva's body, shining gloriously and holding a golden *atmalinga* (the soul of Shiva in the form of a *linga*). Tears flow from Shiva's eyes when he opens them to look at the child, and out of these tears emerge Rudrakshas (replicas of Shiva)—Rudrakanya and Sivasaanis.

Vishnu, Brahma, the goddess Adishakti and other gods pay a visit to see the child. Lord Shiva names him Sasyamuni, teaches him the sacred Panchakshara *mantra*, hands him a *kalasa* (pot), a bell, and a conch, and advises the child to put the *atmalinga* around the neck of one of those present there, and thereby become that entity's spiritual preceptor. Sasyamuni offers salutations to the visiting deities and adorns Jambavan's neck with the *atmalinga*. An elated Jambavan blesses him, declaring Sasyamuni to be his and his descendants' guru. Shiva then offers Rudrakanya, born of his tears, to Sasyamuni as his wife and the Sivasaanis as his devotees, advises him to wear the *atmalinga* and to make all his devotees wear one, and blesses Sasyamuni by declaring that he and his descendants would thenceforth be known as Nulaka Chandayyas, after the *nulaka tadu* (strong cord made of three-strand cotton) used to string the *rudraksha* beads to be worn around their necks.

This myth is the basis of the relationship between Sasyamuni's descendants, known as Nulaka Chandayyas, and those regarded as the descendants of Jambavan—the Madigas.[7]

Historical Origin

As part of the efforts of the philosopher and social reformer Basavesvara (Basava) in the twelfth century AD to encourage access to direct devotional worship of Lord Shiva for everyone, including Shudras and Atishudras, *mutts* (monasteries) for disciples of what came to be known as the Virasaiva movement were established near Shiva temples. One of the disciples was chosen as the *mathaadhipati* (abbot of the monastery), taught the sacred Panchakshara *mantra*, adorned with *rudraksha malas*, the *atmalinga*-carrying sacred thread *jandhyam*, and the three parallel *vibhuti* lines, and he then ordained the other disciples as spiritual preceptors to their respective communities. It is stated in the *Basava Purana*, written by Palkuriki Somanatha during the Kakatiya reign, that:

> The first disciples made by Basava were called Pramadha Ganas. They were from all castes and of both sexes: thus, Kinnuri Brahmaiah was a goldsmith, Bachi Rajayya a carpenter, Bejjuri Brahmaiah a cowherd, Madiwel Machayya a washerman, Gundayya a potter, Harlayya a shoe-maker, Kakkayya a Dhar, Nulaka Chandayya a monk, Sooli Cholakka a concubine (courtesan?) and several others.[8]

All of the disciples mentioned are Lingayats who accepted Virasaivism as their faith and were required to undergo *diksha*—initiatory rites that consisted of *ashtavidhaarchana* or eight sacraments: *vibhuti, rudraksha,* Panchakshara (*Pranava*) *mantra, guru, lingam, jangam, padodaka,* and *prasada.*

Those following the above eight-fold sacraments can be found in the village of Kolanupaka in Nalgonda district, Telangana. The eighteen Saiva monasteries surrounding the Someswara temple in this village belong exclusively to the various castes/sects named 'Pramadha Ganas' in the *Basava Purana.* It is as a continuation of this centuries-old tradition that Nulaka Chandayyas remain, even today, the preceptors and priests of Madiga monasteries.[9]

Today, there are exactly eleven Nulaka Chandayya families and all of them reside in Kolanupaka, performing their caste-based duties for Madigas in the surrounding ghettos while also serving as priests of the *ashtadasa* (eighteen) Saiva *mutts* and taking turns to perform religious rituals in honour of the presiding deities. Over time, they have started performing the rituals in other Saiva temples too. They also visit the villages over which they enjoy exclusive, hereditary, traditional rights, known as *mirasi* rights. These villages are strictly distributed amongst members of dependent castes, such that only someone with *mirasi* rights over a village may be remunerated by that village for his or her services.

A Nulaka Chandayya priest travels on bullock or horse-drawn carts decorated with colourful cloth to conceal him. Upon reaching his destination, he sends word of his arrival to the community chief. The community then accords him a traditional welcome: the womenfolk carry pots of water, lighted lamps, and necessary food items to him, wash his feet with the water from the pots, perform a ritual known as *mangalarati,* and invite him into the *gudem* (ghetto). The priest enters the ghetto alongside his cart, accompanied by drumbeats, and camps in the courtyard of the community chief.[10] The chief, in consultation with other family heads, decides the remuneration to be paid and the number of days over which the Jamba Purana is to be performed, and enters into an agreement with the priest accordingly. However, the priest's daily needs during his stay are not met by anybody from the community.[11] To attend to these, he usually brings along either an unmarried sister or daughter, and this is evidence of the fact that Nulaka Chandayyas consider Madigas untouchables, notwithstanding the latter's higher status as patrons.

The day after entering into the agreement, the priest wakes up before sunrise, completes his ablutions, bathes, wears washed clothes, and starts performing the rituals agreed upon. He first worships Shiva, Jambavan, and Ellamma, necessarily in that order, and then starts narrating the Jamba Purana. In between pauses in the narration, he also resolves problems brought to him by Madiga families, performs ceremonies to ward off misfortunes, fixes auspicious times for family events, designs houses, and appoints locations for cattlesheds. He also advises Madigas about good and bad, to have faith in Shiva, and to visit the temple of Rajanna in Vemulawada and the Madiga monastery in Kolanupaka during the farming off-season or after his return, promising to perform special rituals for them and also fixing the dates for these visits. After completing the rituals, he accepts the remuneration and proceeds to the next village. He carries on in this manner until he has covered all his *mirasi* villages before finally returning to his native village, Kolanupaka.

Dasari or Sangari Madigas

On par with the Nulaka Chandayyas are Sangari Madigas, the Madiga gurus who perform rituals related to the Vaishnava cult,[12] and whose blessings are eagerly sought by Madigas for the health and well-being of their families. Sangari Madigas preach virtues, morality, and good behaviour, officiate rituals in Madiga homes during auspicious and inauspicious events, perform ceremonies to ward off misfortunes, resolve family problems, and fix auspicious times for family events. Their perception of their own caste status is reflected in their insistence that Madigas not sew footwear for Medaris (basket or mat makers) as they deem Medaris to be of a lower status than Madigas and themselves. If a Sangari priest happens to see a Medari wearing footwear, he enquires about the maker and goes to the maker's village to lodge a complaint with the local community chief. The Sangari is pacified only when the chief ostracises the errant cobbler.

Like Nulaka Chandayyas, the Sangari Madiga priest visits villages on bullock or horse-drawn carts. Depending on the number of households in a village, he stays for between three and ten days, either as a guest of the community chief or in a separate accommodation that is thoroughly cleaned, smeared with cow dung or red clay, and decorated with *rangoli* patterns. No Madiga has access to his accommodation, and during his stay all his daily needs are met by the community chief apart from food; he only eats food that is prepared either by his own hands or by his family members. On the day of his departure, the chief arranges for the *mirasi* grain and gets it loaded onto the priest's cart before the Madigas of the village bid him farewell, seeking his bessings.[13]

Gosangis

Gosangis are also known as Goshikas, Gosikollu, or Gosangollu. Edgar Thurston uses the terms Gosangi and Madiga synonymously, and to justify this he provides evidence from the Census Report of 1901 for Madras, which states that members of the 'Kosangi' community seek alms from the Madigas. It seems Thurston may have interpreted this to mean that Gosangis were a Madiga sub-caste, although what it in fact implies is that the Gosangis are dependent on and occupy a lower level in the caste hierarchy than the Madigas.[14]

As mentioned earlier, the term Gosangi derives from the phrase '*go hamsaka*', which means 'one who kills cows'. This claim, made by Siraj Ul Hassan,[15] is supported by Nagendra K. R. Singh, who describes the Gosangis as cowherds who earn their livelihood by selling the meat of the animals they kill,[16] and adds that 'Gosangi' is a corruption of the name 'Gosika'. Singh also notes that Gosangis are found in the Muslim community too, taking on the names 'Sheik', 'Syed', or 'Pathan' after converting, but they too are dependent on alms from Madigas for subsistence.[17] On the basis of these opinions, it can thus be concluded that Madigas were classified into sub-castes based on their occupations and that these sub-castes, over time, split into dependent castes, sub-castes, or castes with their own identities; among them, the Gosangis were those who led the lives of cowherds and sustained themselves through the sale of beef.

Elaborating further on Gosangis, Siraj Ul Hassan claims that Madigas working as soldiers in the armies of the rulers were known as Gosangi soldiers.[18] References to these Gosangi soldiers appear in the history of the Telugu Chodas of medieval India. Besides, according to the *Katamaraju Kadhalu,* a ballad cycle by Tangirala Venkata Subbarao that recounts the heroics of King Katamaraju, a unit of Gosangi soldiers fought for the king in his battle against the Telugu Choda king Nallasiddhi III at Erragaddalapadu.[19] In this battle, a Gosangi warrior from Mangalipadu called Biranidu, the leader of an army of 6,000 Gosangi soldiers, was martyred. According to the epic, Biranidu's unit of soldiers used the same sabre in the battle that they used to kill cows. It can be deduced from the epic that these Gosangis lived in the kingdom of Nallasiddhi III but worked as cowherds and also caretakers of the flocks of cattle that belonged to the Yadava chieftain Katamaraju. It was a break in the covenant between Katamaraju and Nallasiddhi concerning taxes on grazing land that ultimately resulted in the battle at Erragaddalapadu, in which Katamaraju, Biranidu, and many Gosangi warriors lost their lives.[20] The evidence offered by the epic reveals that Gosangis were not just cowherds and traders of meat but also protectors of flocks of cattle and soldiers.

Kommu Madigas

According to Venkata Subbarao's epic, the battle at Erragaddalapadu between Nallasiddhi III and Katamaraju took place on the new moon day (Amavasya) of the month Margasira, according to the Saka calendar, i.e. Tuesday, December 1, 1282.[21] Katamaraju's paternal cousin Bhaktiranna, who was on pilgrimage in Kasi while the battle was on, performed funeral rites for the martyred men after returning, made ceremonial offerings in the Paleru river, and erected a statue of Biranidu along with one of goddess Ganga on a promontory in the river. He then assured the families of the deceased Gosangi warriors that

> henceforth the Kommuvaru families shall be under the patronage of Gollas (Yadavas)—the descendants of Katamaraju. The Kommuvaru shall narrate the ballads of Katamaraju to the Yadavas and shall subsist on the offerings made by the Yadavas. This mendicancy shall be hereditary and will continue as long as the Yadava clan exists. It is obligatory on the part of the Yadava families to honour the Kommuvaru mendicant minstrels ... if any Yadava family fails to oblige this custom, the Kommuvaru shall pitch tents in front of the house, and if the family still disobeys to oblige, the Kommuvaru shall pull down the tents. ... [A]dversity and ruin shall befall the families that fail to honour this order.[22]

The descendants of the Gosangi martyrs of Erragaddalapadu were thus enjoined to sing the ballad cycles of the epic, in return for which they were guaranteed the patronage of the descendants of Katamaraju, and this is indeed how they have sustained themselves as a community since the battle. These mendicant minstrels sing the ballads to the accompaniment of a pair of leather bellows (*tolu titti*), a pair of drums (*pamba jodu*), cymbals (*taalalu*), and the trumpet-like sounds produced by a kind of hollow horn (*kommu*). It is on account of their use of this last instrument that Gosangis are also known as Kommuvaru; the minstrels who sing the ballads of Katamaraju in front of the houses of Gollas are known as Kommulavaru. It is thus that the smaller community of Kommulavaru emerged from the larger Madiga community.

Gosangi Madigas are found in both Telangana and Andhra Pradesh. They are known as Kommulavaru in the areas around Gundlakamma, where the Erragaddalapadu battle took place, and in the areas of Krishna, Guntur, Prakasham, Nellore, and Rayalaseema around Paleru, while in the other regions of the two states they are known as Gosangis or Gosamvaru. Although the ballads of Katamaraju are narrated in both Telangana and Andhra regions, there is a distinct difference between the narrations in both states as well as the use of accompanying musical instruments. The Kommulavaru have *mirasi* (hereditary) rights over Golla villages.

Baindlas

The Baindlas, also known as Kolupulavaru, are another Madiga sub-caste of priests whose members officiate marriages and other ceremonial rites for Madigas. Devotees of Ellamma, they draw *rangoli* patterns in the shrines of the goddess and narrate stories related to her.[23] There are also instances of them serving as mystic healers in villages to halt the spread of contagious diseases like cholera, chicken pox, measles, small pox, etc. by providing talismans, amulets, or sheets of metal with inscriptions of mystic diagrams called *yantras*.[24]

The name 'Baindla' is derived from 'Bhavani', another name for the goddess Shakti (of whom, as has been mentioned, Ellamma is a manifestation); those worshipping the goddess are called Bhavaneeyulu, which over time got corrupted to 'Baindla'. Their principal musical instrument is the *jamidika*, which is also called the *bavanika*; those narrating ballads using the *bavanika* are known as Bavanis.[25] According to one other definition, *bavani* is a dance performed by a class of people during fairs, and those singing fables and providing advice while dancing at the fairs are known as Bavaneedu.[26] The term Baindla also has another definition: those that earn their livelihood by praising or extolling people of lower status.

Baindlas declare themselves to be descendants of Parashurama. Legend has it that when Parashurama chased his mother Renuka (another name for Ellamma), intent upon killing her on the orders of his father, she hid herself in a *landagolem* (the wide-mouthed trough in which animal hide is soaked for treatment) in a Madiga house. On reaching the house, Parashurama picked up a thin layer of skin soaked in the trough and, using the nerves from the leg of a cow, sewed the skin to a *jamidika* and started drumming on it while commanding his mother loudly to emerge from her hiding place. Hearing the sounds emitted by the *jamidika*, the frightened Renuka emerged. Thenceforth, Baindlas say, the *jamidika* became their principal instrument—the one they use while singing the ballads of Ellamma to earn their livelihood. As Parashurama invented the *jamidika* and used it to command Renuka to emerge from her hiding place, Baindlas claim that he is their primogenitor and call themselves his descendants.[27]

Baindlas love consuming meat, including beef and pork, and intoxicants; they are habituated to both in their childhoods. During the festivities they officiate, half of the meat of the sacrificed animal is given to Baindlas by virtue of their position. Similarly, the cockerel used during ceremonies to remove impurities also goes to them. Besides, during the ritualistic worship of the village deity, alcoholic drinks form a part of the remunerations and gifts given to them.[28] Their everyday attire generally consists of *dhoti*s for men and *sari*s for women, although, while narrating ballads, the principal narrator wears a white shirt and a black waistcoat along with the *dhoti*, besides a kerchief tied around his head like a turban, a scourge (*chernakola*) or a small kerchief in one hand, and chains of tinkling bells tied to his ankles. The accompanying singers, while repeating the refrain, play the *jamidika* and harmonium.[29]

Baindlas have *mirasi* rights to a certain number of villages in which only their families have the mandate to perform marriage ceremonies and rituals worshipping the deities. Anyone from a non-Baindla family who violates this mandate is summoned to courts of arbitration administered by the community, which can penalise them and even ostracise them.[30] Just as tax-free lands (*manyalu*) were gifted in the names of presiding deities to temples for their administration, or like *agrahara*s gifted to Brahmins, *manyalu* lands were gifted to Baindlas in the name of Shakti. However, the lands gifted to them were unique in the sense that they were very close to the sluices through which water from local lakes or water tanks flowed out, for the villagers believed that the irrigation of their fields with water that had first flowed through fields dedicated to God would fetch them abundant yields.[31]

The Baindlas' tools of trade are *jamidika*s, harmoniums, wooden planks, and knives. The *jamidika* is shaped like a small bucket or vessel and has traditionally been made from timber (*maddi*), teak, or screw pine (*mogali*). However, these days they tend to be made of bronze. A thin layer of skin extracted from the inner walls of the cow's belly is first dried after applying limestone to it and then fixed to one side of the instrument using a string. To the centre of the skin is affixed a smaller disc of cow skin with a hole through which a string woven using nerves extracted from the cow's neck or limbs is inserted, and one end of the string is tied to a foot-long stick. Two hooks are attached to a leather belt, so that the *jamidika* can be slung over the shoulder. The left side of the *jamidika* is decorated with a string of tinkling bells. The instrument hangs from the left shoulder of the performer, who pulls the foot-long stick with his left hand while plucking the taut string with the fingers of his right hand to produce its distinctive sound. Baindlas use the *jamidika* during festivities in honour of village deities, during marriages, and while cleansing families of ritual impurity. The harmonium serves as an accompaniment to Baindla ballads,[32] while the wooden planks are used as surfaces for making colourful *rangolis* of different patterns, and their knives are used to sacrifice animals and cut lemons.[33]

Significantly, Baindlas use a coded language to communicate among themselves during festivities or other events, when they wish their interactions to remain incomprehensible to others.[34] It is observed that nomadic tribes do use their own coded language.

Services Rendered to Madigas

As stated, Baindlas worship Shakti on behalf of Madigas and also officiate weddings, perform funeral rites, and cleanse members of their patron community of ritual impurities. They do not offer these services to any other community.[35] When Madiga families have settled on a marriage alliance, they approach Baindlas to determine an auspicious time for the wedding; the priest then refers to the almanac, decides on the auspicious day, and prepares the *lagna patrika* or model wedding invitation. Simultaneously, they discuss and decide on the remuneration to be given to the Baindla priest for officiating the marriage ceremony. If Madigas approach the priest for the marriage of their daughter, the latter officiates even the engagement ceremony; if it is the groom's party that approaches him, he performs a ritual to protect the bride and the groom from the evil eye, applies bath powder to them, and bathes them (*mangala snanam*). During the wedding, he cuts their toenails and rubs mango leaves dipped in water on the toes. A new mat (*lagnam polu*) is then spread in front of the house where the ceremony is being held and rice grains are scattered on the mat; this activity is known as *lagnam polu raayuta*. On the *lagnam polu* wooden planks are placed (*peetalu*) as seats for the bride and groom. Also placed on the *lagnam polu* are painted earthen pots (*aireni kundalu*). The priest then ties *basikams* (pieces of string with lockets attached to them) around the foreheads of the bride and groom before supervising all the subsequent activities of the wedding, like *panigrahanam* (the groom enclosing the right palm of the bride in his own right palm),[36] *kanyadanam* (the handing over of the bride by her parents to the groom), *mangalya dharana* (the tying of the *mangala sutram* or auspicious thread around the neck of the bride by the groom), *talambralu* (the mutual showering of the bride and groom with rice mixed with turmeric power), etc. Finally, the invitees offer gifts to the newly-weds.[37]

The Baindla priest officiates the rites performed on the eleventh day of the death of a person to ensure that the departed soul is at peace. On this day, a *chandrapatam* (a decorative pattern drawn using five differently coloured powders) is drawn in a corner of the deceased person's house. Food is then placed near the *chandrapatam* and the family members of the deceased pay obeisance to it before going to the outskirts of the village, where another *chandrapatam* has been drawn and food, arrack, and palm wine have all been placed, and pay obeisance there as well. During the same event, if the deceased person was a husband whose wife survives him, the latter's sacred locket (*puste*) and toe rings (*mettelu*) are removed, initiating her into widowhood. The family takes a bath at a water source near the cremation ground and returns home, but only after a crow touches the food. The Baindla priest collects cow urine in a vessel, dips a branch of *tulasi* in it, and sprinkles it over those present. This concludes the funeral rites of the deceased.[38]

Chindu Madigas

Chindu Madigas, also known as Chinduvaru, Chindollu, Sindollu, or Bhogam Madigas, entertain Madigas by melodiously reciting the Jamba Purana, Ramayana, Mahabharata, and the ballads of Ellamma, Alli Rani, Rukmini Kalyanam, Sita Vanavasam, Bala Nagamma, etc. As remuneration for these recitations, they receive grain, clothes, domestic animals, and cash.[39] They are nomadic, with entire families travelling on bullock carts to the villages over which they have *mirasi* rights, performing their art. They make all the paraphernalia—costumes, ornaments, cosmetics, curtains, maces, bows and arrows, sabres—required for their performances themselves. While people of other castes who come to watch their performances do give them money, it is not customary for audiences to pay for these performances. Rather, the Madiga chief hands over grain and money to the performers according to pre-agreed terms. Chindu Madigas may hike or reduce their remuneration, also called *tyagam*, depending on the concerned community's level of affluence.

Even people of non-Madiga castes, at times, come to agreements with them and arrange for performances related to themes of their choice in front of their houses.[40] Such performances are in addition to the regular ones for the patron caste; Madigas have no say in this matter. Once all the performances are completed in a village, Chindu Madigas meet the community chief of the patrons and discuss and organise festivities for the guardian deity, Ellamma. Although the performances are dominated by men, the role of Ellamma is played by a Chindu Madiga woman of the village. The woman playing the role is believed, for the duration of the performance, to be the deity herself, and a ram and earthen pots filled with food are offered in reverence to her.[41]

While their other performances are presented within the Madiga settlements, recitations of the Jamba Purana are presented at the main junction of the village. The main roles are of Adijambavan, played by a Gosangi and regarded as a sacred role by Chindus, and of an orthodox Brahmin. The performers dress and do their make-up at the house of the Madiga chief. Once ready, they fetch a boulder, which they imagine to be Jambavan, wash it, and pay obeisance to it. The performers then inhale the pleasant smell of burnt benzoin (*sambrani*) and depart for the site of the performance with both the main players concealed by the other actors. The performance itself revolves around an argument between the Gosangi and the Brahmin. The Gosangi, playing the role of Jambavan, offers the Brahmin riddles to solve, and when the latter fails to respond, the former solves them, thus challenging the supremacy of the Brahmin. He even apprises the Brahmin of the thankless drudgery he has endured to serve society, despite which he is considered menial and untouchable. He argues that, notwithstanding this negative perception of him and his people, it is the Brahmin who is the real menial, a position in support of which he cites mythological references from the Jamba Purana, thus boosting the self-respect of Madigas.[42] In the course of this performance, it is also indicated that Jambavan is the primordial man and that the Jamba Purana is the archetypical *purana*.

Dakkalis

Dakkalis are considered untouchables even by Madigas, who themselves suffer the stigma of untouchability. They live in their own ghettos, away from Madigas, and earn their livelihood by narrating, with the help of painted scrolls, the genealogy of Madigas, extolling their virtues and begging for food, money, and grain in return.[43, 44] T. R. Singh, who extensively researched the Madigas of Telangana, states that Dakkalis are regarded as the lowest sub-caste among Madigas. They approach the Madiga chief in the days leading up to their performances and request him to provide them with a livelihood and their *mirasi* grain. In the evenings, they loudly beg for food in front of Madiga houses. Only Madiga men may place food in Dakkali begging bowls; their women are barred from doing so (and also from treading on the footsteps of Dakkalis). Singh goes on to state that the nomadic Dakkalis continue to seek alms from the

Madiga houses of the village until they decide to move on to another village.

Even Chindu and Masti Madigas treat Dakkalis as untouchables. As a result of their lowly status, Dakkalis have traditionally suffered countless restrictions.[45] They are forbidden from sleeping on cots and covering themselves with blankets. In the presence of Madigas, they are not to wear footwear or be seated. They are not to appear before Madigas in the morning, and, when a group of Madigas assembles, Dakkalis must not mingle with the group. They must not draw water from wells on their own; Madigas are expected to draw the water and supply Dakkalis with it. Dakkalis do not seek alms from any community other than Madigas.

Although there is no literary material related to the origins of Dakkalis, the name of the community can be linked once again to the tale of Shiva and Paravati's marriage in the Jamba Purana, although in this case Jambavan's son—whom he cuts up into pieces that are used to make Vishwakarma's tools—is named Heppumuni. At the time of the divine wedding, Parvati, noticing the mournful face of Jambavan's wife and learning about the killing of her son, pleads with Shiva to bring Heppumuni back to life. Shiva obliges and puts life back into the boy's skeletal remains, but when the resurrected Heppumuni enters his house, it goes up in flames. Assuming this to be a bad omen, Jambavan takes Heppumuni back to the burial ground he had emerged from and leaves him there, resigned to the fact that he cannot be recovered or saved—such a person is known as '*dakkanivadu*', and this is the term whose corruption has resulted in the present-day 'Dakkali'.[46]

Dakkalis are allotted *mirasi* rights over certain Madiga ghettos, and, upon reaching there, pitch their makeshift tents at a distance from the ghettos. During the period of their stay, they do not cook; they only beg for food from the Madiga families. After receiving the *tyagam* and performing, they pack up everything and move to the next *mirasi* village, travelling either by foot or on donkeys and using the latter to transport their belongings. They also rear pigs, which they sell. Dakkali women work as agricultural labourers and also weave mats using palm leaves.

Before reaching the *mirasi* ghetto, the Dakkalis inform the Madiga chief of their arrival in advance. The next day, the chief informs the villagers about the Dakkalis' arrival, summons one of the Dakkalis to either his house or to a convenient location, and asks about the quantum of *tyagam* in a manner that is quite unique, involving as it does the use of *gavva* (cowry shells) and *gurivinda ginja* (a red seed with a black spot at one end). Displaying the cowry shells (*gavva darsanam*) to the Dakkali, the Madiga chief announces that each cowry shell is considered the equivalent of Rs 100; then, displaying the seeds (*ginja darsanam*), he declares that each seed corresponds to one *toomu*[47] or four *kunchas*[48] of grain. After the Dakkali selects a certain number of shells and seeds, the chief steps aside, discusses the amount indicated with the family heads of the village, and arrives at a decision about the *tyagam* to be offered. When the chief approaches the Dakkali, the latter spreads his towel over the ground, and into it the chief drops a number of cowry shells and *gurivinda* seeds equivalent to the quantum of *tyagam* the council of family heads had decided. If not satisfied with the offer, the Dakkali may plead for additional cowry shells or seeds. Once the quantum is agreed upon, the Dakkali blesses the community and leaves for his shelter, and commences the narration from the subsequent day.[49]

As stated earlier, the Jamba Purana traces the genealogy of Madigas, who consider it their sacred religious scripture. Dakkalis narrate either three or five stories from the scripture, based on the agreement arrived at. After each day's performance, the narrator takes a day's break so as to prevent his voice from going hoarse. On the first day, the Adishakti Purana is narrated while the second day's narrative is 'Shiva Parvatula Kalyanam', the story of the Shiva–Parvati marriage; on the third day, the narration describes the emergence of the divine cow Kamadhenuvu and Mala Chennaiah (the progenitor of the Mala caste) during the churning of the ocean (*samudra mathanam*); on the fourth, 'Arundhati Kalyanam' (the marriage of Arundhati) or the Vasishta Purana; and on the fifth, 'Balabhadra Vijayam' or stories revealing the genealogies and origins of all castes. The narrations are performed on a makeshift stage displaying images of Jambavan, Adishakti, and the Trimurtis, erected either at the main junction of the ghetto or under the shade of a large tree. The lead artist, accompanied by two or three supporting performers, begins his performance after burning incense sticks, breaking a coconut in front of the images, and paying obeisance to them. All the male performers keep their hair long, like the women of their communities, for these performances. The lead performer wears a white *dhoti*, a long-sleeved *kurta*-like white shirt called *lalchi*, a colourful shawl tied around his head as a turban, a colourful towel around the waist, a handkerchief tied around the little finger of one hand, and strings of tinkling bells around the ankles, and holds a silver-covered baton or pointing stick. The chorus singers also wear white *dhoti*s and black waistcoats and tie kerchiefs around their little fingers. Scrolls depicting scenes from the narrative are hung up on the walls of the stage and are occasionally pointed to by the lead performer during the recital.[50]

For Dakkalis, the performance of their art is their profession and the remuneration they receive for it—in grain or cash—is their only source of livelihood. The remuneration can be of two types—payment on the spot by any patron or payment received as a right whether they perform or not. The latter—*tyagam*—is perpetual and hereditary; the villages covered under this right pass on to the Dakkali's male heirs after him. In case there are multiple heirs, the incomes received from the *tyagam* villages are equitably distributed among all the sons. If the Dakkali has only daughters, the sons-in-law receive these rights, for it is the sons-in-law who have to care for the aged Dakkalis. In the event of a Dakkali not having any children or being inclined to pursue other professions, he has the liberty to sell these rights to another Dakkali. He may also enter into an agreement with others, hand over the *tyagam* from his *mirasi* villages, and continue to receive a specific percentage of it. However, all these agreements will have to be made in the presence of the community elders. *Tyagam* rights are recognised by Dakkalis just as *patta*s are recognised as legal documents proving land ownership, and, for this reason, no Dakkali ventures into the *tyagam* villages of another.[51]

Madiga Mashtis

Madiga Mashtis, who are also spread across both Telangana and Andhra Pradesh, earn their livelihood by performing acrobatic jugglery, making day-to-day domestic implements like wooden articles, ladles, spindles, seating planks, and cots, and receiving *tyagam* as *mirasi* rights from their patron caste.[52]

They appear in historical records as soldiers in the armies of rulers—Gosangi warriors, kettle drummers in battles, and trumpet blowers, with a unique appearance and a unique language.[53] As the British expanded their empire in the country, local rulers began losing their relevance and more and more of their soldiers found themselves out of work. The unemployed infantrymen and cavalrymen formed separate classes of their own; one such class of people is the Mashti caste and members of this caste, along with other untouchables who lost employment as soldiers, became security men for local merchants. However, because of the wresting of the monopoly over commerce and trade from Indians by Europeans, merchants were forced to shift to other professions and the untouchables who had been working until then as their security guards were once again out of work. As they lacked the skills necessary to pursue any other profession, they relied on their traditional skills to perform acrobatics at fairs organised in their villages. Eventually, they restricted themselves to performing in the ghettos meant for Madigas alone. The reasons for this are unclear, but it is possible that Madigas may have objected to Mashtis performing for others, with the consequence that Mashtis became entirely dependent on the patronage of Madigas.

The term 'Mashti' originated from the word '*mushti*', which means 'fist' and also 'seeking alms'.[54] Mashtis can be Shudras or untouchables, or even Vaishyas, as in the case of the Veeramushtis or Veeramashtis; similarly, Gollas have Mashti Gollas, Malas have Mala Mashtis, and Madigas have a dependent caste called Madiga Mashtis or Mashti Madigas. Madiga Mashtis are nomadic people who neither have a permanent place of residence—and hence possess no landed property—nor relationships with any communities other than

Madigas, on whom they depend.[55] Although Madigas do not treat them as untouchables and even dine with them if required, they do not maintain marital relationships with Mashtis. While Mashtis have access to the houses of Madigas and are also served food, being dependents, they squat on the floor in front of their patrons.

As already stated, Mashtis earn by begging and performing acrobatic feats, which is their occupation.[56] A week before the performance, they inform the community chief of the village in which they are to perform. The day before the performance, the troupe goes to the chief's residence and honours him, and he in turn provides them with a space, either in his own cattleshed or on the land beside his house, where they pitch their makeshift tents. Mashtis follow a strict dietary regimen for a week before the performance: they drink milk twice a day, eat as much meat as possible, avoid consuming alcoholic drinks, and keeping practising their acts. The chief summons important members of the village community and together they decide on the quantum of *tyagam* to be offered to the Mashtis. Each family contributes, depending upon its wherewithal, grain to the tune of five to ten *seers*[57] and a cash amount between Rs 10 and Rs 100. If the host ghetto is small in size, the Mashtis get a large measure of grain and nearly Rs 2,000 in cash; if it is a large one, they get a much larger measure of grain and nearly Rs 5,000.[58] Apart from grain and cash, during their temporary stay in the ghetto, they beg for an animal, slaughter it, and consume its meat. They even collect loose change from the audience during the performance and beg for old clothes while not performing.

The time and place of the performance is chosen in accordance with the instructions of the community chief, who is then invited by them to the performance. Before the commencement, they pray to Lord Vighneswara and this is followed by the offering of obeisance to Betala or their ancestors. Initially, rookies perform feats like somersaults and jump over stooping men; at times they pretend to fail in their attempts, creating hilarious situations. The troupe may include seven to eight men, two of them specialists in acrobatic feats using long bamboo sticks and each of the others trained in different skills and feats. The feats they perform include swordplay, boulder-lifting, horse-riding, stilt-walking, pulling seven linked carts with their hair, pulling a bullock cart with a rope that passes through the acrobat's nostrils, breaking rocks with their bare hands, breaking slabs of stones placed on an acrobat's chest, jumping into trenches filled with huge logs of wood, forming human pyramids, two or more people passing through an iron loop that is already around the waist of an acrobat, etc. As the feats seem miraculous, most people think that they use sorcery to perform them, but Mashtis deny this.[59]

After the performances, Mashtis spend seven to ten days begging Madiga families for clothes, cash, grain, ornaments, and food items. On off-days, they repair their equipment—kettle-drums, pestles, iron rings, *pesh-kabz* (long knives), etc. They also move around the village carrying a chisel and a carpenter's adze to make or repair ladles, spindles, seating planks, cots, planks with attached kitchen knives, and bullock cart yokes. In return, they receive jowar, paddy, or cash depending on the kindness and consideration of the concerned family. Though Mashti women do not participate in any of the performances, they go to the nearest rivulets or forest areas and collect vines and palmyra and *moduga* (flame of the forest) leaves, which they bring back to their temporary homes and use to make items of daily use like mats, network slings (*utti*) in which pots are hung, jute ropes, flat dishes (*sibbis*), and leaf plates (*vistarakulu*). They then sell these to the Madiga families in the ghetto.[60]

Conclusion

The strengthening of the occupation-based Indian caste system over time led to the emergence of many sub-castes dedicated to narrating the Kula Puranas—which explain the origins of each caste—through dance or ballads and thereby to the flowering of patron–client relations in Indian society that were hierarchical but characterised by mutual obligations. The patrons were the protectors, sponsors, and benefactors of the clients, who were of inferior social standing. It was even possible that the patrons and clients held the same social rank or status, but the possession of greater wealth, power, and prestige by the former enabled them to help their client castes in return for the performative services provided by the latter. The unwritten remunerative agreement between the patron and dependent castes, known as *tyagam*, is prevalent even to this day in the villages of Andhra Pradesh and Telangana.

The Madiga caste of these two states has more dependent/client castes than any other patron caste in India, and all their client castes are by profession balladeers with rights over certain villages that are passed on from one generation to the next. Under this traditional regime, no family or individual can seek *tyagam* from a village over which another enjoys hereditary rights; any breach of this arrangement is considered a breach of community norms and, hence, it is universally respected. However, it is also a fact that the income provided by the patrons to dependent castes for their services is insufficient, as a result of which Madigas have now switched over to other lines of work—such as business, casual labour, and agricultural wage labour—with recent generations showing greater interest in pursuing education than their traditional callings for economic reasons. These developments may spell the beginning of the end of the patron–client relationships that have anchored the unique, caste-based socio-religious traditions of these regions for centuries.

Notes and References

1. Dwijendra Narayan Jha, *Holy Cow: Beef in Indian Dietary Traditions* (Delhi: Matrix Books, 2002), p. 6; Thalapally Manohar, ed. *Cultural History of Madigas—A Brief Study* (Hyderabad: Pragma Publications, 2016), p. 3.

2. Due to the subcontinent's geographical conditions, winds typically blow from west to east in India. Village ponds, temples, and the homes of upper-caste communities were traditionally built on the western parts of villages. The Shudra *varnas* lived to the west of the upper castes, and, beyond them, on the western outskirts of villages were to be found the dwellings of the untouchables. It was believed that 'pure' air should first pass over the homes of the upper castes, then over the Shudra homes,

and finally over the dwellings of the untouchables. The idea was that air breathed by Brahmins was to be breathed by others, but air already breathed by others was considered impure by Brahmins.

3. 'Adishakti' is considered the source of all energy, the fundamental force responsible for creation.

4. A *jogini* is a woman dedicated to Lord Shiva. After being symbolically married to Lord Shiva, she is expected to engage in sexual relationships with and survive on alms from Saivite devotees.

5. A *matangi* is a woman from the Madiga caste who is dedicated to Ellamma. She is expected to engage in sexual relationships with men from the Madiga community.

6. Syed Siraj Ul Hassan, *The Castes and Tribes of H.E.H the Nizam's Dominions* (Bombay: The Times Press, 1920), p. 409.

7. Pulikonda Subbachari, *Kolanupaka Nulakachandayyala Aadi Jambava Maha Puranam* (Kuppam: Dravidian University, 2008), p. 223.

8. *Ibid,* p. 384. Also see Velcheru Narayana Rao and Gene H. Roghair, trans. *Siva's Warriors: The Basava Purana of Palkuriki Somanatha* (New Jersey: Princeton University Press, 1990), p. 248.

9. *Ibid.*

10. Subbachari, *Kolanupaka Nulakachandayyala, op. cit.,* pp. 4–5.

11. Siraj Ul Hassan, *The Castes and Tribes, op. cit.,* p. 413.

12. *Ibid.*

13. Tulja Ram Singh, *The Madiga: A Study in Social Struture & Change* (Lucknow: Ethnographic & Folk Culture Society, 1969), p. 33.

14. Edgar Thurston and K. Rangachari, *Castes and Tribes of Southern India,* Vol. II (Madras: Government Press, 1909), p. 298.

15. Siraj Ul Hassan, *The Castes and Tribes, op. cit.,* p. 409.

16. Nagendra K. R. Singh, ed. *Global Encyclopedia of the South Indian Dalit's Ethnography,* Vol. I (New Delhi: Global Vision Publishing House, 2006), p. 219.

17. Nagendra K. R. Singh and A. M. Khan, eds. *Encyclopaedia of the World Muslims: Tribes, Castes and Communities,* Vol. I (New Delhi: Global Vision Publishing House, 2001), p. 485.

18. Siraj Ul Hassan, *The Castes and Tribes, op. cit.,* p. 420.

19. Tangirala Venkata Subbarao, ed. *Katamaraju Kathalu,* Vol. I (Hyderabad: Andhra Pradesh Sahitya Akademi, 1976), p. 254.

20. *Ibid.*, p. 201.

21. K. M. Rao, 'The History of Katamaraju and His Times based on Palm Leaf Manuscripts' (Unpublished Ph.D. diss., Osmania University, Hyderabad, 1990), pp. 161–165.

22. *Ibid.*

23. Thurston and Rangachari, *Castes and Tribes of South India, op. cit.*, p. 130; Siraj Ul Hassan, *The Castes and Tribes of H.E.H the Nizam's Dominions, op. cit.*, p. 412.

24. Interview with Vallamdasu Veeraiah, a Baindla of Mandalapuram village, Nakrekal mandal, Nalgonda district, Telangana.

25. Chintala Yadaiah, *Janapada Vignanamlo Bavaneelu* (Hyderabad: Drishti Publications, 1990), pp. 13–14.

26. *Ibid.*, pp. 14–15.

27. Interview with Vallamdasu Veeraiah; and also Chintala Yadaiah, *Janapada Vignanamlo Bavaneelu, op. cit.*, p. 19.

28. Interview with Kandukuri Buchaiah, a Baindla, of Ogodu village, Nakrekal, Nalgonda.

29. Interview with Vallamdasu Veeraiah.

30. Interview with Kandukuri Lakshmi Narsaiah, a Baindla of Ogodu.

31. Interview with Vallamdasu Veeraiah.

32. *Ibid.*

33. Interview with Desapaks Saidulu of Nakrekal village and mandal. They refer to 'loose change' as *kanchikayalu*, 'paddy' as *jigital*, 'arrack' as *kavata*, 'woman' as *sirapa*, 'goat' as *naduvaya*, 'cockerel' as *keraya*, 'cow' as *badisa*, 'dog' as *kaika*, 'deity' as *kasikam*, and 'palm wine' as *kaddee*, and the equivalent of the phrase 'to hide something' in their language is *nagana chey*.

34. Interview with Ramaswami Imadapaka, a Baindla of Chandupatla village, Nakrekal.

35. C. Nagabhushanacharyulu, *Sanchara Jatulu* (Narasaraopet: Dinati Dinula Parisodhana Kendram, 1977), p. 35.

36. This ritual signifies the bride surrendering her heart to the groom.

37. Interview with Imadapaka Ellaiah, a Baindla of Chandupatla village, Nakrekal.

38. Interview with Puli Guruvaiah, a Baindla, of Tatikal village, Nakrekal.

39. Thurston and Rangachari, *Castes and Tribes of South India, op. cit.*, p. 315.

40. Nandu Ram, *Encyclopaedia of Scheduled Castes in India: Vol. I: South India* (New Delhi: Gyan Publishing House, 2007), p. 664.

41. Singh, *The Madiga, op. cit.*, p. 35.

42. Subbachari, *Kolanupaka Nulakachandayyala, op. cit.*, pp. 18–19.

43. Thurston and Rangachari, *Castes and Tribes of South India, op. cit.*, p. 324.

44. Siraj Ul Hassan, *The Castes and Tribes of H.E.H the Nizam's Dominions, op. cit.*, p. 413.

45. Singh, *The Madiga, op. cit.*, p. 36.

46. P. Sayilu, 'Madiga Asrita Kulala Jeevana Vidhanam, Sahityam' (Unpublished Ph.D. diss. Telugu Department, Kakatiya University, 2012), pp. 27–28.

47. An obsolete measure equivalent to 32 *manikas*, which in turn is approximately equivalent to 2.5 kg of grain.

48. An old measure of grain whose value varies from district to district.

49. G. Venkanna, *Patam Kathalu, Kathakulu*, (Warangal: Bhagat Publications, 2011), pp. 61–63.

50. The Jamba Purana performed by Dakkalis during the Dalit Arts Festival held at Nashkal village in Warangal district was turned into a book by the Tribal and Rural Arts Research Centre, Hyderabad, under the supervision of Prof. Jaidhir Tirumala Rao of the Oriental Manuscripts Library and Research Centre. R. B. Rao, K. P. A. Kumar and A. K. Prabhakar, eds. *Dakkali Jamba Puranam* (Hyderabad: Tribal and Rural Arts Research Centre, 1998).

51. Pulikonda Subbachari, *Kula Puranalu – Asrita Vyavastha* (Hyderabad: Prajasakti Book House, 2000), p. 37.

52. Singh, *The Madiga, op. cit.*, p. 35.

53. Chilumuri Srinivasa Rao, *Madigala Charitra – Samskruti* (Tirupati: Jyoti Granthamala, 2010), p. 66.

54. P. Sadanandam, *Art and Culture of Marginalised Nomadic Tribes in Andhra Pradesh*, (New Delhi: Gyan Publishing House, 2008), p. 46.

55. Ram, *Encyclopaedia of Scheduled Castes in India, op. cit.*, pp. 425–426.

56. Siraj Ul Hassan, *The Castes and Tribes of H.E.H the Nizam's Dominions, op. cit.*, p. 412.

57. A measure of weight equivalent to four-fifths of a kilogram.

58. Interview with Itukala Dharmaiah Mashti of Penuganchiprolu village, Krishna district, Andhra Pradesh.

59. Interview with Nagelli Saidulu of Yadgarpalli village, Miryalaguda mandal, Nalgonda.

60. Interview with Nagelli Venkaiah of Jerripotulagudem village, Chilukur mandal, Nalgonda.

9

Non-Brahmin and Adi Dravida Politics

An Uneasy Story of Collaboration and Conflict in Early-Twentieth-Century Tamil Nadu*

Raj Sekhar Basu

The period between the late-nineteenth and early-twentieth centuries was one of great turbulence for Brahminism, which, having been synonymous with social exclusion, encountered during these decades a great deal of resistance from those it had exploited and discriminated against. There are scholars who argue that this resistance was the result of the spread of British colonialism, the integration of the various regions of the subcontinent into the capitalist world order, the spread of liberal ideas filtered through the 'lens of British colonialism', improvements in communication, the emergence of publics, and the release of new social forces through missionary education—all of which countered the ubiquitous social hegemony of Brahminism.[1] Much of the resentment was expressed in journals and other vernacular printed documents; indeed, it was through the use of the vernacular that disadvantaged social groups found a voice for the expression of their antipathy against Brahmin elites, who had been the beneficiaries of English education under the aegis of the colonial state. Various sections of the subjugated populations thus became involved in the construction of an alternative modernity that served to critique the ability of Brahmins to officiate as worthy administrators in the hierarchical bureaucratic structure that had been institutionalised in most parts of south India by the British. As J. Devika has argued, the integration of different linguistic regions with the world system certainly offered the formerly despised communities the opportunity to cast aside identities conditioned by the notions of 'low birth' and historical 'unaccountability'[2] in favour of modernisation. Counterintuitively, the result of this modernising pursuit was, in most cases, a more distinct feeling of belonging to a particular caste or community.[3]

Old, traditional social arrangements mediated by notions of caste hierarchy, purity, and pollution showed signs of breaking down during this period. It was clear that the social critique of caste would also lead to a critique of a political order that offered greater space for Brahminical dominance. The '*avarna*' social groupings that had borne the brunt of caste oppression were clearly opposed to the continuation of Brahminical superiority in the political sphere. However, despite all their polemical outbursts against the '*savarna*' Hindu castes, their preferred allies in this cause were the elites among the non-Brahmins. David Washbrook has expressed the opinion that the social transformations underway in the last decades of the nineteenth century brought together different non-Brahmin groups in a bid to challenge the domineering presence of Brahmins in modern institutions of government education and various public fora. Indeed, *avarna* intellectuals ran their own journals to establish a more broad-based and inclusive 'Adi Dravida' identity that would serve as a politico-ideational mechanism of resistance against the upper-caste elitism represented by nationalism.[4]

Tamil society was largely ordered along the lines of beliefs and customs that were significantly influenced by religious and cultural perceptions of Brahminism. The most visible outward manifestation of this religio-cultural philosophy is to be found in the importance accorded to Sanskritic texts like the Dharma Shastras and the Manusamhita. Despite their material standing, privileged non-Brahmin castes had to accept their caste status, and the ritual superiority of Brahmins, within the Brahminical *jati* order.[5]

Non-Brahmins sought to address the preponderance of Brahmins in public services by requesting that preferential status be accorded by the colonial bureaucracy to non-Brahmin communities, who were educationally and socially 'backward' in comparison to Brahmins. This construction of a monolithic non-Brahmin caste cluster was based on the popularisation of myths of Dravidian cultural origins and decline, and prefigured the formation of a political party that could vouchsafe the interests of non-Brahmin communities in the Madras Legislative Council. The political philosophy of the movement was largely shaped by the intellectual inputs of educated landholding non-Brahmin elites, who placed a singular emphasis on social backwardness to create common bonds of affinity between different communities within the cluster.[6] However, despite this sort of cultural engineering, caste and class differences continued to serve as obstacles to the realisation of this projected homogeneity. The fact was that non-Brahmin/Dravidian politics, rather than being a leveller of different and disparate identities, turned out to be a platform for the voicing of different social identities, despite the outward efforts of the different groups to identify themselves as 'Dravidian' races and communities.[7] Although it was culturally constructed to bring to light the economic and social marginalisation of the erstwhile 'lower castes', the notion of a homogenised identity failed to reconcile inter-caste differences and to identify forms of dissent within the majoritarian forms of Dravidian politics.[8, 9]

The contradictions within the non-Brahmin cultural sphere were indicative of a hesitation in dismantling the foundations of Brahminism. The non-Brahmin elite leadership might have shown great passion for reviving the Saiva Siddhanta philosophy and popularising Tamil in place of Sanskrit, but it is doubtful whether all these ideas were accepted by the Adi Dravida cultural elites of the late-nineteenth and early-twentieth centuries. As Ravi Vaitheespara has pointed out, the Saivite revivalist projects differed from the more radical Dravidian ideological streams, especially the Self-Respect Movement launched by E. V. Ramaswamy Naicker, in terms of the extent to which they critiqued hierarchical structures based on caste.[10] Intellectuals from 'untouchable communities' seemed less interested in the philosophical issues than the religious ones discussed by Saivite scholars, especially because they were more interested in problematising caste and social hierarchy within larger cultural, economic, historical, and material contexts. As Gajendran Ayyathurai has pointed out, the prominent strands of early-twentieth-century Dalit assertion were primarily concerned with the communities' liberation from their positions of marginality. It was but natural that a cultural onslaught against the institution of caste would involve attacking both Brahmin and non-Brahmin upper-caste dominance in the Tamil-speaking regions of the Madras Presidency, and it was this very oppositional discourse from the margins that led to a refashioning not only of the Adi Dravida past(s) but also of the notion of liberation from caste-based ideological hegemony.

This Dalit cultural resurgence may be regarded as an expression of Dalit modernity, which, within a space of few years, went beyond the discourses of Brahminism and non-Brahminism in its questioning of cultural constructions.[11] More importantly, however, by the early years of the twentieth century, while the political expression of non-Brahminism was steadily gaining ground, there were sections within Tamil society that were steadily making use of colonialism and the transformations generally associated with it to acquire a measure of self-esteem and dignity.[12] There were indications that the projected non-Brahmin identity would face counter-challenges from Panchama intellectual elites, who were steadily infiltrating the elite disciplines of history-writing, epigraphy, numismatics, and textual hermeneutics. The non-Brahmin version of history was itself fractured, and the exercise of recovering the past(s) by Panchama intellectuals had the potential to lead to Adi Dravida–non-Brahmin political rivalries and differences.

In this chapter, I would like to argue that, even though Paraiyar intellectuals initially supported the notion of a shared Dravidian/ Tamil identity, their positions did not remain the same over time. A number of issues caused rifts to emerge between them and the elite non-Brahmin leadership of the Justice Party. Depressed class leaders worked to expose the weaknesses of non-Brahmin identity, propagating their Adi Dravida identity to foreground their separateness from the grand homogenised representation of non-Brahminism. By the early 1920s, there were visible signs of fissures within the Adi Dravida–non-Brahmin alliance. Paraiyar community leaders—the driving force behind Adi Dravida politics in Tamil Nadu—raised a number of social and political issues, including issues related to representation in public services and elected bodies, which earned the ire of the non-Brahmin leadership. However, internal differences within the Adi Dravida bloc forestalled the emergence of an autonomous brand of politics that would be completely separate from and independent of the political objectives of the Justice Party. In fact, it was the trajectory of institutional politics that prevented them from taking a bold, separatist political line vis-a-vis the non-Brahmin political leadership. This possibly explains the endorsement by Adi Dravida political leaders of temporary alliances with groups representing different political streams—the Justice Party, the Self-Respect Movement, and the Congress.

The Beginnings of the Non-Brahmin Movement

The non-Brahmin movement in Madras Presidency owed its origins to certain developments in the early decades of the twentieth century. Although the Madras United League and the Dravidian Association did try to vocalise non-Brahmin interests in the early 1910s,[13] the foundation of a strong non-Brahmin political organisation emerged only when non-Brahmin leaders, seeking to counter the Brahmin stranglehold on public representation and public services, met on November 20, 1916 at Victoria Public Hall in Madras.

At this conference, attended by thirty non-Brahmin leaders, C. Natesa Mudaliar, secretary of the Madras Dravidian Association, brought together two well-known leaders, T. M. Nair and P. Theagoraya Chetti, to form a non-Brahmin political action group. The deliberations led to the formation of the South Indian Peoples' Association, whose primary objective was to publish newspapers in English, Tamil, and Telugu, highlighting the viewpoints of non-Brahmins in Madras Presidency. The conference also proposed to establish a political association under the banner of the 'South Indian Liberal Federation'.[14]

The South Indian Peoples' Association noted in its manifesto that '[t]he time has come when an attempt should be made to define the attitude of several Non-Brahmin Indian communities in this Presidency towards what is called the Indian Home Rule Movement.'[15] The manifesto also pointed out that, though non-Brahmins constituted a large proportion of the population in Madras Presidency and the majority of taxpayers, they did not play an important role in the realm of politics. It expressed the need for a proper political organisation of non-Brahmins, since their political interests differed greatly from those of Brahmins, who had a minuscule presence in the total population of the Presidency.

The majority of non-Brahmin leaders shared an apprehension that reforms in the direction of self-government would only strengthen Brahmin dominance over the administration and polity, and this caused them to oppose the nationalist movement, which was inspired by the ideology and political programmes of the Congress. A prominent non-Brahmin newspaper observed in December 1916, 'We do not want Home Rule for it will bring about the condition of ancient India, when the Sudras were kept suppressed. ... Our goal is the goal of self-government, but we want to be led there by the British.'[16]

Thus, by the end of 1916, the non-Brahmin political identity had assumed an element of distinctiveness. The aversion to the Brahmin-dominated Congress shared by non-Brahmin leaders was the most important factor in the emergence of this identity; it was the political machinations of the Congress leadership to keep non-Brahmins away from membership of elected bodies that encouraged non-Brahmin leaders to demand a greater share of political power. Dr T. M. Nair's successive defeats in elections to the Madras Legislative Council and the Imperial Legislative Council validated, to a large extent, the apprehensions of a possible 'Brahmin Raj'.

It has often been argued that Annie Besant's Home Rule movement greatly influenced the course of early-twentieth-century non-Brahmin politics in Madras Presidency. Her repeated emphasis on the Brahminical ideals of karma and *varna* led the majority of non-Brahmin leaders to believe that she and her followers were trying to revive the logic of caste to maintain the superiority of Brahmins.[17] Fears of a rejuvenated 'Brahmin oligarchy' caused a great deal of consternation among all sections of non-Brahmins.[18] The Madras Adi Dravida Jana Sabha, claiming to represent the interests of six million untouchables, criticised Home Rule propaganda and requested the government to grant special concessions to socially despised communities. The middle-class leadership of the Madras Adi Dravida Jana Sabha, comprising mostly traders, teachers, and journalists, forcefully stated that efforts by the government in the sphere of education alone could ensure the uplift of the untouchable population. They also favoured communal representation in the local bodies and the legislature.[19] Subsequently, on the eve of the Montagu–Chelmsford Reforms, non-Brahmin political elites, in their quest to build a broader political constituency, expressed strong support for Adi Dravida demands for social equality. Influential non-Brahmin leaders organised several conferences to bring the Adi Dravidas closer to their ideology, propounding that the uplift of untouchables had to be one of the most important items on the agenda of the non-Brahmin movement. They also exhorted the depressed classes to reject Brahminical injunctions outright and to claim equality of status with other classes of society. T. M. Nair, addressing a gathering of the depressed classes at the Spur Tank in Madras, bitterly denounced the Home Rule movement, expressing the opinion that it was a ploy on the part of some influential Brahmins to enforce an oppressive hierarchical social system on the majority of the population. He observed:

> Our contention is that until all the members of your community [the Panchamas] and the educated are brought to a condition when you can realise what is going on, realise your responsibility and use your votes in a discriminating manner, the British power must continue to hold the scales … instead of leaving you to the tender mercies of the so called superior castes in this country[.] … [Y]ou must at least have the courage to resist all attempts

on the part of the small oligarchy in this country to snatch the powers of Government in their hands.[20]

Nair also broached the idea of a committee comprising representatives of the non-Brahmin communities and the depressed classes. These moves towards a broader coalition were evolved with the definite objective of convincing the colonial bureaucracy of the injustices being faced by the majority,[21] and they ultimately yielded political dividends for the non-Brahmin leaders. The Adi Dravida Jana Sabha supported the stand taken by the South Indian Liberal Federation on constitutional changes and subsequently demanded election instead of nomination to the legislature as well.[22]

The Montagu–Chelmsford Reforms and the Issue of Responsible Government

On August 20, 1917, the Secretary of State for India announced that the British government's plan to implement policies aimed at increasing Indian participation in the governance of the country. This official stance evoked a series of responses from different non-Brahmin groups in Madras Presidency. The non-Brahmin elites organised conferences to uphold the principle of equality of rights and opportunities for different groups in society. These conferences prepared the ground for discussions on non-Brahmin representation on the eve of Montagu's visit to Madras. The non-Brahmin elite drew up an elaborate list of demands to influence the British and also tried to strengthen the rural base of the Justice Party, emphatically stating that lack of unity among non-Brahmins was the main cause of their political subordination to the Brahmin-dominated Congress, launching virulent attacks against institutions drawing sustenance from classical Hinduism, and reminding the colonial authorities that the purpose of responsible government would not be served unless non-Brahmins were provided representation on a communal basis.

In December 1917, Lord Chelmsford, the viceroy, and Edwin Montagu, the secretary of state, made a visit to Madras. The South

Indian Liberal Federation, the mouthpiece of the non-Brahmin political elite, was the first political organisation to present a political memorandum to the Viceroy, expressing the need for political reforms but hesitating to demand full-scale self-government. Dr T. M. Nair, a founding member of the Justice Party, explained to Montagu the farcical nature of elections, given the power and prestige enjoyed by the Brahmins.

Despite these strong assertions, however, the Montagu–Chelmsford Report rejected the plea for separate non-Brahmin electorates.[23] The report firmly opposed the principle of communal representation on the ground that it would strengthen communal divisions within Indian society, thereby stalling India's advancement towards self-government. However, the non-Brahmin political elite felt that, by setting aside the opinions of non-Brahmins, the colonial bureaucracy had expressed its inability to comprehend the links between caste and politics in Madras Presidency. Interestingly, a section of the bureaucracy in the Presidency also seemed to be in sympathy with the political demands of the non-Brahmins.

While the debate over communal representation for non-Brahmins continued, the Government of India, in 1918, formed a committee under Lord Southborough to examine the issues of separate electorates, constituencies, and franchises. Two Indian members were inducted into the committee, both of whom were Brahmins as well as members of the Congress. The decision immediately gave rise to controversy in the political circles of Madras. The non-Brahmins criticised the government for involving Brahmins in vital issues, particularly ones related to their own political demands, and the South Indian Liberal Federation hurriedly summoned a session in October 1918 to voice its protest against this.[24]

In this memorandum, the non-Brahmin elite also strongly argued that neither direct elections nor the extension of the franchise would be of any real benefit to their communities. They felt not only that a non-Brahmin electorate would ensure the return of a larger number of non-Brahmin legislators but also that it would guarantee that only those who were sincerely interested in the welfare of their communities found a place on the council.[25] A more rigid stand on this issue was taken by the Adi Dravida Jana Sabha, which observed, 'We would fight to the last drop of our blood, any attempt to transfer the seat of authority in this country from the British hands to the so called caste Hindus, who have been oppressing us in the past and would do so again but for the British Government.'[26]

However, the Southborough Franchise Committee expressed the opinion that, as non-Brahmins outnumbered Brahmins 4:1, they could secure the election of their own candidates and that separate electorates for non-Brahmins would have the counterproductive result of effectively creating separate electorates for Brahmins.[27] Thus, the adoption of the principle of communal representation for non-Brahmins was characterised by the committee as totally unreasonable.

The Government of India, however, did not endorse the opinions of the Franchise Committee, opining that at least fifty per cent (thirty out of sixty-one) of the general non-Muhammadan seats in the Madras Legislative Council needed to be reserved for non-Brahmins. The Governor of Madras adopted a more rigid stand on the recommendations of the committee; the Madras government, in its correspondence with the Government of India, expressed the opinion that even if the size of the electorate was enlarged, it would not be of much benefit to the Panchama communities, Muhammadans, Indian Christians, and Anglo-Indians. A section of the colonial bureaucracy felt that such a policy was not justifiable, since non-Brahmin caste Hindus believed that territorial electorates would favour Brahmins.[28] Influential members of the Indian Civil Service (ICS) lobby in Madras opined that the educational superiority of Brahmins would give them greater advantage at the time of canvassing, while their traditional social and religious pre-eminence as well as their organisational skills would help them extend their political influence beyond their own class.[29]

Alexander Cardew, a prominent ICS officer and a member of the Madras Executive Council, communicated to the Government of India the difficulties of achieving democracy in a caste-ridden society. Highlighting the fact that the place of an individual in Indian society was determined by the merits or demerits of previous births, he observed:

> [C]losely connected with the doctrine that each man's place in the present birth has been determined by his actions in the past existence is the institution of caste which has the effect of stereotyping and fixing unalterably the position of each individual in the social scale. Thus a man born a Brahmin cannot be other than a Brahman and a man born a Pariah can never be other than a Pariah. Equality of opportunity is impossible under such conditions and it is neither recognized nor desired by Indian public opinion.[30]

Furthermore, it was argued that the policy of neutrality and impartiality pursued by the British administration in India had only strengthened Brahmin hegemony over society and polity. In fact, reformist colonial bureaucrats insisted that in societies marked by great social and political disparities, the introduction of modern democratic institutions and practices would prove to be far more oppressive to socially despised communities.[31] These opinions were also echoed in the demands of the non-Brahmin political elite for communal representation. The Government of India and the Executive Council of Madras did concede that the ritual superiority of Brahmins would always give them an advantage in any democratic representational scheme. However, a final decision on the matter remained to be taken.

Finally, in 1919, a Joint Parliamentary Committee was appointed in London to make recommendations regarding future constitutional reforms for India, and the non-Brahmin opinion in favour of communal representation, presented in the form of a memorandum by K. V. Reddi Naidu,[32] won over the top echelons of the colonial bureaucracy. Subsequently, the Government of India Act, 1919, while reserving seats for non-Brahmins in the Madras Legislative Council, left it to the contending parties to decide on the number of seats to be reserved, but the Brahmin–non-Brahmin dialogue on this matter failed to yield the desired result. The non-Brahmin leaders firmly contended that, though they constituted a numerical majority, the overwhelming nature of the reality of Brahmin supremacy prevented them from exercising their political rights.[33]

In the meantime, Lord Willingdon, the governor of Madras, gave his consent to the reservation of fifty per cent of the total seats in the legislature for non-Brahmins. The South Indian Liberal Federation immediately thereafter lodged a protest against the decision, demanding the reservation of seventy-five per cent of the seats. Both the Brahmin and non-Brahmin lobbies levelled allegations and counter-allegations against each other of creating confusion over the number of reserved seats. K. V. Reddi Naidu argued that non-Brahmins would not be able to secure meaningful political power as long as Brahmins continued to enjoy an undue advantage in matters related to representation.[34]

While the debate over representation reached a point of acrimony, the hesitation of the colonial bureaucracy in Madras gave rise to many complications. This element of indecision was reflected in the opinions of the governor, Lord Willingdon, who, along with several other high officials, felt that broadening the size of the electorate would not be of much benefit to the Panchamas, the Muhammadans, the Indian Christians, and the Anglo-Indians. His comments drew the ire of the non-Brahmin political elites, who alleged in their mouthpieces that the Governor was acting at the behest of the Brahmins.[35] In the midst of this furore, the Government of India, at the request of the Madras government, appointed Lord Meston to find a solution. After hearing the views of a select group consisting of both non-Brahmins and Brahmins on matters related to the reservation of seats, Lord Meston rejected the non-Brahmin allegations of 'Brahmana tyranny' and the demand that a limit be placed upon the number of Brahmin candidates who could be re-elected. Instead, the recommendation of Brahmin propagandists like C. P. Ramaswami Iyer that seats be reserved for non-Brahmins in each constituency were favoured.[36]

Lord Meston's judgment was, to a great extent, influenced by some of the election results of 1919 and 1920. In the August 1919 elections to the Madras Legislative Council and in the Madras Corporation elections of 1920, non-Brahmin candidates were elected in large numbers, with voters voting across community lines. These trends might have convinced Lord Meston that non-Brahmins were making impressive gains even without the benefit of any special protection.[37]

The Meston Award, which granted twenty-four seats to non-Brahmins, was greeted with protests by the non-Brahmin lobby. Leaders with important portfolios in the Justice Party bitterly opposed the award, issuing statements exhorting non-Brahmin electorates to vote for only non-Brahmin candidates.[38] Lord Meston's observations regarding the efficacy of communal representation provoked non-Brahmin mouthpieces to adopt a more rigid stand on the issue.[39] Several associations joined protest meetings organised by the non-Brahmin leadership to express their resentment, and resolutions condemning the award as a Brahmin-influenced one were adopted.[40] Significantly, the arguments advanced by the non-Brahmin leaders reflected the peculiarities of the minority problem in Madras Presidency. The non-Brahmin leaders tried to bolster their arguments by invoking their status as both a majority—by number—and a minority—in terms of political backwardness. Their views on communal representation led to ill-will between them and the Brahmins.

The government tried to broker a compromise by supporting the policy of reserved seats in plural-member constituencies, somewhat of a halfway house between the separate communal electorates demanded by the non-Brahmins and the free general constituencies demanded by the Brahmins, who had had every reason to be happy, as the principle of communal electorates was not extended to them. On the other hand, the non-Brahmins, despite their disagreements with the colonial bureaucracy, also scored a major political victory, since their demand for the adoption of special safeguards in matters related to representation was given statutory recognition.

The Justice Party Ministry and the Issue of Panchama Identity

The first election in Madras Presidency under the reforms was held in November 1920. The Justice Party participated in the election with a definite political programme. Its task was made easy by the Congress Party's decision to not field candidates, although several Congress members defied this decision and ran for office as independents and some of them even returned to the council. Despite this, the Justice Party registered a comfortable victory, winning sixty-three out of the ninety-eight seats;[41] this victory owed a great deal to the efforts of its leaders to exploit the non-Brahmin sentiment of 'self-respect'. The non-Brahmin elite were successful in conveying the impression that nationalism and freedom from colonial rule could not be regarded as the sole issues of political significance in Madras, particularly in the context of their efforts to build a distinct non-Brahmin constituency based on cooperation and understanding between upper-caste non-Brahmins and untouchables. This constituency not only responded to the call of the non-Brahmin political ideology and the insistence of the leaders that the social and political implications of the *varna-jati* ordering needed to be analysed from an altogether new perspective, but also to the fundamental need to survive.

In December 1920, A. Subbarayalu Reddiar, Ramarayaningar, and K. V. Reddi Naidu assumed their ministerial offices under Governor Willingdon. The choice of non-Brahmin ministers provoked a great deal of reaction from the pro-Brahmin press, but despite such provocations, Lord Willingdon preferred to continue with his three non-Brahmin minsters[42] and urged the non-Brahmin representatives to present themselves as a single political entity during deliberations in the Madras Legislative Council. Such efforts, aimed at unifying the diverse non-Brahmin communities, received a far greater impetus from the decisions taken by the Raja of Panagal in his capacity as Minister for Local Self-Government. He made full use of his official powers to make nominations to the local boards and distributed largesse in the form of lucrative licenses and government contracts among his supporters.[43]

In a bid to retain political power, the Justice Party, under the influence of consensualists, secured the passage of the Hindu Religious Endowments Act during its first term in office. The ministry also supported the Civil Marriages Bill introduced in the Legislative Council to legalise inter-caste and other forms of marriage not recognised by traditional customs. At the same time, the ministry issued a 'Communal Government Order' to secure communal representation for all the communities in public services.[44] It also recognised the nomenclatures chosen by the so-called 'untouchable' communities and 'backward classes', whose previous nomenclatures had had pejorative connotations.[45]

However, the partial lack of political will on the part of the non-Brahmin leaders impeded the aims and objectives of the Justice Party ministry. The consensualists did not favour the implementation of radical measures. The ministry's policies on elementary education, the development of public facilities, and the representation of untouchables in local bodies did not fulfil the expectations of the untouchables, who constituted an important section of the non-Brahmin population in the Presidency. The elite non-Brahmin leadership of the Justice Party failed to comprehend their demands, and this scuppered the efforts to build non-Brahmin solidarity.[46]

Depressed class leaders like M. C. Rajah frequently complained that the interests of the 'untouchable' communities were not being served by public bodies. He argued that, in most cases, the presidents of the Local Boards were caste Hindus and that they generally ignored the demands of the untouchable communities. On the other hand, the consensualists felt that local institutions as formulators of local policy and moulders of public opinion could serve as catalysts for social change and believed that any reform intending to eliminate caste distinctions and to integrate untouchables into the local community would have to emanate from local groups through a consensus-building process.

In the early 1920s, the Justice Party leaders, drawn mostly from the upper castes, failed to bridge the gaps between different non-Brahmin communities with varying interests. The strong casteist bias of the influential non-Brahmin leaders led to a decline in the Justice Party's electoral fortunes.[47] The discontent of the communities categorised as 'depressed' or as 'untouchables' with the Justice Party's policies brought about the split in the non-Brahmin coalition, catalysing the realisation among the socially and economically marginalised non-Brahmin communities that the call for a homogeneous non-Brahmin bloc would not be of much benefit to them.[48]

The Politics of Identity

The leaders of the Paraiyar community, representing the largest and most articulate group among the socially ostracised communities, popularised the Adi Dravida identity across the entire depressed class or 'Panchama' population of Tamil Nadu towards the end of the nineteenth century.[49] The emergence of the Justice Party in the late 1910s gave fresh impetus to this identity, but the unresponsive attitude of some of the influential non-Brahmin leaders sometimes sparked caste tensions. The consensualists, led by the Raja of Panagal, did not show much interest in mitigating the grievances of the untouchable communities. Their insensitivity meant that the untouchables were denied the opportunity to exercise their influence over decision-making processes, particularly in local bodies. This situation led to some untouchables expressing their mistrust of the Justice Party's emphasis on a homogeneous non-Brahmin bloc.[50]

Thus, the task of building a non-Brahmin–Adi Dravida coalition proved to be a difficult one for the Justice Party leadership. Non-Brahmin leaders like T. M. Nair faced great difficulties in mobilising Adi Dravidas to join a broader non-Brahmin bloc.[51] In fact, several Adi Dravida leaders expressed the opinion that neither 'Brahmin-sponsored Home Rule' nor 'non-Brahmin-sponsored Home Rule' would bring about changes in the conditions of the communities that for centuries had been regarded as untouchable.[52] Notwithstanding such differences of opinion, the majority of Adi Dravidas, who owed allegiance to the Madras Adi Dravida Janasabha, responded favourably to the Justice Party's ideological and political overtures.

At the same time, the Adi Dravidas made it clear that they did not favour the merger of their political identity with the broader political mainstream represented by the Congress and the Justice Party. In October 1917, the Adi Dravidas requested the Justice Party to support social reform and treat them as their own brethren.[53] Adi Dravida leaders also reminded the non-Brahmin Congress leaders of the Madras Presidency Association (MPA) that they needed to be accorded equality in terms of prestige and social status. The MPA leaders did not show much interest in accepting these demands and their differences with the Adi Dravidas remained irreconcilable.[54]

By 1918, rifts had also surfaced between the Adi Dravidas and the Justice Party. Adi Dravida leaders who owed allegiance to the Adi Dravida Mahajana Sabha sought to maintain a distance from the Justice Party. The efforts of the Adi Dravida Mahajana Sabha to raise the demand for separate electorates reflected its eagerness to maintain a distinct political identity rather than a composite non-Brahmin identity.[55] Thus, it became fairly evident that the Adi Dravidas preferred a measure of political autonomy, and their choice of the appellation 'Adi Dravida' over 'Dravida' reflected the desire for a distinct political and social identity. Though they had an understanding with the Justice Party, the leaders of the Madras Adi Dravida Mahajana Sabha pointed out that their interests were not always the same as those of other non-Brahmin communities. They preferred a more complex politics of identity. M. C. Rajah and other like-minded Adi Dravida leaders felt that there was a need to reconstruct Panchama history in order to preserve the distinct identity of the untouchable communities within the vortex of non-Brahminism.[56]

Historicising the Past: Reinvigorating the Panchama Identity

By the late 1910s, the new historical exercise of rediscovering the Panchama past had generated powerful critiques of both Brahminism and non-Brahminism. The Paraiyar community leaders not only attacked Brahminical notions of hierarchy and purity but also brought to the fore the issue of the subordination of Adi Dravidas at the hands of upper-caste non-Brahmins. *Adi Dravidan*, a journal launched early in 1920, expressed the economic and social demands of the Adi Dravidas, publishing a series of articles that sought to initiate a new debate over the meaning of the term 'Sudra'.

In an article published in April 1920 entitled 'Are We Sudras?', an unnamed *Adi Dravidan* author tried to advance the opinion that the term 'Sudra' had mostly been used to denote those races that had been vanquished by Aryan invaders from the north. It was argued that this term could not be applied to the Tamil people, since they had never tasted defeat at the hands of the Aryans. There were attempts to establish that the Adi Dravidas were the original inhabitants of south India and had enjoyed a superior social status in the past because of their close connections with Tamil ruling groups.[57]

Adi Dravida leaders also tried to inculcate religious virtues among untouchable communities. The spiritual attainments of saintly figures like Tiruvalluvar and Nandanar were frequently discussed in the pages of *Adi Dravidan* to vindicate the claim that social superiority was not dependent on birth; rather, it was determined by the qualities and actions of individuals.[58] Adi Dravida intellectuals rejected the Brahminical logic underlying the notion of an Aryan invasion of south India. The intellectual premise of this thesis was based on the argument that the pre-Aryan Dravidian civilisation was culturally superior to the nomadic civilisation of the Aryans.[59] Subsequently, Adi Dravida intellectuals also tried to link incidents of rural violence to the institution of caste. Growing incidents of caste violence in the southern Tamil-speaking districts led to angry outbursts from Adi Dravida leaders. They strongly criticised the Justice ministry's failure to quell these disturbances in rural areas.[60] These incidents also gave rise to debates among Adi Dravida reformers and community leaders. While reformists like Swami Sahajananda stressed cleanliness and moral virtues, others like Swami Advaidananda argued that 'reform of Hinduism', as advocated by Gandhi, would not be of much benefit to their community.[61] These debates also acquired distinctly political overtones, with the Adi Dravida leaders unanimously stating that no real purpose could be served by joining either the Congress or the Justice Party. The concept of a homogeneous non-Brahmin bloc, as propounded by the Justice Party leadership, came in for sharp criticism by the Adi Dravida leaders, who felt that a wide gulf separated the non-Brahmin upper castes from the untouchables.[62]

Thus, a section of Adi Dravida leaders and intellectuals made use of 'caste' journals to establish their distinct socio-political identity. The debates revolving around the Panchama past as well as the socio-economic conditions of untouchable communities convinced them that their uplift could only be attained through the formation of their own caste associations. There was an expectation that the formation of such caste associations would enable Adi Dravidas to gain preferential treatment from the government.[63]

The politics of identity centred on and following the rediscovery of the Panchama past generated a lot of controversy in political circles. The government's decision to induct M. C. Rajah into the Madras Legislative Council under the provisions of the Montford reforms sparked protests from Home Rule Leaguers, who criticised the government's decision to nominate an 'avowed Brahmin hater'.[64] They proposed instead V. G. Vasudeva Pillay, a Congressman as the representative of the depressed classes in the Madras Legislative Council. The Brahmin-dominated Congress tried to engineer a conflict between the two rival groups of the depressed classes to scuttle the projection of a distinct Adi Dravida identity, with Congress leaders seeking to establish that not all sections of depressed classes favoured a distinct identity as expressed through the usage of terms such as 'Authee Dravidas'.[65] Significantly, these controversies did indeed cause splits in the depressed class leadership. Those opposed to M. C. Rajah felt that attempts to establish an exclusive 'Authee Dravida' identity represented the opinions of only a section of the untouchable communities.[66] They argued that such efforts could win special privileges for them but would not place them on an equal footing with caste Hindus. In an article published in *New India,* a depressed class author stated that Rajah's attempt to foist an Adi

Dravida identity on all untouchable communities would denigrate them further in the eyes of the colonial bureaucracy.[67]

In the early 1920s, the issue of Adi Dravida identity proved to be of immense political significance. Adi Dravidas who enjoyed proximity to the Congress felt that nomenclatures such as 'Authee Dravida', representing an inclination for a distinct brand of politics, were unacceptable as they were overtly communal. On the other hand, the non-Brahmin political elite expressed the opinion that, though Adi Dravidas were attempting to project a distinct political identity, the non-Brahmin–Adi Dravida political coalition needed to be given a proper shape through the creation of a monolithic non-Brahmin bloc.[68]

For Rajah and others who had close connections with the Madras Adi Dravida Mahajana Sabha, the preservation of a distinct identity seemed to be the most important route to political success. Rajah felt that the 'Panchamas' would fail to win special concessions and adequate representation in elected bodies if their distinctive identity was not maintained. At the same time, he pointed out that despite differences between them, temporary alliances with non-Brahmins could be worked out to stall the all-pervasive Brahmin supremacy and to attain the political status that was rightfully theirs. By the early 1920s, as Adi Dravida identity gained prominence, the conflict with non-Brahmins became more and more pronounced. In most cases, the alienation of the Justice Party was a result of the reluctance of upper-caste non-Brahmins to accord a position of honour and pride to the depressed classes. Their domineering attitude made the prospects of a historic non-Brahmin bloc appear bleak.

Caste and Class: The Buckingham and Carnatic Mills Strike and the Fracture in the Non-Brahmin Polity

The formation of the Madras Labour Union in April 1918 was a significant step forward in the history of the labour movement in south India.[69] By 1920, the Madras government, in its correspondence with the Government of India, was pointing to increasing instances of conflict between the managerial and labour classes. In the early part of the same year, a strike in the Buckingham and Carnatic Mills in Madras, run by the British firm Binny and Co., set off fears of a wave of sympathetic strikes. The government promptly appointed an arbitration team, but the mills' management was not willing to cede the workers' demands. The governor's attempts to persuade the employees to resume work met with success, but only temporarily. On October 21, 1920, the labourers of Buckingham mill struck work again, and when their management refused to grant them any concessions, the protests intensified. On December 9, the government ordered the police to shoot striking workers who were indulging in violence. The government justified the police action as self-defence against violence by the workers.[70]

The following year witnessed more strikes and lockouts in the mills, sparked by the refusal of the management to recognise the union formed by their employees and the engagement by them of labourers from outside.[71] The strike, which gave way to a major conflict, began on May 21, 1921. Workers in the spinning department struck work because the management refused to discuss wage demands. Subsequently, fearing trouble, the management decided to close the mills. But trade union members were divided over the strike[72], and this division coincided with the caste loyalties of upper-caste Hindus and the Adi Dravidas.

The decision of the Adi Dravidas to abstain from the strike met with strong criticism from the nationalist press in Madras, which interpreted this as a conspiracy that had been hatched by the Binny management in collusion with government officials and Adi Dravida politicians.[73] However, the decision was in fact largely dictated by the economic interests of the Adi Dravidas. Bereft of the tactical mobility enjoyed by the caste Hindus, Adi Dravidas found that the recurrent strikes were causing their economic resources to rapidly dwindle. The predicament of the Adi Dravida workers was perhaps best explained by M. C. Rajah, who was then a member of the Madras Legislative Council. Rajah observed:

> In my presence the Adi Dravida labourers unanimously decided that they could not join the strike. ... And they in a body wrote

> a letter to the President of the Labour Union stating that they were extremely poor, that they had no means of livelihood except working in the Mills and they could not join the strike since they had suffered considerably during the last strike, when even the little property they had, had to be placed in the hands of the Marwaris [moneylenders].[74]

The majority of the Adi Dravida labourers defied both the management and the workers' union. Most of them believed that the Binny management did not discriminate against them as much as the Indian mill owners did and, in fact, that British rule had given them greater opportunities to rise out of their lowly economic positions. The links between the caste Hindu-dominated union and the leadership of the national movement also strengthened the fears and suspicions of the Adi Dravidas. They had little interest in the anti-British agitation and resented being forced to take part in political meetings and demonstrations organised by the Congress.[75] By June 1921, it was clear that economic factors as well as differences along caste lines would disrupt the united struggle of the workers against the foreign management of the Buckingham and Carnatic Mills.[76]

The Adi Dravidas initially faced challenges in defying the instructions of the union. Being a community long accustomed to traditions of subservience and oppression, they found it difficult to pursue an independent line of action. Nonetheless, their procrastination gave way once a sizeable number of workers from their community, unable to bear the economic distress, broke away from the rest of the labour force. Subsequently, the Adi Dravidas who lived in *cheris* (slums) and shared a strong sense of community started acting as a group. Soon, the battle between the strikers and the strike-breakers assumed serious proportions. In this battle, the caste Hindus allied with the Muslims while the Adi Dravidas were in alliance with the Indian Christians.[77]

The cooperation between the Adi Dravidas and the mill management aroused jealousy among the upper-caste striking mill-hands. Towards the end of June 1921, Adi Dravida leaders like M. C. Rajah alleged that the mill-hands who owed allegiance to the union had been intimidating the Adi Dravidas to prevent them from joining the mill as workers. Fearing violent reprisals from the union, the Adi Dravidas started marching in groups from their *cheris*, armed with crude weapons, to their places of work.

The conflict escalated on June 28, 1921, when a mob attacked the Puliyanthope *cheri* with stones and bottles. At night the same day, a mob set fire to nearly a hundred huts belonging to the Adi Dravidas and went on a rampage, shouting slogans like 'Gandhi *ki jai*!' (Victory to Gandhi!)[78] Soon after, realising the gravity of the situation, the government decided to evacuate the affected Adi Dravida families from the *cheris*.[79] Despite these preventive measures, the clashes between Adi Dravidas and Muslims took an ugly form. This violence, however, had little connection with the labour dispute, being a direct fallout of tensions that had been brewing between the two communities over other issues.[80]

The trade union leaders strongly condemned the attacks on the Adi Dravida workers and suspected the incidents to be the handiwork of a few hooligans. The government, however, refused to accept the assurances provided by the union leaders. Lord Willingdon, the governor, summoned the union leaders and warned them that they would be personally held responsible for any such untoward incidents in the future. The government also made it clear to them that it was in favour of a return to normalcy in the mills and the acceptance of the conditions laid down by the Binny management.[81] The government took upon itself the responsibility of evacuating and housing the homeless Adi Dravidas in government camps at Vyasarpadi, a suburb of Madras.[82]

The anti-labour policies of the mill management further embittered relations between the government and trade union leaders. The leaders, most of whom were nationalists, felt that the working class movement needed to be more closely integrated with the political programmes of the Congress. However, ordinary members of the union favoured a compromise with the management, which enjoyed the patronage and support of the colonial bureaucracy. Efforts to reach a compromise between the union and the management did not fully succeed, with the communal strife in the city also posing a challenge.[83]

In the midst of this uneasy calm, Gandhi made a visit to Madras in September 1921. His visit proved ineffective, since he could neither win back jobs for the workers nor extract assurances of financial support from the management. His speech in favour of non-violence and the adoption of a conciliatory approach towards the Adi Dravidas also went unheeded. The conflict between the Adi Dravidas and caste Hindus continued, with the government frequently resorting to police firing.[84] On October 21, 1921, the striking workers finally surrendered. In a general body meeting addressed by a prominent anti-Congress politician, the workers were exhorted to return to work unconditionally. The mills started functioning and the Adi Dravidas were clearly the gainers.[85]

The end of the mill strikes witnessed a tussle between political parties in Madras. They accused each other as well as the government of deliberately mishandling the issue. The nationalists criticised the colonial government for engineering splits within the labour movement, arguing that it was in defence of British commercial interests that the bureaucracy had adopted a repressive attitude towards labour. This interpretation was contradicted by both the government and the Justice Party. Leaders of the party, critical of the involvement of both the Congress and the government in the labour disputes, blamed the politics of non-cooperation for producing violent labour unrest. They believed that the government's pronounced partiality towards the Adi Dravidas, especially in the aftermath of the Puliyanthope riots, was a deliberate attempt to break non-Brahmin solidarity.[86]

While differences of opinion continued to prevail between the Congress and the Justice Party, the Indian press stepped up its demand for an impartial enquiry into the government's high-handedness against unarmed striking workers. In response to repeated pleas, the government decided to appoint a three-member committee headed by Sir William Ayling. The two other members of the committee were a Brahmin and a non-Brahmin, both known for their moderate views.[87]

The appointment of the enquiry committee did not meet with much favour from the general public, for there was a widespread feeling that it would not discharge its responsibilities impartially. Thus, it was in the midst of public apathy that the Ayling Committee began its fact-finding mission. Prominent non-Brahmin leaders like Theagoraya Chetti, O. Thanikachalam Chetti, and V. Shanmughan Mudaliar also visited the riot-torn Adi Dravida *cheri*s and submitted a memorandum to the government based on their own observations, arguing that the government's decision to segregate the Adi Dravidas from caste Hindus and Muslims was the most important factor in the spread of violence. They also expressed the opinion that the 'Authee Dravidas' were far more restive than any other community. Subsequently, it was also stated that the Adi Dravidas had inflicted injuries on their own bodies to draw the government's attention and benevolence.[88]

The Justice Party memorandum made several interesting recommendations. It demanded that the free feeding of Adi Dravidas in government camps be stopped and a proclamation be issued to the effect that offenders of all castes were going to be punished. The memorandum also demanded that erring officials like the Assistant Commissioner of Labour and Inspector Hankinson, responsible for police atrocities on innocent citizens, be transferred and a large number of workers who had been dismissed during the strikes be reinstated.[89]

The Ayling Committee's report blamed the striking workers for the senseless violence and loss of human lives. It supported the government's view that the Adi Dravidas had been the worst victims of this violence.[90] However, the findings of the committee fell far short of public expectations. Public disenchantment with the Ayling Committee report affected the course of deliberations in the Madras Legislative Council. Non-Brahmin representatives of the Justice Party were successful in forcing a debate on the issue. Leaders like O. Thanikachalam Chetti criticised the government for its laxity in mitigating the problems faced by untouchable communities. Several other non-Brahmin leaders expressed the opinion that strikers and non-strikers should both have been accorded equal protection.[91]

In the course of these deliberations, the Adi Dravidas constantly critiqued the Congress' attempts to brand them 'appendages' of the government. M. C. Rajah argued that, though the Congress and Justice Party leaders blamed the Adi Dravidas for the violence, the government records clearly showed that the untouchables had been the worst victims.[92] In the midst of such allegations and counter-allegations, the Home Member, Sir Lionel Davidson, expressed the opinion that, as caste Hindus had launched attacks on the Adi Dravidas, the police had been left with no option but to intervene. He refuted the allegation that the violence had erupted out of a labour dispute, upholding the view that it was triggered by 'a faction inflamed by caste prejudice'.[93] It was also pointed out that, far from being blatantly partial, the government had been neutral all through in its handling of the riots.[94]

But the government's version of the Puliyanthope incidents failed to pacify the Congress. V. K. Kalyanasundara Mudaliar, who was closely connected with the Madras Labour Union, argued that the Congress' stance of non-cooperation had never been a catalyst of violence. He alleged that the disturbances had been caused by the government's machinations to divide the workers along caste lines.[95] This opinion was not shared by Annie Besant and her followers. Besant criticised the non-cooperators in the provincial Congress for their refusal to testify before the Ayling Committee. She was stronger, though, in her criticism of the Justice Party leaders, arguing that the disturbances would not have occurred had the Adi Dravidas not emulated the Justicites in imbibing the politics of hate. Besant alleged that the Adi Dravida urge to project a distinct identity had also been responsible for violence along caste lines. The Justice ministry was also criticised for conniving with the executive regarding the deployment of armed police in the Puliyanthope *cheri*. It was alleged that Justice Party legislators and ministers had been part of the official conspiracy to cause a split in the working class movement.[96]

The consensualists within the Justice Party refuted the allegations made against them by the Congress leadership. Represented by the Raja of Panagal, Theagoraya Chetti, and O. Thanikachalam Chetti, they argued that the actions of the Labour Commissioner had alienated the untouchables from the other non-Brahmin communities and that an influential section of the colonial bureaucracy, by displaying overt sympathies for the Adi Dravidas, had tried to wreck the homogeneous non-Brahmin bloc in south India.[97] Adi Dravida leaders like M. C. Rajah were also criticised for openly supporting the partisan attitude of the Labour Department.[98]

In fact, it was the Justice Party that was most affected by the incidents at Puliyanthope. The Justice Party leaders tried to cover up the growing differences between the non-Brahmins and Adi Dravidas by highlighting the disruptive features of the Non-Cooperation movement in Madras. The non-Brahmin elites argued that the Congress had deliberately adopted such a political line to prevent the Justice Party from fulfilling its agenda of good governance. They also stated that the non-Brahmin caste-Hindu workers were innocent victims of the political sins committed by the Congress. But, while the Justicites tried to espouse the interests of the non-Brahmin classes, they made hardly any attempt to comprehend the complex interplay of class and caste factors behind the labour strikes. Failure to recognise the implications of these factors led the non-Brahmins to level stringent criticisms against the Adi Dravidas.

Significantly, with the ideology of non-Brahminism gradually losing its political sway, differences with the Adi Dravidas acquired sharper overtones. The Adi Dravida leader M. C. Rajah launched an attack on the Justice Party's style of political functioning. *Adi Dravidan* published a series of editorials condemning the pronounced upper-caste bias of the Justice Party. One such editorial stated that all talk of a non-Brahmin brotherhood was nothing but a ploy aimed at misleading Adi Dravidas. It was emphatically asserted that, instead of being a part of the non-Brahmin fraternity, Adi Dravidas would be better served developing programmes for their own social and political elevation.[99] The non-Brahmin elites were also criticised for advocating the abolition of the post of Commissioner of Labour, who, along with his subordinates, was characterised in the editorial as having done a commendable job of protecting the lives of innocent Adi Dravida workers.[100]

By mid-1922, relations between non-Brahmin elites and Adi Dravidas were at their lowest ebb. M. C. Rajah blamed Justice Party leaders for betraying the trust reposed in them by Adi Dravidas in Madras, asserting that the casteist bias of the Justice Party leadership had led to the oppression of Adi Dravidas. His ire was mainly directed against O. Thanikachalam Chetti, who had made remarks calling for the abolition of the department of the Commissioner of Labour during a speech at the Adi Dravida Conference in Palayamkottai.[101] Reacting to Chetti's comments, Rajah emphatically stated that non-Brahmin elites were trying to influence the government to revise its policies towards Adi Dravidas. He also argued that non-Brahmin leaders were out to spoil the good work initiated by Dr T. M. Nair for the establishment of a broad, non-Brahmin political coalition.

Rajah argued that, even as non-Brahmins and Brahmins vied with one another to secure the support of Adi Dravidas, the 'untouchable' population rarely benefited in terms of representation. The real beneficiaries were the non-Brahmin caste Hindus. He also criticised the attitude of the Justice Party leadership towards the unfortunate incidents at Puliyanthope. Rajah and his supporters were peeved by the Justice Party's decision to not tender any apology for the role it played during the riots. Subsequently, it was argued that the Justice Party leadership had been overtaken by casteist bias and had extended support to non-cooperating Hindu workers even though the Adi Dravidas had defied this proposal. This casteist bias, it was believed, was manifest in the Justice Party leadership's demand for the abolition of the department of the Commissioner of Labour, which had been seriously engaged in the socio-economic amelioration of untouchable communities.[102]

The antipathy of the Adi Dravidas towards the Justice Party found expression in deliberations over several other issues. M. C. Rajah criticised the Elementary Education Act passed by the Madras government on the ground that it did not include any idea of social reform. He argued that, though the Justicites professed wanting Adi Dravidas to take advantage of the Act, they were not in favour of untouchables giving up their old vocations or professions.[103]

The suggestion of the non-Brahmin elite that closing down the department of the Commissioner of Labour would help secure larger funds for Adi Dravida welfare was also strongly criticised.

Rajah stated that such suggestions were part of a larger conspiracy to prevent Adi Dravidas from improving their economic and social status. Several other depressed class leaders also accused the Justice Party of practising a form of 'political blackmail' against untouchable communities.[104]

In a conference at Chingleput, Adi Dravida leaders expressed the opinion that, in view of the attitude of the Justice Party leaders, the untouchable communities needed to think of new means of social and political elevation based on self-respect. However, some among them refused to wholly condemn the Justice Party. Adi Dravida leaders like Madurai Pillai accused M. C. Rajah of exploiting the Puliyanthope incidents to further his own political interests. On the other hand, some 'dissenting' Justicites supported the allegations made by Rajah. O. Kandaswamy Chetti opined that, after its resounding success, the Justice Party leadership had done little to preserve the ideological content of the non-Brahmin movement. The Justice Party thus stood on the threshold of a horizontal divide, with O. Kandaswamy Chetti, J. S. Kanappar, and J. N. Ramanathan on one side and O. Thanikachalam Chetti and the Raja of Panagal on the other.[105]

This debate in the aftermath of the Puliyanthope incidents revealed beyond all doubt that years of discrimination at the hands of upper-caste non-Brahmins had forced untouchables to side with the British. The Justice Party, despite its dream of a homogeneous non-Brahmin bloc, did not make much of an effort to bridge disparities between untouchables and other non-Brahmin communities. Indu Rajagopal has pointed out that the absence of dialogue between the members and the leaders and between the district units and the party headquarters in Madras made decision-making in the Justice Party too simplistic an affair.[106] In the early stages of the non-Brahmin movement, the consensualists believed that it would not always be possible to satisfy the aspirations of the different non-Brahmin communities. Therefore, only those interests which aligned with their ideology were given importance. This elitist bias led them to adopt a rigid stand towards Adi Dravidas both during and after the

Puliyanthope riots and undoubtedly stifled all chances of a political compromise with Adi Dravidas.

The Age of Depressed Class Conferences

By the early 1920s, the depressed classes (mostly including the untouchable communities) were displaying great interest in organising conferences to promote cooperation amongst themselves. In 1921, the Adi Dravida Mahajana Sabha organised a gathering of depressed classes to protest against a resolution supporting the proposal to change caste appellations like 'Pariah' and 'Panchama' to 'Adi Dravida'. Depressed class leaders like V. G. Vasudeva Pillai, P. Venkatachalam, and S. Somu Pillai opposed the move on the ground that the opinions of various depressed class organisations needed to be ascertained before taking such a decision. It was felt that such unilateral efforts on the part of a section of the non-Brahmin elite would generate more communal discord than solidarity. In fact, it was opined that the term 'Adi Dravida' would lead to controversy, for the proposal was to integrate within it the depressed classes as well as the aboriginal tribes and other socially depressed communities. It was felt the term 'Dravida' was better suited to expressing the distinct identity of the depressed classes.[107]

The hue and cry over these abrupt moves brought the issue of depressed class identity to the forefront. Depressed class leaders increasingly favoured a different brand of politics, distinct from the politics of non-Brahminism. The conflict between the non-Brahmins and the untouchable communities over the issue of nomenclature coincided with efforts to organise depressed class conferences. These conferences were mostly organised in the remote and interior parts of South Arcot and Tanjore districts. At some of them, enlightened Brahmin social reformers like Justice T. Sadasiva Iyer suggested that terms such as 'Thirukulathar' and 'Nandanarkulathar' could be adopted as substitutes for pejorative terms such as 'Pariah' and 'Panchama'. The government, however, adopted the term 'Adi Dravida' for the untouchable communities in Madras Presidency.[108]

The Adi Dravidas utilised these conferences to vent their grievances. The government was requested to enact special labour legislations for the benefit of the agricultural labourers. Resolutions were also adopted requesting the colonial administration to initiate legislations to eliminate social segregation. Adi Dravida leaders known for their reformist zeal, like Swami Sahajananda, utilised the conferences to popularise the concepts of cleanliness, sanitation, and religious devotion among untouchable communities. They also pleaded for temple entry rights for members of their community.[109]

Search for a New Identity: The Adi Dravidas in the Early 1920s

The Adi Dravida inclination to preserve a distinct socio-political identity often found expression through social movements seeking to repudiate the logic of the hierarchical Hindu social order. In June 1921, Adi Dravidas, under the leadership of the reformist leader Jagannatha Swami, became involved in a mass movement. From the very beginning, this movement directed its attack against the oppression of agricultural labourers, who belonged mostly to the 'untouchable' communities, by upper-caste landlords. The followers of Jagannatha Swami distributed pamphlets among agricultural labourers, instructing them to discontinue the practice of prostrating themselves before upper-caste landlords. The swami also instructed his followers to lead a respectable life and abstain from the use of alcohol and other intoxicants. These instructions often gave rise to conflicts between the agricultural labourers and the upper-caste landlords. In Kurumballur *taluk* of Trichinopoly, the conflict assumed the form of riots, and Adi Dravida settlements were subjected to senseless acts of mayhem and destruction. In most cases, the upper-caste landlords retaliated by issuing threats of social boycott, evictions, and cancellation of employment contracts.[110]

The Collector of Trichinopoly intervened to prevent the deterioration of law and order. He assigned lands for both habitation and cultivation purposes to the Adi Dravida families to ameliorate their economic and social status. Despite such official actions, the movement spearheaded by the Paraiyars continued. Though other untouchable communities like the 'Pallars' and 'Chucklers' withdrew from the movement, the Paraiyars seemed to be in no mood for reconciliation with the landlords. Their resilience was partly a result of the belief that, by opposing unjust social practices, they were upholding the egalitarian traditions of the British Raj in India.[111]

Subsequently, the involvement of Adi Dravida leaders like M. C. Rajah strengthened the movement. In a short period of time, the movement spread to the neighbouring South Arcot and Salem districts. Although it failed to retain popularity for long, it remained a significant episode, since it inculcated a vision of an egalitarian social order among the untouchables. The widespread popularity of this movement indirectly forced the government to pay attention to the emerging Adi Dravida consciousness in Madras Presidency.

The growing Adi Dravida consciousness found expression in the depressed class conferences organised throughout Tamil Nadu. At these conferences, Adi Dravida leaders expressed the opinion that representation in local bodies on the basis of their numerical strength would put an end to the social discrimination they faced. The insignificant presence of untouchable communities in the local bodies had led to an indifferent attitude on the part of the upper castes. M. C. Rajah argued that the government's policy of generally nominating members not belonging to the untouchable communities had not been of any real benefit to Adi Dravidas. In other words, it was felt that such a policy deprived Adi Dravidas of the benefits of real representation.[112]

The conferences also paved the way for political tussles between the Adi Dravidas and the Justice Party. In 1923, M. C. Rajah, leading a deputation of Adi Dravidas, presented a memorandum to Lord Willingdon highlighting the injustices committed by the Justice Party against Adi Dravidas in the context of their representation in elected bodies and public services. It also stated that, despite public pronouncements about the ideals of the non-Brahmin movement, the Justice Party leaders tried to keep Adi Dravidas under their control. It was argued that Adi Dravidas, as descendants of the original Dravidian races of south India, looked upon the British Raj as a providential blessing, for they felt that British rule had provided them with the opportunity to familiarise themselves with institutions of self-government.[113]

Conclusion

The story of the emergence of depressed class politics in early-twentieth-century Madras Presidency brings several issues to the forefront. The depressed class leadership was critical of both elitist non-Brahmin politics and of the proponents of Vedic Brahminism who argued that their ideology was the basis of Indian unity and nationalism. The elite leadership of the Justice Party and the Brahmin-dominated Congress too often ignored the humanitarian and egalitarian traditions represented by diverse religious streams. The defence of nationalism by both Brahmin and non-Brahmin elites enabled the traditionally dominant castes to project their own selfish ideas, whether in the form of non-Brahminism or Congress nationalism.

The depressed class consciousness and depressed class politics that emerged during this time incorporated traditions of resistance, equality, and dignity. Subsequently, depressed class politicians became increasingly interested in doing away with caste and other forms of social divisions and sought to restore confidence and dignity amongst the oppressed populace. Indeed, there were also attempts to establish a new order based on a composite non-Brahminical tradition, which accommodated and integrated the interests of the Shudras and those of the '*antajas*' or depressed sections of society. This vision of a single, monolithic non-Brahminism was not endorsed by Justice Party politicians, who belonged to the elite strata of Hindu castes.[114] However, despite their opposition, depressed class leaders tried to understand the past in terms of the present and vice-versa. Their perceptions of history were shaped by their contemporary social and political experiences. This became part of a bigger project of inventing and reinventing the past. In other words, it was through their own construction of history/the past that the depressed classes strengthened their claims to an appropriate share in the power structure of the colonial state and society. The past represented the living experiences of these communities, their comprehension based on their own reality, and all this was integrated to forge an element of connectivity with their own selves that later found expression in a community identity. Such historiographic exercises enabled the depressed class leadership in south India, as in other parts of the subcontinent, to develop critiques of the relationship between oppressor and oppressed, between a citizenry that had long been marginalised and the homogeneous nation-state projected by elite nationalists. Lastly, it was through their political conflicts with the dominant non-Brahmin caste groups and through their own narratives of the past that the depressed classes were able to project their own identity, which was different from those of Brahmins and upper-caste Hindus. Indeed, all this provided them with a framework for advancing claims to an appropriate share in the power structure of the colonial state.

Notes and References

*An earlier version of this article was published in *Social Scientist* 39(7–8) (July–August 2011). I am grateful to the editorial board of *Social Scientist* for granting me permission to reproduce substantial portions of the earlier version in the form of a revised chapter in this book.

1. J. Devika, 'Identity Assertions and Print in Malayalam and Tamil Speaking Regions in the Early Twentieth Century: Some Comments', *South Asia Chronicle* 11 (2021): 61–68.

2. The notion that the 'despised castes' did not have a history of their own led to their being identified as casteless, 'broken people' or communities that were beyond the frontiers of human civilisation.

3. For more details see *ibid*, p. 62.

4. David A. Washbrook, *The Emergence of Provincial Politics: The Madras Presidency, 1870–1920* (Cambridge: Cambridge University Press, 2008), pp. 6–16.

5. Eugene F. Irschik, *Politics and Social Conflict in South India: The Non-Brahman Movement and Tamil Separatism, 1916–1929* (Los Angeles: University of California Press, 1969), p. xv.

6. Bernard Bate has argued that, by 1920, politics in Madras had undergone a major transformation and non-Brahmin communities like the Chettiars, Pillais, Naidus, Naiyakars, and Mudaliars were coming together to set up a non-Brahmin bloc whose politics was characterised by the use of the vernacular language. Dr P. Varadarajulu Naidu, a non-Brahmin leader, undertook a major vernacular-speaking tour of the Tamil country in 1970. It was clear that non-Brahmin politicians were increasingly in favour of Tamil as a medium of oration, since they now wanted to mobilise the vast majority of *pamara makkal* (illiterate or poor people) engaged as farmers and labourers—including women, Dalits (Adi Dravidas), and others—who had previously been entirely left out of politics. For more details see Bernard Bate, 'To Persuade Them Into Speech and Action: Oratory and the Tamil Political, Madras, 1905–1919', *Comparative Studies in Society and History* 55(1) (January 2013): 145–146.

7. R. Saravana Raja, 'Vanniyar Claims to Mobility in Pluralist Tamil Nadu, 1900–1935'. *South Asia Research* 40(1) (February 2020): 22.

8. *Ibid*, p. 23.

9. For more details see Malarvizhi Jayanth, 'Struggling for Freedom from Caste in Colonial India: The Story of Rettaimalai Srinivasan', *Caste: A Journal on Social Exclusion* 3(1) (April 2022): 140–141.

10. Ravi Vaitheespara has tried to draw an interesting comparison between the ideas of nineteenth-century Saivaite figures like Ramalingar Swamigal and the twentieth-century Saivite intellectual Maraimalai Atigal. There is little doubt that Atigal's recasting of Saivism and Saiva Siddhanta had both similarities and differences with that of Ramalingar. The most visible difference was that Ramalingar's religiosity was clearly more practice-oriented and focused on disciplining the body and mind, whereas Atigal seems to have emphasised more the intellectual exploration and explication of Saivism and Saiva Siddhanta. Atigal's interpretation of Tamil literary works brought him into conflict with the Vedantists, but it skilfully established the fact that Tamil Saivism could not be subsumed under the broader umbrella of Brahminical Hinduism. Atigal tried to oppose the challenges emanating from Aryan-Sanskrit hegemony by highlighting the status of the Tamil language and tradition. However, it remains doubtful

whether Atigal's critique of Brahminism could override the importance of caste and social hierarchy in the consciousness of the Tamil public. For more details see Ravi Vaitheespara, 'Maraimalai Atigal and the Genealogy of the Tamilian Creed', *Economic and Political Weekly* XLIV(14) (April 4–10, 2009): 45–51.

11. For more details see Gajendran Ayyathurai, 'Foundations of Anti-Caste Consciousness: Pandit Iyothee Thass, Tamil Buddhism and the Marginalised in South-India' (Ph.D. diss. Columbia University, 2011), pp. 1–3.

12. V. Geetha and S. V. Rajadurai, 'Dalits and Non-Brahmin Consciousness in Colonial Tamil Nadu'. *Economic and Political Weekly* 28(39) (September 1993): 2091–2098.

13. The Madres United League was started in the early years of the twentieth century by some clerks of the Revenue Board Office in Madras. The induction of Dr C. Natesa Mudaliar as secretary of the League led to the induction of some non-Brahmins as members. By 1914, it was renamed the Dravidian Association, which tried to involve itself mostly in representing student interests. Its fund-collecting drives and periodical meetings attracted only a small group of urban and rural non-Brahmin elites. See Indu Rajagopal, *The Tyranny of Caste* (Delhi: Vikas Publishing House, 1985), pp. 34–35. See also S. G. Manavala Ramanujan, 'The Origin of the Justice Party' (Madras: Justice Party Golden Jubilee Souvenir, 1968), pp. 89–90; and P. Rangaswami Naidu, 'The Origin of the Justice Party' (Madras: Justice Party Golden Jubilee Souvenir, 1968) pp. 259–60.

14. *The Hindu*, December 20, 1916.

15. T. Varadarajulu Naidu, comp. *The Justice Movement 1917* (Madras: Dravida Kazhagam, 1991), p. 1.

16. Non-Brahmin, 3 December 1916, cited in Srinivasan Saraswathi, *Minorities in Madras State: Group Interests in Modern Politics*, (Delhi: Impex India, 1974), p. 69.

17. Rajagopal, *The Tyranny of Caste, op. cit.*, p. 19.

18. *Common Weal* expressed certain views that led to a considerable degree of resentment among non-Brahmins. It observed that 'the word "non-Brahmana" itself is unnatural and not very complementary to those who seem to take glory in it. Although there is not much in a name, yet it must be admitted that the name "Dravidian" is much better, as it at once brings before the mind's eye the great part played by the Dravidians

in the building up of the great spiritual civilisation in India. How much poorer the Indian nation would have been but for the Dravidian pioneers of civilisation.' S. Kasturiranga Iyengar, who was deeply involved with the Home Rule movement, also made some observations that were deeply critical of non-Brahmin politics in Madras Presidency: 'the non-Brahmana movement was started with distinctly official support and guidance to produce cleavage into that community [south Indian society as a whole] and to protest against the national Congress' scheme; conferences have been organised with official help in several places.' For more details, see the November 30, 1917 and December 28, 1917 issues of *Common Weal: A Journal of National Reform*, edited by Annie Besant.

19. Address presented to the Governor General and the Secretary of State by the Madras Adi Dravida Jana Sabha, 1917, preserved in the form of a pamphlet in the Nehru Memorial Museum and Library (hereafter NMML), New Delhi.

20. *The Hindu*, 1 October 1917.

21. It has been argued that this broad alliance of non-Brahmins was formed with a definite aim to invoke the concepts of minority and majority before the colonial bureaucracy. The enormous power and prestige wielded by Brahmins, despite their minuscule population strength, was highlighted by the non-Brahmins as the real reason behind the unequal distribution of power and privilege in Madras Presidency. For more details, see Saraswathi, *Minorities in Madras State, op. cit.*, p. 75.

22. Joint Select Committee of Government of India Bill, Volume III, p. 96. 1919. London: His Majesty's Stationery Office (hereafter HMSO).

23. *Ibid.*, p. 20; Saraswathi, *Minorities in Madras State, op. cit.*, pp. 72–73.

24. The non-Brahmin elite felt that the selection of a Tamil Brahmin Congressman, V. S. Srinivasa Sastry, would lead to the brahminisation of politics and services. It was argued that such attempts at strengthening the political supremacy of the Brahmins would be detrimental to the progress of the non-Brahmin communities. The colonial government needed to be more sympathetic to the latter, who saw the continuance of the British Raj as more conducive to the improvement of the majority of the population that was suffering from poverty and illiteracy. For more details see *The Justice*, 16 May 1919; G.O. No. 1019-1020, Public Department, 7.11. 1918, TNA.

25. G.O. No. 854-855, Public Department, 19.9.1918, TNA.

26. Indian Constitutional Reforms: Report of the Franchise Committee, 1918, Calcutta, 1919, Appendix XIV.

27. Indian Constitutional Reforms, Report of the Southborough Committee (also referred to as the Report of the Franchise Committee), Calcutta, 1919, p. 9.

28. G.O. No. 1146, Public Department, dated 31.12.1918, TNA.

29. The Chief Secretary to the Government of Madras highlighted the fact that the results of the elections held for filling the seats reserved for non-officials to the Madras Legislative Council in 1909, 1912, and 1916 revealed the supremacy of the Brahmins. For instance, in 1916, Brahmins secured as many as ten seats and non-Brahmins could bag only five. He also pointed out that, though non-Brahmin voters outnumbered Brahmin voters, the former's numerical superiority was not reflected in the election results. Thus, arrangements in favour of territorial electorates would be unlikely to ensure a meaningful representation of all sections in the society. For more details, see *ibid*.

30. The views of Alexander Cardew have been discussed in detail in a separate enclosure along with the correspondences of the Acting Chief Secretary to the Government of Madras with the Home Department of the Government of India. For more details, see *ibid*. See also Reports of the Southborough Committee and the Government of India's Dispatches on them (1918–1919), Calcutta, 1919, pp. 124–25.

31. Since the early 1910s, Alexander Cardew had been vocal about the monopolisation of public services by Brahmins in Madras Presidency. He also expressed the opinion that simultaneously holding ICS examinations in India and England would give Brahmins a greater opportunity to establish bureaucratic monopoly in the Presidency. He observed, 'It is necessary[,] however[,] to see whether they [reform-minded bureaucrats] have not done so [substituted the bureaucracy with an oligarchy] even without any such intention, for it would be a travesty of liberal principles to surrender the 10 millions of downtrodden, non-caste people to the control of the upper caste without any adequate safeguards. ... Is it wise to entrust the happiness and progress of the downtrodden and illiterate Pariah and Panchama community or even of the ill-educated and politically backward Non-Brahmin Hindu castes, to an assembly in which the majority will probably be largely composed of and controlled by Brahmins and in any case be drawn from the literate community representing only about 7.5%

of the population?' See C. R. Reddy Papers, File No. 45, NMML, New Delhi, cited in Rajagopal, *The Tyranny of Caste, op. cit.*, p. 22.

32. For more details see Saraswathi, *Minorities in Madras State, op. cit.*, p. 76; V. Geetha and S. V. Rajadurai, *Towards a Non-Brahmin Millennium: From Iyothee Thoss to Periyar* (Calcutta: Samya, 1998), p. 156.

33. G.O. No. 142, Public Department (Confidential), dated 28.2.1920, TNA.

34. *Ibid.*

35. *Dravidan*, 28 January 1920.

36. Geetha and Rajadurai, *Towards a Non-Brahmin Millennium, op. cit.*, p. 160.

37. *Ibid.*

38. *New India*, 23 March 1920.

39. The Justice Party leadership almost unanimously felt that the award amounted to a betrayal of the non-Brahmin cause and that all its labours over the three preceding years had been in vain. *The Justice*, a non-Brahmin mouthpiece, observed, 'It [Meston Award] is a tragedy. It can never afford them protection, while however the stigma of social discrimination sticks to them.' For more details, see *The Justice*, 18 March 1920.

40. *The Hindu*, 23 March 1920.

41. Rajagopal, *The Tyranny of Caste, op. cit.*, p. 45.

42. David Arnold has argued that Willingdon's decision on this matter might have been influenced to a great extent by his eagerness to successfully implement the Montagu-Chelmsford reforms in Madras. For more details, see David Arnold, *The Congress in Tamilnadu: Nationalist Politics in South India, 1919-37* (New Delhi: Manohar, 1977), pp. 56–58.

43. In fact, non-Brahmin leaders, from the very inception of the Justice Party ministry, exhibited great eagerness to utilise their political power to find new supporters among the rising middle classes. Therefore, they were bent upon extracting promises from the government that non-Brahmins would be given preference over Brahmins in public service appointments and promotions. For more details, see *ibid.*

44. Rajagopal, *The Tyranny of Caste, op. cit.*, p. 47.

45. The Justice Ministry backed the proposals of some 'untouchable' communities—Pariahs and Panchamas—that their names be changed to 'Adi Dravida.' See G.O. No. 1955, Law (General) Department, dated 19.11.1921, TNA; G.O. No. 817, Law (General) Department, dated 25.3.1922, TNA.

46. Geetha and Rajadurai (*Towards a Non-Brahmin Millennium, op. cit.*, pp. 174–75) point out that non-Brahmin attitudes towards the Adi Dravidas were mediated through a vortex of material interests, and this probably undermined the efforts to construct an imagined non-Brahmin fraternity.

47. *Ibid.*, pp. 48–50.

48. David Arnold has pointed out that in several parts of Tamil Nadu, the depressed classes showed signs of shifting tacit political allegiances to the Congress. See David Arnold, *The Congress in Tamilnad, op. cit.*, p. 67.

49. The 'untouchable' communities utilised various nomenclatures to express their distinct social identities. Some of them referred to themselves as depressed classes and Panchamas. The Paraiyars, who were numerically the largest among the 'untouchable' communities, preferred to identify themselves in the early part of the twentieth century as Adi Dravidas or the original inhabitants of south India. The term 'Adi Dravida' was favoured because it was felt it would enable them to regain their lost status and free themselves of the pejorative connotations of terms such as 'Paraiyan'.

50. Arnold, *The Congress in Tamilnad, op. cit.*, p. 67.

51. For more details, see D. Gopala Chettiar, *Adi Dravida Poorva Charitam* (Madras, 1920), pp. 31–32.

52. Irschik, *Politics and Social Conflict in South India, op. cit.* p. 178.

53. *Ibid.*, p. 71.

54. Surinder K. Gupta, *The Scheduled Castes in Modern Indian Politics: Their Emergence as a Political Power* (New Delhi: Munshiram Manoharlal, 1985), p. 187.

55. The Madras Adi Dravida Mahajana Sabha observed, 'We are particularly desirous of a separate electorate being created for us. Representation by nomination is no representation at all.' New India, 9 January 1919.

56. Geetha and Rajadurai, *Towards a Non-Brahmin Millennium, op. cit.*, pp. 180–81.

57. In 'Are We Sudras?', the author vehemently argued that term 'Sudra' had been applied to tribal races such as the Kols, who were vanquished by the Aryans. The author pointed out that there were several references in ancient Tamil literature which proved that the Brahmin–non-Brahmin divide was not very stringent. In the ancient Tamil epic *Silappathigaram*, a Brahmin lady called Devanti is shown to be a close confidante of Kannagi's.

Brahmins also worked in the house of danseuses. For more details, see *Adi Dravidan* (Tamil), April 1920, pp. 26–32.

58. In an article that appeared in *Adi Dravidan* on June 15, 1920, it was stated that Tiruvalluvar and Nandanar had crossed the barriers of untouchability through their unparalleled devotion or *bhakti*. In another article that appeared on July 15, 1920, an author by the name S. V. N. Alvar demolished the myth of the Aryan invasion of south India. He asserted that the indigenous people of south India, i.e. the Dravidians, possessed a culture of their own which was by no means inferior to the cultural elements of Aryan civilisation. In other words, there was an attempt to emphasise the links between the Dravidian civilisation and the Indus Valley Civilisation.

59. *Adi Dravidan* (Tamil), 15 August 1920, pp. 93-95.

60. In fact, there were a series of caste riots in Ramnad involving the dominant rural groups and the Adi Dravidas, who were mostly 'untouchable' agricultural labourers. For more details, see *ibid*, pp. 95–97.

61. Swami Advaidananda was particularly critical of Congress leaders for treating the problems from an entirely moralist perspective. He felt that instead of exhorting the Adi Dravidas to lead a life of virtue, Gandhi could have initiated a thorough overhauling of the social system by undertaking movements in favour of temple entry by all classes of the society. *Adi Dravidan*, 15 May 1921, pp. 30-39.

62. *Adi Dravidan* (Tamil), 15 June 1921.

63. *Adi Dravidan* (Tamil), 17 August 1921, pp. 82-84. 55.

64. A report published in *New India* on August 2, 1919, objected to the nomination of M. C. Rajah for two reasons. In the first place, Rajah was labelled an anti-nationalist, since he did not believe in the Indian nation. Secondly, he was condemned for his anti-Brahmin sentiments and for his attempts to establish a distinct 'Authee Dravida' identity.

65. *New India*, 23 December 1920.

66. R. T. Ramakrishna Pillay, in *New India* (23 July 1920), observed: 'When there is a divided opinion on the subject and when there is a single representative in the [Madras] Corporation who can advocate one of the two sides, it is unfair for the Corporation to dispose of the case without hearing the other side. No non-Brahmana can represent the other side unless the Panchamas are playing into their hands.'

67. *Ibid.*

68. For more details, see Geetha and Rajadurai, *Towards a Non-Brahmin Millennium, op. cit.*, pp. 176–77.

69. The Madras Labour Union was formed on April 27, 1918 by B. P. Wadia, T. V. Kalyanasundaram, and others, as a result of the combined efforts of the Home Rule Leaguers and Congress propagandists. For more details, see Christopher S. Krishna, *Labour Movement in Tamilnadu, 1918–1933* (Calcutta: K. P. Bagchi & Co, 1989), p. 57. Also see Rakhahari Chatterjee, *Working Class and the Nationalist Movement in India: The Critical Years* (New Delhi: South Asia Publishers, 1984), p. 84.

70. Rajagopal, *The Tyranny of Caste, op. cit.*, p. 129.

71. For more details, see E. D. Murphy, 'Class and Community in India: The Madras Labour Union 1918-1921', *Indian Economic and Social History Review* 14(3) (July 1977): 306–308.

72. For more details, see, G.O. No. 1912, Law (General) Department, dated 27.6.1924, TNA.

73. *The Hindu*, 22 June 1921.

74. Madras Legislative Council Proceedings (hereafter MLCP), Vol. Ill, 12 October 1921, p. 1012.

75. G.O. No. 1844, Law (General) Department, dated 2.8.1922, TNA.

76. By the end of May 1921, M. C. Rajah and Swami Desikananda exhorted the Adi Dravida mill hands residing in the Puliyanthope *cheri* not to participate in the strike. The Assistant Commissioner of Labour was also present at these meetings. MLCP, Vol. Ill, p. 1012.

77. Murphy, 'Class and Community in India', *op. cit.*, p. 314.

78. *The Hindu*, 12 August 1921.

79. G.O. No. 671, Public Department, dated 7.10.1921, TNA.

80. The violence between the Muslims and the Adi Dravidas, who lived in close proximity in the *cheris*, was particularly intense. Some of them worked together in the slaughterhouse in Perambur. In March 1921, on *hartal* day observed to condemn the imprisonment of Yakub Hasan, Adi Dravidas in the slaughterhouse refused to obey the Muslims' demand to stop slaughter. In the ensuing conflict, an Adi Dravida was killed and in retaliation Adi Dravidas burnt four Muslim huts in the *cheris*. See Murphy, 'Class and Community in India', *op. cit.*, p. 315.

81. *The Hindu*, 9 July 1921.

82. Murphy, 'Class and Community in India', *op. cit.*, p. 315.

83. *Ibid.*, p. 316.

84. *Madras Mail*, 17 September 1921; Murphy, op. cit., p. 317.

85. When the mills resumed their operations, nearly 5,000 Adi Dravidas remained in their jobs, thereby excluding many of the caste Hindus and Muslims. For more details, see *Madras Mail*, 21 October 1921.

86. Geetha and Rajadurai, *Towards a Non-Brahmin Millennium, op. cit.*, p. 183.

87. G.O. No. 671, Public Department, dated 7.10.1921, TNA.

88. Geetha and Rajadurai, *Towards a Non-Brahmin Millennium, op. cit.*, p. 185.

89. *Ibid.*

90. The committee pointed out that the Adi Dravidas were the worst sufferers and that only about one-sixth of the huts belonging to Muslims and caste Hindus had been razed to the ground. G.O. No. 671, Public Department, dated 7.10.1921, TNA.

91. MLCP, Volume III, 12 October 1921, pp. 1005–1008, 1022.

92. Rajah observed: 'If [the Adi Dravidas] had been with the rioters in their rioting, they would have certainly lost their lives. The very fact that no Adi Dravida was shot clearly indicates that the Adi Dravidas were not creating the mischief[,] ... but my friend Mr Thanikachalam Chettiyar has said nothing about the throwing of bombs which has become the fashion of the rioters. How many lives have been lost by the throwing of bombs, who threw them, these are questions which my honourable friend ought to have put before the Council.' For more details, see *ibid.*, pp. 1012–13.

93. *Ibid.*, p. 1028.

94. The government strongly stated that its law enforcement agencies had never been soft or partial towards the Adi Dravidas, but had treated them on an equal footing with the Muhammadans and caste Hindus. For more details, see *ibid.*

95. Geetha and Rajadurai, *Towards a Non-Brahmin Millennium, op. cit.*, p. 187.

96. *New India*, 13 October 1921.

97. Justice Party leaders like Rao Bahadur A. S. Krishna Rao Pantulu, P. Theagaraya Chetty, and O. Thanikachalam Chetty argued that it was not within the rights of the Labour Commissioner as a civil officer to persuade the Adi Dravidas not to participate in the strike. See MLCP, Volume III, 1921, pp. 1023, 1032.

98. The progressive Justicites also stated that the British members of the Cabinet had greater decision-making powers than the Indian ministers. They felt that neither the Indian ministers nor the legislature could change the labour policies, which had resulted in the secession of the 'untouchables' from non-Brahmin communities. For more details, see MLCP, Volume III, 21 October 1921, p. 1013.

99. *Adi Dravidan* complained that the slogan of non-Brahminism could never really solve their problems, as long as the domination of the Pillais, Mudaliars, and Reddis continued in the organisational structure of the Justice Party. For more details, see *Adi Dravidan* (Tamil), 15 November 1921, pp. 131–32.

100. *Adi Dravidan* (Tamil), 15 December 1921, p. 156.

101. At this conference, O. Thanikachalam Chetti demanded the abolition of the Department of Labour. He argued that the functioning of the department had resulted in conflicts between Non-Brahmin communities and Adi Dravidas. For more details, see *New India*, 23 May 1922.

102. *New India*, 21 July 1922.

103. For more details, see Geetha and Rajadurai, *Towards a Non-Brahmin Millennium*, *op. cit.*, p. 195.

104. Rajah blamed the Justice Party leaders for the underrepresentation of Adi Dravidas in the Madras Legislative Council and the local bodies. He argued that all the important political and administrative positions had been monopolised by Justice Party ministers and their supporters. As a consequence, the principle of communal representation could never be translated into reality. For more details, see *ibid.*, p. 196.

105. *Ibid.*, pp. 196–97.

106. Rajagopal, *The Tyranny of Caste*, *op. cit.* p. 133.

107. In fact, it was argued that the term 'Dravida' would not create much confusion, since there was a clear-cut distinction with the caste Dravidas, who happened to be 'clean' Non-Brahmin Hindus possessing distinct caste appellations. For more details, see G.O. No. 1680, Law (General) Department, dated 20.10.1921, TNA.

108. The government differed with the suggestion of the high-caste Hindu reformers that the term 'Dravida Samanyas' be used for addressing the depressed class population. However, it did agree that terms such as 'Pariah' and 'Panchama' carrying an element of stigma ought to be

eliminated through the use of new terms such as 'Adi Dravida'. For more details, see G.O. No. 785, Law (General) Department, dated 7.7.1921, TNA.

109. Swami Sahajananda advised the untouchables to adopt clean habits. He felt that, by practising such habits, the depressed classes could gain social respectability in the eyes of high-caste Hindus. But a few others felt that the untouchable communities also needed temple entry rights in order to be socially equal to the caste Hindus. It was suggested that temples usually managed by upper-caste Hindus could divert a part of their surplus revenue towards building schools accessible to children of all communities. For more details, see *Adi Dravidan* (Tamil), 15 May 1921 and 15 November 1921.

110. G.O. No. 138, Public Department, dated February 14, 1922, TNA; see also Fortnightly Reports For the First Half of July, 1921 (Confidential), TNA.

111. *Ibid.*

112. Depressed class leaders like M. C. Rajah, supported by organisations like the Adi Dravida Mahajana Sabha, pressurised the government to constitute a separate electoral roll for the depressed classes to ensure proper representation for them in the local bodies. The government, however, made it clear that the District Municipalities and Local Board Act of 1920 safeguarded the interests of the depressed classes by securing the appointment of their members to nominated seats in local bodies. The government stated that, as early as November 1919, the Madras Legislative Council adopted a resolution instructing collectors to nominate suitable candidates of these classes to various local bodies and municipalities. The government also reiterated the view (vide G.O. 2525, Local and Municipal Department, dated 12.12.1922) that it had requested collectors and presidents of the District Boards to ensure proper representation of the depressed classes in these bodies. For more details, see G.O. No. 1431, Local and Self Government Department, dated June 21, 1923, TNA.

113. G.O. No. 1070, Law (General) Department, dated March 27, 1924, TNA.

114. Non-Brahmin politicians and ideologues were interested in invoking the greatness of Tamil literary texts like the *Tirukkural* and *Silappathigaram* to downsize the superiority of Brahminical religious

texts. However, even if radical non-Brahmin intellectuals were interested in a critical engagement with Brahminism, their privileged status often prevented them from presenting a critique of caste and advocating its irrelevance to contemporary Tamil society. For more details see Karthick Ram Manoharan, *Periyar: A Study in Political Atheism* (Hyderabad: Orient BlackSwan, 2022), p. 18.

10

The History and Politics of Dalit Sub-Classification in India*

YAGATI CHINNA RAO

Caste has long been an important dimension of political mobilisation in India, particularly in the domain of electoral politics. In the post-colonial period, caste has been at the centre of intense debates triggered by various commissions on reservations and their recommendations. The reservation policy in India has been a bone of contention and conflict in different circles, ranging from the academic and the political to civil society, and the politics of reservation has also been articulated through literary and cultural debates. In recent times, however, a significant shift has been noticed, with reservations transforming from a source of conflict between the reserved and non-reserved categories to one between different reserved communities. This intra-caste conflagration amongst reserved communities has been fuelled to a great extent by the state and its political power-mongers. Thus, the Dalit movement during the post-colonial period has been confronted with the dilemma of having to forge Dalit unity against the oppressive upper castes while engaging with divisive forces emanating from within the Dalit community.

As per the Constitution, the term 'Scheduled Castes' denotes specifically the castes listed in Article 341. It is important to note at the very outset that, except for limited powers to exclude castes from or include castes in the list by an act of Parliament, no provision in Article 341 deals with sub-dividing, sub-classifying, or sub-grouping the castes listed. Evidently, the framers of the Constitution conceived all the listed castes to be members of one overarching group for the purposes of Article 15 and Article 16(4) of the Constitution of India—any further classification by way of sub-classification is not constitutionally mandated or even permissible. The discourse around the sub-classification of Dalits, thus, poses simultaneously an old question and a new challenge. Although it has been an existential issue for Dalits since the colonial period, the magnitude of the present crisis is relatively new.

It should be mentioned here in passing that, while Article 330 guarantees the reservation of seats for Scheduled Castes in the Lok Sabha and in all state assemblies, there is no reservation in the Rajya Sabha and in state legislative councils despite long-standing and persistent demands for the same.

Issues of Identity

As mentioned, issues related to the identity and identification of untouchables have been recurrent in Dalit politics and in public discourse since the colonial period. The labels or nomenclatures used to identify untouchables in India have witnessed several changes over time, and each time a new nomenclature has emerged it has added a new, salient dimension to Dalit identity. This dynamic reinvention of identity has featured more prominently in the history of untouchables than that of any other social group in India, and it is intertwined with intellectual developments in a wider milieu.

While caste or sub-caste (or *jati*) identities connote discrete communities, homogeneous categories were deployed by various agencies to express a generic untouchable identity that cut across regional and intra-untouchable distinctions. It is useful to understand the evolution of these multiple identities and nomenclatures in a historical context. Historically, four major categories of nomenclatures among Dalits can be discerned.[1] The first is the discrete caste or *jati* identity, e.g. Jatav, Chamar, Mala, Madiga, Mang, Mahar, and so on, which emanates from the lore of community traditions or myths explaining their origins and status. The second is the identity related to their structural exclusion and inferior status, indicated by Brahminical texts through the use of names like 'Atchut', 'Asprishya', 'Antyaja', 'Chandala', 'Asura', 'Dasa' or 'Dasya', 'Rakshasa', 'Pariah',[2] 'Harijan', 'Panchama', etc. The third category consists of terms like 'Depressed Classes', 'Exterior Castes', 'Scheduled Castes', and so on—the result of the administrative and political policies of the colonial and post-colonial states, which had far-reaching effects on political and social discourses. The terms by which untouchables were known during the colonial period—Depressed Classes, Harijans, and Scheduled Castes—were political responses to multifarious compulsions, ranging from the colonial necessity of official documentation to the cultural movements of caste-Hindu and untouchable communities; in the post-colonial period, of course, they were officially given the name 'Scheduled Castes'.

The fourth and last category is that of the generic identities that untouchables themselves adopted. These can be divided into two categories, each pertaining to a different period. One, emerging in the early decades of the twentieth century, was built around the 'Adi' ideology, which propagated the notion that untouchables were the original inhabitants of the land and, consequently, the rest of the populace could be regarded as outsiders or immigrants. This gave rise to a set of distinct regional and linguistic identities: the Adi Andhras and Adi Dravidas in the Telugu-speaking and Tamil-speaking regions respectively of Madras Presidency, the Adi Hindus in the dominions of the Nizam of Hyderabad and in the United Provinces, the Bhumiputras in what was to become Maharashtra, and so on across the country. The second generic identity was the 'Dalit' itself, which came into vogue in 1972 in Maharashtra with the formation of the Dalit Panthers. 'Dalit' literally means 'trampled'—squeezed, crushed, or broken, reduced to pieces[3]—and is, politically, a symbol of change and revolution. A new antinomianism in the early post-colonial era saw the birth of a radical ex-untouchable who believed in humanism and rejected the existence of God, rebirth, soul, and sacred books that wove discrimination into teachings about fate and heaven. Representing as it does the country's exploited populations,[4] 'Dalit' is a more secular identity than any other. Although originally used to denote a class rather than a caste identity, it is used today in political and academic debates and discourses to refer to all ex-untouchables.

The Historical Roots of 'Scheduled Castes'

It would be pertinent to briefly recapitulate the history of the nomenclature 'Scheduled Caste'. Untouchability, with all its manifold manifestations, is rooted in religious and cultural notions of purity and pollution which are believed to have developed in the later Vedic period (1,000–500 BC), when the Brahminical scriptural canon emerged in the form of the Smritis, Samhitas, and the Upanishads. The advent of British rule ushered in crucial transformations, although the orientation of the colonial government towards Dalits was not initially guided by clearly spelt-out policies or by a conscious political objective. The benefits that accrued to the Dalits can be understood as unintended positive effects of a policy that was not specifically formulated for the purpose of yielding those benefits.

The first definite and deliberate attempt to ascertain the size of the population of untouchables was made by the census commissioner in 1911, who instructed census superintendents of different provinces to separately enumerate castes and tribes that were classified as Hindus but did not conform to certain standards and were subject to certain disabilities. These enumerations were to enlist, according to official criteria, those who:

> (1) denied the supremacy of the Brahmins; (2) did not receive the *Mantra* from [a] Brahmin or other recognized Hindu Guru; (3) denied the authority of the Vedas; (4) did not worship the great Hindu Gods; (5) were not served by good Brahmins; (6) have no Brahman priests at all; (7) have no access to the interior of the ordinary Hindu temple; (8) cause pollution; (9) bury their dead; and (10) eat beef and do not revere the cow.[5]

The 'official criteria' as enlisted above left no room for speculation. In 1930, the Indian Statutory Commission defined these castes as partly functional—comprising those who followed occupations described as unclean or degrading, such as scavenging and leather work—and partly tribal, i.e., aboriginal tribes absorbed into the Hindu fold and transformed into castes that were imposed on them.[6] With regard to the issue of identity/nomenclature, Ambedkar pointed out that 'the existing nomenclature of Depressed Classes is objected [to] by the members of the Depressed Classes who have given thought to it and also by outsiders who take interest in them'.[7] Ambedkar argued that the usage of such nomenclature has 'degrading and contemptuous' connotations, and suggested that, instead, 'they should be called "non-caste Hindus", "protestant Hindus" or "non-conformist Hindus" or some such designation'.[8]

The term 'exterior castes' appeared for the first time in the 1931 census of India. This term for the Hindu castes hitherto known as 'depressed' was originally suggested by C. S. Mullan, the census superintendent for Assam, and was adopted in the census report of 1931 as the most satisfactory alternative to the label 'depressed classes'. It was criticised for being the same term as 'outcaste', only with five instead of two syllables, and it must be admitted that 'exterior' is but 'out' writ large. At the same time, it is here submitted that 'outcaste', with an 'e', does not carry the implications of the quite differently derived 'outcast', with no 'e'. The former, if correctly interpreted, seems to mean no more than 'one who is outside the caste system (and is therefore not admitted to Hindu society)'. But, in practice, the 'exterior castes' also included those who had been *cast out* from the Hindu social body for some breach of caste rules; 'outcaste' and 'outcast' were in some cases synonymous and the derogatory implications of the latter term unjustly coloured the former. This taint is not conveyed by its substitution with the word 'exterior', which may connote exclusion but not extrusion.[9]

The instructions of the Government of India for the conduct of the 1931 census concluded with a rejoinder that 'the Government of India also desires that attention be paid to the collection of information conducive to a better knowledge of the backward and depressed classes and of the problem involved in their present and future welfare'.[10] It was explained that the depressed castes were those with whom

> contact would prompt purification rites on the part of high caste Hindus. It was not intended that the term should have any reference to occupation as such. But it referred to those castes who, by virtue of their traditional position in Hindu society are denied access to temples or have to use separate wells or [are] not allowed to sit inside a school building and have to remain outside or suffer similar social disabilities. These disabilities vary in degree in different parts of India with south of India reporting more severe forms. At the same time, the castes which belong to this class are generally known and can in most parts of India be listed for a definite area, though perhaps the lists for India as a whole will not coincide.[11]

The question of the preparation of lists for each province was discussed at a meeting of the superintendents of census operations in January 1931 before the census took place. It was decided that each province should prepare a list of castes that suffered disabilities on account of their low social status and on account of being debarred from temples, schools, or wells. Neither was a specific definition of depressed castes framed nor was a precise instruction issued to the superintendents, because it was realised that conditions varied greatly from province to province and even from district to district within some provinces. Thus, it was thought unwise to tie down the superintendents of census operations with overly detailed instructions; the general procedure prescribed was one of local enquiry into which castes were regarded as depressed and why.

The 1931 census played a decisive role in Dalit history for several reasons. Enumerations of untouchables in census reports prior to 1931 suffered great limitations and were merely estimations. Each new estimate either suggested an increase in their strength or added to the existing mess of conflicting statements. For instance, the census commissioner in 1921 provided what he described as the minimum number of depressed classes in various provinces and estimated their total population to be 52,680,000. This figure, he stated, 'must be taken as [a] low estimate', since it did not include all those who should have been included, and he added that 'we may confidently place the numbers of these Depressed Classes, all of whom are considered impure, at something between 55 and 60 millions in India proper.'[12] Out of the 52.6 million for whom the census commissioner gave actual figures, less than 43.5 million were to be found in British India. This figure concurs with the figure of 42 million arrived at by the Franchise Committee of 1919, and is also not at great variance with the 1929 Nair Central Committee's approximate estimation of 44.5 million. However, it varies considerably from the Hartog Committee's figure of 30 million. Significantly, these estimations by governmental agencies were related to specific administrative purposes. For instance, the data compiled by the Seventh Quinquenniel Review was for a programme for the educational uplift of the depressed classes, while the data collected by the home department was for the partial implementation of a resolution on the general amelioration of Dalits moved in the Imperial Legislative Council. Thus, such estimations were indubitably approximate figures. The 1931 census, on the other hand, was meant to procure more definite figures than the estimations hitherto employed and, although it was difficult to arrive at an accurate number of Dalits, in the process of ascertaining the number of people who belonged to the depressed classes, a 'schedule' with certain criteria was prepared. This was an important development, as the category 'depressed classes', while in use prior to 1931, had neither been conceptualised nor clearly defined until then.

Criteria for 'Scheduled Castes'

The fundamental question in relation to the lists of Scheduled Castes and Scheduled Tribes arises with regard to the basis on which a community is listed so. The term 'Scheduled Castes' appeared officially for the first time in the Government of India Act of 1935, and, in April 1936, the British government issued the Government of India (Scheduled Castes) Order, listing certain castes, races, and tribes as Scheduled Castes in Assam, Bengal, Bihar, Bombay, the Central Provinces and Berar, Madras, Orissa, Punjab, and the United Provinces. The terms for inclusion in this schedule were those mentioned in the census report of 1931:

> (1) Whether the caste or class in question can be served by the barbers, water carriers, tailors, etc., who serve the caste-Hindus; (2) Whether the caste or class in question can be served by clean Brahmin or not; (3) Whether the caste in question pollutes a high caste Hindu by contact or by proximity; (4) Whether the caste or class in question is one from whose hands a caste Hindu can take water; (5) Whether the caste or class in question is debarred from using public conveniences, such as roads, ferries, wells or schools; (6) Whether the caste or class in question is debarred from the use of Hindu temples; (7) Whether in ordinary social inter-course a well educated member of the caste or class in question is treated as an equal by high caste; (8) Whether the caste or class in question is merely depressed on account of its own ignorance, illiteracy or poverty and but for that would be subject to no social disability and;(9) Whether it is depressed on account of the occupation followed and whether but for that occupation it would be subject to no social disability.[13]

It is clear from the above that those communities which were socially, educationally, and economically backward on account of the traditional practice of untouchability were grouped together and listed invariably as a homogeneous category. The sole criterion, in other words, was untouchability, and the investigation conducted by the census commissioners was unambiguous about this determining criterion, which was then used by the census operators to ascertain the exact number of Dalits. Though the exercise was complicated by the diversity and specific local characteristics of communities and the very modus operandi of obtaining such information, the use of disability or discrimination as the crucial indicator signalled a significant shift.

The absence of any single criterion for identifying untouchables provoked a variety of responses to the Franchise (Lothian)

Committee.[14] However, the majority of the committee, adhering to the basic criterion, i.e. denial of access to temples and causing pollution by touch or approach, reiterated its conviction that the depressed classes should include only such untouchables and not those Hindus who were economically poor and in other ways backward but not regarded as untouchables.[15] All those untouchable groups were listed or 'scheduled' in 1936 for the purposes of giving effect to the provisions for special electoral representations in the Government of India Act 1935. These 'scheduled' groups of communities were later designated 'Scheduled Castes', and this designation was adopted by independent India for legal and official purposes. It is stated in Article 341 of the Constitution, which governs the listing of Scheduled Castes, that

> (1) The President [may with respect to any State [or Union territory], and where it is a State, after consultation with the Governor thereof] by public notification,[16] specify the castes, races or tribes or parts of or group within castes, races or tribes which shall for the purposes of this Constitution be deemed to be Scheduled Castes in relation to that State [or Union territory, as the case may be].
> (2) Parliament may by law include in or exclude from the list of Scheduled Castes specified in a notification issued under clause (1) Any caste, race or tribe or part of or group within any caste, race or tribe, but save as aforesaid a notification issued under the said clause shall not be varied by any subsequent notification.[17]

Thus, it was under the provisions of Article 341 of the Constitution that the first list of Scheduled Castes for a state/UT was made by a notified order of the president. Any subsequent modifications in the list could be made only by an act of Parliament. While introducing Article 341 during a discussion in the Constituent Assembly on September 17, 1949, Ambedkar said:

> The objective of these two articles, as I stated, was to eliminate the necessity of burdening the Constitution with long lists of Scheduled Castes and Scheduled Tribes. It is now proposed that the President, in consultation with the Governor or Ruler of a

> State should have the power to issue a general notification in the Gazette specifying all the castes and tribes or groups thereof deemed to be Scheduled Castes and Scheduled Tribes for the purpose of the privileges which have been defined for them in the Constitution. The only limitation that has been imposed is this: that once a notification has been issued by the President, which, undoubtedly, ... will be issued in consultation with and on the advice of the Government of each State, thereafter, if any elimination was to be made from the List so notified or any addition was to be made, that must be made by Parliament and not by the President. The object is to eliminate any kind of political factors having a play in the matter of the disturbance in the Schedule so published by the President.[18]

As we will see, these observations continue to be of great relevance today.

Historical Context of Sub-Classification

Different communities clustered under the generic identity of 'Scheduled Castes' have had different experiences of socio-political and economic development. For instance, the Mahars in Maharashtra, Malas in Andhra, Pariahs in Tamil Nadu, and Chamars in Uttar Pradesh are relatively better-off than other competing communities within the Scheduled Castes. This gave rise to a tenuous relationship between various discrete communities, leading to disputes, allegations, and counter-allegations to such an extent over a period of time that even the leadership of Ambedkar, as a member of the leading community among the Dalits, came to be questioned.

The Mahars, numerically the largest among the Scheduled Castes of Maharashtra, commonly provided a variety of services for villages, some of which were considered highly polluting, like the flaying of carcasses. They were forced by their abject poverty to eat carrion, and it lowered their status considerably. The other major untouchable castes of Maharashtra were the Mangs (rope makers) and the Chambhars (leather workers), who were economically better-off than the Mahars, as the traditional occupations they pursued were essential to the livelihoods of agrarian caste Hindus. Perhaps because they were independent of caste Hindus, unlike Mahars, Chambhars felt that they were superior to Mahars in the caste hierarchy. Mangs and Chambhars often allege that Ambedkar focused his attention on his own caste fellows, i.e. the Mahars. They believe that Ambedkar's efforts led to Mahars getting a disproportionate share of benefits that should have been rightly dispersed among all Scheduled Caste groups, particularly in *watan inam* cases.[19, 20]

However, throughout his career, Ambedkar operated as a representative of Dalits as a whole rather than as a parochial agent or a Mahar leader. Although he hardly referred to his own community in his addresses, his arguments and formulations, influenced by his experience and background, were misconstrued in particular instances as showing excessive concern for Mahars. For instance, on March 20, 1927, at a conference organised by the Kolaba District Depressed Classes, he asked the members of his audience to improve their general demeanour with a specific Mahar-oriented injunction: '[T]ake a vow from this movement to renounce eating carrion.'[21] The misconception, due to such injunctions, that he was a Mahar leader was to have an adverse impact on Ambedkar's credibility.[22]

The intensified internal conflict among Dalits was reflected in the deliberations of the Round Table Conference (hereafter RTC). Politically, this conflict was articulated by the Congress, especially Gandhi, who refused to recognise Ambedkar as a spokesperson of the entire Dalit community while projecting himself in that role, as one possessing the moral authority and genuine claims to represent them. Gandhi rejected Ambedkar's claim that 'the Congress had not so far done anything tangible for the Depressed Classes'.[23] At the RTC, Ambedkar repudiated the Congress claim to speak on behalf of the depressed classes and insisted on separate electorates and special representation, as were enjoyed by other minorities.[24] At this juncture, Gandhi and the Congress encouraged rebel untouchable sub-castes to find among themselves alternative leaders who could speak on behalf of the Congress. At a meeting of the depressed classes of the Bombay suburbs, held in Lower Parel, a resolution was passed 'expressing full confidence in Mahatma Gandhi and repudiating Dr. Ambedkar's claim to represent all the "Depressed" Classes',[25] and similar instances surfaced in Punjab,[26] Banaras,[27] and other places where certain communities expressed confidence in Gandhi instead of Ambedkar. However, the delegates of the depressed classes at the RTC in London stated that they had received fifty-four telegrams from members of the depressed classes from different parts of India—including Ahmedabad in Gandhi's home state of Gujarat—protesting against Gandhi's claim to represent the depressed classes, and expressing confidence in Ambedkar and Srinivasan, besides demanding special representation through provisions for separate electorates.[28] But, by then, considerable internal tension had been created by the political manoeuvring of Gandhi and the Congress, which had the advantage of material resources and institutional tactics. In the years after the RTC, Gandhi's sudden love for untouchables manifested in the form of 'Harijan Tours' and Harijan Sevak Sanghs, through which he pushed his accommodative politics and selectively appropriated untouchable activists and leaders from across the country. These developments did not go unnoticed. Ambedkar was suspicious and concerned about such manoeuvres and noted 'the policy of the Congress and the Hindu Mahasabha of creating leaders for the Depressed Class for their own purposes and by their own propaganda and then trying to foist them on the Depressed Classes'.[29]

Gandhi's reformist endeavours and politics of 'inclusion' culminated in a 'Harijan movement' that became a major national campaign between 1932 and 1936.[30] One of the major fallouts of this movement was the encouragement of 'nationalist' anti-Ambedkarite Dalit organisations,[31] most notably the All-India Depressed Classes League, founded in 1935 in Kanpur, and the Bihar Khet Mazdoor Sabha, founded in 1937, both of which were under the leadership of Jagjivan Ram. The Harijan Sevak Sanghs evolved out of a hastily called meeting of caste Hindu representatives in Bombay on September 25, 1932, presided over by Madan Mohan Malaviya, calling on caste Hindus to 'secure by legitimate and peaceful means an early removal of the social disabilities of untouchability, including temple entry'.[32] On September 30, a public meeting resolved to set up an 'All India Untouchability League' seeking to get public wells, roads, schools, and crematoriums opened up for untouchables. The league was set up in Delhi on October 26, 1932, and Gandhi later on changed its name to 'Harijan Sevak Sangh'. But Ambedkar opposed the league/sangh on two counts: first, he insisted that the goal of any organisation working on the problems of the Dalits had to be not simply the 'removal of untouchability' but the eradication of the caste system itself; and second, he insisted that the leadership be in the hands of untouchables. These demands were, as usual, unacceptable to Gandhi because the primary purpose of the Sangh as envisioned by him was not to be an organisation for Dalit emancipation but a body for the reform of Hinduism.[33]

The differences between Ambedkar and Gandhi that first appeared at the RTC crystallised in the post-Poona Pact years, with the Congress moving ahead with its plans to create an alternate leadership for Dalits, and anti-Ambedkarite organisations through 'Harijan' programmes. By doing so, the Congress successfully fostered sharp differences amongst the different untouchable communities, differences that widened in the following years. Ambedkar on many occasions pleaded for unity among Dalits and made conscious efforts to demonstrate that he was not discriminating against any group. While addressing a meeting at R. M. Bhat High School in Parel, Bombay, Ambedkar said, 'It was regrettable that there should be difference of opinion among the different sections of the depressed classes.'[34] He said the work he did was 'not meant for a particular section but for the benefit of the whole community'.[35] Perhaps the Congress and Gandhi were alarmed; they saw a potential threat in Ambedkar, who clearly stated that 'the goal of the Depressed Classes is sharing of the power of the Government of the country'.[36] Ambedkar warned his community that the great obstacles in their path were Gandhi and the Hindus, who accepted the demand of the Muslims for their due share in government but not a similar demand made by the depressed classes.[37] Ambedkar believed and made it clear to the British government that a real 'national government' would have to be one constituted of Hindus, Muslims, and other communities, including the depressed classes, emphasising that 'the Depressed Classes did not lag behind any other community in their love for India's freedom but they wanted the independence of their community along with the independence of the country'.[38]

On his way to the Matang Conference, Ambedkar said in a speech at Sholapur in Karkam district on December 31, 1937:

> First, it is a misfortune for all of us that there is no unity among the various castes, such as Mahar, Chambhar, Bhangi, etc., prevailing among the untouchables. The real reason for absence of this unity is the existence of caste distinction (*jati-bhed*) in the Hindu society. Mahars, Mangs, Chambhars or Bhangis are not responsible for this caste discrimination. Caste discrimination is the gutter of dirty water (*gatar ganga*) flowing to us from above. This is the hell (*narak*) flowing towards us. ... The painful part of it is that Hindus not only do not remove caste discrimination among themselves, but on the contrary, strive to strengthen the differences among the untouchables, taking undue advantage of their ignorance. They support Mangs and raise them against Mahars; they support Chambhars and raise them against Mahars and Mangs. They spread their policy of discrimination among us and thus prevent our unity. Though the original responsibility for caste distinctions is on Hindu society, for us to forget our responsibility would be suicidal. It is our foremost duty to remove the caste distinctions among ourselves and prevent the entry of any policy of discrimination among us. Unless we achieve this, we will never prosper. We must completely abolish the ban on inter-dining and inter marriage among the Mahars and Mangs. If every caste sticks to its own caste for its pride, if Mahars remain Mahar and Mangs remain Mang, we will not be able to fight the injustice against us. What is so great about the names Mahar and Mang that you should feel proud of it? What bright history comes in front of your eyes by uttering these names that you should strive for preserving old traditions? The entire society considers these names contemptible. Today, you do not have the value even of garbage. So you must not take pride in these names. You should

> understand that both our societies are getting crushed under one common grinding stone and work unitedly. Mahars are not willing to follow any caste distinction. They are ready to inter-dine and inter-marry with Mangs, Chambhars, or Bhangis. And if they are hesitant, I undertake that I will compel them.[39]

Despite Ambedkar's efforts, the splintering initiated by the Congress and Gandhi was successful: in the first Lok Sabha elections held under the auspices of the Constitution of the Republic of India, the Congress candidate N. S. Kajrolkar, a Chambhar by caste, defeated Ambedkar.[40]

Gandhi went on establishing Harijan Sevak Sanghs across the country during his 'Harijan' tour in the 1930s. Karnataka was at the forefront of the Harijan movement, with branches of the Sangh being set up in Bijapur, Belgaum, Karwar, Mangalore, Coorg, Bellary, and its headquarters in Hubli.[41] By conducting Harijan *bhajan* meetings, promoting temperance and sanitation, and organising medical relief camps through the Sangh, the Congress accommodated all the workers of the depressed classes and moulded them in its Hinduistic mode of reform while also preparing them to oppose Ambedkar.

In Jagjivan Ram's own state of Bihar, the post-Emergency socialist movement initially weaned away non-Chamar castes like Dushad and Paswan and threw up non-Chamar leaders like Ramvilas Paswan. Jagjivan Ram himself became a part of the anti-Congress Janata Party and shifted Chamars to that fold. The Chamars of Bihar have since either remained with the Janata Party and its later variants like Lalu Prasad's Rashtriya Janata Dal or shifted to the Bahujan Samaj Party of Kanshi Ram.

Indeed, it is striking to note how the effects of seeds of division planted during the nationalist movement persisted even in the post-colonial era. It was in the 1930s that first-generation educated Dalit leaders were accommodated into the Congress Party; Arigay Ramaswamy and B. S. Venkata Rao were the first,[42] and Naralasetti Devendrudu and Vemula Kurmayya were made joint secretaries of the Harijan Sevak Sangh. In fact, these leaders were earlier active and played a major role in the Adi Andhra movement of the 1920s.[43] Mala leaders were the first beneficiaries of the accommodative politics of the Congress Party. But the post-colonial Madiga sub-caste leadership sought political space and tried to exploit Congress antipathy towards Ambedkar and his Scheduled Castes Federation (SCF), which had a significant presence in Andhra Pradesh until the late 1960s. For this purpose, they equated themselves with the Chamars of north India and claimed to share the same sub-caste lineage as Jagjivan Ram. The Madigas' desire for political space led them to discard Ambedkar as their leader. The Madiga Reservation Movement that took shape in the 1990s continued in the same vein and promptly elevated Jagjivan Ram to the position of Ambedkar's equal for the purpose of their agitation. To reinforce their claims, they started erecting statues of Jagjivan Ram and demanded a public holiday on his birthday. Meira Kumar, daughter of Jagjivan Ram and a Congress leader, added fuel to such claims and encouraged Madiga Congress leaders during her tenure as Congress general secretary in charge of Andhra Pradesh affairs during 1990–1992. Later, in her role as Union Minister for Social Justice and Empowerment (2004–2009), she encouraged and worked to secure separate Madiga reservations in Andhra Pradesh, probably for the same parochial reasons—Madigas were the only Scheduled Caste to elevate Jagjivan Ram to the level of Ambedkar. Meanwhile, the people of Meira Kumar's own caste—Chamars—discarded Jagjivan Ram in north India.[44]

However, Dalits have been divided not only along sub-caste lines but also along party lines. In the post-colonial period, primarily three types of divisions have been perceptible: the accommodation of Dalit leaders in major political parties, the encouragement of Dalit associations as the sister organisations of those political parties, and the splitting and conversion of Dalit organisations into cadre organisations. These complex machinations can be seen at work in contemporary Andhra society. For example, Jupudi Prabhakara Rao, president of the Mala Mahanadu, was an ally of the then Chief Minister Dr Y. S. Rajasekhara Reddy of the Congress, while Karem Shivaji, who also staked claims to the state presidency of the Mala Mahanadu, was with Reddy's rival G. V. Harsha Kumar, also of the Congress and a sitting Member of Parliament.[45]

What is perhaps most striking about the differences in the development trajectories of different Dalit communities across the country is that only the communities that were influenced by the Ambedkarite movement have shown substantial progress. Common to Mahars in Maharashtra, Malas in Andhra, Chamars in north India, Adi Dravidas or Pariahs in Tamil Nadu, and Dushads and Paswans in Bihar is the fact that they all adopted the Ambedkarite ideology. Incidentally, the anti-Ambedkarite groups of communities that picked alternative leadership have remained relatively backward.

The Context of Sub-Classification

The issue of reservations has always been controversial for the upper castes. Since the adoption of the Constitution, there have been a plethora of judgments both in favour of and against reservations, starting with the Champakam Dorairajan case in 1951, which led to the first ever amendment to the Constitution and the insertion of Article 15(4). But all these interventions have been driven by the non-reserved categories. Now, to add to the complications, the issue of sub-classifications within reservations has also caught the imagination of the ruling classes.

To be clear, the implementation of reservations for Scheduled Castes (SC) in educational, governmental, and democratic institutions was never seriously challenged. However, a shift in the discourse around reservations became discernible in Punjab in the 1960s and 1970s. Reservations had until then been based on a 'first come first served' merit policy, with no preference being shown to any particular listed castes on any grounds. During the 1960s in Punjab, Dalits across political lines, representing a demographic that comprised more than 30 per cent of the state's total population, started asserting themselves and staging walkouts in unison, protesting against atrocities and demanding a separate budget for Dalit uplift. The Congress government under the leadership of Zail Singh, the chief minister, responded by sub-dividing the SC list in 1975, sowing the seeds of divisive politics. The assertive

30-per-cent-strong Dalits were split into the Ad-Dharmi-Ravidasi and Mazhabi-Balmiki groups, and inter-group animosities pushed them into virtual political insignificance, with no decisive say in Punjab politics. The decision was processed without any deliberations or transparent procedures; the state government simply planned it and issued a notification.[46]

Haryana, partly carved out of Punjab, also adopted this policy in response to the rise and spread of the Bahujan Samaj Party (BSP) in Uttar Pradesh and adjacent regions. Under the leadership of Bhajan Lal, the Haryana Congress government in 1994 revised the state's SC list and introduced internal divisions;[47] the 20-per-cent-strong Dalit population that was reclassified has not had a significant voice in Haryana politics since, because oppositional groups led by dominant Chamar and Balmiki castes were at loggerheads over the distribution of benefits.

What becomes clear, in view of the above examples, is that the Congress certainly adopted the colonial policy of divide and rule. More than any ideological basis or concern for the genuine welfare of Dalits, the modus operandi of the state governments indubitably point to a more vulgar political praxis that arose out of anxiety about the potential dangers of Dalit unity. Larger political considerations were outweighed by short-term political games that were played routinely and unabashedly, as illustrated by the absence of any transparent process of deliberations and consultations in redesigning constitutional provisions to the detriment of Dalit interests. For about three decades after the decision to divide Dalits had first been operationalised, this issue—the political growth and implications of these divisions—was conspicuously evaded by social scientists and academia.[48] Ironically, a sizeable population of literate Dalits in Punjab and Haryana are also unaware of the implications of the government's policy of classification and division.

It is in this context that the case of Andhra Pradesh is not only important but quite interesting in several ways. The Karamchedu massacre[49] of 1985 led to the organisation of Dalits into a movement led by the Dalit Mahasabha,[50] which was further strengthened after the Tsundur incident of 1991.[51] What is worth noting here is that the Dalit Mahasabha leadership was drawn from a class of organic intellectuals who were not associated with any established political camp and could be considered the most progressive of the Dalit vanguards in the period after the Maharashtra awakening in the post-colonial era.[52] It created a ground-level leadership faction that was all set to move into the political arena. In 1994, after the BSP victory in the UP elections the previous year, a victory rally was organised in Hyderabad. This victory rally of BSP supporters in Andhra Pradesh forced the ruling TDP leader N. T. Rama Rao to shake hands with Kanshi Ram, leading to Dalit intellectuals envisioning the possibility of an alliance between them in Andhra Pradesh, which could have changed the face of national politics. This possibility, however, dissipated.[53] Like most caste-based coalitions that have failed to crystallise in the nation's electoral history, the coalition of the Dalits of Andhra Pradesh under Kanshi Ram's BSP and N. T. Rama Rao's TDP did not fructify despite NTR's offer to share 40 out of 294 seats in the 1994 assembly elections. This pre-poll arrangement, brokered by Devendra Goud[54] and a Dalit journalist,[55] was frittered away by Kanshi Ram to focus only on Uttar Pradesh, leaving Andhra Pradesh in a huff. And yet, this abortive attempt at a coalition led to the next phase of Dalit politics, for the June 5 victory rally or '*pradarshana*' of BSP supporters in Hyderabad, which witnessed lakhs of Dalits coming together under one 'united' front, shocked the governments and political parties of the time and forced them to pilot another political experiment in division. Dramatically, on July 27, 1994 at, in Edumudu village, Prakasam district, incidentally the same district where a Dalit massacre gave birth to the Dalit Mahasabha, a new organisation known as the Madiga Reservation Porata Samiti (MRPS) emerged.

One of the causes to which the formation of the organisation has been attributed is the seething discontentment among Madigas over their relatively backward status. They complained that Malas were gaining benefits from reservation that were disproportionate to their population. To counter this trend, Madigas initiated a movement popularly known as 'Madiga Dandora'[56] and proclaimed a distinct identity, separate from the rest of the Dalit community. They added prefixes to their activities and programmes: 'Madiga Dandora Rally', 'Madiga Dandora Meeting', etc. Consequently, the MRPS leadership explicitly formulated a political agenda around the demand for a reasonable share in the SC quota and vociferously argued for it at meetings, rallies, and *padayatras* (walking tours).[57] Through vigorous efforts, popular mobilisation, and the staunch support of the ruling TDP, they brought considerable pressure to bear on the government and finally won an announcement by the chief minister in the state assembly of the appointment of a commission to look into the matter.[58]

Particularly intriguing here is the manner in which the chief minister of Andhra Pradesh appointed a commission, issued directions to it, and laid down guidelines regarding what was to follow. In other words, it was not a regular case of a commission deciding to classify Dalits into certain categories after an enquiry and investigation into the issue. On the contrary, this commission simply facilitated the political designs or directions of the state government. It is worth mentioning in this connection the statements of the chief minister on the floor of the assembly on September 2, 1996: 'there have been persistent demands from a certain section of persons belonging to Scheduled Castes ..., [as] disproportionately large number of benefits have gone to a particular sub-caste ... for categorisation of the sub-castes among Scheduled Castes into A, B, C, and D.'[59] Following this statement, a one-man commission of enquiry was constituted, headed by Justice P. Ramachandra Raju, to ascertain whether a disproportionate number of benefits had gone to any group among the SCs of the state and, if so, to recommend the steps required to ensure an equitable distribution. The commission, in its May 1997 report, declared that there was indeed a disproportionate distribution of reservation benefits in as much as the Malas and Adi Andhras were over-represented both in public employment and in educational institutions. The commission also recommended that the SC communities of the state be categorised into four groups, A, B, C, and D, leaving little doubt that it had simply followed the instructions of the chief minister.

The appointment of the commission—the entire process, from the chief minister making an announcement, through the rounds of consultation, to the stage of formal appointment—was completed in record time: a mere eight days. On the other hand, the commission itself took eight months to submit its report to the government.[60] Surprisingly, the cabinet sub-committee appointed on June 2, 1997 to go over the report green-lit the commission's recommendations that same day. Consequently, a government order (GO) to implement the recommendations was ready in five days.

Then came a twist: in September 1997, responding to several writ petitions challenging the sub-categorisation, a full bench of the state high court quashed the GO as ultra vires because the National Commission for Scheduled Castes (NCSC) was not consulted in the matter by the state government.[61] The Andhra Pradesh government filed an appeal before the Supreme Court on October 13 and simultaneously approached the NCSC to solicit its concurrence. In accordance with the NCSC's advice, the government withdrew the petition before the Supreme Court on January 4, 1998.

The NCSC observed that the findings of the Raju Commission were based on limited and inadequate data and no scientific method had been adopted to arrive at a holistic picture of the varying levels of development among different SC communities. It averred that any orders based on such findings and recommendations could not be treated as rational. However, in spite of these observations, the Government of Andhra Pradesh accepted the Raju Commission's recommendations and promulgated an ordinance in June 1997, sub-classifying all the fifty-nine SC communities in the state into the aforementioned four groups—A, B, C, and D—based on relative backwardness and fixing separate reservation quotas in state services and seats in state educational institutions for each of the four groups. Consequently, this ordinance was challenged in the Andhra Pradesh High Court.

In the meanwhile, i.e., during the pendency of the challenge, the state government replaced the ordinance in May 2000 with the Andhra Pradesh Scheduled Castes (Rationalisation of Reservation) Act, 2000, also known as the A.P. Act of 2000.[62] The validity of this act, though challenged, was upheld by the high court in its judgment in November 2000, after which an appeal against this order was filed in the Supreme Court (E. V. Chinnaiah vs. State of Andhra Pradesh and Others). A five-judge bench of the Supreme Court struck down the act by a unanimous judgment on November 5, 2004,[63] mainly on the grounds that the sub-categorisation of Scheduled Castes is not provided for in Article 341(1). The apex court also said that it was beyond the power of the state to sub-classify a class—SCs—already recognised by the Constitution to be 'homogeneous' on grounds of subjection to untouchability and to allot portions of the already reserved quota to sub-classes created by the state from within the list of SCs. For the 're-grouping of Scheduled Castes', stated the court, the state cannot rely upon Articles 15(4) and 16(4) or on entry 41 of List II or entry 25 of List III of the Seventh Schedule. The act was, therefore, beyond the legislative competence of the state and also violative of Article 14 of the Constitution, according to the court, and all three states—Punjab, Haryana, and Andhra Pradesh—withdrew their respective orders.[64]

After the Supreme Court judgement, the Andhra Pradesh legislative assembly unanimously resolved on December 10, 2004 to 'recommend to the Government of India' that the matter of the 'categorization of Scheduled Castes as recommended by Justice Ramachandra Raju Commission' be taken up in Parliament.[65] On March 28, 2005, the Ministry of Social Justice and Empowerment, examining the matter, sought the views of the Ministry of Law and Justice, which obtained the opinion of the Attorney General for India (AGI). The AGI felt that the case was similar to one concerning the insertion of Article 16(4A) into the Constitution through the 77th Amendment Act, 1995, consequent to the decision in the Indra Sawhney case that reservation in promotions would violate Article 14 of the Constitution. In the light of this opinion, the Ministry of Social Justice and Empowerment prepared a note for the Cabinet Committee on Political Affairs (CCPA), dated January 16, 2006, seeking consideration of and a decision on further action from among the following options:

1. the aforesaid judgment of the Supreme Court be deemed the final legal position and no further steps be initiated towards neutralising its effect;
2. in view of the unanimous resolution passed by the Andhra Pradesh assembly, a suitable law be enacted by the Government of Andhra Pradesh and a proposal be made to the Central government for placing the act in the Ninth Schedule of the Constitution; and
3. in view of the opinion of the AGI, the Government of Andhra Pradesh be advised to commission research studies—to indicate the necessity for such sub-classification and to generate unimpeachable evidence that some groups among the SCs have received disproportionately large benefits—and to recommend further action on the basis of the studies.[66]

On March 9, 2006, the CCPA submitted the decision that it would be best for a retired judge of the Supreme Court to be appointed to examine all aspects of the matter. Accordingly, the Ministry of Social Justice and Empowerment prepared a note for the Union cabinet dated August 28, 2006, seeking approval to set up a 'National Commission to examine the issue of Sub-Categorization of Scheduled Castes'. The commission's proposed terms of reference included the examination of the constitutional, statutory, and legal ramifications of the demand for sub-classification of SCs in other states/Union Territories. The Union cabinet, in a meeting on September 7, 2006, approved a modified version of the proposal in which the directive to examine said issues in the contexts of other states/Union Territories was deleted, and a resolution for constituting such a commission was notified on November 15, 2006.

The NCSC met the president of India and demanded that, if the centre were considering the constitution of a commission, then a retired Supreme Court judge belonging to a Scheduled Caste be appointed to head it. When the president sought the opinion of the Ministry of Social Justice and Empowerment in this matter, the ministry informed the president that it had asked the Department of Justice to provide the names of judges who had demitted office in the past two years. The justice department furnished a list of eight retired judges and also conveyed to the ministry that it did not keep a caste-wise list of judges. While opposing the demand of the NCSC for the appointment of a Scheduled Caste judge, the Haryana Scheduled Castes (Block A) Forum said that only a non-Scheduled Caste retired judge of the Supreme Court could be entrusted with the responsibility of looking into the entire ambit of the reservation policy.[67]

However, as the process of appointing the chairperson of the commission showed no progress, the ministry, in a note to the Union cabinet dated May 16, 2007, sought an expansion in the scope of its November 15, 2006 resolution, so as to make eligible for the role a retired chief justice of India, chief justice of a high court, a retired judge of the Supreme Court or a high court, or any other person of eminence with an understanding of the subject. On November 16, 2006, the Government of India constituted the new commission through a gazette notification, following which the Union cabinet, in a meeting held on May 17, 2007, approved the proposal, and, on May 19, 2007, a retired judge of Delhi High Court, Usha Mehra, was appointed as chairperson of the commission—reportedly after two former Supreme Court chief justices and one former Supreme Court judge declined the position—for one year from the date of taking charge.[68] The commission, technically known as the 'National Commission to examine the issue of Sub-Categorization of Scheduled Castes in Andhra Pradesh' (NCSCSC), had its first meeting with Meira Kumar, minister of social justice and empowerment, on May 21, 2007. In attendance were the secretary, additional secretary, and officers of the Ministry of Social Justice and Empowerment. It was decided at this meeting that the mandate of the commission was:

1. to examine the various facets of the demand for sub-categorisation of SCs in Andhra Pradesh;
2. to examine the constitutional, statutory, and legal ramifications of the demand; and

3. to make recommendations regarding the future course of action, clearly specifying the grounds and the criteria on which these recommendations were based.

The commission submitted its report on May 1, 2008, just twenty days before the end of its tenure.[69] As per its recommendations, a proposal for the amendment of Article 341 of the Constitution and the addition of clause 3 thereto was suggested:

> Parliament may by law provide for sub-categorization or de-sub-categorization of caste, race or tribe or part of or group within any caste, race or tribe specified in a notification issued under clause (1) or by law made by Parliament under clause (2), upon receiving a resolution from legislature of a State/U.T. passed unanimously.[70]

The NCSCSC proposed, in other words, that the Constitution be amended on the basis of recommendations made by the legislatures of the affected states by way of a unanimous resolution regarding the exact percentage of reservation in state services and educational institutions to be allocated to various SCs. Further, it was suggested the amendment mention that the state legislatures were to make such recommendations on the basis of the data collected by them through a judicial commission headed by at least a sitting or retired high court judge.

It is to be noted that the report of the commission was incomplete as it did not address the second term of reference: the constitutional, statutory, and legal ramifications of the demand for the sub-classification of SCs. In fact, the report seems to be merely an extension of the Ramachandra Raju Commission report, aside from a few procedural tactics on the part of the former, e.g. its visits to eleven districts and the commissioning of a study—'Evaluation study on the extent of benefits accrued to all the Scheduled Castes Communities included in the Constitution (Scheduled Castes) Order 1950 in Andhra Pradesh'—by the Indian Institute of Economics, Hyderabad. As mentioned above, the Usha Mehra Commission largely provided a foundation for the recommendations that had already been made, despite the rejection of those recommendations by the Supreme Court. While the technique deployed to arrive at a rational basis was limited even in idea, with only eleven districts covered, in reality it was even less impressive, with Dalit habitations only having been visited in only in three districts.[71]

Similarly, the Indian Institute of Economics, to which the commission entrusted a study, focused on thirty-six communities, excluding twenty-four from its purview. The commission report was, thus, also limited, despite its professed commitment to the provision of a holistic picture. The overall profile of SCs in the second chapter of the report is uncritically based on data that is three decades old, and the profiles of individual communities are silent about several crucial indicators like literacy rate, educational attainments, and work participation rates, in the absence of which any comparison among the communities is flawed. The fundamental issue, however, remained: how could a retired high court judge examine a decision arrived at by a Constitution bench of the Supreme Court, which declared SCs to be a homogeneous class, especially given that the Constitution does not provide for the sub-classification of SCs, the NCSC had rejected the proposal on two occasions, and sub-classification was likely to create administrative problems?

Similarly, there was a deviation between what the NCSCSC intended to recommend and what it actually recommended. The scope of the commission was to look into the issue of disproportion in the accrual of the benefits of reservation to Dalit communities in state services and educational institutions, if any, but the proposed recommendation encompassed the entire reservation policy, i.e., reservations in services, educational institutions, and in bodies like panchayati raj institutions.

The NCSCSC, in its report, declared SCs to be a heterogeneous group, which was legally untenable, as the Supreme Court had[72] officially taken the position that the SCs were not an amalgam of castes but 'a class apart[,] having the common features of socio, economic and educational backwardness arising out of the traditional practice of untouchability'.[73] Further reservation in services was to be given to those communities which were not adequately represented in the services of the state, but the NCSCSC had not indicated anywhere in its report that any of the communities listed as SCs in Andhra Pradesh had become 'forward' on account of their adequate representation in the services of the state and were no longer socially, educationally, and economically 'backward'. If all the communities notified as SCs in Andhra Pradesh remained inadequately represented in the services and socially, economically, and educationally backward, no rationale existed for restricting by sub-classification any of the listed communities' claims to reservation. The Usha Mehra Commission did not clarify or respond to the Supreme Court's objection to the sub-classification of SCs on the grounds that it was in violation of Articles 14, 15, and 16 of the Constitution and that it was impermissible under the doctrine of reasonable classification. Rather, the commission depended on defence counsel arguments and on the 'Report of the Advisory Committee[74] on the revision of the list of Scheduled Castes and Scheduled Tribes, 1965', not realising that the recommendations and findings of this advisory committee (popularly known as the Lokur Committee) were superficial and thus not worthy of practical use. One of the incredible aspects of the Mehra Commission's flawed methodology was its incorporation of irrelevant data from various sources. For example, a list of studies sponsored by the Ministry of Social Justice and Empowerment in Andhra Pradesh during the years 2001–2004 was attached to the sixth chapter of the report, but this list was in no way connected to the issue under consideration. One can discern several such superfluous additions, like Ambedkar's views on the caste system and on the insertion of word 'backward' in Article 16(4) and extracts from Supreme Court decisions in a number of arbitrary cases.

The NCSCSC, in support of its recommendations, argued that SCs, STs, and Other Backward Classes (OBCs) had all been placed together under Article 16(4) and that, in the Mandal case, the Supreme Court had held that the OBC communities could be sub-classified. It is indeed a fact that, for the purpose of reservations in services, SCs, STs, and OBCs have been clubbed together under the term 'Backward Classes', but it is also a fact that they are three distinct groups having no affinities. The criteria for inclusion in each group are different, and, therefore, what is applicable in the case of OBCs does not hold good for the other categories.[75] Further, this exact argument was adduced by the state of Andhra Pradesh in E. V. Chinnaiah's case and rejected by the Supreme Court.

The report of the NCSCSC was referred to the NCSC on May 23, 2008. The NCSC, under the chairmanship of Sardar Buta Singh, stated in a letter dated December 4, 2008 to the Ministry of Social Justice and Empowerment, that

> ... Article 16(4) of the Constitution of India is an enabling provision which enables the State to provide for making of the reservation in appointments and if the State does so, it also decides its proportion. The State Government of Andhra Pradesh may adopt provisions of afore-said Article of the Constitution. The Government of Andhra Pradesh is advised that most educationally and socially backward castes of Andhra Pradesh listed under the Presidential Orders ... may be given proportionate share in the reservation in the State of Andhra Pradesh only.[76]

This opinion, reached on the basis of a faulty report, remains legally questionable, because Article 16(4), which provides for adequate representation in services and posts under the state for SCs and STs not adequately represented in the opinion of the state, is a fundamental right; as adjudicated in the E. V. Chinnaiah case, any sub-classification of the list is a violation of Article 16, while any similar erroneous suggestion with regard to the education sector would necessitate an amendment to Article 15(4) and (5).

Though the NCSC did not explicitly specify its position on the matter, it would appear from its opinion that it did not support the recommendation of the NCSCSC to amend Article 341 of the Constitution, which identifies the procedure for adding or deleting castes and is not amenable to provisions relating to sub-classification. It was precisely on the grounds that Parliament cannot abdicate to states the power to tamper, based on political considerations, with SC lists that Ambedkar argued for Article 341 as a special case. The opinion of the NCSC would have adverse and irrevocable implications on the constitutional provisions in Article 15(4) and (5), Article 16(4), and Article 341, which would not survive the scrutiny of the Supreme Court. The question for consideration here is whether the suggestions made by this commission for the reorganisation, redistribution, or apportionment of benefits amongst various SCs would in fact be tantamount to contempt of court.

Commissions for Sub-Classification in Other States

Punjab

The executive order of the Government of Punjab initiating the policy of sub-classification of Scheduled Castes in 1975 mentions that the

> government has decided that henceforth, fifty percent of vacancies of the quota reserved for Scheduled castes would be offered to Balmikis and Mazhabi Sikhs, if available, as first preference from amongst the Scheduled Caste candidates, in direct recruitment only and not in promotion cases. It has also been decided that promotion cases already decided in the light of aforesaid instructions are not to be opened.[77]

Haryana

It was in 1994 that the Government of Haryana followed suit,[78] revising the state's reservation policy in cases of direct recruitment to government services as follows:

> For the purpose of reservation in services, the scheduled castes in Haryana will be put in two categories i.e. Block 'A' and Block 'B'. Block 'B' will consist of Chamars, Jatia Chamars, Rahgars, Ramdasias or Ravidasias. Block 'A' will consist of the remaining 36 scheduled castes including Balmiki, Dhanak, Nat etc.
>
> Within the quota reserved for scheduled castes in direct recruitment to Govt. jobs 50% vacancies will be offered to

candidates from Block 'A'. In case suitable candidates from Block 'A' are not available, candidate from Block 'B' may be recruited against these vacancies.

Similarly, candidates from Block 'B' will be given preference in respect of the remaining 50% vacancies. In case suitable candidates from Block 'B' are not available, candidates from Block 'A' may be recruited against these vacancies.

The inter seniority of the candidates from Block 'A' and Block 'B' will be as per the common merit list prepared by the recruiting agency. It will not be necessary to fix the roster points separately for each of the Blocks within the present roster system.

If on a particular occasion the total number of vacancies meant for Scheduled castes is odd, say 9, five of them will go to Block 'A' and 4 to Block 'B'. On the next such occasion, however, the position would …, that is 4 of them will go to Block 'A' and 5 to Block 'B'.[79]

Uttar Pradesh

In 2001, Uttar Pradesh Chief Minister Rajnath Singh of the BJP initiated a process of sub-classification in the state as a tactic to influence his party's political fortunes and to settle scores with his political rivals—Mulayam Singh Yadav of Samajwadi Party (SP) and Mayawati of Bahujan Samaj Party (BSP)—and their vote banks. On June 28, he announced his intention to give effect to a 'quota within quota' policy for SCs and the most backward castes among OBCs. To formulate this as a provision, he constituted a Social Justice Committee headed by Hukum Singh[80] and co-chaired by Ramapati Shastri.[81]

The terms of reference of the committee included an overview of the programmes, facilities, and systems available for the benefit of the SCs, STs and OBCs, suggestions for changes to their quotas according to changes in the state's population after the creation of the separate province of what was then Uttaranchal, a look at the status of recruitments against the quotas available for these categories, an estimation of the representation of different castes under the existing reservation policy, and suggestions to improve the lot of these categories, especially those that had been deprived of benefits.[82] Entrusted with the task of carrying out a caste-based census in the state to decide the quantum of reservation for the most backward sections among SCs and OBCs, the commission, constituted on June 28, 2001, completed its work in a record period of two months and submitted its report on August 31, 2001.

It proposed the classification of Dalits into two schedules—Schedule A, comprising Chamars, Jatavs, and Dhusias, and Schedule B, comprising the sixty-five other castes in the SC category—and the division of the existing quota of 21 per cent between the two schedules, such that 10 per cent be reserved for the castes in Schedule A and 11 per cent for those in Schedule B. The castes in Schedule A constituted the traditional support base of the BSP. It was alleged that, although they constitute only about 50 per cent of the Dalit population in the state, they unfairly enjoyed almost 80 per cent of the benefits of reservation owing to their relatively well-off status and the patronage of leaders such as Mayawati. Since these communities had in general never voted for the BJP, the party was not likely to be affected by their resentment against the committee's report.[83]

It was further observed that the major share of the benefits of reservations for SCs in the state had gone to Jatavs, Chamars, and Pasis, while castes like the Valmikis, the Dhobis, and the Khatiks had not benefited. Both Pasis and Jatavs were noted to be politically more influential and monetarily more prosperous than the other castes. Besides, owing again to the political patronage of leaders like Mayawati, a Jatav, and Ram Vilas Paswan, a Pasi, these castes had emerged more assertive than the rest.

Rajnath Singh made no secret of his expectation of political benefits from the report and the redesigned reservation policy. He unabashedly claimed, 'I would not be surprised if we crossed the 200-mark [in the next state assembly elections].'[84] In raking up the issue of 'quota within quota', Singh not only relied on the reports of earlier commissions and committees but also drew parallels to classification models followed in Andhra Pradesh, Karnataka, and Bihar.

Karnataka

Following in the footsteps of Uttar Pradesh, the Government of Karnataka appointed a judicial inquiry committee under the chairmanship of Justice Sadashiva to study the imbalances in the utilisation of reservation facilities by different SCs and STs.[85] Its broad parameters were specified by Justice Sadashiva, and no new communities were to be included in the SC list. The government set a deadline of September 27, 2007 for the commission's report, and, although it is known that the commission held sittings and recorded the pleas of different communities in seventeen of the state's twenty-seven districts and was scheduled to complete public hearings in the remaining ten districts before the end of February 2007, later developments remain ambiguous.

Bihar

In Bihar, the Nitish Kumar government set up a 'Maha Dalit Commission' in August 2007 to suggest ways of uplifting the most deprived communities from amongst the SCs. The commission, headed by Vishwanath Rishi,[86] submitted its 186-page report comprising 116 recommendations in November the same year. Of the twenty-two Scheduled Castes of Bihar, the commission identified eighteen castes as 'Maha Dalits', i.e., Dalits among the Dalits, and sought a series of affirmative action initiatives by the state government for their upliftment. The castes deemed to be in need of special attention included Musahars, Bhuiyans, Mehtars, Doms, Rajwars, Nats, and Halal Khors, while 'dominant' castes like Paswans, Dhobis, Chamars, and Pasis were excluded from the most deprived group.[87] It is no coincidence that all these four excluded sub-castes are known to have political affiliations.[88] Rishi even acknowledged that 'this could ... have political repercussions', but hastened to add that 'the commission has been set up with no political reasons' and was genuinely concerned with the empowerment of Maha Dalits. Rishi pointed out that

> none of the members of these communities had made it to the civil services or any medical and engineering examinations. Their representation in Panchayats is almost nothing. Let alone doctors and engineers, there are no high school teachers from these communities. These communities need special help to climb up the social and economic ladders.[89]

As regards the political repercussions he had referred to, Rishi claimed that the constitution of the Maha Dalit Commission and its subsequent developments would empower Maha Dalits and admitted that 'they may begin taking political decisions independent of the [other] Dalits'.[90] Strangely, in a move unprecedented in the electoral history of independent India, the commission recommended that a provision be made for special polling stations for Maha Dalits, since it was assumed to be difficult for them to go to polling stations for the general populace and exercise their franchise freely. Other recommendations included setting up a grain bank to provide them with grain on loan, boiled rice instead of wheat under rural developmental schemes, and bank financing on a priority basis and organising special loan *melas* and opening schools—with free books, scholarships, uniforms, food, and teachers possibly belonging to Maha Dalit castes—in Maha Dalit areas.[91]

Tamil Nadu

Tamil Nadu was the latest to join the league, appointing a commission under the chairmanship of Justice M. S. Janardhanam, a retired judge of Madras High Court, on March 25, 2008 to study gross enrolment and drop-out rates at educational institutions and representation in politics and in professional fields like medicine and engineering. Based on the survey conducted, the commission submitted its report on November 22, 2008—in about eight months, again betraying a sense of urgency. It professed to have 'gone into all aspects of the issue' in detail and took the position that the Arundathiyar community—which included the Chakkiliar, Madhari, Adi Andhra, Pagadai, Madia, and Thotti sub-sects—needed to be empowered, as they were backward in many regards.

Although Jayalalithaa, the former chief minister and AIADMK leader, called it a 'political fraud', Chief Minister M. Karunanidhi claimed that his government had simply adopted the policy that had been introduced by the Punjab government.[92] In an all-party meeting on November 28, Karunanidhi announced that the state cabinet had 'accepted in principle' the report. In effect, this meant a separate reservation of 3 per cent for Arundathiyars and a few other sub-sects within the existing quota (18 per cent) for the Scheduled Castes.[93] Implemented in 2009, this policy continues to work well, although there was a writ petition to review and repeal the sub-classification. As of now, this might be the best possible way of addressing the sub-classification issue.

Historical Wonder and a Historical Blunder

When examining political developments in connection with the sub-classification issue, one wonders about the urgency with which state governments consistently acted, across political lines. It would not be incorrect to state that, if all the political parties—communal, secular, right, left, and centrist—came together unanimously on any single issue in the history of independent India, it was indubitably this one. The Andhra Pradesh legislative assembly successively passed not one or two but three historical and unanimous resolutions supporting the apportionment of Scheduled Caste reservations among four groups. In other words, the issue of classifying or dividing Dalits has been considered of fundamental significance by all political parties—more important than any other issues of national importance, such as calamities, corruption, communalism, human rights violations, atrocities on Dalits, the Babri Masjid, the Mandal Commission, reservations in the private sector, extremism, minorities, or even national security issues like border conflicts. Unlike in the case of Dalit sub-classification, none of these other issues was treated as morally or politically critical enough to garner a cross-party political consensus.

The unique manner in which this issue was formulated and the procedures followed illustrate the workings of the state in this regard. First, the Andhra Pradesh legislative assembly passed a resolution on April 22, 1998, unanimously agreeing on the need to classify the Scheduled Castes and their reservations into groups A, B, C, and D, as recommended by the Raju Commission. Then the assembly unanimously passed the Scheduled Caste Reservation (Rationalisation) Act of 2000 on April 1, 2000. Third, and perhaps most importantly, in the light of the Supreme Court judgment of November 2004, the assembly passed a unanimous resolution on December 10, 2004 recommending to the Government of India that it take up the matter in Parliament, resulting in the appointment of the Usha Mehra Commission.

It is evident that neither the government nor the commission, or even the institutes commissioned to study the matter, ever reflected on the specific reasons for the emergence of generic identities on which the provisions were formulated. For instance, in the case of Andhra Pradesh, 'Adi Andhra' is a generic term and the sub-caste of Adi Andhras is basically an offshoot of the Mala and Madiga castes.[94] They are the descendants of the educated and socio-politically conscious untouchables of the early decades of the twentieth century. Influenced by the Dravidian movement, they identified themselves as Adi Andhras, claiming to be the original inhabitants of the land based on the theory of 'sons of the soil'.[95] While the 1921 census mentions no distinct sub-caste of Adi Andhras in official enumerations, they emerged in the 1931 census with a remarkable strength of 665,000 (see Table 10.1 below). Though the term Adi Andhra began to be popularised in 1917, it was only in 1922 that the Madras government accepted the appeal of Dalits to delete the terms used to refer to them, like 'Panchama' and 'Pariah', from government records and replace them with 'Adi Andhra' or 'Adi Dravida', reflecting their regional identity and their status as the original inhabitants of those regions.[96] The legislative council of the Government of Madras, in a meeting on January 20, 1922, resolved to recommend 'to the Government that the terms "Panchama" or "Paraya" used to designate the ancient Dravidian community in

Southern India should be deleted from Government records, etc., and the term "Adi-Dravida" in the Tamil and "Adi-Andhra" in the Telugu districts be substituted instead.'[97] The Government of Madras undertook that it had 'no objection to call[ing] the members of this community ... "Adi-Andhra" in Telugu districts if they prefer to be called so' but also accepted its inability 'to re-edit the old records'. In other words, the idea of introducing this nomenclature was to bring all the untouchable communities together under one name that erased the negative connotations of the names hitherto used to refer to them—a fact that has been overlooked by state governments, sundry commissions, and commissioned studies amidst the discontent and conflict of the post-classification political scenario.

Table 10.1: Population of selected 'untouchable' castes in Madras Presidency, 1921–1931 (in thousands)

Caste	Year	
	1921	**1931**
Cheruman	248	215
Holeya	92	50
Madiga	737	612
Mala	1,493	838
Parayan	2,387	1,117
Thoti	154	2
Adi Andhra	–	665
Adi Dravida	50	1,619
Adi Karnataka	–	1

Source: *Census of India, 1931*: Vol. 14: Madras, Part I: Report, p. 349.

The Raju Commission, the state government, the Mehra Commission, and even the Indian Institute of Economics, Hyderabad, which was chosen to study 'the extent of benefits accrued to all the Scheduled Caste Communities included in the Constitution (Scheduled Castes) Order 1950 in Andhra Pradesh', all left unexplained the history of such an important generic identity, encouraging misconceptions and prejudices based on fallacious notions.[98] One can easily infer from the data in Table 10.1 that, when all the other communities witnessed a decline in numbers between 1921 and 1931, only the populations of three communities or sub-castes' showed a remarkable increase, deviating from the general trend. This was clearly the result of the emergence of new communities or sub-castes that were considerable forces, at least in the cases of Adi Andhras and Adi Dravidas.[99] The category 'Adi Andhra' illustrates the flux that resulted from political developments, with groups of Malas and Madigas embracing a new identity. Unlike the authentic, empirical caste or sub-caste category, this was an exercise in identity-building misconceived as the formation of a separate caste by colonial enumerators, and Adi Andhras have continued to be treated as an exclusive sub-caste through the post-colonial period[100] despite these erroneous conceptions on the part of the state and the commissions.

Contemporary Dalit politics is entangled in a conflict around categorisation that fails to recognise the distinct nature of the categories that are being fought over. Given the self-conscious assertion of the Adi Andhras as early as 1920s, it goes without saying that they were more developed than any other group among the Scheduled Castes in the state, but this generic identity does not necessarily suggest the validity of recognising them as a separate sub-caste or *jati*. It is a matter of some concern that the government-sponsored or -appointed commissions and commissioned institutes failed to recognise this colonial legacy and repeated this historical blunder to gain legitimacy or consensus. The suspicions of castes that attribute their backwardness to other Dalit castes are thus misplaced, leading to a great deal of ambiguity and the growth of prejudices that have an adverse impact on emancipatory praxis.

Present Status of the Issue

The purpose of the proposed amendment is to permit, once sub-classification of Scheduled Castes of a state/UT is enacted by law, the equitable sub-allocation, among the sub-categories of its Scheduled Castes, of the overall reservation quota for Scheduled Castes in: (i) appointment to services in connection with the affairs of that state/UT; and (ii) admission to educational institutions run or substantially funded by that state/UT. However, the state/UT-specific sub-classification will not be applicable in appointments in Central services and in admission to Central educational institutions. A provision to that effect also seems necessary in the proposed amendment to the Constitution.

It has accordingly been proposed that two new clauses be added to Article 341 of the Constitution: clause 3 on the lines suggested by the NCSCSC and clause 4 to address the above-mentioned concern. Accordingly, the proposed text of the Constitutional amendment is as follows:

> 341. Scheduled Castes
> (3) Parliament may, by law, provide for sub-categorization or de-sub-categorization of the castes, races or tribes, or part of or group within any castes, races or tribes specified in a notification issued under clause (1), or by law made by Parliament under clause (2), in respect of a State or Union Territory, upon receiving a resolution from the legislature of that State or, as the case may be, Union Territory passed unanimously, recommending such sub-categorization or, as the case may be, de-sub categorization.
> (4) Upon the Scheduled Castes of a State/Union Territory being sub-categorized as per clause (3) above, it shall, notwithstanding anything contained in clauses (1) and (2) above, be lawful for such sub-categories to be treated as a distinct entity for the purpose of reservation in the services in connection with the affairs of that State or, as the case may be, Union Territory, in pursuance of clause (4) of Article 16, and in admission to educational institutions run or substantially aided by the Government of that State or, as the case may be, Union Territory, in pursuance of clause (5) of Article 15.[101]

Once the above constitutional amendment is enacted, guidelines regarding procedure will be issued along the lines, mutatis mutandis, of the 'approved modalities' for modification of the list of Scheduled

Castes. The gist of the above-mentioned 'approved modalities' was approved in 1999 by the Cabinet Committee on Scheduled Castes, Scheduled Tribes and Minorities. The procedure at the Central level includes obtaining the views and considerations of the NCSC and the Registrar General of India. The guidelines issued to the states and UTs in this regard would specify, inter alia, that the legislature's resolution should be obtained only after a detailed investigation by an independent commission headed by a serving/retired judge of a high court into the relative backwardness of various Scheduled Castes of the state/UT and that the conclusion of the commission should be based on 'unimpeachable evidence' that will stand judicial scrutiny.

It is learnt from reliable sources that the draft note for the cabinet was prepared for inter-ministerial consultations and circulated to the ministries of Home Affairs, Tribal Affairs, and Human Resource Development, and Departments of Personnel and Training, and Legal Affairs by the government in the period between 2020 and 2024. The Ministry of Tribal Affairs has also been requested to obtain the views of the National Commission for Scheduled Tribes. Cabinet approval has been solicited for the introduction of a Constitution Amendment Bill inserting clauses 3 and 4 in Article 341, with such drafting modifications as the Ministry of Law and Justice may consider necessary. This note is believed to have been seen and approved of by the Minister of Social Justice and Empowerment and received the approval of the NCSC. Given that these two constitutional bodies have no objections, it is unlikely that any other ministry will raise its voice against this issue, as it is unrelated to their concerns—it will, in other words, be approved in no time. As has been illustrated, the political/bureaucratic masters are shockingly efficient in this regard.

There is growing suspicion about the intentions of the state, since these sub-classifications have only further divided Dalits into splinter groups, thereby dissipating their power. What are the alternatives? How can reservations or the distribution of reservations be rationalised? One could, on the basis of relative parameters of 'development' in the fields of educational or employment, frame policies to empower the most backward amongst these Scheduled Castes, as in the case of the model envisaged by Tamil Nadu, for instance. Dalits were once a strong political force (e.g. in Punjab in the 1950s and 1960s, and in Andhra Pradesh in the 1980s and early 1990s), demonstrating their strength and bargaining power, whether in terms of claiming their share of resources or developmental schemes or demanding the strict implementation of existing provisions. However, divisions into sub-classes have changed the destiny of Dalits, leaving them a spent force, imprisoned, and scattered into defused blocks. This is foreshadowed in what we witness now in Andhra politics, where each block is divided into several groups and has become an addendum to established political parties.

Given the polarisation, it seems there are only two issues that can unite Dalits—the vandalism of Ambedkar statues, and anti-reservation voices. Even these issues could not bring them together in the recent past, more particularly when the issue of the 'reservation bill 2008' came up. In Punjab, when political activists and intellectuals proved their strength together in the 1950s and 1960s, they were divided. When Kanshi Ram tried to bring all these scattered groups together, he was accused of being a Ravidasi. In Haryana, Dalit leaders divided as per their party loyalties, which further weakened their strength. In Andhra Pradesh, it appears that Dalit politics has reached a stage that is beyond redemption now.

Concluding Remarks

As a result of the so-called sub-classification phenomenon, Dalits have alienated themselves from a collective identity shaped by pain, agony, and the trauma of centuries of subjugation and oppression. The frantic and hasty responses of states (some extremely successful, others abortive, while still others have evolved novel models) point to a new, dangerous trend in caste politics. While states have deftly deployed the rhetoric of democratic redistribution or historic justice, these developments have resulted in mistrust, hatred, and shifting alliances, thus ensuring irreparable damage to the cause of Dalits in general.

Dalits have been systematically split and realigned in every state, with upper-caste parties vying to reap the results of this volatile division. Unfortunately, though the issue of sub-classification has consumed a great amount of Dalit intellectuals' and activists' time and energy, they have demonstrated an inability to confront it together and to join forces. As all political parties shift towards a consensus on the dilution of reservations, the day is not far when they will broach the question of ending reservations. The issue of reservations in the private sector has quietly withered on its own, and the manner in which the Scheduled Castes and Scheduled Tribes Reservation Bill, 2008 was passed in the Rajya Sabha in less than three minutes, with no discussion or debate, makes it undeniable that the Dalit force has weakened, as there was no protest against it. It should be recalled that Ambedkar, during his lifetime, was disillusioned with the divisive tendencies within the Dalit movement. In one such instance, he expressed his anguish by saying,

> with great difficulty I have brought the caravan where it is seen today. Let the caravan march on, despite the hurdles, pitfalls and difficulties that may come its way. If my people, my lieutenants are not able to take the caravan ahead, they should leave it where it is seen today, but they must not, under any circumstances, allow the caravan to go back.[102]

It remains to be seen if Dalits will be capable of reflecting on this crucial moment in history and evolving alternatives to carry their rich legacy forward as a new phase of politics unfolds, or whether they will succumb to the divisive tactics of the state.

Notes and References

1. For details, see Yagati Chinna Rao, 'The "Self" and the "Other": Towards Dalit Identity', *Human Rights Global Focus* 3(1) (2006): 30–37.

2. In the modern period, European visitors to India noted the existence of despised groups, and the Tamil word '*pariah*' lent itself to the English

vocabulary as a synonym for 'social outcaste', a person of low caste or of no caste. See Albert Sydney Hornby, *Oxford Advanced Learners Dictionary of Current English* (Delhi: Oxford University Press), p. 608.

3. See *Molesworth's Marathi-English Dictionary,* 1975 (reprint of 1831 edition), cited in Eleanor Zelliot, *From Untouchable to Dalit: Essays on the Ambedkar Movement* (New Delhi: Manohar, 2005 [1992]).

4. Gangadhar Pantawane, 'Evolving a New Identity: The Development of Dalit Culture', in *Untouchables! Voices of Dalit Liberation Movement,* ed. B. R. Joshi (New Delhi: Zed Books, 1986), pp. 79–87.

5. B. R. Ambedkar, 'Untouchables—Their Numbers', in *Dr. Babasaheb Ambedkar: Writings and Speeches,* Vol. 5, eds. H. Narake, N. G. Kamble, M. L. Kasare and A. Godghate (New Delhi: Dr. Ambedkar Foundation, 2019 [1979]), p. 7.

6. Report of the Indian Statutory Commission, Vol. 1, p. 37. 1930.

7. H. Narake, N. G. Kamble, M. L. Kasare, and A. Godghate, 'Role of Dr. B.R. Ambedkar in Bringing the Untouchables on the Political Horizon of India and Laying a Foundation of Indian Democracy', in *Dr. Babasaheb Ambedkar: Writings and Speeches,* Vol. 17, Part 1 [Dr. B.R. Ambedkar and His Egalitarian Revolution], eds. H. Narake, N. G. Kamble, M. L. Kasare, and Ashok Godghate (New Delhi: Dr. Ambedkar Foundation, 2019 [1979]), p. 123.

8. *Ibid.* In Mahad, Ambedkar and his followers had to confront violence in their fight for the right to enter the temple tank and temple premises.

9. For details see J. H. Hutton, 'Exterior Castes'. Report in *Census of India 1931*, Vol. I, Part I (1933), pp. 471–501. The appendices of this volume are particularly informative.

10. *Ibid.*

11. *Ibid.*

12. *Census of India 1921*, Vol. I, Part I, paragraph 193.

13. *Census of India 1931*, Vol. I, Part I (Appendix I), p. 472. Also see P. K. Nambiar, *Census of India 1961—Madras,* Vol. 9, Part V-A(i) [Scheduled Castes and Tribes (Report & Tables)] (1964), pp. 5–6. Madras: Superintendent of Census Operations. http://lsi.gov.in:8081/jspui/bitstream/123456789/6480/1/45989_1961_SC.pdf (accessed on March 30, 2023).

14. Report of Indian Franchise Committee, Vol. 1 (1932).

15. The Government of India (Scheduled Castes) Order (1936).

16. See the Constitution (Scheduled Castes) Order, 1950 (C.O. 19), the Constitution (Scheduled Castes) (Union Territories) Order, 1951 (C.O. 32), the Constitution (Jammu and Kashmir) Scheduled Castes Order, 1956 (C.O. 52), the Constitution (Dadra and Nagar Haveli) Scheduled Castes Order, 1962 (C.O. 64), the Constitution (Pondicherry) Scheduled Castes Order, 1964 (C.O. 68), the Constitution (Goa, Daman and Diu) Scheduled Caste Order, 1968 (C.O. 81), and the Constitution (Sikkim) Scheduled Castes Order, 1978 (C.O. 110).

17. For more details see P. M. Bakshi, *The Constitution of India (15th Edition)* (Gurgaon: Universal Law Publishing, 2018), p. 371.

18. *Constituent Assembly Debates*, Vol. 9; *Constituent Assembly Debates: Official Report*, Vol. 9, Book 4, (New Delhi: Lok Sabha Secretariat, 2014), pp. 1591–1673.

19. '*Watan*' means 'service lands'. *Watan* lands are those given to a person or a family for their work and shall always remain in their possession. As village servant, the Mahar was bound to the village as a whole. Ambedkar perceived this to be caste bondage and felt that, if the *watan* were abolished, Mahars could be freed from their oppressive ties to villages.

20. Neera Burra, 'Was Ambedkar Just a Leader of the Mahars?', *Economic and Political Weekly* 21(10–11) (March 8–15 1986): 429–431.

21. Dhananjay Keer, *Dr. Ambedkar: Life and Mission* (Bombay: Popular Prakashan, 1954), p. 70.

22. Burra, 'Was Ambedkar Just a Leader of the Mahars?', *op. cit.*, p. 429.

23. 'Depressed Classes: Dr Ambedkar Sees Mr Gandhi', *The Times of India* (15 August 1931). Also see B. G. Kunte, comp. *Source Material on Dr. Babasaheb Ambedkar and the Movement of Untouchables*, Vol. I (Bombay: Dr. Babasaheb Ambedkar Source Material Publication Committee, 1982), p. 52; B. R. Ambedkar, 'I Have No Homeland', in *Dr. Babasaheb Ambedkar: Writings and Speeches*, Vol. 5, eds. H. Narake, N. G. Kamble, M. L. Kasare and A. Godghate (New Delhi: Dr. Ambedkar Foundation, 2019 [1979]), p. 55.

24. 'Segregating Untouchables', *The Times of India* (18 August 1931); 'Depressed Classes Disclaim Ambedkar: Separate Electorate Not Wanted, Full Faith in Gandhi', *The Free Press Journal* (11 October 1931).

25. This meeting was presided over by Mr Sukharam Buwa, and the resolution was moved by Mr B. J. Deorukhkar. For details, see 'Dr Ambedkar Repudiated', *The Bombay Chronicle* (12 October 1931);

'No Confidence in Ambedkar', *The Free Press Journal* (21 October 1931); cited in Kunte, *op. cit.*, pp. 60–61.

26. The president of the Dayanand Dalit Uddhar Mandal (Dayanand Depressed Classes Uplift Association), Punjab, sent a cable to the prime minister and Gandhi saying, 'The Depressed Classes do not want Separate Electorates. They will be satisfied with adult franchise and they have no confidence in Dr. Ambedkar.' See 'Punjab "Depressed Classes": Have No Confidence in Dr Ambedkar', *The Bombay Chronicle* (17 October 1931).

27. The secretary of the Untouchability Committee, Banaras, sent a cable to Gandhi saying, 'Public meeting of Depressed Classes of Benares expresses no confidence in Dr. Ambedkar and supports Congress demands.' For details see 'No Confidence in Ambekdar', *The Free Press Journal* (28 October 1931).

28. 'Despicable', *The Bombay Chronicle* (27 November 1931).

29. 'Nothing to Do with Mr Rajah: Dr Ambedkar's Statements', *The Times of India* (22 September 1932), cited in Kunte, *op. cit.*, pp. 90–91.

30. Atul Chandra Pradhan, *The Emergence of the Depressed Classes* (Delhi: Bookland International, 1986), p. 250.

31. Gail Omvedt, *Dalits and the Democratic Revolution: Dr. Ambedkar and the Dalit Movement in Colonial India* (Delhi: Sage, 1994), p. 262.

32. One can only marvel at the promptness with which the Congress initiated actions to stop Ambedkar and his followers from emerging as a strong force. The Poona Pact was signed only on September 24, 1932, and the meeting was convened by the Congress the very next day, September 25. B. K. Jha, 'Negotiating Malaviya's Place in Modern Indian History' (Nehru Memorial Museum and Library Occasional Paper [History and Society, New Series 107] 2021), p. 29; B. Pattabhi Sitaramayya, *History of the Indian National Congress*, Vol. I (New Delhi: Gyan Publishing House, 2016 [1946]), p. 536. For more details, see Jagdish Chandra Mandal, *Poona Pact and the Depressed Classes* (Calcutta: Sujan Publishers, 1999).

33. Omvedt, *Dalits and the Democratic Revolution, op. cit.*, p. 263.

34. 'Differences among Harijans Deplored: Dr. Ambedkar's Plea for Unity'. *The Times of India*, July 5, 1939; cited in Kunte, *Source Material on Dr. Babasaheb Ambedkar, op. cit.*, p. 215.

35. *Ibid.*

36. He made these statements at a meeting organised by the Hyderabad State Scheduled Castes Federation to welcome him to Hyderabad on

September 20, 1944. For more details see 'Dr. Ambedkar's Plea: Harijan's Share in Power'. *The Times of India*. September 22, 1944; cited in Kunte, *Source Material on Dr. Babasaheb Ambedkar, op. cit.*, p. 283.

37. *Ibid.*

38. *Ibid.*

39. 'Mang Community Conference at Sholapur', *Bombay Secret Abstract* (8 January 1930), cited in Kunte, *Source Material on Dr. Babasaheb Ambedkar, op. cit.*, p. 163.; also see M. F. Ganjare, *Dr. Babasaheba Ambedkaranci Bhashane*, Vol. III (Nagpur: Sanganak Prakashan, 1975), p. 130.

40. Eleanor Zelliot, 'Learning the Use of Political Means: The Mahars of Maharashtra', in *Caste in Indian Politics*, ed. R. Kothari (New Delhi: Orient BlackSwan), p. 53.

41. For details see G. S. Halappa, *History of the Freedom Movement in Karnataka*, Vol. II (Mysore: Government of Mysore, 1966).

42. P. R. Venkataswamy, *Our Struggle for Emancipation*, Vol. II (Secunderabad: Saraswati Press, 1955), p. 656.

43. M. B. Gautam, 'The Untouchables Movement in Andhra Pradesh', *Harijan Conference Souvenir* (Hyderabad, 10–12 April 1976), pp. 71–72.

44. Chamars and Jatavs of Uttar Pradesh joined the Bahujan Samaj movement of Kanshi Ram in a big way in the early 1980s and had shifted completely towards the Bahujan Samaj Party (BSP) by 1990. Kanshi Ram accused Jagjivan Ram of being a *chamcha* (stooge) of the Congress and published *Chamcha Age: An Era of Stooges*—on the Congress government's role in undermining Dalit politics—in 1982, on the fiftieth anniversary of the Poona Pact. Kanshi Ram weaned Chamars and Jatavs away from the Congress, bringing them back to the Ambedkarite fold (they had supported Ambedkar's Scheduled Castes Federation (SCF) in Uttar Pradesh until the end of the 1960s).

45. There is also a third group within the Mala community, under the leadership of Mrs Prameela Devi, wife of the late P. V. Rao.

46. For details, see Yagati Chinna Rao ed., *Dividing Dalits: Writings on Sub-categorization of Scheduled Castes* (New Delhi/Jaipur: Rawat Publications, 2009), Appendices 1 and 2.

47. *Ibid.* Appendix 3.

48. The one and only exception is by Surinder S. Jodhka and Avinash Kumar, and even that was written after three decades of divisions had

played out. For details see Surinder S. Jodhka and Avinash Kumar, 'Internal Classification of Scheduled Castes: The Punjab Story', *Economic and Political Weekly* 42(43) (October 27–November 2 2007): 20–23.

49. The first-ever Dalit massacre organised by the Telugu Desam Party, which is backed by members of the Kamma caste.

50. For details see K. Srinivasulu, *Caste, Class and Social Articulation in Andhra Pradesh: Mapping Differential Regional Trajectories* (London: Overseas Development Institute [Working Paper 179], 2002).

51. This massacre took place under Congress rule, with the Reddy caste ruling the state.

52. See Adapa Satyanarayana, *Andhra Pradesh lo Noorendla Dalita Charitra* (Hyderabad: Hyderabad Book Trust, 2009).

53. I owe these ideas to Raja Sekhar Vundru, whose critical reflections on the issue provided crucial insights. For details see R. S. Vundru, 'Andhra may see a historic handshake'. *Mail Today*, 14 July 2008, p. 15.

54. Devendra Goud was the most powerful and influential member of the TDP in his time, after N. T. Rama Rao and N. Chandrababu Naidu. Goud later left the TDP to launch his own party after the outbreak of the Telangana statehood issue. His party later merged with Chiranjeevi's Praja Rajyam Party.

55. Mallepali Laxmaiah, who contributes regularly to *Andhra Jyothi* and other Telugu dailies and is also an important functionary at the Centre for Dalit Studies, Hyderabad, having been associated with it since its inception in various capacities (governing body member, chairman, etc.).

56. The term '*dandora*' literally means 'pronouncement' or 'proclamation' and refers to the hereditary profession of Madigas, who traditionally made announcements in the village about all kinds of events—from the selling of pulses to the summoning of the village panchayat—to the accompaniment of drumbeats. The drum or *dappu* is the most common traditional percussion instrument used in Andhra society for this purpose. All rituals and festivals also invariably feature the *dappu*, both while the rituals are taking place and during the associated processions. For details see M. Nagabhushana Sarma, *Folk Performing Arts of Andhra Pradesh* (Hyderabad: Telugu University, 1995), pp. 50–51.

57. For details see Yagati Chinna Rao, 'Neo-Reservation Movement in Contemporary India: A Case Study of Andhra Dalits', *Contemporary India* 4(3) (2005): 53–76.

58. Rao ed., *Dividing Dalits, op. cit.,* Appendices 4 and 5.

59. For the complete details of the statement, see *ibid.,* Appendix 4.

60. *Ibid.,* Appendix 6.

61. Andhra Pradesh High Court judgment (18 September 1997) in B. Narayana and Others. vs State of Andhra Pradesh.

62. See Rao ed., *Dividing Dalits, op. cit.,* Appendix 8.

63. For the extracts of the judgment, see Rao ed., *Dividing Dalits, op. cit.,* Appendix 9.

64. *Ibid.* Andhra Pradesh Government withdrawal orders of Rationalisation (Sub-Category) Act of 2000, dated, 23rd December, 2004; Withdrawal of Subcategory-wise Reservation by the Punjab Government, Dated 5th October, 2006; and Withdrawal of Sub-Category-wise Reservation by the Government of Haryana, Dated 7th June, 2007. For more details, see Rao, ed. *Dividing Dalits, op. cit.,* pp. 341–351.

65. https://eparlib.nic.in/bitstream/123456789/575982/1/80957.pdf (accessed on April 2, 2023).

66. A pamphlet entitled 'The Report of the Justice Usha Mehra Commission – An Exercise in Futility: The Remedy is Worse than the Disease: A Memorandum' (Hyderabad: Association for Social Action, Andhra Pradesh, undated).

67. Y. Gupta, 'Panel of 8 Judges formed: Issue of Sub-Categorisation of SCs', *The Tribune* (September 7 2006).

68. It is reported that Justice Doraiswami Raju, Justice S. Rajendra Babu, and a retired chief justice from Punjab declined to head the Commission. For details see S. Ghildiyal, 'Judge refuses to head panel to sub-categorise Scheduled Castes', *The Times of India* (December 5 2006).

69. 'The Report of the Justice Usha Mehra Commission – An Exercise in Futility', in Rao ed., *Dividing Dalits, op. cit.,* Appendix 14.

70. For more details, see 'Justice Usha Mehra Commission Recommendations', in Rao ed., *Dividing Dalits, op. cit.,* pp. 352–362.

71. V. Pathak, 'SC Quota Fissures to Widen'. *The Hindustan Times,* June 1, 2008.

72. Rao ed., *Dividing Dalits, op. cit.,* pp. 363–370.

73. See Supreme Court judgment (November 5, 2004) in E. V. Chinnaiah vs State of Andhra Pradesh and Others [Case No: Appeal (civil) 6758 of 2000].

74. The Government of India had appointed this 'Advisory Committee', headed by then law secretary B. N. Lokur and therefore popularly known as the 'Lokur Committee', on June 1, 1965 to study the implementation of reservations in all the states and to revise the lists of Scheduled Castes and Scheduled Tribes in a rational and scientific manner, if needed.

75. Rao ed., *Dividing Dalits, op. cit.*, pp. 363–370.

76. Supreme Court judgment (November 5, 2004) in E. V. Chinnaiah vs State of Andhra Pradesh and Others [Case No: Appeal (civil) 6758 of 2000]; also see Rao ed., *Dividing Dalits, op. cit.*, p. 26.

77. Letter 1786-3WI-75/23005 (September 19, 1975), from the secretary to the Government, Punjab Scheduled Caste and Backward Classes to all the heads of departments, commissioners, and divisions district and sessions judges, deputy commissioners and Registrar, Punjab and Haryana High Court and copy to others.

78. Rao ed., *Dividing Dalits, op. cit.*, pp. 290–291.

79. Letter 22/55/90-3GS-III (November 9, 1994), from the chief secretary of the Government of Haryana to all heads of departments and commissioners of Ambala, Hisar, Rohtak, and Gurgaon Divisions and all deputy commissioners and sub-divisional officers (civil) in Haryana.

80. Hukum Singh, a member of the Gujjar caste and minister for parliamentary affairs.

81. Ramapati Shastri, a Dhobi by caste and minister for health and family affairs.

82. P. S. Tripathi, 'Counting on Quota', *Frontline* 18(16) (2001).

83. *Ibid.*

84. P. S. Tripathi, 'A new calculation in Uttar Pradesh', *Frontline* 19(16) (2001).

85. Special Correspondent, 'Sadashiva Commission recommends internal reservation among SCs', *The Hindu* (15 June 2012).

86. Vishwanath Rishi, a three-time legislator, was the state welfare minister in 1989.

87. A. Srivastava, 'Caste Controversy', *India Today* (January 5, 2008).

88. J. P. Yadav, 'Nitish all set to carry forward his "Maha Dalit" Agenda', *Bihara* (January 5, 2008).

89. Srivastava, 'Caste Controversy', *op. cit.*

90. Yadav, 'Nitish all set to carry forward his "Maha Dalit" Agenda', *op. cit.*

91. TNN, 'Maha Dalit Panel Submits Report', *The Times of India* (21 November 2007).

92. K. Venkataraman, 'Karunanidhi—A Champion of Social Justice, Caste Amity', *The Hindu* (28 November 2021).

93. S. Viswanathan, 'Separate Slice', *Frontline* 26(1) (2009). https://frontline.thehindu.com/social-issues/article30183414.ece (accessed on 5 November 2024).

94. S. R. Sankaran, 'The Mala–Madiga Controversy: An Appeal to the Scheduled Castes', *Sanghika Sankshema Samacharam* (June–July 1998): 14–15. Also see Gail Omvedt, *Dalits and the Democratic Revolution, op. cit.*; Yagati Chinna Rao, *Dalits' Struggle for Identity: Andhra and Hyderabad* (New Delhi: Kanishka, 2003).

95. Yagati Chinna Rao, 'Change in Nomenclature: A Historical Note', in *Dalits: Assertion for Identity*, ed. A. Pinto (New Delhi: Indian Social Institute, 1999), pp. 84–95; also see Yagati Chinna Rao, 'Introduction', in *Dalit Studies: A Bibliographical Handbook* (New Delhi: Kanishka, 2003).

96. Proceedings of Law Department, Government of Madras, Law (General) Department, G.O. No. 817, March 25, 1922, [Legislative Council Resolution – January 1922]. Also see M. B. Gautam, *Bhagyodayam: Maadari Bhagya Reddi Varma, Life Sketch and Mission* (Hyderabad: Adi-Hindu Social Service League Trust, 1991).

97. *Ibid.*

98. Rao, 'Introduction', in *Dalit Studies, op. cit.*

99. The exact number of Adi Andhras in 1931 was 6,64,844. J. H. Hutton, *Census of India, 1931*: Vol. 1: India, Part I: Report, p. 477. Madras: Registrar Census Commissioner for India, 1933).

100. The caste certificates of this particular 'sub-caste' read 'Adi-Andhra Mala' or 'Adi-Andhra Madiga'. One can see this in the caste certificates issued in the districts of East Godavari, West Godavari, Krishna, and Guntur, where these particular 'sub-caste' communities are prevalent. Even when it comes to marriage, in which context the sub-caste/*jati* is considered most important, an Adi-Andhra Mala marries only a Mala of neighbouring districts/regions, and an Adi-Andhra Madiga marries only a Madiga of neighbouring districts/regions, irrespective of the religion they profess.

101. Rao, 'Introduction', in *Dalit Studies, op. cit.*

102. http://news.ambedkar.org /?p=10 (accessed on April 2, 2023).

Notes on the Contributors

S. Victor Babu is Professor of History at Babasaheb Bhimrao Ambedkar University, Lucknow. His published works include *Popular Culture and Religion in Medieval India* (2006), and the co-authored volume *Social Exclusion and Inclusion: A Journey from Past to Present* (with R. C. Sobti et al., 2017).

Raj Sekhar Basu is Professor of History at the University of Calcutta. His published works include *Nandanar's Children: The Paraiyans' Tryst with Destiny, Tamil Nadu 1850–1950* (2011), and the edited volumes *Narratives from the Margins: Aspects of Adivasi History in India* (with Sanjukta Dasgupta, 2011), *Medical Encounters in British India* (with Deepak Kumar, 2013), and *Dalit Intellectuals: Ideas, Struggles and the Vision* (with Yagati Chinna Rao, 2022).

Sudarshana Bhaumik is Assistant Professor of History at Birsa Munda College, Darjeeling. A recipient of the Charles Wallace India Trust Grant Fellowship (2018), she is the author of *The Changing World of Caste and Hierarchy in Bengal: Depictions from the Mangalkavyas, c. 1700–1931* (2023).

Rajesh Komath is Associate Professor Social Sciences at the Mahatma Gandhi University, Kerala, where he teaches social theory and folkloristics. He is a performer of *theyyam* who has researched extensively on the art form, and the author of *Theyyam: The Other Gods* (with Bhawani Cheerath-Rajagopalan, 2020).

P. Sanal Mohan, former Professor of History at Mahatma Gandhi University, Kerala, served as Director of the Kerala Council for Historical Research (2019–2020), and was the Smuts Visiting

Research Fellow at University of Cambridge (2017–2018). He is the author of *Modernity of Slavery: Struggles against Caste Inequality in Colonial Kerala* (2015).

THALLAPALLY MANOHAR is Professor of History at Kakatiya University, Warangal. His published works include *Land Issues in Telangana: A Selected Village* (2016), and *Traditional Economy and Religious Life of Leather Working Madigas* (2018), edited by him. In recognition of his contributions to the agrarian, social and cultural history of Telangana, he was conferred the Best Teacher Award by the Government of Telangana in 2023.

ROSHNI PADMANABHAN is Assistant Director, Kerala State Planning Board. Her publications include the book *Padikkatha Pandangal: DPE Pyude Parinithiyum Parimithiyum* (in Malayalam), and the chapter 'Learning to Learn: Dalit Education in Kerala' in *Development, Democracy and the State: Critiquing the Kerala Model of Development* (edited by K. Ravi Raman, 2010).

YAGATI CHINNA RAO is Professor at the Centre for the Study of Social Exclusion and Inclusive Policy (CSSEIP), Jawaharlal Nehru University. He served as chairperson CSSEIP (2014–2024), member secretary of the Indian Council for Historical Research (2008); he was visiting professor at Nelson Mandela Metropolitan University, Port Elizabeth (2011), Sapienza Universita di Roma, Rome (2016), and at Kaunas Technological University, Kaunas (2017 and 2023), among others. His recent published works include the edited volumes *Dividing Dalits: Writings on Sub-Categorisation of Scheduled Castes* (2009), *The Past of the Outcaste: Readings in Dalit History* (with Sabyasachi Bhattacharya, 2017), *Towards Inclusivity: Essays on Social Exclusion and Discrimination* (2022), *Dalit Intellectuals: Ideas, Struggles and the Vision* (with Raj Sekhar Basu, 2022), and *Labour, Diaspora and Marginality: Essays in Honour of Sabyasachi Bhattacharya* (with Hitendra K. Patel, 2024).

B. RAMA CHANDRA REDDY retired as Head of the Department of History, Kanchi Mamunivar Government Institute of Postgraduate Studies and Research, Puducherry, in 2023. His published works include *Tribal Revolts in Colonial Andhra* (2015), *Traditional Economy and Religious Life of Leather Working Madigas* (2018); and the edited volumes *Telangana in 19th Century (Select Documents)*, and *Musings on South India: Festschrift to Konda Srinivasulu* (with Yagati Chinna Rao and Venkateswara Reddy, 2016).

PRIYADARSHINI VIJAISRI is a cultural historian, was a Fellow at the Nantes Institute for Advanced Studies (2011–2012), and is Associate Professor at the Centre for the Study of Developing Societies, New Delhi. Her published works include *Recasting the Devadasi: Patterns of Sacred Prostitution in Colonial South India* (2004), *Dangerous Marginality: Rethinking Impurity and Power* (2014), and *Essays on Violence: Pollution, Sacrifice and Madness* (2024).

Index